Dealing with the Challenges of Macro Financial Linkages in Emerging Markets

A WORLD BANK STUDY

Dealing with the Challenges of Macro Financial Linkages in Emerging Markets

Otaviano Canuto and Swati R. Ghosh, editors

THE WORLD BANK
Washington, D.C.

Contents

Boxes

Figures

Tables

Acknowledgments

This study grew out of a joint World Bank and Bank Indonesia conference in Bali, Indonesia in November 2011. We would like to thank Dr. Darmin Nasution, then Governor of Bank Indonesia, Dr. Muliaman Haddad, then Deputy Governor, Bank Indonesia, Dr. Halim Alamsyah, Deputy Governor, Bank Indonesia, Dr. Wimboh Santoso, Director of Banking Research and Regulation, Bank Indonesia, and their staff.

The study benefitted enormously from the insightful comments and suggestions we received from the conference participants. We are grateful to the high-level policy makers who took their valuable time to join the discussions, as we are to our International Monetary Fund and World Bank colleagues and to Amar Bhattacharya, Director of the Secretariat of the Intergovernmental Group of Twenty-Four (G-24). The conference would not have been possible without the excellent collaboration and contribution of the Jakarta World Bank office, particularly the finance team: P.S. Srinivas, Djauhari Sitorus, Alexandra Drees-Gross, and Erly Tantontos.

We are especially grateful to Stijn Claessens for his participation in the conference and his invaluable suggestions and comments throughout the preparation of this volume.

We would also like to thank Faraz Usmani for his excellent research assistance during the editing and production process.

About the Authors *(in order of chapter appearance)*

Hyun Song Shin is the Hughes-Rogers Professor of Economics at Princeton University. He has a PhD in Economics from Oxford University. His research interests cover financial institutions, risk and financial stability issues, topics on which he has published widely in both academic and policy outlets. He is the author of *Risk and Liquidity: the 2008 Clarendon Lectures in Finance*, and coauthor of the 2009 *Geneva Report on the Fundamental Principles of Financial Regulation*. Before moving to Princeton in 2006, he was based in the United Kingdom, holding academic positions in Oxford and the London School of Economics. Professor Shin is a Korean national. In 2010, he took leave from Princeton to serve in a policy role in Korea as the Senior Adviser to President Lee Myung-bak on the international economy. He is a fellow of the Econometric Society and of the British Academy.

Viral Acharya is Starr Professor of Economics at New York University, Stern School of Business. Prior to joining NYU Stern, Professor Acharya was a Professor of Finance and Academic Director of the Private Equity Institute at the London Business School, a research affiliate at the Center for Economic Policy Research and an academic advisor to the Bank of England. He was appointed Senior Houblon-Normal Research Fellow at the Bank of England to conduct research on efficiency of the interbank lending markets during the summer of 2008. He holds a PhD in Finance from the New York University Stern School of Business. Professor Acharya has received recognition and numerous awards for his research. He has published articles in the *Journal of Finance; Journal of Financial Economics; Review of Financial Studies; Journal of Business; Rand Journal of Economics; Journal of Financial Intermediation; Journal of Money, Credit and Banking;* and *Financial Analysts Journal*. His coedited books include *Restoring Financial Stability: How to Repair a Failed System* (2009); *Regulating Wall Street: The Dodd-Frank Act and the New Architecture of Global Finance* (2010); and *Dodd-Frank: One Year On* (2011). He is also the coauthor of *Guaranteed to Fail: Fannie Mae, Freddie Mac and the Debacle of Mortgage Finance* (2011).

Stijn Claessens is Assistant Director in the Research Department of the International Monetary Fund. Mr. Claessens holds a PhD in business economics from the Wharton School of the University of Pennsylvania and an MA from

Erasmus University, Rotterdam. He started his career teaching at New York University's business school in 1987 and then worked for 14 years at the World Bank in various positions (1987–2001). He taught for three years at the University of Amsterdam (2001–04), where he remains a Professor of International Finance Policy. Prior to his current position, he was Senior Adviser in the Finance and Private Sector Vice-Presidency of the World Bank (2004–06). His research has been published in the *Journal of Financial Economics, Journal of Finance,* and the *Quarterly Journal of Economics.* He has edited several books, including *International Financial Contagion* (2001), *Resolution of Financial Distress* (2001), *A Reader in International Corporate Finance* (2006), *Macro-Prudential Regulatory Policies: The New Road to Financial Stability,* and *Understanding Financial Crises.* He is an associate editor at the *IMF Economic Review,* and has been an editor of the *Journal of Financial Services Research,* and associate editor at the *World Bank Economic Review* and other journals. He is also a fellow at the London-based Center for Economic Policy Research, the European Corporate Governance Institute, Brussels; the Asian Institute for Corporate Governance, Seoul: and the Wharton Financial Institutions Center, University of Pennsylvania.

Swati R. Ghosh is Adviser in the Poverty Reduction and Economic Management (PREM) Network at the World Bank. She has a PhD in Economics from Oxford University, and an MSc in Economics from the London School of Economics. She has published in the areas of macroeconomic policy coordination, private capital flows, macro financial linkages, financial crises, and structural vulnerabilities. She has been a core team member of several World Bank publications including the policy research report *Private Capital Flows: The Road to Financial Integration* and was the lead author of the World Bank publication *East Asian Finance: The Road to Robust Markets.*

Otaviano Canuto is Senior Advisor on BRICS Economies in the Development Economics Department at the World Bank. He previously served as the World Bank's Vice President and Head of the Poverty Reduction and Economic Management (PREM) Network. He also served as Executive Director of the Board of the World Bank from 2004 to 2007. Outside the Bank he has held leadership positions at the Inter-American Development Bank, where he was Vice President for Countries, and for the Government of Brazil, where he was Secretary for International Affairs at the Ministry of Finance. He also served as Professor of Economics at the University of São Paulo and University of Campinas in Brazil. Recently he has published on the emerging market economies and the global economic crisis, fiscal policy and growth, monetary policy and financial regulation, natural resource-led development, middle-income growth traps, subnational finance, sovereign ratings and debt restructuring, and gender equality.

Matheus Cavallari works for the Poverty Reduction and Economic Management Network at the World Bank. Since joining the Bank in 2012, he has written about competitiveness and natural resource richness; monetary policy and macro prudential regulation in emerging markets; and macro financial stability and public debt management in Africa. Previously, he was partner at one of the pioneer hedge funds in Brazil, Claritas Investments, where he worked as chief economist, macro strategist, and portfolio manager. In 2008, he was a member of the Portfolio Management subcommittee at the Brazilian Financial and Capital Markets Association. He holds a Master of economics degree from Pontificia Universidade Catolica of Rio de Janeiro, where he specialized in optimal fiscal and monetary policies.

Roxana Mihet is a graduate student specializing in international macroeconomics and macro-finance at the University of Oxford, Nuffield College. Previously she worked in the Research Department at the International Monetary Fund (2010– 12) and in the Office of the Chief Economist at the European Bank for Reconstruction and Development (2013). She completed her B.A. (Hons) in Economics at the University of Chicago in 2010.

Luiz Awazu Pereira Da Silva is currently Deputy Governor, in charge of international affairs and financial regulation, at the Central Bank of Brazil. Before that he was Deputy Finance Minister, in charge of international affairs at Brazil's Ministry of Finance; Chief Economist at Brazil's Ministry of Budget and Planning; Regional Country Director at the World Bank (Southern Africa Department 2); and Advisor to the Chief Economist of the World Bank. He also worked as a visiting scholar at the Institute of Fiscal and Monetary Policy of the Ministry of Finance, Tokyo and as Director of the Country Risk and Economic Analysis Department at the Export-Import Bank of Japan, Tokyo. He holds a PhD in Economics and a Master of Philosophy from the Université de Paris-I Sorbonne. He graduated from the Ecole des Hautes Etudes Commerciales and the Institut d'études politiques in Paris.

Ricardo Eyer Harris is a Deputy Advisor at the Central Bank of Brazil with extensive experience on banking supervision, payment system and foreign exchange regulation. Mr. Harris has actively participated in developing most of the macro prudential measures implemented by the Brazilian government since 2010. Prior to joining the Central Bank, Mr. Harris worked at Flemings Bank and Banco Espírito Santo structuring Mergers & Acquisitions and Project Finance transactions. Ricardo Harris holds an MBA from Fundação Getúlio Vargas and is a Chartered Financial Analyst charter holder.

Jong Kyu Lee is currently the Deputy Director of Economic Research Institute at the Bank of Korea. He was previously in the Institute of Foreign Affairs and National Security in the Ministry of Foreign Affairs and Trade, head of the Finance Studies Office in the Institute for Monetary and Economic Research, and Deputy Director General in the Monetary Policy Department. He completed his PhD in Economics at the University of Hawaii, and his BA in Business Administration at Seoul National University, Korea. His publications include *Another Currency Crisis in Korea: A Victim of Sudden Stops in the Wake of Global Financial Turmoil* (2008) and *Recurring Economic Crisis in Korea* (2008).

Abbreviations

AAA	prime bond credit rating
ABCP	asset-backed commercial paper
ABS	asset-backed securities
ACs	advanced countries
BCB	Central Bank of Brazil
BCBS	Basel Committee on Banking Supervision
BHCs	bank holding companies
BIS	Bank for International Settlements
CAR	capital adequacy ratio
BNDES	Brazilian Development Bank (Banco Nacional de Desenvolvimento Econômico e Social)
BOK	Bank of Korea
bps	basis points
BRL	Brazilian real
CDO	collateralized debt obligation
CDs	certificates of deposit
CEPR	Center for Economic Policy Research, London
CFM	capital flow management
CG	credit growth
CGFS	Committee on the Global Financial System
CMN	National Monetary Council (Conselho Monetário Nacional)
CoVaR	value at risk (VaR) of the financial system *conditional* on institutions being in distress
CP	commercial paper
CVM	Securities Commission of Brazil (Comissão de Valores Mobiliários)
DC	domestic currency
DSGE	Dynamic Stochastic General Equilibrium models
DTI	debt-to-income ratio
ECB	European Central Bank

EL	expected loss
EMPI	Exchange Market Pressure Index
EMs	emerging markets
EWE	early warning exercise
FBBs	branches of foreign banks
FDI	foreign direct investment
FIR	financial interrelations ratio
FSAP	Financial Sector Assessment Program
FSC	financial stability contribution
FSI	financial stress index
FX	foreign exchange
G-20	Group of Twenty Finance Ministers and Central Bank Governors
GDP	gross domestic product
GSEs	government-sponsored enterprises
HELOC	home equity line of credit;
ICMB	International Center for Monetary and Banking Studies
IMF	International Monetary Fund
IOF	Brazilian tax on financial operations (imposto sobre operações financeiras)
IRB	internal ratings based approach
LCFIs	large complex financial institutions
LCR	foreign currency liquidity coverage ratio
LCR	liquidity coverage ratio
LF	Letras Financeiras
LTD	loan-to-deposit ratio
LTROs	long-term refinancing operations
LTV	loan-to-value ratio
MaPPs	macro prudential policies
MBS	mortgage-backed security
MES	marginal expected shortfall
NAV	net asset value
NBER	National Bureau of Economic Research
NBFIs	nonbank financial institutions
NFAs	net foreign assets
NPL	nonperforming loan ratios
NPV	net present value
NSFR	net stable funding ratio

OFR	Office of Financial Research
OTC	over the counter
PA	advanced payment (pagamento antecipado)
PD	probability of default
QOQ	quarter-on-quarter
ROE	return on equity
RRs	reserve requirements
RWA	risk-weighted assets
RWF	risk-weight factor
SCAP	Supervisory Capital Assessment Program
SEC	Securities and Exchange Commission (U.S.)
SELIC rate	Brazil's domestic interest rate, the Special Clearance and Escrow System (Sistema Especial de Liquidação e Custodia)
SIFIs	systemically important financial institutions
SIVs	structured investment vehicles
SME	small- and medium-size enterprises
SOFSM	Self-Organizing Financial Stability Map
TBTF	too big to fail
URR	unremunerated reserve requirements
VaR	value-at-risk
YOY	year-on-year

Dealing with the Challenges of Macro Financial Linkages in Emerging Markets
http://dx.doi.org/10.1596/978-1-4648-0002-3

Overview

Introduction

The 2008 financial crisis has highlighted the challenges associated with global financial integration and emphasized the importance of macro financial linkages. Specifically it has shown how the real sector (business cycles) can interact with and be amplified by the financial sector, resulting in high procyclicality and a buildup of systemic risk in the financial sector that manifests itself during economic downturns.

Although boom-bust cycles in asset prices and credit were observed prior to the recent global crisis, they did not seriously challenge the prevailing paradigm. In the macro arena, the general view was that keeping monetary policy focused on price and output stability would deliver the best feasible outcome (Bernanke and Gertler 1999, 2001), although some proponents argued in favor of "leaning against the wind" (Blanchard 2000; Borio and White 2004). In the financial sector, prudential policies in most economies focused narrowly on the soundness of individual financial institutions.

Policies in both the macroeconomic and financial sector arenas are now being debated and reviewed (see Blanchard, Dell'Ariccia, and Mauro 2010, 2013 for overviews). In the financial sector, attention is being directed toward macro prudential regulations that are geared toward the stability of the financial system as a whole. Some of the proposed measures under The Third Basel Accord (Basel III)[1] aim to dampen the procyclicality of the financial sector and to reduce cross-sectional systemic risks partly by introducing measures to address liquidity and issues of banks being too big to fail. In the macro arena, the facts that price stability was not sufficient to guarantee macroeconomic stability and that financial imbalances developed despite low inflation and small output gaps have highlighted the need for additional tools (macro prudential policies) to complement monetary policy in countercyclical management. They have also raised questions about the respective roles and interactions between the monetary and macro prudential policies when either policy operates imperfectly or is constrained.

The policy debate is currently taking place largely, if not exclusively, in the context of the advanced industrial countries. However, emerging markets face different conditions and have key structural features that can have a bearing on the relevance and efficacy of the measures being discussed. Also important, because they suffered earlier financial crises, many emerging markets have had greater experiences with macro prudential and other policies aimed at ensuring financial stability. As such, emerging markets can offer valuable lessons. The chapters in this volume discuss the challenges of dealing with macro financial linkages and explore the policy toolkit available for dealing with systemic risks with particular reference to emerging markets.

Macro Financial Linkages and Systemic Risk

What are the mechanics through which interactions between the financial and real sectors take place and how do these lead to a buildup of systemic risks?

The financial sector is inherently procyclical—that is, it amplifies the business cycle. Interactions between the financial sector and the real sector "causing" this procyclicality largely operate through changes in the value of assets and leverage. As Hyun Shin elucidates in chapter 1, financial intermediaries are not typical of the textbook rational portfolio optimizer who decides on the asset holdings based on an assessment of some fundamental value. Instead, banks and other financial intermediaries have quite perverse portfolio choice behavior—their asset holdings depend on their "balance sheet capacity" and their demand for an asset tends to rise when the price of the asset rises and falls when the price of the asset falls. Balance sheet capacity depends on two things: the amount of bank capital and the degree of permitted leverage. During a boom, balance sheet capacity is bolstered for two reasons. First, bank capital is bolstered by increased profitability of the bank, or the capital gains implied by the increase in asset prices. Second, lowered measured risks during the tranquil up-phase of the financial cycle raise banks' leverage. In particular, if the bank is managing asset risk through managing its value-at-risk (VaR), then a fall in measured risk translates directly into an increase in bank leverage, that is, leverage itself is procyclical. If all banks respond in the same way, the increased demand for assets raises their prices, further fuelling the cycle and leading to a generalized expansion of banks' assets (credit). The amplifying, procyclical nature of banking sector balance sheet management has far-reaching implications for financial stability.

Although banks' balance sheet management is a key element underlying the procyclicality of the financial sector, several other factors can give rise to market failures and externalities that exacerbate the generalized expansion of bank assets (or contraction in a downturn) as discussed by Viral Acharya in chapter 2 and Claessens, Ghosh, and Mihet in chapter 5. Indeed, some aspects of micro prudential regulations that are designed to ensure the stability of individual financial institutions can in fact aggravate both the cyclical and cross-sectional dimensions of systemic risks.

During an upturn or boom period, the financial system as a whole can become vulnerable, by becoming exposed to balance sheet weaknesses or mismatches such as liquidity, maturity, and foreign exchange. These vulnerabilities manifest themselves in the face of shocks (or a downturn in the economy). Thus, as lever-age in the financial sector increases, bank portfolios can become highly exposed to particular asset classes (often real estate), and as discussed by Hyun Shin in chapter 1, on the liabilities side, the ratio of noncore-to-core liabilities tends to rise. Core liabilities can be defined as the funding on which the bank draws dur-ing normal times and which is sourced (in the main) domestically. What consti-tutes core funding will depend on the context and the economy in question, but retail deposits of the household sector are a key candidate. When banking assets are growing rapidly, core funding is likely to be insufficient to finance the rapid growth in new lending (because retail deposits tend to grow in line with aggre-gate household wealth). Thus, other sources of (noncore) funds need to be tapped—usually in the form of interbank liabilities or liabilities to a foreign credi-tor (capital inflows). As Shin documents in chapter 1, very often the source of the increase in noncore funds is from foreign creditors. Prior to the 2008 financial crisis, branches of foreign banks in the United States raised significant amounts of U.S. dollar funding in the U.S. capital markets that were then shipped to their headquarters. Although some of these borrowed dollars found their way back to the United States to finance purchases of mortgage backed securities (MBS) and other assets, much of it flowed to Europe, Asia, and Latin America where global banks are active local lenders. Even for liabilities to domestic creditors, if the creditor is another intermediary, the claim tends to be short term. The distinction between core and noncore liabilities becomes meaningful once there are differ-ences in the empirical properties of the two types of liabilities, with noncore liabilities generally exhibiting less "stickiness" and greater volatility in the face of shocks.

As mentioned, the vulnerability then manifests itself in the face of a negative shock or downturn (fall in asset prices, stops in capital inflows, or sudden with-drawal of funds). Even a small shock, such as declines in collateral values during a downturn, can trigger systemwide problems once financial institutions' balance sheets become weak. If equity buffers are insufficient to absorb losses, for exam-ple, banks may be forced to deleverage, creating systemwide declines in the sup-ply of external financing. The reduced credit extension, in turn, can exacerbate an economic slowdown, raising the probability of default for all other borrowers and can set off an adverse cycle of bank losses, further credit contraction and economic slowdown. Alternatively, a negative shock that shakes depositors' con-fidence can expose banks to the risk of runs, forcing them to hoard liquidity or sell assets at depressed market prices to meet withdrawals, if the systemwide maturity transformation (lending long and borrowing short) or reliance on wholesale funds (noncore funding) is high. Negative externalities related to fire sales can then come into play as a generalized sell-off of financial assets causes a decline in asset prices, which in turn further impairs the balance sheets of inter-mediaries, further amplifying the contractionary phase of the cycle.

The cross-sectional dimension of systemic risk arises from the interconnected-ness of financial institutions and markets, as outlined by Acharya in chapter 2. Given their interconnectedness, the contemporary market-based financial sector should be thought of not only as the deposit-taking, loan-making activities of commercial banks but also as investment banks, money-market funds, insurance firms, and potentially even hedge funds and private equity funds. Even though the financial sectors of emerging economies consist primarily of traditional commercial banks, recent evidence from China and India shows that when commercial banks are restricted in risk taking and leverage growth, emerging economies tend to have an outgrowth of "shadow banking," that is, nonbank financial intermediaries (money market funds and nonbank finance operations) that often remain outside the scope of regulators.

Several types of systemic risks can arise from the failure of interconnected financial institutions, such as counterparty risk, especially in interbank markets; spillover risk due to forced asset sales in asset- or market-based economies; the risk of runs on the shadow-banking system; or simply the inability to resolve failed banks by selling them to better-capitalized firms (given their dearth in a systemic crisis) leading to a credit crunch or regulatory forbearance and the creation of "zombie" institutions that do not allocate resources effectively given their debt overhang problems.

Unless the external costs of such systemic risks imposed on the rest of the financial sector as well as the rest of the economy are internalized by each financial institution, an incentive will remain to take risks whose costs are borne by others. A financial institution's risk is a negative externality on the entire system. Thus, financial regulation should be not only micro prudential but also macro prudential in nature, focused on limiting systemic risk. Absent such macro prudential regulation, economies run the risk of excessively large amplifiers over and above the normal cyclical macroeconomic fluctuation. However, the issue is often not so straightforward. For instance, even if a domestic regulator penalized a multinational financial firm for producing systemic risk locally, the impact of this penalty may not carry through to all the international markets in which the firm operates. This situation makes a case for more severe penalties for firms whose actions can lead to systemic consequences elsewhere. But financial institutions' propensity to conduct regulatory arbitrage across national jurisdictions (that is, if institutions are more strictly regulated in one jurisdiction they may move their base for financial intermediation services to jurisdictions that are more lightly regulated) means such institutions expose all jurisdictions to their risk taking. Individually, jurisdictions may prefer to be regulation "lite" in order to attract more institutions and thereby jobs.

Systemic risk concerns caused by interconnected firms are as important, if not more so, in emerging markets as in advanced economies. As the role of emerging markets in the global economy rises, the importance of risk spillovers across these markets has also grown. It is thus important to look for emerging pockets of macro prudential risk, not just within economies but also outside them. Acharya discusses in greater detail such potential spillovers and global linkages and provides a possible blueprint for achieving better international coordination of macro prudential regulation.

Often, cyclical and cross sectional systemic risks grow in tandem. In a boom, when credit is growing rapidly, the growth of bank balance sheets outstrips the growth in the pool of retail deposits. As a result, the growth of bank lending results in greater lending and borrowing between the intermediaries themselves, or results in "sucking in" of foreign debt. Thus, the "cross-section" dimension of risk, in which banks are vulnerable to a common shock, is closely related to the "time-series" dimension of risk having to do with procyclicality of the balance sheet where assets are larger during the peak of the financial cycle.

Are the Challenges of Macro Financial Linkages Greater in Emerging Markets?

The contributions of Shin and Acharya provide the theoretical foundations for the use of macro prudential policies. The adoption and application of these tools, however, remains at an early stage of analysis. Nonetheless, it seems clear that emerging markets are more likely to need such tools.

Although the 2008 global financial crisis originated in the advanced economies—highlighting the fact that reaping the benefits of financial integration without incurring the costs remains a key challenge for all economies[2]—Stijn Claessens and Swati R. Ghosh argue in chapter 3 that, in general, emerging markets (EMs) tend to face even greater challenges with respect to managing the implications of macro financial linkages, notably with regard to procyclicality. This tendency is for two reasons: their greater exposure to shocks and their institutional characteristics.

Not only are EMs more prone to shocks—particularly capital flows, surges, and stops, but also commodity-price and terms-of-trade shocks—but the magnitude of these shocks, both positive and negative, is often large relative to their domestic economies and the size and depth of their financial sectors. For example, on average, total net private capital flows relative to M2[3] over 2000–10 has been some factor 100 times that for advanced countries (ACs). As a share of local capital markets, financial flows in EMs are thus much larger than in ACs, and certainly more volatile. Also foreign bank presence is greater—more than double—in EMs than in ACs. Unsurprisingly, therefore, shocks to capital flows and foreign banks' operations can have significant impacts on EMs' domestic financial and real sectors. Perhaps more importantly, the amplification of shocks tends to be larger in EMs.

In turn, both susceptibility to external shocks and amplifying transmission mechanisms can, to a significant extent, be traced to structural and financial market characteristics generally prevailing in emerging markets as well as to their institutional environments and policies.

One reason is because financial sectors in most EMs are still largely bank dominated and bank lending against collateral is generally more prevalent than in ACs. In EMs and developing countries, 72–85 percent of loans require collateral, higher than in ACs. Hence, when asset prices and collateral values change, other things being equal, they are more likely to affect lending by banks in EMs than those in ACs. Because borrowers are otherwise constrained, that is, given more limited alternative sources of financing, this change in bank lending is likely to have a greater impact on the real economy in EMs.

More broadly, shocks tend to get amplified and propagated more easily in EMs because of their structural and institutional characteristics. Although EMs have made substantial progress, they still lag behind ACs in measures of overall quality of institutions and have weaker legal regimes and enforcement. Market discipline of financial institutions may not work as well in EMs, given lower information disclosure and transparency, and greater prevalence of insider-type corporate governance arrangements, including firms often linked to financial institutions. These factors, in addition to narrower investor bases and less developed capital markets, and greater financial sector limitations and imperfections, such as limited availability of hedging instruments, tend to amplify and transmit shocks more easily. In the face of uncertainty or a shock, investor confidence fluctuates significantly or can even evaporate. Capital inflows and the potential for sudden stops are especially key sources of risk and shocks for EMs.

Claessens and Ghosh explore and document what these factors mean for the nature of the links between various financial cycles—domestic credit cycles, asset price cycles, and private capital movements—financial crises, and domestic business cycles in emerging markets and contrast them with those in advanced economies. They find that, indeed, the interaction of real and financial cycles tends to be greater in EMs (both in terms of an overlap of recessions with financial events and of recoveries with financial events) (figures O.1 and O.2).

Figure O.1   Recessions Associated with Different Financial Events

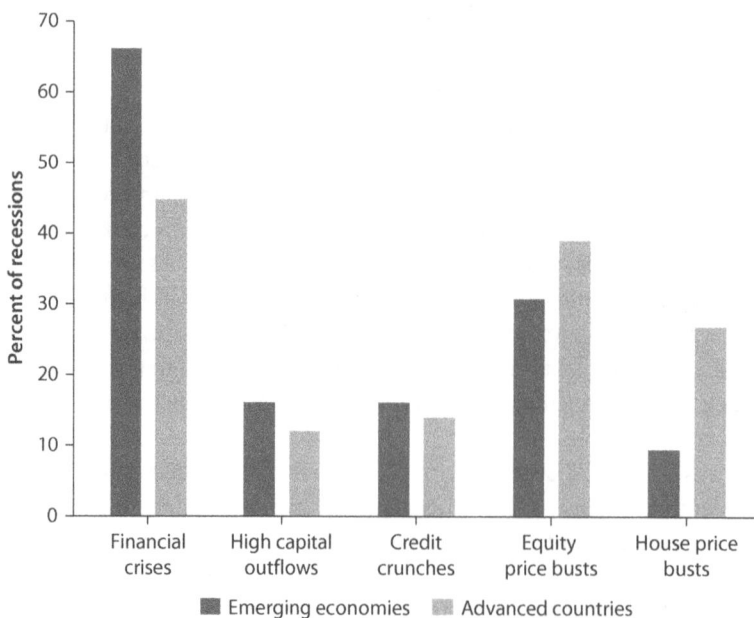

Source: Based on data in chapter 3, calculated from table 3.1.

Figure O.2 Recoveries Associated with Different Financial Events

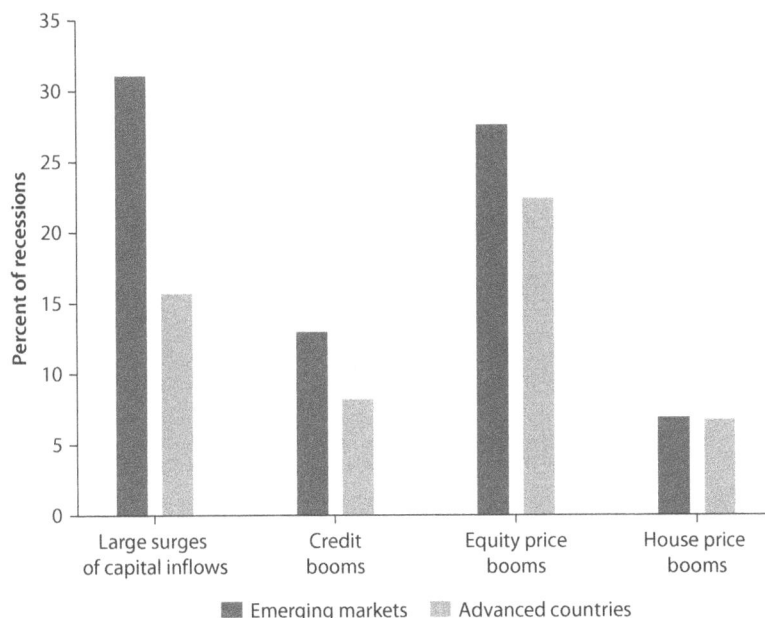

Source: Based on data in chapter 3, calculated from table 3.1.

Moreover, the impact in terms of both favorable and adverse outcomes is much larger in EMs. The stronger link is probably because gyrations in domestic financial markets are often associated with large swings in the direction and volume of capital flows. Indeed, in terms of adverse events, the worst outcomes in EMs are associated with sudden capital outflows where output declines by some 9.5 percent, whereas large capital outflows in advanced economies are associated with a mean drop in output of 2.8 percent; likewise cumulative output losses are 19.4 and 5.8 percent for EMs and ACs respectively (figure O.3).

Broad Policy Toolkit: Monetary and Macro Prudential Policies and their Interactions

How has the global financial crisis and growing recognition of systemic risks altered views on what constitutes an appropriate policy framework? In chapter 4, Otaviano Canuto and Matheus Cavallari discuss the new paradigm for monetary and macro prudential policies. Their discussion takes stock of where monetary and exchange rate policies are heading as a result of recent experiences and revisit theoretical monetary tenets. As they note, the precrisis principles for a monetary policy framework did not give due attention to how financial markets and their channels of interconnectivity affect macro stability. Although many argued in favor of monetary policy "leaning against the wind" from financial developments, the prevalent opinion was that difficulties in detecting bubbles would outweigh the advantages of doing so and that furthermore, monetary

Figure O.3 Cumulative Output Losses Associated with Different Adverse Financial Events

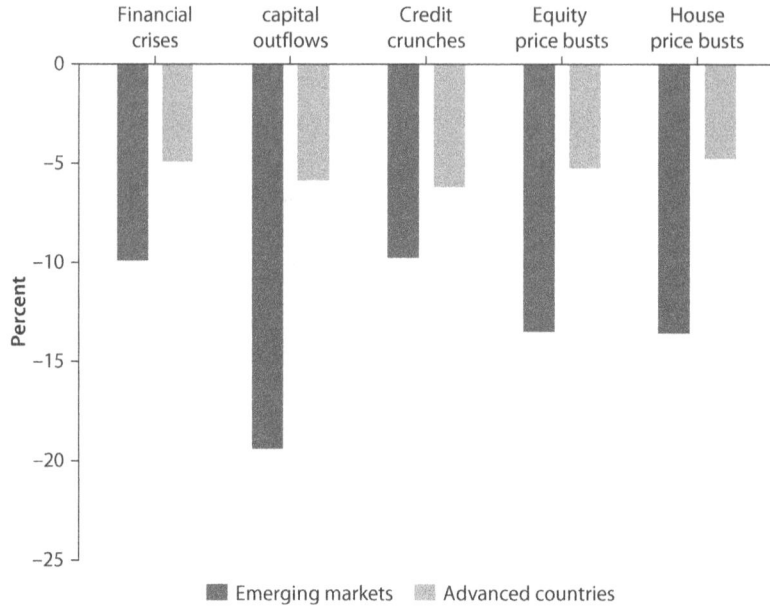

Source: Based on data in chapter 3, calculated from table 3.1.

policy tools would be too blunt to curb the rise of bubbles, because correspondingly sharp interest rate hikes would have harmful unintended consequences on
output growth and volatility. Thus, the best approach would be to have monetary
policy react only if and when "mopping up" or "cleaning up" the financial mess
after bubble bursts was necessary.

Since the crisis, there is growing recognition that a framework of flexible inflation targeting and micro prudential regulations is not sufficient to ensure financial and ultimately macroeconomic stability. Given the high costs associated with
asset price busts, including the possibility of protracted negative feedback
between unsound private balance sheets and public sector imbalances and/or
foregone employment and gross domestic product, attention is now being directed toward addressing this failure. Canuto and Cavalleri explore whether or not
addressing this failure implies that central banks should incorporate indicators of
financial stability into their reaction function in an "augmented Taylor rule." They
then consider whether macro prudential policies alone can reduce financial instability and guarantee both financial and macro stabilities.

As they note, most practitioners have expressed the view that a combined
(articulate) use of both monetary and macro prudential policies is superior to a
standalone implementation of either (Canuto 2011). Both policies are needed as
neither one alone can achieve the two objectives. Monetary policy alone cannot
achieve financial stability because the causes of financial instability are not
always related to the degree of liquidity (which monetary policy can fix).
Mitigating the effects of financial distortions or pricking an asset price bubble can
require large changes in policy rates and when financial distortions (individual

behavior that is distorted giving rise to excessive risk taking and externalities) are more acute in some sectors of the economy than others, monetary policy is too blunt a tool. Conversely, the use of macro prudential policies primarily for managing aggregate demand may in fact cause additional distortions by imposing constraints on behavior beyond areas where financial distortions originate (Claessens and Valencia 2013).

At the same time, the two policies can have impacts on each other's objectives. For instance, monetary policy can affect financial stability when it pursues its primary objective by (1) shaping ex ante risk-taking incentives of individuals through leverage, short-term borrowing or foreign currency borrowing; or (2) affecting ex post the tightness of borrowing constraints and possibly exacerbating asset price and exchange-rate externalities and leverage cycles. Macro prudential policies also have side effects. By constraining borrowing and hence expenditures in one or more sectors of the economy, macro prudential policies affect overall output (Claessens and Valencia 2013).

The existence of side effects implies that the new paradigm needs to take into account how the conduct of both policies is affected in the presence of their interactions. If macro prudential policies have strong effects on output, more accommodative monetary policy can offset these effects as necessary. If changes in the monetary stance affect incentives too much, the relevant macro prudential policies would need to be tightened.

A number of models surveyed by the International Monetary Fund suggest that when both policies are available, it is desirable to keep monetary policy primarily focused on price stability and macro prudential policies focused on financial stability, while taking into account the impact that each has on the other's objectives. In particular, these models suggest that the optimal calibration of the reaction to monetary policy to output and inflation does not change markedly when macro prudential policy is also used, even when different shocks are considered. In other words, the sole presence of side effects has no major implications for the conduct of both policies.

However, as Claessens and Valencia highlight, these models assume that both policies operate perfectly. In practice, policies face constraints. Macro prudential policies may not operate perfectly, especially given the still-limited knowledge about their quantitative impact, which makes calibration difficult, and they may not fully offset financial shocks or distortions; institutions are imperfect and time inconsistencies can arise. Should these weaknesses prove important, monetary policy may have to take a greater role in preserving financial stability and accept the associated trade-offs. Similarly, where monetary policy is constrained—as within currency boards and in many small open economies—there will be greater demands on macro prudential policies. Thus, as Canuto and Cavalleri note in their chapter, "instead of a corner solution where one instrument is devoted entirely to one objective, the macro stabilization exercise must be viewed as a joint optimization problem where monetary and regulatory policies are used in concert in pursuit of both objectives" (CIEPR 2011).

In chapter 4, Canuto and Cavalleri also explore the challenges of dealing with cross-country spillovers in the context of the new policy paradigm. As they mention, cross-border capital flows and the potential transmission of asset price booms and busts via interconnected balance sheets imply additional layers of complexity as opposed to purely domestic asset price cycles. Canuto and Cavalleri propose that capital controls and exchange rate interventions can be seen as options to be combined with monetary and macro prudential policies, options that can even increase, or at least help, with the effectiveness of the latter. Claessens and Ghosh, who also look at the challenges of dealing with cross-border flows in emerging markets in chapter 3 and document how large surges of capital inflows are associated with increased financial sector vulnerability across several dimensions, also reach the conclusion that for most EMs receiving large inflows, it is likely that a combination of macroeconomic, macro prudential, and capital flow management policies is needed to avoid trade-offs and limitations associated with each individual policy instrument. Both chapters emphasize that the appropriate combination will clearly depend on the vulnerability identified, country-specific conditions, and constraints on individual policies. Canuto and Cavalleri conclude chapter 4 with a discussion on the new challenges faced broadly by central banking in emerging markets.

Macro Prudential Framework and Efficacy of Macro Prudential Measures

In chapters 1 and 2, Shin and Acharya discuss what constitutes a macro prudential framework. They highlight that it requires two elements: a set of indicators that can inform judgments on the degree of vulnerability to financial instability and hence serves as the informational basis for policy actions; and the associated macro prudential policy tools or automatic stabilizers that can kick in when circumstances warrant to anticipate and mitigate the vulnerabilities.

From a procyclicality perspective, given the centrality of the banking sector and its potential for amplifying business cycles and exacerbating systemic vulnerability in the process, as Shin notes, the pace of asset growth is of first-order interest. The challenge for policy makers, therefore, is knowing when asset growth may be "excessive" and finding policy tools that can address and counter excessive growth in a timely and effective manner.

Various potential indicators of vulnerability are discussed. Given that noncore liabilities play a key role in the funding of financial institutions' asset expansion during a cyclical upturn, a key indicator of vulnerability discussed in the chapter is the ratio of noncore-to-core liabilities. As Shin points out in chapter 1, what constitutes core and noncore liabilities will vary from country to country and will be context specific; he explores what may be relevant for an economy such as the Republic of Korea and also what may be relevant in countries where regulations restrict the banking sector from having access to the global banking system.

From a cross-sectional perspective, Acharya highlights in chapter 2 the value of using market-based signals of systemic risks. These measures are generally based on stock market data because it is most regularly available and least affected by bailout expectations. For instance, the marginal expected shortfall (MES) measure estimates the loss that the equity of a given firm can expect if the broad market experiences a large fall. A firm with both a high MES and high leverage will find its capital most depleted in a financial crisis relative to required minimum solvency standards and, therefore, faces high risk of bankruptcy or regulatory intervention. It is such undercapitalization of financial firms that leads to systemic risk. Notably he shows how the MES can be used to identify institutions that can pose risks to the system as a whole and shows how the information can be used to guide regulation in the U.S. banking system. Similar results are applicable for European institutions. He also explores how these measures may be adapted and used in emerging markets.

Efficacy of Macro Prudential Measures: Empirical Evidence to Date

Little empirical evidence exists to date on the efficacy of macro prudential policies, notably as to what policies work best in a country-specific context. This issue is explored in chapter 5 by Claessens, Ghosh, and Roxana Mihet. They first review the motivations for macro prudential policies. Then, following a review of the empirical literature on the effectiveness of various macro prudential policies, they report the results of their own analysis, based on an econometric estimation involving a sample of 2,800 banks in 48 countries (advanced and emerging) during the period 2000–10. In particular, they examine the effectiveness of different macro prudential policies—limits on loan-to-value (LTV) ratios, caps on debt-to-income (DTI) ratios, limits on credit growth, limits on foreign currency lending, reserve requirements, restrictions on profit distribution, countercyclical capital requirements, and dynamic provisioning—on reducing financial sector vulnerabilities. Their analysis looks at three dimensions through which the financial sector can become vulnerable: namely increase in leverage, growth in assets, and increase in noncore-to-core liabilities. In assessing the effectiveness of macro prudential policies they also distinguish by the stage of the financial cycle (upturn or downturn), on emerging-versus-advanced economies and in open-versus-closed capital account economies.

Their regression results suggest that many of the macro prudential measures can help control banking system vulnerabilities. However, their analysis also suggests that macro prudential policies are much more effective in booms than in busts, with many coefficients statistically significant in expansionary periods and much fewer in contractionary periods. In principle, tools such as reserve requirements could provide liquidity cushions, while dynamic provisioning could help build capital buffers during upturns, supporting lending during downturns. Other tools such as limits on profit redistribution could also have countercyclical, buffer effects, helping banks' willingness to maintain, or at least reduce less,

Dealing with the Challenges of Macro Financial Linkages in Emerging Markets
http://dx.doi.org/10.1596/978-1-4648-0002-3

their balance sheets in bad times. However, their regressions show that very few policies affect with any statistical significance the speed of decline when the credit cycle reverses. There are actually some negative signs, meaning that having a policy in place worsens the declines.

As they note, the fact that macro prudential policies are mostly effective only in expansionary times may not be surprising, since most macro prudential policies are not designed to mitigate contractionary periods. It could even be that tools like LTV limits actually act perversely during periods of credit contractions and asset price declines. Unless these limits are adjusted quickly in a rightly calibrated manner, that is, without unduly increasing systemic risks, their effects may be perverse.

Regarding the differences in effectiveness of macro prudential policies in emerging markets versus advanced economies, and in open- versus closed-capital-account economies, they do find some differences—including that LTVs are less effective in reducing asset growth in open economies and DTIs are less effective in reducing leverage growth in emerging markets and open economies.

Case Studies: Brazil and the Republic of Korea

The two final chapters deal with the country experiences of Brazil and the Republic of Korea, which deployed macro prudential policies to address their unique macro financial challenges.

In chapter 6, Luiz Perriera da Silva and Ricardo Harris analyze and document Brazil's experience. Brazil fared well during the global financial crisis. By 2010, its GDP was growing at 7.5 percent year-on-year (YOY) and its investment at over 11 percent YOY. But the strong V-shaped recovery—coupled with increased global liquidity, high commodity prices, and strong capital inflows—began to give rise to inflationary pressures, and by 2011 the economy was showing signs of overheating. In addition, an intensified flow of foreign financing increased the potential of financial instability within the economy, which was already going through an extended period of rapid credit expansion (over 22 percent per year between 2005 and 2011).

In this context, Pereira da Silva and Harris outline Brazil's unique experience deploying macro prudential policy to complement existing monetary and fiscal policy tools to address its financial challenges. Brazil increased bank reserve requirements to dampen the transmission of excessive global liquidity to domestic credit markets; increased credit requirements for specific segments of the credit market to address with the aim of stemming the deterioration in the quality of loan origination; and enacted reserve requirements on banks' short-spot foreign exchange positions and taxed specific inflows to correct imbalances in the foreign exchange market as well as to address intensified, volatile inflows of capital. Enacted in addition to policy rate hikes and credible commitments to reduce the public-debt-to-GDP ratio, these measures were successful in reducing the growth of household credit to a more sustainable pace. They affected not only the volume of new loans but also their interest rates and average maturities.

Global financial deterioration in the second half of 2011 (and extending into 2012) gave Brazil an opportunity to fine-tune its deployed macro prudential regulations to tailor them to the new economic outlook, but this proved a difficult task. Indeed, Brazil's experience in this regard is indicative of the incomplete understanding of the economics profession of how systemic financial risks develop and how macro prudential tools impact those risks, particularly in emerging markets. For example, the bulk of the macro prudential regulations enacted by Brazil dealt with the time-series dimension of systemic risk, that is, with the procyclicality of the financial system. However, given the high degree of conglomeration in the Brazilian financial system, experience quickly showed that that cross-section risks arising from the interconnectedness of the financial system and the real economy also would need to be addressed.

Brazil's experience as outlined by Pereira da Silva and Harris is illuminating, especially for emerging markets. Brazil was innovative during and after the peak of the global financial crisis, not least in exploring the boundaries of Tinbergen's separation principle, using two instruments (the base rate and a set of macro prudential tools) to address two objectives (price stability and financial stability). The country's experience exemplifies the need for regulators and central bankers to be "ahead of the curve" in dealing with ongoing financial stress in the present context of the global economy.

This mindset may be illustrated by the experience of Korea, as described by Jong Kyu Lee in chapter 7. Korea operated several macro prudential policy instruments prior to the advent of the financial crisis in 2008. Although not based on the concept of financial stability as currently discussed, these instruments did take forms similar to those now in vogue. For example, as part of its systematic macro prudential framework, Korea applied several types of liquidity ratio regulations as early as 1997 aimed at addressing potential weakness in domestic banking and foreign exchange transactions. Later, with a housing boom becoming apparent, Korean authorities also introduced an LTV ratio and, finally, a DTI ratio.

These arguably prudent measures notwithstanding, Korea faced a round of crisislike events in 2008. The economy had accumulated a new type of financial imbalance in domestic banking as well as in foreign exchange transactions, associated in part with the housing market boom. Banks had raised funds through noncore liabilities and expanded their lending to households in line with strong housing prices. Meanwhile, to meet the growing demand for foreign exchange derivatives transactions, banks had simultaneously begun to rely increasingly on short-term foreign borrowing. Lee thus assesses that the macro prudential measures "were unable to achieve the ultimate goal of 'preventing systemic events.'"

Lee identifies a number of factors to which this failure may be attributed. The micro rather than macro prudential objectives of the measures are noted first. Another reason may have been the governance of the measures. Supervisory

Dealing with the Challenges of Macro Financial Linkages in Emerging Markets
http://dx.doi.org/10.1596/978-1-4648-0002-3

authorities, whose purview rests in micro prudential territory, were responsible for handling these measures and, thus, were not targeting macro level variables or events critical to financial stability. Chapter 7 outlines these and other factors in more detail, providing lessons for the rapidly evolving macro prudential policy arena.

That being said, Lee does find that these policy measures had some impact. He finds that the limits on LTV and DTI ratios helped maintain the soundness of financial institutions during the global crisis, but that these measures had only a temporary effect in dampening housing prices and housing loan volumes in the period prior to the crisis.

The Korean experience offers important lessons about the potential as well as the limitations of these types of regulations. Above all, the Korean experience serves as a basis for evaluating several macro prudential measures from a variety of viewpoints. For a well-defined macro prudential framework, the objective, scope, and other elements of the policy need to be specified. The choices of operational options, such as single versus multiple measures, broad-based versus targeted risks, and fixed versus time-varying application can also impact the effectiveness of macro prudential tools. In this regard, the Korean experience is a good illustration of not only how macro prudential tools may be deployed but also what can go wrong in the deployment of macro prudential measures with respect to the factors outlined above.

Notes

1. The Third Basel Accord is a global, voluntary regulatory standard on bank capital adequacy, stress testing, and market liquidity risk.

2. The buildup of banking systems vulnerabilities in advanced economies prior to the global crisis took place through complex chains of financial intermediation and involved large gross capital flows. Global banks, particularly European banks, were key players in this process, raising funds in U.S. wholesale markets and then lending these back to U.S. residents through purchases of securitized claim on U.S. borrowers, mostly related to residential mortgages. While net capital flows—that is, the net of gross inflows and outflows—were relatively small, gross exposures ended up being very large. The shock that originated in the U.S. subprime market quickly affected many financial systems around the world. As banks were vulnerable on their funding side to wholesale markets and developments in the U.S. dollar shadow-banking system, liquidity shortages quickly spread. These disturbances lead to major real sector dislocations as the tightening of funding spurred a downward cycle of balance sheet contractions and deleveraging declining asset prices and declining economic activity (Claessens and others 2012).

3. M2 is the sum of currency held by the public and transaction deposits at depository institutions (which are financial institutions that obtain their funds mainly through deposits from the public, such as commercial banks, savings and loan associations, savings banks, and credit unions), savings deposits, small-denomination time deposits (those issued in amounts of less than $100,000), and retail money market mutual fund shares.

References

Bernanke, Ben, and Mark Gertler. 1999. "Monetary Policy and Asset Price Volatility." *Economic Review*, Federal Reserve Bank of Kansas, Fourth Quarter.

———. 2001. "Should Central Banks Respond to Movements in Asset Prices?" *American Economic Review* 91 (2): 253–57.

Blanchard, Oliver. 2000. "Bubbles, Liquidity Traps and Monetary Policy." http://economics.mit.edu/files/718.

Blanchard, Olivier, Giovanni Dell'Ariccia, and Paulo Mauro. 2010. "Rethinking Macroeconomic Policy." Staff Position Note SPN/10/03, International Monetary Fund, Washington, DC.

———. 2013. "Rethinking Macro Policy II: Getting Granular." Staff Discussion Note SPN/13/03, International Monetary Fund, Washington, DC.

Borio, Claudio, and William White 2004 "Whither Monetary and Financial stability? The Implications of Evolving Policy Regimes." Working Paper 147, Bank for International Settlements, Basel, Switzerland.

Canuto, Otaviano. 2011. *How Complementary Are Prudential Regulation and Monetary Policy?* Washington, DC: World Bank.

CIEPR (Committee on International Economic Policy and Reform). 2011. *Rethinking Central Banking.* Washington, DC: Brookings Institution.

Claessens, S., G. Dell'Ariccia, D. Igan, and L. Laeven. 2012. "A Cross-Country Perspective on the Causes of the Global Financial Crisis." In *The Evidence and Impact of Financial Globalization*, 737–52. The Netherland: Elsevier.

Claessens, Stijn, and Fabian Valencia. 2013. "The Interaction of Monetary and Macroprudential Policies." Column, March, Voxeu.org. http://www.voxeu.org/article/interaction-between-monetary-and-macroprudential-policies

CHAPTER 1

Adapting Macro Prudential Approaches to Emerging and Developing Economies

Hyun Song Shin*

Introduction

Traditionally, the focus of prudential policy has been on the solvency of individual financial institutions. Indeed, prior to the global financial crisis of 2007–09 the overall approach and reasoning underlying prudential regulations could have been broadly characterized by the following set of propositions:

- Minimum capital requirements serve as a buffer against loss of bank assets, thereby protecting depositors from loss. The fact that risk-weighted assets are used as the denominator in the capital ratio reveals the purpose of the capital requirement as setting a buffer against loss for the senior creditors, especially the depositors. If deposits are insured by the government, the bank capital requirement also serves as a buffer against loss by taxpayers.
- Minimum capital requirements ensure that the banks' owners have a stake in the value of the bank's assets, thereby ensuring that owners have sufficient "skin in the game" to deter moral hazard on their part toward excessive risk taking.
- Having ensured financial stability through bank capital requirements and in the presence of well functioning international capital markets, the role of monetary policy is to focus on macroeconomic stabilization by setting interest rates to stabilize components of aggregate demand such as consumption and investment.

The global financial crisis has raised questions regarding the adequacy of a policy framework based on these propositions alone, and has spurred a reassessment of the purpose and effectiveness of prudential regulations. However, the

* **Hyun Song Shin** is Hughes-Rogers Professor of Economics at Princeton University. He thanks Swati R. Ghosh and Stijn Claessens for comments and guidance on this chapter.

thinking has not yet borne fruit in terms of any fundamental shift in the debate concerning prudential policy.

Thus, the Third Basel Accord (Basel III), the new capital and liquidity framework for banks, has continued the tradition of basing banking regulation on building buffers against loss. The centerpiece of the new agreed framework is a strengthened common equity buffer of 7 percent together with newly introduced liquidity requirements and a leverage cap to be phased in over an extended timetable running to 2019 (BCBS 2010).

Basel III also incorporates a countercyclical capital surcharge in the range of 0–2.5 percent that can be introduced at the discretion of national regulators. The rationale for the countercyclical surcharge is to lean against the procyclicality of the financial system by demanding a higher capital buffer at the peak of the financial cycle. Basel III also envisages additional requirements on systemically important financial institutions (SIFIs) in the form of capital surcharges, leverage caps or levies designed to impose a higher margin of safety on institutions that are deemed "too big to fail."

However, neither the countercyclical capital requirement nor the SIFI surcharge has found universal and consistent acceptance among the member countries of the Basel Committee on Banking Supervision (BCBS). In the case of the countercyclical capital requirement, disagreement among the BCBS member countries on a uniform rate of the capital surcharge has meant that countries can, in effect, opt out of the requirement. The countercyclical capital surcharge is left to the discretion of the national regulators, who can impose them within a range of 0–2.5 percent. In the case of SIFIs, discussions are currently focused on the imposition of a possible capital surcharge on global SIFIs (G-SIFIs), such as large banks with cross-border operations. Discussions have revolved around the difficulties of cross-border resolution and, hence, the need to overcome the moral hazard engendered by the banks being too big to fail. For emerging or developing countries, though, the issues raised by cross-border banking are somewhat different and have to do with their impact during booms and their role in creating excess liquidity as discussed later.

Overall, the common denominator in Basel III that applies universally (that is, not considering the countercyclical capital or SIFI surcharges) is almost exclusively micro prudential in its focus, that is, concerned with the resilience of individual banks, rather than being macro prudential and concerned with the resilience of the financial system as a whole. Its focus remains on "loss absorbency" of bank capital.

Achieving greater loss absorbency by itself is almost certainly inadequate to achieving a stable financial system for two reasons:

- Loss absorbency does not address directly the procyclicality of the financial system and the *excessive asset growth* during booms.
- Preoccupation with loss absorbency diverts attention from the *liabilities* side of banks' balance sheets and vulnerabilities from the reliance on unstable short-term funding and short-term foreign currency funding.

These two shortcomings have special importance for developing and emerging economies given their susceptibility to global liquidity conditions and the relatively early stage of the development of their financial systems. Indeed, the Basel process has focused almost exclusively on the imperatives of advanced-country financial systems, rather than on the needs of emerging markets and developing countries.

This chapter discusses the principles behind macro prudential policies and how these principles can be translated into a policy framework. It is intended primarily as a conceptual document that lays out the economic principles that underpin macro prudential policy rather than as a "how to" manual that details an exhaustive list of possible policy measures and relevant country experiences.

Analytical Background

In keeping with its conceptual focus, the chapter begins by outlining salient elements of the theory and practice of balance sheet management by financial intermediaries. Against this background of financial institutions' balance sheet management, the next section discusses how global liquidity conditions and the external environment affect banks' funding options and their implications for financial stability.

Balance Sheet Management

The banking system occupies a pivotal role for financial stability. Principles of balance sheet management that can inform policy discussions are described here.[1]

In textbook discussions of corporate financing decisions, the set of positive net present value (NPV) projects is often taken as given, with the implication that the size of the balance sheet is fixed and determined exogenously. In a simplified setting, the choice can be depicted as in figure 1.1. The assets are fixed, given exogenously by the set of projects (assets) in grey that have positive NPV. Having fixed the asset side of the balance sheet, the discussion turns on how those assets are financed—that is, on the liabilities side of the balance sheet.

The left-hand panel of figure 1.1 shows a balance sheet in which the assets are financed predominately by equity. The arrow indicates a shift in the funding mix to a state in which some of the equity is replaced by debt. One way this could be accomplished is through the repurchase of equity by using the

Figure 1.1 Choice of Mix of Debt and Equity Financing

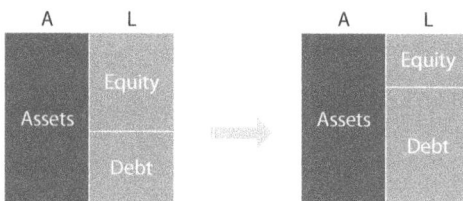

proceeds of a debt issue. The leverage of the firm is defined as the ratio of assets to equity. Hence the shift depicted in figure 1.1 leads to an increase in the leverage of the firm but without any change in the size of the balance sheet as a whole.

However, figure 1.1 is not a good description of the way banking sector leverage varies over the financial cycle. The distinguishing feature of banking sector leverage is that it fluctuates through changes in the total size of the balance sheet. Credit increases rapidly during the boom phase and increases less rapidly (or even decreases) during the downturn. Some of the variation in the size of banking assets can be accounted for by the fluctuations in the size of the pool of positive NPV projects but some of the fluctuation is caused by shifts in the bank's willingness to take on risky positions over the cycle—that is, on the bank's risk appetite.

Adrian and Shin (2010, 2011) show that shifts in the leverage of financial intermediaries conform more closely to figure 1.2 in which leverage increases by an expansion of *assets*, taking the equity of the bank as a given.

One plausible scenario with empirical backing that is consistent with the change depicted in figure 1.2 is when the bank manages the size of its loan book so that its risk-weighted assets are maintained to be equal to its capital. If the bank assesses that the risks of lending have declined, it can expand its lending without breaching its minimum capital requirements.

Consider, for example, what happens when the equity of the bank itself is subject to shocks—both positive and negative. During the upward phase of the financial cycle, greater profitability of the bank bolsters its capital position. This bolstered capital position constitutes a positive shock to equity. (Conversely, during the downward phase of the financial cycle, losses or provisioning for bad debt constitutes a negative shock to equity.) Even if the bank were to target a fixed leverage ratio, the positive shock to equity would cause the bank to increase the size of its balance sheet. For instance, suppose that a financial intermediary manages its balance sheet actively so as to maintain a constant leverage ratio of 10 and that the initial balance sheet is as follows: the intermediary holds $100 worth of assets and the bank holds marketable securities, which have been funded with debt worth $90 and equity of $10 as in figure 1.3.

Figure 1.2 Increased Leverage through Expansion in Assets

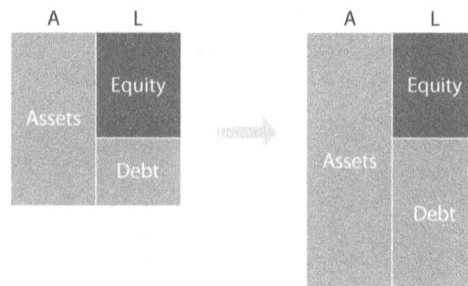

Now assume that the value of the debt is approximately constant for small changes in total assets. First, let's assume that the price of securities increases by 1 percent to 101. This shock impacts the balance sheet as depicted in figure 1.4.

Leverage falls to 101/11 = 9.18. If the bank targets leverage of 10, then it must take on additional debt of D to purchase D worth of securities on the asset side so that:

$$\text{Assets/equity} = (101+D)/11 = 10, \text{ which implies that } D = 9.$$

The bank takes on additional debt worth $9 and with the proceeds purchases securities worth $9. Thus, an increase in the price of the security of $1 leads to an increased holding worth $9. The demand response for the assets held by the bank is upward sloping. After the purchase, leverage is back up to 10 (figure 1.5).

If the bank's assets consist of loans rather than securities, then the increase in equity is better viewed as a result of improved profitability of the bank, when some of the net income is accumulated into bank equity. The practice of "marking to market," where assets are valued according to prevailing market prices, will mean a more immediate reflection of the asset value increase on the bank's equity position.

Figure 1.3 Initial Balance Sheet

Assets	Liabilities
Securities, 100	Equity, 10
	Debt, 90

Figure 1.4 Price of Securities Increases

Assets	Liabilities
Securities, 101	Equity, 11
	Debt, 90

Figure 1.5 Bank Adds Debt

Assets	Liabilities
Securities, 110	Equity, 11
	Debt, 99

The mechanism works in reverse on the way down. Suppose there is a shock to the price of securities so that the value of security holdings falls to $109. On the liabilities side, it is equity that bears the burden of adjustment, since the value of debt stays approximately constant (see figure 1.6).

Dealing with the Challenges of Macro Financial Linkages in Emerging Markets
http://dx.doi.org/10.1596/978-1-4648-0002-3

Figure 1.6 Value of Securities Falls

Assets	Liabilities
Securities, 109	Equity, 10
	Debt, 99

Figure 1.7 Bank Sells Securities

Assets	Liabilities
Securities, 100	Equity, 10
	Debt, 90

Leverage is now too high ($109/10 = 10.9$). The bank can adjust down its leverage by selling securities worth \$9 and paying down \$9 worth of debt. In this way, a fall in the price of securities leads to a sale of securities. The supply response is downward sloping, unlike the textbook case of an upward sloping supply response. The new balance sheet is hence restored to where it stood before the price changes and leverage is back down to the target level of 10 (figure 1.7).

In this way, maintaining constant leverage entails upward-sloping demand responses and downward-sloping supply responses for the assets held by the bank. *The perverse nature of the demand and supply curves is even stronger when the leverage of the financial intermediation is procyclical, that is, when leverage is high during booms and low during busts.* As demonstrated in Adrian and Shin (2010, 2011), banks' active management of their balance sheets and their use of value-at-risk (VaR) models results in procyclical leverage because the boom (downturn) reduces (increases) measured risk and hence induces banks to increase (decrease) their leverage.

If, in addition, there is the possibility of feedback, the adjustment of leverage and of price changes will reinforce each other in amplification of the financial cycle. If greater demand for the assets tends to put upward pressure on its price, there is potential for feedback in which a stronger balance sheet triggers greater demand for the asset (that is, greater lending), which in turn raises the asset's price and leads to stronger balance sheets. In the case of banks with loans rather than securities on the balance sheet, the amplification goes through the greater profitability of the banks during the up-phase of the financial cycle.

The mechanism works in reverse in downturns. If greater supply of the asset tends to put downward pressure on its price, then weaker balance sheets lead to greater sales of the asset, which depresses the asset's price and leads to even weaker balance sheets. Figure 1.8 illustrates the amplification mechanism in both the upward and downward phases of the financial cycle.

Figure 1.8 Amplification Mechanism

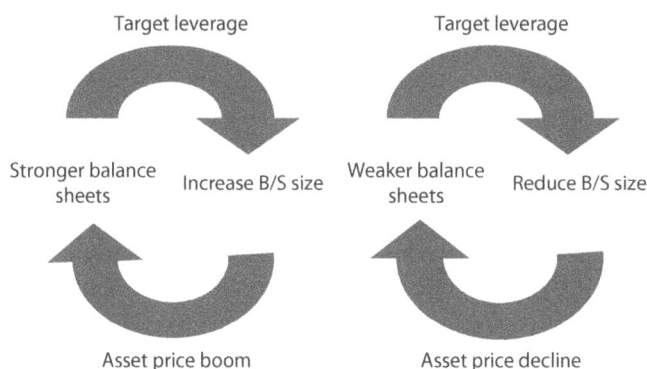

The amplifying nature of banking sector balance sheet management has far-reaching implications for financial stability. Financial intermediaries are not typical of the textbook rational portfolio optimizer who decides on the asset holdings based on an assessment of some fundamental value. Instead, banks and other financial intermediaries have quite perverse portfolio choice behavior where the holding of assets depends on their "balance sheet capacity." Balance sheet capacity depends on two things: the amount of bank capital and the degree of permitted leverage.

During a boom, balance sheet capacity is bolstered for two reasons. First, bank capital is bolstered by increased profitability of the bank, or the capital gains implied by the increase in asset prices. Second, lowered measured risks during the tranquil up-phase of the financial cycle raise banks' leverage. In particular, if a bank is managing asset risk through managing its value-at-risk, then a fall in measured risk translates directly into an increase in bank leverage (Adrian and Shin 2009).

This perspective of the banking sector balance sheet capacity also sheds light on one finding regarding the financial stability implications of banking-sector foreign direct investment (FDI) (see Ostry and others 2010). FDI flows are usually equity stakes held by foreign investors and are conventionally associated with long-term financing that has beneficial effects. In this sense, FDI is normally regarded as being a benign form of capital inflow. However, banking-sector FDI appears to have a more destabilizing influence. This point is especially relevant with respect to the experience of emerging Europe during the recent global crisis. Ostry and others (2010) find in their empirical analysis that financial-sector FDI is associated with larger stocks of debt liabilities of the banking sector and does not have the conventionally expected beneficial effect. Indeed, countries with larger financial FDI fared worse in the current crisis, while those with larger nonfinancial FDI fared better. The vulnerability of emerging Europe in the wake of the recent crisis and the region's heavy dependence for capital on foreign banking groups, particularly those from Western Europe, gives some clues on the likely mechanism. Larger financial-sector FDI in the form of greater inflows of banking sector capital is the base on which larger banking sector balance sheet capacity will be built. Thus, the banking-sector FDI inflow will be accompanied by the debt financing that builds up the banking sector's total lending capacity. If the local savings pool (say, through local retail deposits) is not large enough to finance the expansion in lending, the parent bank will supply intragroup funding through wholesale deposit funding or other wholesale funding. In this way, financial-sector FDI in the banking sector is inextricably bound with greater debt flows into the banking sector and leads to a growth in the nondeposit funding used by the local banking system. Ostry and others (2010) find that both debt and financial FDI are strongly associated with credit booms and foreign exchange (FX)-denominated lending by the domestic banking system, which in turn is associated with greater vulnerability. Both are key channels through which a country becomes susceptible to crises. The greater vulnerability to crises holds even controlling for credit booms and FX-denominated lending, perhaps because households and firms may borrow directly from abroad (or flows are intermediated through nonbank financial institutions).

External Environment and Global Liquidity

External financial conditions provide the backdrop to domestic financial conditions, especially when the domestic banking system is open to funding from internationally active banking groups with cross-border operations and also purely domestically focused banks with cross-border financial activities. This section outlines the ways in which the external environment and global liquidity impact on financial stability.

The low interest rates maintained by advanced-economy central banks in the aftermath of the global crisis have ignited a lively debate about capital flows to emerging markets. One of the distinguishing features of the credit boom that preceded the global financial crisis of 2008 was the role played by banking sector inflows. Banking sector inflows surged during the period leading up to the Lehman Brothers bankruptcy, in contrast to the Asian crisis and in the immediate aftermath of the current crisis, when banking-sector inflows accounted for less than 20 percent of capital inflows (see IMF 2011). Understanding the external environment and the role of cross-border banking is important in putting the recent crisis in context.

The U.S. dollar bank funding market has special significance in this debate. As well as being the world's most important reserve currency and invoicing currency in international trade, the U.S. dollar is also the currency that underpins the global banking system. It is the funding currency of choice for global banks. The United States hosts branches of about 160 foreign banks whose main function is to raise wholesale dollar funding in capital markets and then ship it to their head offices.

Some of the borrowed dollars return to the United States to finance purchases of mortgage-backed securities (MBS) and other assets. But much of it flows to Europe, Asia, and Latin America where global banks are active local lenders (figure 1.9). In this way, global banks become the carriers for the transmission of

Figure 1.9 Role of Global Banks

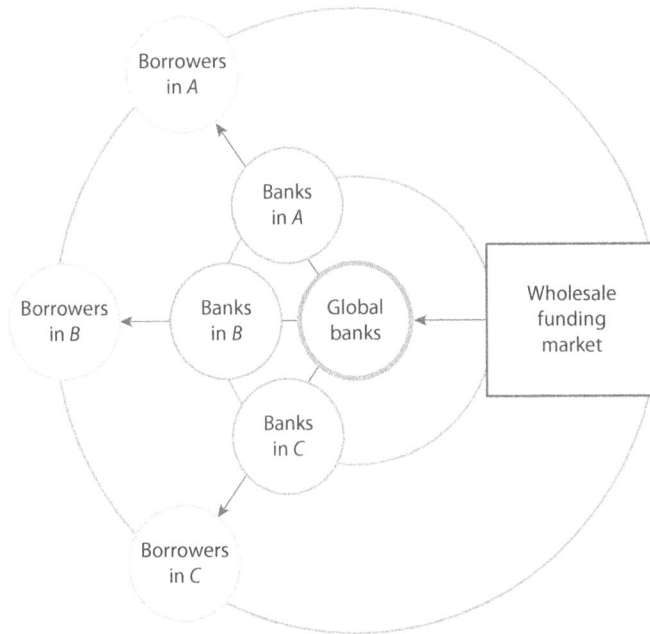

liquidity spillovers across borders. At the margin, the shadow value of bank fund-ing will be equalized across all regions through portfolio decisions of global banks so that global banks become the carriers of dollar liquidity across borders. As such, permissive U.S. liquidity conditions are transmitted globally and U.S. mon-etary policy becomes, in some respects, global monetary policy.

Foreign bank branches raise over US$1 trillion of funding, of which over US$600 billion is channeled to their headquarters (CGFS 2010). This figure cov-ers just the branches of foreign banks, not their subsidiaries. If the funding shipped to the parent by the U.S.-based subsidiaries is also considered, the total funding shipped to headquarters would be substantially higher. A key quantity is the inter-office assets of foreign bank branches in the United States—the lending by branch-es to headquarters—as shown in figure 1.10. Interoffice assets increased steeply in the last two decades, saw a sharp decline in 2008, but bounced back in 2009.

What is remarkable about the U.S. dollar funding market is that even in net terms, foreign banks have been channeling large amounts of dollar funding out of the United States to their respective head offices. Figure 1.11 shows net interoffice assets of foreign banks in the United States. Net interoffice assets measure the net claim of the branch or subsidiary of the foreign bank on its parent. Normally, net interoffice assets would be negative, as foreign bank branches act as lending outposts. However, we see that the decade 2001–11 was exceptional, when net interoffice assets turned sharply positive, before reversing into negative territory during the height of the European crisis in 2011. In effect, between 2001 and 2011, foreign bank offices became funding sources for the

Figure 1.10 Interoffice Assets of Foreign Bank Branches in United States

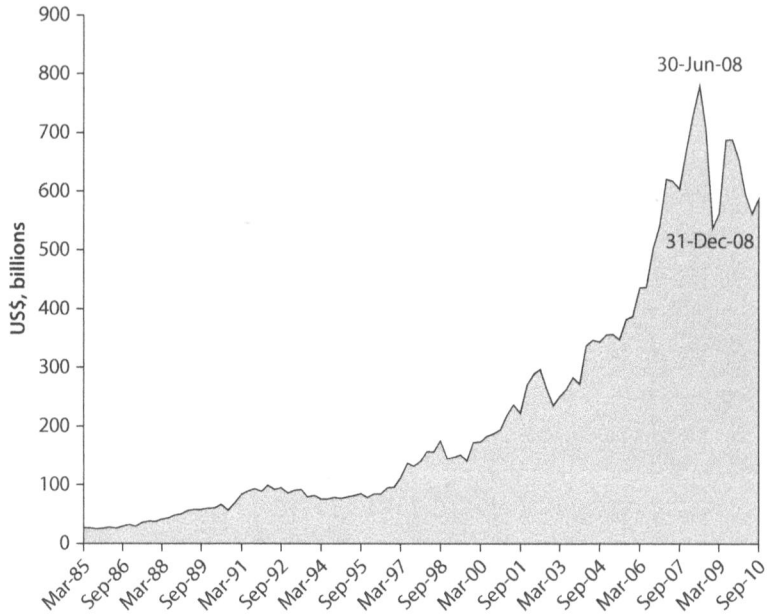

Source: Federal Reserve.

parent, rather than lending outposts. As noted in a recent Bank for International Settlements (BIS) report, many European banks use a centralized funding model in which available funds are deployed globally through a centralized portfolio allocation decision (BIS 2010a). The net interoffice position of foreign banks in the United States therefore reflects the extent to which global banks were engaged in supplying U.S. dollar funding to other parts of the world.

We thus face an apparent paradox: although the United States is the largest net debtor in the world, it is a substantial net creditor in the global banking system. In effect, the United States is borrowing long (through treasury and other securities) but lending short through the banking sector. This situation is in contrast to countries such as Ireland and Spain that financed their current account deficits through their respective banking sectors and that have subsequently paid the price through runs by wholesale creditors on their banks.

In this chapter we will make frequent use of the net interoffice account position of foreign banks in the United States as an empirical proxy for the availability of wholesale funding provided to borrowers in the capital-recipient economy. Bruno and Shin (2011) conducted an empirical study of the sensitivity of capital flows to global factors.

Although there is a large degree of synchronization of banking-sector flows across different geographical regions and countries, there is also some diversity in the pattern of banking flows. Emerging Europe saw the most rapid increase in banking-sector inflows, followed by countries such as Turkey and the Republic of Korea. One factor in the diverse regional experiences has to do with the divergent business models pursued by cross-border banks that form the bridge between a

Figure 1.11 Trends in Assets of Foreign Banks in the United States

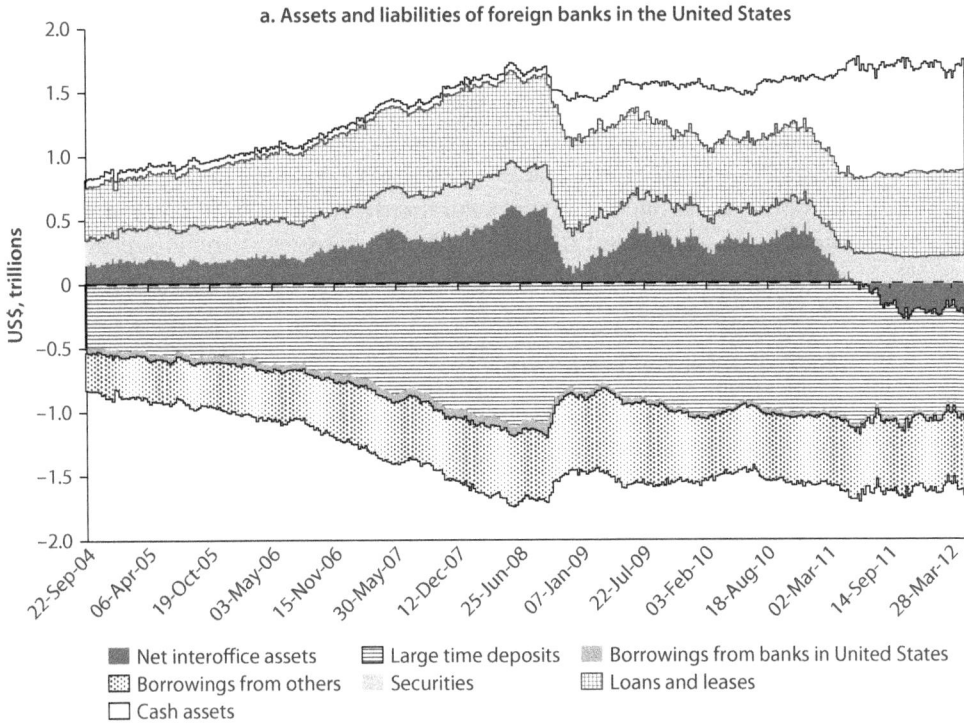

a. Assets and liabilities of foreign banks in the United States

Legend:
- Net interoffice assets
- Large time deposits
- Borrowings from banks in United States
- Borrowings from others
- Securities
- Loans and leases
- Cash assets

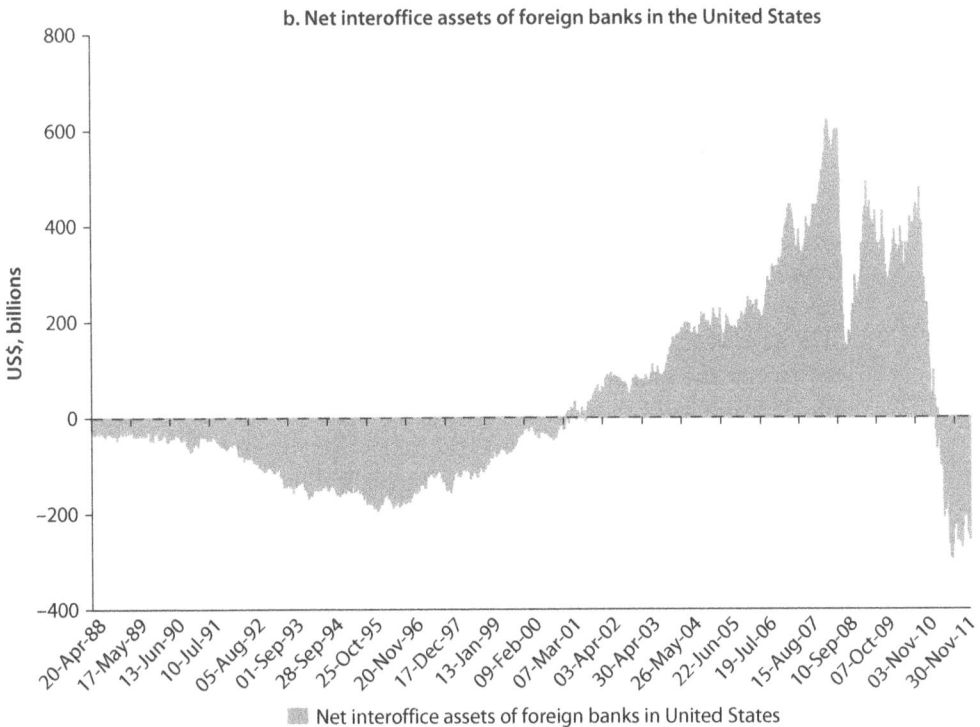

b. Net interoffice assets of foreign banks in the United States

Net interoffice assets of foreign banks in United States

Source: Federal Reserve Board H8 series on commercial banks.

Dealing with the Challenges of Macro Financial Linkages in Emerging Markets
http://dx.doi.org/10.1596/978-1-4648-0002-3

particular region and the global banking system. Another BIS paper on funding patterns of global banks draws a distinction between global banks that operate a centralized portfolio allocation model and those that pursue a more decentralized operational model (BIS 2010b). Spanish banks that have large local subsidiaries in Latin America are cited as an example of the decentralized mode of operation, where the local subsidiaries draw on local deposit funding and operate largely independently from the parent in terms of its asset allocation. In contrast, European banks operate a more centralized portfolio allocation model where the portfolio allocation and funding decisions are made at the group headquarters and the banking group's global portfolio decision follows a centralized pattern.

Macro Prudential Framework

Drawing on the analytical background discussed earlier, we turn to the elements of a macro prudential framework. A macro prudential framework encompasses two key elements:

- A set of indicators that can inform judgments on the degree of vulnerability to financial instability and hence serve as the informational basis for policy actions
- An associated set of policy tools or automatic stabilizers that can kick in when circumstances warrant to anticipate and mitigate the vulnerabilities.

Macro Prudential indicators

Given the centrality of the banking sector and its potential for amplifying the procyclicality of the financial system, the pace of asset growth is of first-order interest. The challenge for policy makers is knowing when asset growth may be "excessive" and finding policy tools that can address and counter the excessive asset growth in a timely and effective manner.

Ratio of Credit Growth to GDP

Indicators that capture some notion of the ratio of total private sector credit to GDP have been discussed. This ratio has been shown to be a useful indicator of the stage of the financial cycle, as demonstrated by the work of BIS economists, notably Borio and Lowe (2002, 2004).

Under the Basel III framework, the ratio of credit to GDP has been given a central role in the framework for countercyclical buffer. The initial consultation document (BCBS 2009) issued by the Basel Committee in December 2009 first proposed a countercyclical capital buffer surcharge to act as a further buffer against loss during the upswing of the financial cycle. Subsequent development of the concept focused on the credit-to-GDP ratio as a measure of procyclicality that would trigger increased capital requirements on banks. The final version of the Basel III framework left the implementation of the countercyclical capital buffer to the discretion of national regulators, with the additional buffer in the range of 0–2.5 percent.

Conceptually, it is natural that credit growth should be scaled by normalizing it relative to some underlying fundamental measure. Normalizing credit growth by GDP has many advantages. GDP is an aggregate flow measure of economic activity that reflects current economic conditions, and one that is readily available under basic national income calculations. Moreover, it is a measure that is highly standardized across countries, which helps in competition and level-playing field disputes in the consistent implementation of international banking regulation rules.

However, there are measurement challenges, even for the concept of credit growth. To serve as a signal of procyclicality, credit growth should mirror the risk-taking attitudes of market premiums, where they are relevant. The need for judgment is important in emerging and developing countries where long-term structural changes through financial development may render credit growth statistics less useful as a gauge of risk appetite. For instance, if the ratio of private credit to GDP shows rapid increase because of informal credit arrangements moving into the formalized banking sector, such a development has benign consequences for financial stability. In contrast, if the ratio of private credit to GDP increases because of a housing boom that is fed by cheap credit and the recycling of funding by nonfinancial companies, the financial stability implications are more worrying. The simple credit-to-GDP ratio may suffer from the fact that the aggregate measures of credit growth may mask some subtleties that cannot be summarized in one simple aggregate. It is also conceivable that there may be endogenous changes in economic relationships if the reduced-form economic relationships that underpin credit and GDP are used for policy purposes.

A possible counterargument to the accusation that the credit-to-GDP ratios may be too blunt is that any policy maker would exercise judgment when interpreting figures. Also, it could be argued that there is an asymmetry between the upswing part of the financial cycle and the downswing part. During the upswing, it may be argued that the policy of "leaning against the wind" can utilize information contained in the rapid growth of the credit-to-GDP ratio.

Assenmacher-Wesche and Gerlach (2010) present an opposing viewpoint to the emphasis placed by Borio and Lowe (2002, 2004) on the credit-to-GDP ratio as an informative signal of the buildup of vulnerabilities in the economy. Assenmacher-Wesche and Gerlach (2010) take a skeptical line on the link between credit growth and property price increases. Although they find that credit shocks are associated with increases in real GDP and equity prices, they do not find evidence that credit growth has a large impact on property prices. The authors take this result as evidence that the bulk of the variation in credit growth is related to expected future changes in real economic activity, and they conclude that the widely accepted view that fluctuations in credit growth have been a major driver of property price shocks seems not to be supported by the data. Assenmacher-Wesche and Gerlach's (2010) study uses data from the Organisation for Economic Co-operation and Development (OECD) countries covering the period 1986–2008. Hence, their study applies to advanced economies rather than to developing and emerging economies. However, the difficulty of finding conclusive evidence for the link between credit and property prices may be more widely applicable.

The fundamental difficulty is that a simple credit-to-GDP ratio lacks a conceptual framework that can easily link the measurement to measures of financial vulnerability. The skeptic could always argue that a surge in credit could either be caused by a structural change in the economy, the increase in positive net present value projects, and hence the *demand* for credit that is fully justified by the fundamentals, or simply by the migration of lending relationships to the formal banking sector that were previously taking place in the informal sector. Further research will be necessary to determine to what extent the simple credit-to-GDP ratio can serve as a finely calibrated signal that can support the use of automatic tightening of bank capital standards, as envisaged in the Basel III framework.

Bank Liability Aggregates

Because of the difficulties in using the simple credit-to-GDP ratio as the appropriate signal of the stage of the financial cycle, alternatives may be preferable. Measures derived from the *liabilities side* of banking-sector balance sheets show promise. In particular, the growth of various components of noncore-to-core liabilities of the banking sector may be especially useful in gauging the stage of the financial cycle, as argued by Shin and Shin (2010). The following discussion draws closely on this study.

Although traditional monetary aggregates such as M1 and M2[2] are also liability-side aggregates of the banking sector (measuring mainly the deposit liabilities), there are reasons to believe that such traditional monetary aggregates can be refined and improved upon so as to serve as effective indicators that underpin effective macro prudential policy.

Banks are the most important financial intermediaries in emerging and developing economies. Traditional monetary aggregates give a window on the size and composition of bank liabilities. Key monetary aggregates such as M2 track the size of the deposit base of the domestic banking system, and hence can serve as a proxy for the claim of the household sector on the banking sector. In more advanced financial systems where market-based debt instruments are more developed, the claims on the intermediary sector could include money market funds and other short-term claims held by the household sector.

To the extent that monetary aggregates reflect the size and composition of the banks' balance sheets, they may play a role in macro prudential policy. Central banks that continue to give some attention to monetary aggregates in their policy frameworks have increasingly emphasized the financial stability properties of monetary aggregates, moving away from the more traditional rationale for focusing on monetary aggregates based on the quantity theory of money and the association with inflation.

Traditional classifications of monetary aggregates focus on the transactional role of money as a medium of exchange. As such, the criterion is based on how close to cash—how "money-like"—a particular financial claim is. The classic study by Gurley and Shaw (1960) emphasized the distinction between "inside money," which is a liability of a private sector agent, and "outside money," (such as fiat currency) which is not. The traditional focus of monetary analysis has been on money as a medium of exchange.

Demand deposits are the archetypal money measure, since such liabilities of the banking sector can be quickly transferred from one person to another. Savings deposits are less moneylike, and hence figure in broader notions of money, such as M2, but even here they fall outside the M2 measure if the depositor faces restrictions on easy access to the funds. In this way, the traditional hierarchy of monetary aggregates goes from cash to the very liquid claims such as demand deposits and continuing to more illiquid claims such as term savings deposits. The criterion is how easily claims can be used to settle transactions. In the context of the quantity theory of money and the main quantity theory accounting identity $MV = PY$, the traditional monetary aggregate is more appropriate in identifying the extent to which inflation is likely.

For financial stability purposes, however, an alternative classification system for liability aggregates may be needed that is conceptually a better fit for the vulnerability to financial shocks and their propagation. The key task would be to draw on existing knowledge of the behavior of financial intermediaries (as discussed in the balance sheet management section of this chapter) and to find the counterparts in banking sector liability aggregates that have implications on the procyclicality of financial system. Traditional transaction-motivated monetary aggregates may not be the most useful measure in this respect.

Core and Noncore Bank Liabilities

One clue can be obtained from our earlier examination (in the external environment and global liquidity section of this chapter) of the role of external funding conditions in influencing banking-sector behavior. A useful distinction is that between *core* and *noncore* liabilities of the banking sector. Core liabilities can be defined as the funding that the bank draws on during normal times, and is sourced (in the main) domestically. What constitutes core funding will depend on the context and the economy in question, but retail deposits of the household sector would be a good first conjecture in defining core liabilities.

When banking sector assets are growing rapidly, the core funding available to the banking sector is likely to be insufficient to finance the rapid growth in new lending. This shortage is because retail deposits grow in line with the aggregate wealth of the household sector. In a lending boom, when credit is growing very rapidly, the pool of retail deposits is not likely to be sufficient to fund the increase in bank credit. Other sources of funding must then be tapped to fund rapidly increasing bank lending. The state of the financial cycle is thus reflected in the composition of bank liabilities.

To better focus the discussion around the key concepts, we first lay out an accounting framework for the financial system as a whole that will be useful later in distinguishing between core and noncore liabilities.

Suppose there are n banks in the domestic banking system. The term "bank" should be interpreted broadly to include firms in the intermediary sector generally. The exact composition of the sector will depend on the country's financial system, including its degree of openness and financial development. We denote the banks by an index that takes values in the set $\{1, 2, \ldots, n\}$. The domestic creditor sector (for example, households and domestic pension funds) is given the index $n+1$. The foreign creditor sector is given the index $n+2$.

Bank i has two types of assets. First, there are loans to end users such as corporations or households. Denote the total loans by bank i to such end users of credit as y_i. Next, there are the claims against other financial institutions. Call these the "interbank" assets, although the term covers all claims on other intermediaries. The total interbank assets held by bank i are

$$\sum_{j=1}^{n} x_j \pi_{ji}$$

where x_j is the total debt of bank j and π_{ji} is the share of bank j's debt held by bank i.

Note that $\pi_{i,n+1}$ is the proportion of the bank's liabilities held by the domestic creditor sector (for example, in the form of deposits), while $\pi_{i,n+2}$ is the proportion of the bank's liabilities held by foreign creditors (for example, in the form of short-term foreign currency-denominated debt). Since "banks" $n+1$ and $n+2$ are not leveraged, we have $x_{n+1} = x_{n+2} = 0$. The balance sheet identity of bank i is given by

$$y_i + \sum_{j=1}^{n} x_j \pi_{ji} = e_i + x_i$$

The left-hand side of the equation is the total assets of the bank. The right-hand side is the sum of equity and debt. Letting $x = [x_1 \quad \ldots \quad x_n]$ and $y = [y_1 \quad \ldots \quad y_n]$, we can write in vector notation the balance sheet identities of all banks as

$$y + x \prod = e + x$$

where $\prod$ is the matrix whose (i,j)th entry is π_{ij}. Solving for y,

$$y = e + x(I - \prod).$$

Define leverage as the ratio of total assets to equity, given by

$$\frac{a_i}{e_i} = \lambda_i.$$

Then defining Λ as the diagonal matrix with λ_i along the diagonal, we have

$$y = e + e(\Lambda - I)(I - \prod)$$

where $\prod$ is the matrix of interbank liabilities. By post-multiplying the above equation by the unit column vector

$$u = \begin{bmatrix} 1 \\ \vdots \\ 1 \end{bmatrix}$$

we can sum up the rows of the vector equation above, and we have the following balance sheet identity:

$$\sum_i y_i = \sum_i e_i + \sum_i e_i z_i (\lambda_i - 1)$$

where z_i is given by the ith row of $(I - \Pi)u$. Here, z_i has the interpretation of the proportion of the bank's liabilities that come from outside the banking sector, that is, the proportion of funding that comes either from the ultimate domestic creditors (for example, deposits) or the foreign sector (for example, foreign currency-denominated banking-sector liabilities).

Therefore, we can rewrite the aggregate balance sheet identity in the following way:

Total credit = Total equity of banking sector + Liabilities to nonbank domestic creditors + Liabilities to foreign creditors.

This accounting framework helps us understand the connection between (1) the procyclicality of the banking system, (2) systemic risk spillovers, and (3) the stock of noncore liabilities of the banking system.

Within this accounting framework, the *core liabilities* of a bank can be defined as its liabilities to nonbank domestic creditors (such as through retail deposits). Thus, the *noncore liabilities* of a bank are either (1) a liability to another bank or (2) a liability to a foreign creditor. Two features distinguish noncore liabilities. First, noncore liabilities include claims held by intermediaries on other intermediaries. Second, they include liabilities to foreign creditors, who are typically the *global* banks, and hence also intermediaries, albeit foreign ones. Even for liabilities to domestic creditors, if the creditor is another intermediary, the claim tends to be short term. The distinction between core and noncore liabilities becomes meaningful once there are differences in the empirical properties of the two types of liabilities.

Table 1.1, taken from Shin and Shin (2010), is a two-way classification of banking sector liabilities that distinguishes the traditional concern with the liquidity of monetary aggregates for transaction purposes together with the question of whether the liabilities are core or noncore. The distinction between core and noncore liabilities has widespread applicability, but the precise demarcation line between core and noncore funding depends on the particular economy and the context of financial development. For advanced economies with developed financial systems, noncore liabilities will include nondeposit funding that is raised in the wholesale bank funding market.

It would be reasonable to conjecture that core liabilities are more stable (or "sticky") than noncore liabilities. For instance, retail deposits of household savers

Table 1.1 Classification of Core versus Noncore Liabilities

	Core liability	Intermediate	Noncore liability
Highly liquid	Cash Demand deposits (households)	Demand deposits (nonfinancial corporate)	Repos Call loans Short-term FX bank debt
Intermediate	Time deposits and CDs (households)	Time deposits and CDs (nonfinancial corporate)	Time deposits and CDs (banks and securities firms)
Illiquid	Trust accounts (households) Covered bonds (households)	Trust accounts (nonfinancial corporate)	Long-term bank debt securities (banks and securities firms) ABS and MBS[a]

Source: Shin and Shin 2010.
Note: CDs = certificates of deposit.
a. ABS is asset-backed securities; MBS is mortgage-backed securities.

would be more stable than corporate deposits, which in turn could be subdivided into nonfinancial company deposits and financial institution deposits. Again, it would be a reasonable conjecture that nonfinancial corporate deposits are more "sticky" than financial company deposits. Indeed, there is considerable empirical support for the different properties of bank liabilities depending on who holds the claim.

Hahm et al. (2010) examine the components of Korean banks' liabilities, subdivided into the two-dimensional categorization illustrated in table 1.1, that is, by classifying liabilities into how liquid they are and who holds them. They present evidence of a clear hierarchy within each liquidity category of the relative "stickiness" of the liability, depending on whether the liability is due to the household sector, nonfinancial corporate sector or financial corporate sector.

As mentioned, the dividing line between core and noncore liabilities will depend on the financial system in question and its degree of openness and the level of development of its financial markets and institutions. For a developed financial system like the United States or Western Europe, the distinction between core and noncore liabilities seems reasonably well captured by the distinction between deposit and nondeposit funding. Figure 1.12, which is taken from Shin (2009), shows the composition of the liabilities of Northern Rock, the U.K. bank whose failure in 2007 heralded the global financial crisis.

In the nine years from 1998 to 2007, Northern Rock's lending increased 6.5 times. This increase in lending far outstripped the funds raised through retail deposits with the rest of the funding gap being made up by wholesale funding (securitized notes and other lending as shown in figure 1.12). Northern Rock's case illustrates the general lesson that during a credit boom, the rapid increase in bank lending outstrips the core deposit funding available to a bank. As the boom progresses, the bank resorts to alternative, noncore liabilities to finance its lending. Therefore, the proportion of noncore liabilities of banks serves as a useful indicator of the stage of the financial cycle and the degree of vulnerability of the banking system to a downturn of the financial cycle.

For emerging or developing economies, more thought is needed to find a useful classification system between core and noncore liabilities. In an open emerging

Figure 1.12 Northern Rock Bank's Liabilities, 1998–2007

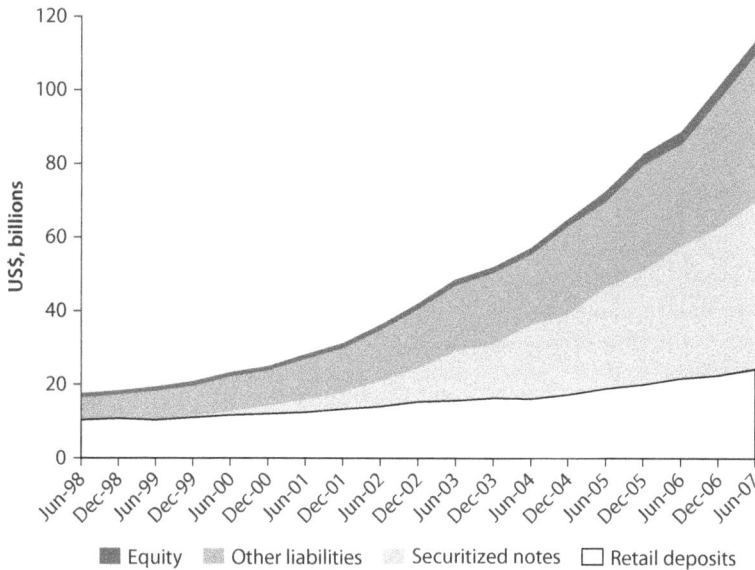

Source: Shin 2009.

economy where the banking system is open to funding from global banks, rapid increases in the noncore liabilities of the banking system would show up as capital inflows through increased foreign exchange-denominated liabilities of the banking system. For this reason, foreign exchange-denominated liabilities of the banking sector can be expected to play a key role in diagnosing the potential for financial instability.

For the case of Korea, Shin and Shin (2010) proposed a definition of noncore liabilities as the sum of (1) foreign exchange-denominated bank liabilities, (2) bank debt securities, (3) promissory notes, (4) repos, and (5) certificates of deposit.[3] Note that this measure of noncore liabilities is an approximation of "true" noncore liabilities defined in our accounting framework above, as the classification is still based on financial instruments rather than actual claim holders. For instance, bank debt securities such as debentures and certificates of deposit (CDs) can be held by households, and must be excluded from the noncore liabilities. Figure 1.13 charts the noncore liabilities of the Korean banking sector, taken from Shin and Shin (2010) with the FX liabilities shown as "other FX borrowing." It is noticeable how the first peak in noncore liabilities coincides with the 1997 crisis. After a lull in the early 2000s, noncore liabilities increase rapidly in the runup to the 2008 crisis.

Note that the major peak occurs some weeks after the outbreak of the crisis because the total amounts are measured in Korean won, and the outbreak of the crisis coincides with a rapid depreciation of the won, which implies an increase in the won value of the foreign currency-denominated bank liabilities.

The pronounced procyclicality of the noncore liability series for Korea should not come as a surprise, given what we know (see earlier discussion in this chapter)

Figure 1.13 Noncore Liabilities of the Korean Banking Sector

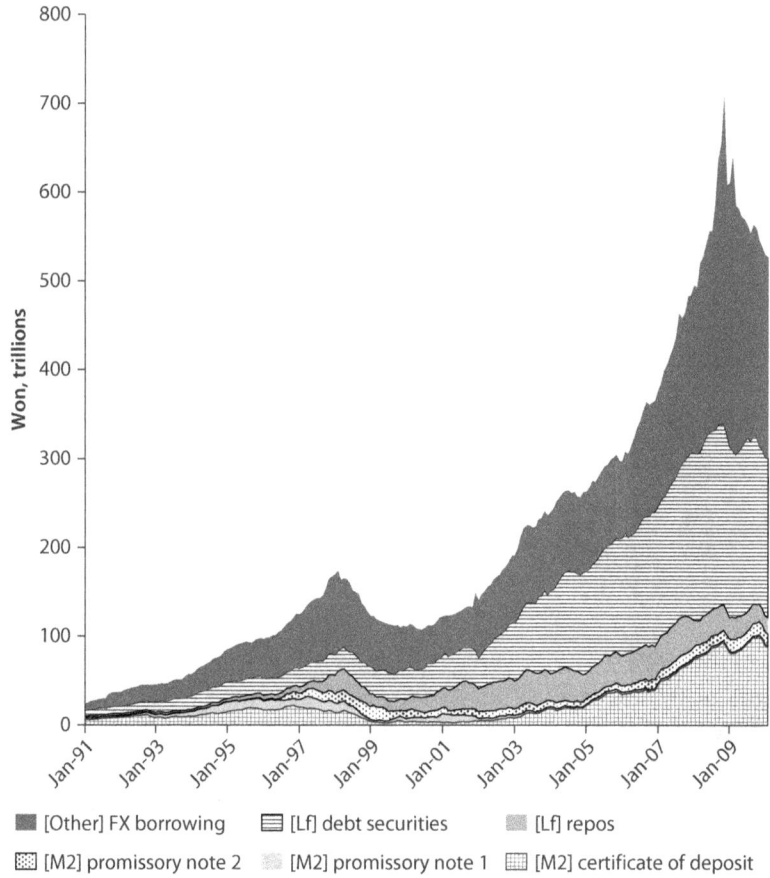

Source: Shin and Shin 2010.

about the balance sheet management practices of banks and the perverse nature of the demand and supply responses to asset price changes and shifts to measured risks. During a credit boom, when measured risks are low and funding from global banks is easy to obtain, we would expect to see strong credit growth fuelled by capital inflows into the banking sector, often in foreign exchange.

Figure 1.14 shows how capital flows associated with foreign currency liabilities of the banking sector played a key role in the foreign exchange liquidity crisis of 2008 in Korea. Figure 1.14 plots and compares the net of capital inflows and outflows for two sectors: the equity sector and the banking sector. The equity sector actually saw *net inflows* during the crisis in the autumn of 2008. Contrary to the common misperception (perpetuated by television broadcasts from the stock exchange after turbulent trading) that the exit of foreign investors from the Korean stock market is the main reason for capital outflows, we can see that the flows in the equity sector was *net positive* immediately after the crisis.

There are good reasons for why the equity sector should see net positive flows during a crisis. Equity outflows have two mitigating factors. During a crisis, not

Figure 1.14 Net Capital Flows of Equity and Banking Sector in Korea

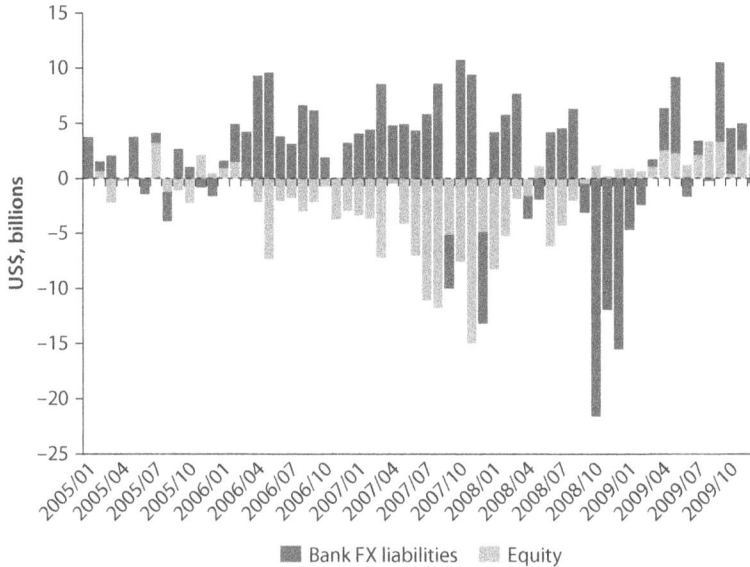

Source: Shin and Shin 2010.

only do stock prices fall sharply but there is a steep depreciation of the local currency relative to U.S. dollars. For both reasons, foreign investors suffer a "double whammy" if they withdraw from the local stock market. Provided that the exchange rate is allowed to adjust, equity outflows will not be the main culprit in draining foreign currency reserves. When Korean investors have equity investments abroad, the repatriation flows back to Korea will outweigh the outflows from foreign investors.

However, the banking sector is different for three reasons. First, foreign currency liabilities of the banks have a face value that must be met in full. Second, the face value is in foreign currency. Third, the dynamics of deleveraging set off amplifying effects through price changes and shifts in measured risks.

For all three reasons, the deleveraging of the banking sector is associated with precipitous capital outflows. Unlike long-term investors, such as pension funds, mutual funds, and life insurance companies, leveraged institutions are vulnerable to erosion of their capital, and hence engage in substantial adjustments of their assets even to small shocks. The feedback loop generated by such reactions to price changes amplifies shocks.

As figure 1.14 shows, the banking sector in Korea saw substantial capital outflows in the aftermath of the Lehman crisis. In the three months following the Lehman bankruptcy, the outflow from the banking sector was US$49 billion, which more than accounts for the decrease in Korea's foreign exchange reserves from over US$240 billion before the Lehman crisis to US$200 billion at the end of 2008. Deleveraging by banks and the associated amplification effects have figured prominently in emerging economy financial crises.

Cross-Section Measures of Risk and Core and Noncore Liabilities

In a boom when credit is growing rapidly, the growth of bank balance sheets outstrips the growth in the pool of retail deposits. As a result, the growth of bank lending results in greater lending and borrowing among the intermediaries themselves, or results in the "sucking in" of foreign debt. Thus, the "cross-section" dimension of risk where banks are vulnerable to a common shock is closely related to the "time-series" dimension of risk having to do with procyclicality of the balance sheet where assets are larger during the peak of the financial cycle.

To illustrate the principle that the cross-section and time-series dimensions of risk are closely related, consider the simple case where there is no foreign creditor sector. Figure 1.15 depicts a stylized financial system with two banks: Bank 1 and Bank 2. Both banks draw on retail deposits to lend to ultimate borrowers. They can also hold claims against each other, if they so choose.

Imagine a lending boom in which the assets of both banks double in size, but the pool of retail deposits stays fixed. Then, the proportion of banking-sector liabilities in the form of retail deposits must fall. In other words, rapidly expanding bank assets are mirrored by increased cross-claims across banks. The growth in bank assets and increased systemic risk are two sides of the same coin.

The relationship between banking-sector assets and increased cross exposure across banks holds more generally in the accounting identity described earlier. Recall our definition of core and noncore liabilities. The *core liabilities* of a bank are its liabilities to claimholders who are not financial intermediaries themselves, such as retail deposits. Any liability of an intermediary held by another intermediary would be a *noncore liability*.

From our earlier accounting identity for the financial system as a whole, we can define the total core liabilities of the banking sector as:

$$\text{Total core liabilities} = \sum_{i=1}^{n} e_i z_i (\lambda_i - 1)$$

where, as before, e_i is the equity of bank i, λ_i is the leverage of bank i, z_i is the ratio of bank i's core liabilities to its total liabilities, and n is the number of banks in the banking system. Since total core liabilities (such as retail deposits) are slow moving, a rapid increase in total bank assets (equity multiplied by leverage) must result in lower z_i values, implying a greater reliance on noncore funding. More generally, in the presence of a foreign creditor sector, the increase in bank lending will result not only in increased cross lending between banks but also in

Figure 1.15 Cross-Claims between Banks

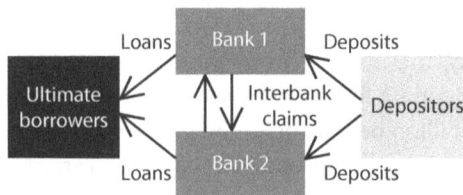

the sucking in of foreign debt. In this way, there are close conceptual links between procyclicality, systemic risk spillovers, and the banking system's stock of noncore liabilities. The stage of the financial cycle is reflected in the composition of the liabilities of the banking sector. In a boom, we have the conjunction of three features:

- Total lending increases rapidly
- Noncore (especially foreign currency) liabilities increase as a proportion of total liabilities
- Systemic risk increases through greater cross holdings between intermediaries.

Measures of cross exposures across intermediaries (such as the CoVaR measure, the value-at-risk (VaR) of the financial system *conditional* on institutions being in distress measure due to Adrian and Brunnermeier [2009]) may be useful complementary indicators, bearing in mind that cross exposures themselves are procyclical, and track noncore liabilities. The study of cross exposures across financial institutions is still in its infancy, but there has been a growing interest in this issue, especially from researchers in central banks from advanced economies that suffered financial distress during the recent financial crisis. Among advanced-economy central banks, the Bank of England has been one of the most active in research into the systemic risk generated by cross exposures between financial intermediaries. In November 2009, the Bank of England published a discussion paper on the role of macro prudential policy that discusses the issues and policy concerns regarding the United Kingdom's experience with the failure of Northern Rock bank and the subsequent intervention and resolution in the U.K. banking system (Bank of England 2009). Although there is a gap between the concerns of an advanced economy and those of an emerging economy, many of the lessons on excessive asset growth and the growth of volatile market-based liabilities are common themes.

Nonfinancial Corporate Deposits as a Measure of Noncore Liabilities

The discussion so far is appropriate for an economy (such as Korea) in which the domestic banking sector has access to funding from the global banking system. However, in financial systems at an early stage of development or where the banking sector is restricted by regulation from having access to the global banking system, the distinction between core and noncore liabilities of the banking system may look different, although the principles from the systemwide accounting framework will apply.

When the domestic banking sector is mostly closed from the global banking sector, deposits will constitute the lion's share of banking-sector liabilities, and traditional monetary aggregates such as M2 itself becomes highly variable and procyclical, encompassing volatile banking liabilities. In such instances, it may be more meaningful to decompose M2 into its core and noncore components. The noncore component may include the deposits of nonfinancial companies that recycle funding within the economy and hence become integrated into the intermediary sector. China and India are two examples of countries where the distinction between core and noncore liabilities may be usefully employed. In both cases, foreign exchange-denominated bank liabilities or market-based funding instruments play a much smaller role than in a more open economy such as Korea.

Somewhat paradoxically, perhaps, one way to illustrate the role of nonfinancial firms in financial intermediation is to draw on the experience of Japan in the 1980s during the liberalization of its financial sector. Japan's 1980s experience was taken up by Hattori, Shin, and Takahashi (2009), who examined the role of the nonfinancial corporate sector in amplifying the financial cycle. Some themes that overlap with macro prudential policy are worth mentioning.

The focus of Hattori, Shin, and Takahashi (2009) is on corporate lending following the sectoral changes that took place in Japan after the liberalization of the securities markets and the accompanying liberalization of the rules governing bank deposits.

As a result of the financial liberalization of the 1980s, securities markets enabled the opening up of new funding sources—both domestic and foreign—for companies that had traditionally relied on the banking sector. Of particular interest is the role played by Japan's large manufacturing firms. Before the 1980s, manufacturing firms in Japan received most of their financing from the traditional banking sector, both for long-term investment and short-term liquidity needs. However, with the liberalization of the securities market beginning in the mid-1980s, nonfinancial companies were able to tap new sources of funding from outside the traditional banking sector. New issuance of equity, corporate bonds, warrants, and commercial paper (CP) increasingly became important sources of funding for nonfinancial firms. The new funding was supplied by both domestic savers and other nonleveraged financial institutions, such as life insurance companies who purchased the bonds and other securities issued by Japanese companies. Foreign investors also figured prominently among the new funding sources.

However, the sequencing of reforms meant that the liberalization of nonfinancial corporate funding proceeded ahead of the liberalization of the banking sector. As new funding sources opened up to large manufacturing firms, it became profitable for them to recycle liquidity and act as *de facto* financial intermediaries by raising funding in the capital markets through securities, and then depositing the funds in the banking system through time deposits. Through this channel, the financial assets of nonfinancial corporations increased dramatically together with their financial liabilities in the late 1980s (see Hattori, Shin, and Takahashi 2009 for details). Figure 1.16 illustrates the change in financial structure entailed by the recycling of liquidity.

When nonfinancial firms play the role of *de facto* financial intermediaries, the stock of M2 will see rapid increases due to the increasing deposit claims on the banking sector. Meanwhile, the banking sector itself will be under increasing pressure to find new borrowers, since its traditional customers (the manufacturing firms), no longer need funding, instead have undergone a reversal of roles and are pushing deposits into the banks, rather than receiving loans from the banks.

Figure 1.16 Structural Change in Financial Intermediation in Japan, 1980s

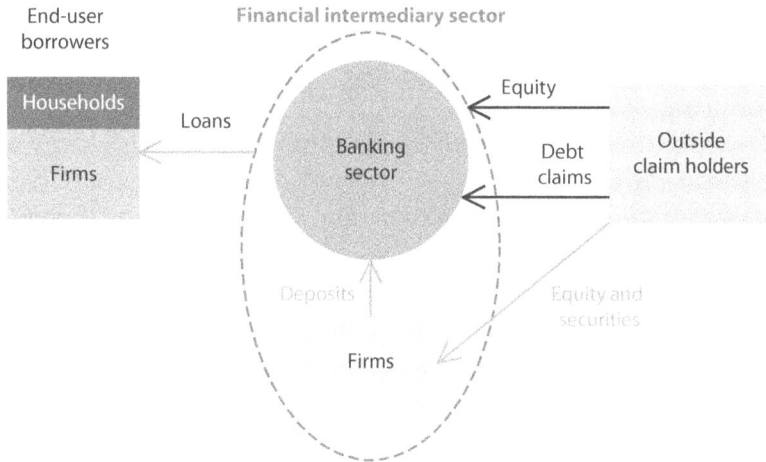

Source: Hattori, Shin, and Takahashi 2009.

Under such circumstances, the distinction between core and noncore banking sector liabilities does not coincide neatly with the distinction between deposit and nondeposit liabilities.

In many developing countries that are at an earlier stage of financial development, or are more closed to the global banking system, the principle behind the distinction between core and noncore liabilities is better expressed as the distinction between:

- The *retail deposits* of the household sector and
- The *wholesale deposits* of nonfinancial companies.

The new liquidity requirements on banks contemplated under the Basel III rules (the net stable funding ratio [NSFR] and the liquidity coverage ratio [LCR]) recognize that retail deposits are much more "sticky" and are less likely to run, whereas the wholesale deposits of corporates are more "flighty" (BCBS 2010).

Adapting Monetary Aggregates and Macro Prudential Indicators

Traditional monetary aggregates were defined around their legal form, and how liquid they are in transactions. For the reasons outlined earlier, these traditional aggregates will be less effective as a macro prudential monitoring tool without further adaptation.

The particular adaptations may be usefully summarized in the following three points:

- For countries with open capital markets, international capital flows into the banking sector will be key indicators of financial vulnerability. During a boom when bank assets are growing rapidly, the funding required outstrips the growth of the domestic deposit base, and is often met by capital flows from the international banks, which is reflected in the growth of short-term foreign currency-denominated liabilities of the domestic banking system. As such, short-term foreign currency-denominated bank liabilities can be seen as the volatile noncore liabilities of the banking sector.

- For countries with relatively closed financial systems, where domestic banks do not have ready access to funding provided by the global banking system, a better approach would be to adapt existing conventional monetary aggregates to address financial stability concerns. The key distinction is not how *liquid* the claims are, but rather *who holds the claims*. The distinction between household retail deposits and corporate deposits in the banking sector will play a particularly important role in this regard.

- More generally, invoking the accounting principle that defines core versus noncore liabilities of the banking sector may prove useful in guiding classification exercises. Core liabilities are the claims of the household sector on the intermediary sector. Noncore liabilities are the claims of the intermediary sector on itself. There may be ambiguities in applying this principle (as exemplified by the case of 1980s' Japan).

As a practical matter, the classification into core and noncore is not clear cut. Bank deposits of a small or medium-size enterprise with an owner-manager could be seen as household deposits. However, a larger firm with access to market finance might be able to issue bonds and then deposit the proceeds of the bond sale in the banking system, as happened in Japan in the 1980s, for instance. The latter case should not be counted as a core liability, since the creditor firm is acting like an intermediary who borrows in the financial markets to lend to the banks.

Other ambiguities are presented by items such as trust liabilities of the banking sector. Much of the trust liabilities are to nonfinancial corporates and face many of the definitional hurdles. In addition, it may be better to have a more graduated distinction between core and noncore liabilities, allowing an intermediate category to take account of such ambiguities.

Nevertheless, the distinction between core and noncore bank liabilities provides a better window on the actual exposure of the banking sector to financial risk and its willingness to increase exposures. As such, the relative size of noncore liabilities can be used as a monitoring tool to reflect the stage of the financial cycle and the degree of vulnerability to potential setbacks.

Macro Prudential Tools

Macro prudential policy tools aim to mitigate the buildup of vulnerabilities to financial instability. For the reasons outlined earlier, the primary aim of macro prudential policy is to secure financial stability by leaning against permissive financial conditions (should they be deemed excessive), and to lean against excessively rapid loan growth by the banking sector. Macro prudential policies complement existing tools in banking regulation, such as minimum capital ratios.

An important consideration in formulating macro prudential policy is the link with broader macroeconomic stabilization policy, and especially with the conduct of monetary policy. The role of monetary policy in securing financial stability has broad resonance, both in advanced and in developing and emerging countries.

In this section, we focus on the specific tools of macro prudential policy and their link to the debate on capital controls. To the extent that the external environment in the global banking system is a key determinant of the vulnerability of the economy to financial excesses, considerations of macro prudential policies cannot easily be separated from the currently active debate on the merits of capital controls. The International Monetary Fund (IMF) has recently suggested the more neutral term "capital flow management" (CFM) policies (IMF 2011), rather than the more emotive term "capital controls," reflecting the more receptive attitude by the IMF to the imposition of capital controls. Indeed, some macro prudential tools have many similar attributes to the tools used in capital controls. For this reason, it is useful to adapt the three-part taxonomy in the recent IMF report (IMF 2011, 41) on capital flows:

- *Prudential tools*. These tools encompass existing or new tools of prudential regulation that have a primarily domestic focus and are not aimed primarily at correcting capital flow distortions. Examples include LTV rules, caps on the loan-to-deposit ratio, and leverage caps.
- *Currency-based tools*. These tools are prudential measures that address vulnerabilities that originate from distortions in the external environment such as global liquidity conditions, but which restrict activity or impose costs based on currency distinctions rather than on the residency of the investor. An example is the levy on short-term foreign exchange-denominated liabilities of the banking sector implemented by Korea (the "macro prudential levy").
- *Residency-based tools*. These tools are the traditional capital control (capital flow management) tools that restrict activity or impose costs based on the residence of the investor. Examples include administrative restrictions on ownership, taxes on portfolio inflows, such as Brazil's tax on financial operations (Imposto sobre operações financeiras; IOF). Capital controls raise a complex set of issues concerning their ultimate objectives, that is, whether the objective is to hold down the exchange rate, or to limit the total volume of inflows to slow down the appreciation of the exchange rate. These issues merit a separate discussion, and will not concern us here. In this chapter, we will focus exclusively on the financial stability impact of macro prudential policies.

Prudential Tools

Capital Requirements that Adjust Over the Cycle

The balance sheet management of banks is inherently procyclical, as explained earlier in this chapter. The rise in asset values that accompanies a boom results in higher capital buffers at financial institutions, supporting further lending in the context of an unchanging benchmark for capital adequacy. In a bust, the value of this capital can drop precipitously, possibly even necessitating a cut in lending.[4]

Capital requirements as currently constituted, therefore, can amplify the credit cycle, making a boom and bust more likely. Capital requirements that, instead, lean against the credit or business cycle, that is, rise with credit growth and fall with credit contraction, can thus play an important role in promoting financial stability and reducing systemic risk.

We have commented on some of the measurement issues associated with the implementation of countercyclical capital buffers. The framework for countercyclical capital buffers as envisaged in the Basel III framework has focused on the ratio of credit growth to GDP. There are two preconditions for the successful implementation of such countercyclical measures. First, the quantitative signals that trigger actions must reflect accurately the features (such as excessively loose lending conditions) that are being targeted by policy makers. Second, the implementation procedure should be such that policy makers can move decisively and in a timely manner in heading off the buildup of vulnerabilities. We have commented on the first point, and here we focus on the second point.

If the triggering of countercyclical capital requirements is predicated on the exercise of discretion and judgment by the authorities, the political economy problems associated with the exercise of such discretion can put the authorities under pressure from market participants and other interested parties. The political economy problem is similar to that of central banks that tighten monetary policy to head off property booms. Since private-sector participants (such as construction companies or property developers) are the beneficiaries of the short-term boom, they can be expected to exert pressure on policy makers or engage in general lobbying. The political economy problems will be more acute if there are controversies on the exact stage of the financial cycle or the degree of conclusiveness of the empirical evidence invoked by the policy authorities.

Thus, the two issues mentioned above—the accuracy of the quantitative indicators and the political economy problems—are closely related. One of the disadvantages of the countercyclical capital buffer is that it relies on triggering additional capital requirements in response to quantitative signals. Although such quantitative measures are relatively straightforward in simple theoretical models, there may be considerable challenges to smooth and decisive implementation in practice.

Forward-Looking Provisioning

Forward-looking provisioning requires the buildup of loss-absorbing buffers in the form of provisions at the time of making the loan, and shares similarities with the countercyclical capital buffer. However, a key difference between provisioning and equity is in their accounting treatment. In the case of forward-looking provisioning, the provision is not counted as bank capital, and hence is less likely to influence bank management that targets a specific return on equity (ROE) level. To the extent that the bank uses its capital as the base on which to build its total balance sheet, a larger equity base will result in a larger balance sheet, and hence greater use of debt to finance the assets. During the credit boom, the buildup of greater assets using debt financing will contribute to the buildup of vulnerabilities.

The accounting treatment of the loss buffer as a provision rather than as equity thus has a potentially crucial effect on bank behavior. By insisting on forward-looking provisioning, the bank's equity is reduced by the amount of the provision. During a boom, such a reduction of bank capital can play an important role in "letting off steam" in the pressure to build up the bank's balance sheet by removing some of the capital base of the bank.

Although forward-looking provisioning has been important in cushioning the Spanish banking system from the initial stages of the global financial crisis, it remains to be seen whether building up loss-absorbing buffers, by itself, can be sufficient to cushion the economy from the bursting of a major property bubble, as Spain discovered in the recent financial crisis in Europe.

Loan-to-Value and Debt-Service-to-Income Caps

When monetary policy is constrained, administrative rules that limit bank lending such as caps on loan-to-value (LTV) ratios and debt-to-income (DTI) ratios may be a useful complement to traditional tools in banking supervision. LTV regulation restricts the amount of the loan not to exceed some percentage of the value of the collateral asset. DTI caps operate by limiting the debt service costs of the borrower not to exceed some fixed percentage of verified income.

Conceptually, it is useful to distinguish two motivations for the use of LTV and DTI rules. The first is the consumer protection motive, where the intention is to protect household borrowers who may take on excessively burdensome debt relative to the reasonable means to repay them from wage income. Under this motivation, LTV and DTI rules would be similar to the rules against predatory lending to uninformed households. Although this motivation is an important topic in consumer protection policy, it is not relevant for macro prudential policy, and is not discussed in this chapter. Instead, the macro prudential rationale for imposing LTV and DTI caps is to limit bank lending to prevent the buildup of noncore liabilities to fund such loans, and also to lean against the erosion of lending standards associated with rapid asset growth.

It is important to reiterate why conventional micro prudential tools such as minimum capital requirements are insufficient to stem excessive asset growth. Minimum capital requirements rarely bite during a lending boom when bank profitability is high, and when measured risks are low.

Whereas LTV ratio caps are familiar tools, the use of DTI caps is less widespread. For Korea and some Asian economies such as Hong Kong SAR, the use of DTI ratios has been an important supplementary tool for macro prudential purposes. DTI rules have the advantage that bank loan growth can be tied (at least loosely) to wage growth in the economy. Without this fundamental anchor, an LTV rule by itself will be susceptible to the amplifying dynamics of a credit boom, which interacts with an increase in the value of collateral assets during a housing boom. Even though the LTV rule is in place, if house prices are rising sufficiently fast, the collateral value will rise simultaneously, making the constraint bind less hard.

In the case of Hong Kong, the use of DTI rules takes on added significance because Hong Kong's currency board is based on the U.S. dollar, and hence does not have an autonomous monetary policy. Thus, monetary policy shocks are transmitted directly to Hong Kong.

Leverage Caps and Loan-to-Deposit Caps

Caps on bank leverage may be used to limit asset growth by tying total assets to bank equity (Morris and Shin 2008). The rationale for a leverage cap rests on the role of bank capital as a constraint on new lending rather than the Basel approach of bank capital as a buffer against loss.

The experience of Korea holds some lessons in the use of leverage caps and loan-to-deposit ratio caps. In June 2010, the Korean regulatory authorities introduced a new set of macro prudential regulations to mitigate excessive volatility of foreign capital flows. Specific policy measures included explicit ceilings on foreign exchange derivatives positions of banks, regulations on foreign currency bank loans, and prudential regulations for improving foreign exchange risk management of financial institutions. These policy measures were intended to limit short-term foreign currency-denominated borrowings of banks.

Korea's leverage cap on bank FX derivative positions introduced in June 2010 was aimed at limiting the practice of banks hedging forward dollar positions with carry trade positions in Korean won funded with short-term U.S. dollar debt.

A related measure in Korea is the cap on the ratio of loans to deposits. The Korean supervisory authority announced in December 2009 that it would reintroduce the loan-to-deposit ratio regulation that had been scrapped in November 1998 as a part of the government deregulation efforts. According to the regulation, the ratio of Korean won-denominated loans to won-denominated deposits should fall to below 100 percent by 2013. The rationale for this policy was to restrict loan growth, by tying the growth of lending to the deposit base.

Since the deposit base constitutes the baseline, the definition of what qualifies as deposits has strict guidelines. For instance, negotiable certificates of deposit are not included in the measure of deposits in the denominator in computing the ratio. Although the requirement to meet the 100 percent ceiling was set for the end of 2013, banks anticipated the eventual cap and began reducing their loan-to-value ratios in anticipation of the implementation of the cap.

However, a potential weakness of the regulation is that it does not apply to the Korean branches of foreign banks. Since foreign bank branches supply a substantial amount of foreign exchange-denominated lending to Korean banks and firms, the exemption of foreign bank branches leaves a gap in the regulation. However, this gap would not have been easily plugged within the framework of a loan-to-deposit cap because foreign bank branches, by their nature, rely mostly on funding from headquarters or from wholesale funding, rather than local deposit funding.

For domestic banks, the loan-to-deposit ratio cap has two effects. First, it restrains excessive asset growth by tying loan growth to the growth in deposit funding. Second, there is a direct effect on the growth of noncore liabilities, and hence on the buildup of vulnerabilities that come from the liabilities side of the balance sheet. In this respect, there are similarities between the loan-to-deposit cap and the levy on noncore liabilities, to be discussed later. Indeed, at the theoretical level, the loan-to-deposit cap can be seen as a special case of a noncore liabilities levy where the tax rate is kinked, changing from zero to infinity at the threshold point. However, the comparison with the noncore liabilities levy is less easy because the loan-to-deposit cap applies only to loans, not total assets or total exposures (including off-balance-sheet exposures).

Currency-Based Tools
We now turn to the currency-based tools that have been used as capital control means, as well as for prudential reasons.

Unremunerated Reserve Requirements
Perhaps the best-known traditional form of capital control has been unremunerated reserve requirements (URR), through which the central bank requires importers of capital to deposit a certain fraction of the sum at the central bank. The prevalence of the URR is largely because the central bank has been in charge of both prudential policy and macroeconomic management, and because the central bank normally has had discretion to use URR policies without going through the legislative procedures associated with other forms of capital controls, such as levies and taxes.

The recent IMF staff discussion note (Ostry and others 2011) has a comprehensive discussion of countries' experiences in their use of URRs. Most central banks impose some type of reserve requirement for deposits, especially when the deposits are under government-sponsored deposit insurance. The rationale for the reserve requirement is that it is an implicit insurance premium paid by the bank in return for deposit insurance.

The macro prudential motivation for URR is to impose an implicit tax on components of financial intermediary liabilities other than insured deposits that are likely to impose negative spillover effects. The introduction of a reserve requirement for the nondeposit liabilities of banks would raise the cost of nondeposit funding for banks, and thereby restrain the rapid growth of such liabilities during booms. In this respect, the reserve requirement on nondeposit liabilities would have a similar effect to a tax or levy on such liabilities, to be discussed later. Recent examples of the use of URR are discussed in Ostry and others (2011, 28).

Although the URR is an implicit tax on a balance sheet item, the implied tax rate itself will vary with the opportunity cost of funds, and hence with the prevailing interest rate. The variability of the implicit tax rate necessitates some adjustment of the reserve rates, and the requirements will need to be raised to a high level when interest rates are low. This is potentially one disadvantage of the URR relative to other measures.

Another issue is the challenges of managing the central bank's balance sheet as a consequence of URRs. The reserves would have to be held on the central bank's balance sheet as a liability, with implications for the fluctuations in the money supply in line with the private sector's use of nondeposit liabilities, and the selection of counterpart assets on the central bank's balance sheet.

Although not central, there are also differences in the revenue implications between the reserve requirement and a levy or tax. The reserve requirement would raise revenue to the extent that the net income on the assets held by the central bank that is funded by the reserves would be positive. Hence, the bigger the interest spread between the asset and liability, the larger the income.

One advantage of the reserve requirement is not shared by the levy: the banks would have access to a liquid asset in case there is a liquidity shortage or run in the financial market. In this respect, the reserve requirement has some of the features of the Basel III liquidity requirement on banks (BCBS 2010).

A disadvantage of the reserve requirement is that it applies only to banks, rather than to the wider group of financial institutions that use noncore liabilities. When faced with the possibility of arbitrage, or with structural changes that shift intermediation activity from banks to the market-based financial intermediaries, the reserve requirement would be less effective.

Levy on Noncore Liabilities

As discussed earlier, the stock of noncore liabilities reflects the stage of the financial cycle and the extent of the underpricing of risk in the financial system. A levy or tax on the noncore liabilities can serve to mitigate pricing distortions that lead to excessive asset growth. The financial stability contribution recommended by the IMF in its report (IMF 2010b) on the bank levy to the Group of Twenty Finance Ministers and Central Bank Governors (G-20) in June 2010 is an example of such a corrective tax.

The levy on noncore liabilities has several features that impact overall financial stability. First, the base of the levy itself varies over the financial cycle. The levy bites hardest during the boom when noncore liabilities are large, so that the levy has the properties of an automatic stabilizer even if the tax rate itself remains constant over time. Given the well-known political economy challenges to the exercise of discretion by regulators, the automatic stabilizer feature of the levy may have important advantages.

Second, the levy on noncore liabilities addresses financial vulnerability while leaving unaffected the essential functioning of the financial system in channeling core funding from savers to borrowers. By targeting only noncore liabilities, the levy addresses externalities associated with excessive asset growth and systemic risk arising from interconnectedness of banks. In other words, the levy addresses the "bubbly" element of banking sector liabilities, rather than the core liabilities of the banking system.

Third, the targeting of noncore liabilities can be expected to address the vulnerability of emerging economies with open capital accounts to sudden reversals in capital flows caused by deleveraging by banks. Indeed, for many emerging economies, the levy on noncore liabilities could be aimed more narrowly at the foreign currency-denominated liabilities. Shin (2011) discusses some of the potential advantages of a levy on noncore liabilities of this sort.

The revenue raised by the levy is a secondary issue. The main purpose of the levy is to align incentives. A good analogy is with the "congestion charge" used to control car traffic in central London. Under this charge, car drivers pay a daily fee of £8 to drive into central London. The purpose of the charge is to discourage drivers from bringing their cars into central London, thereby alleviating the externalities associated with traffic congestion. In the same way, the noncore liabilities bank levy should be seen primarily as a tool for aligning the incentives of banks more closely with the social optimum. The revenue raised by the levy would be of benefit (perhaps for a market stabilization fund) but is a secondary issue.

In December 2010, Korea announced that it would introduce a *Macro Prudential Levy* aimed at the FX-denominated liabilities of banks, both domestic banks and the branches of foreign banks. The proposal passed the legislative process in April 2011, and implementation began in August 2011.[5] The rate for the Korean levy has been set at 20 basis points for short-term FX-denominated liabilities of up to one year, falling to 5 basis points for long-term liabilities exceeding five years. The proceeds from the levy will be held in a special account of the preexisting Exchange Stabilization Account, managed by the finance ministry. The proceeds may be used as part of the official foreign exchange reserves.

There is a key difference between Korea's macro prudential levy and the outwardly similar levy introduced by the United Kingdom. In the United Kingdom, the revenue goes into the government's general fiscal account, hence can be regarded as a revenue-raising measure. In contrast revenue from the Korean levy is ring-fenced for specific use in financial stabilization.

Figure 1.17 plots the recent history of capital flows to the Korean banking sector. Since Korea's June 2010 introduction of macro prudential controls, there has been a moderation of short-term flows. There have been continued outflows of short-term liabilities, as seen by the negative value of the bars for short-term flows. Longer-term liabilities have replaced the short-term liabilities. These data do not establish the success of Korean macro prudential policies, as we have not controlled for the broader backdrop in capital markets. However, Bruno and Shin (2013) show that Korea's moderation can be considered exceptional in that a more detailed panel study revealed that capital flows into Korea became less sensitive to global factors, even as capital flows to other advanced and emerging economies experienced an increased sensitivity of to global factors. This finding lends support to the hypothesis that Korea's macro prudential policies were successful in moderating the inflows of volatile short-term liabilities of the banking sector.

Dealing with the Challenges of Macro Financial Linkages in Emerging Markets
http://dx.doi.org/10.1596/978-1-4648-0002-3

Figure 1.17 Capital Flows to Korean Banking Sector

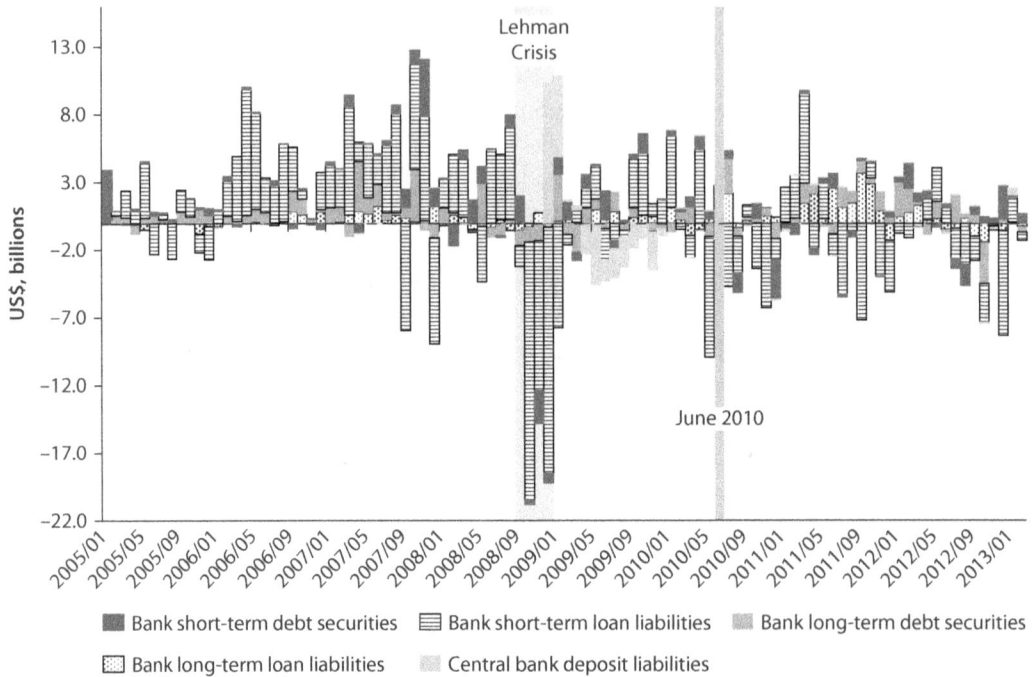

Source: Bruno and Shin 2013, data from Bank of Korea balance of payment statistics.

Relative Merits of URR versus Levies and Taxes

The time delay in implementing the macro prudential levy in Korea offers useful lessons on the relative merits of unremunerated reserve requirements compared with levies and taxes. The legislative process required to implement a levy can entail considerable delays in the introduction and effectiveness of the policy. In Korea, the process took 18 months: initial discussions began in February 2010; announcement of implementation followed in December 2010; legislative hurdles were cleared in April 2011; and implementation was set for August 2011.

When the external environment is changing rapidly, such long delays make the new introduction of a levy cumbersome and impractical as the first line of defense. Nevertheless, as in Korea's case, alternative measures that rely on existing legislation or other temporary measures can be used in the interim until longer-term policy measures come into force.

In practice, the choice between URR and levies or taxes is driven by practical administrative expediency, rather than by matters of principle. Typically, the central bank is the best established policy institution that has direct contact with the financial markets and institutions. The long-established status of the central banks in most countries explains why URRs have been more prevalent than levies or taxes.

There are, however, exceptions to this rule. Brazil's tax on financial operations (IOF) was introduced some time ago (in 1993), and the legislation has been in effect since. Although the tax rate has been set at zero at times, the infrastructure remained in place to "dust it off" as circumstances demanded.

Unlike a tax, a URR can usually be removed (or set to zero) more easily because the budget is not directly reliant on its revenues. Similarly, the macro prudential levy set by Korea has been designed so that the revenue does not have budgetary implications, precisely in order to forestall potential political economy concerns.

Residency-Based Tools

Capital controls have two broad rationales. The first is as a macroeconomic policy tool aimed at leaning against the appreciation of the exchange rate. The second is as a prudential tool, used for financial stability objectives. The distinguishing feature of capital control tools is that they discriminate on the basis of residence of the investor—that is, on whether the investor is domestic or foreign. The tools include inflow taxes such as Brazil's IOF, as well as administrative measures that restrict or ban certain activities or investments that foreign investors can hold.

Although capital controls have been employed to affect the pace of exchange rate appreciation, evidence of their effectiveness remains controversial. However, there is much better evidence on the financial stability implications of capital controls.

Regarding the financial stability objective, a recent IMF position paper finds a strong empirical association between capital controls on the one hand and less

Table 1.2 Taxonomy of Macro Prudential Tools

	Policy tool	Advantages	Drawbacks
Asset-side tools[a]	Loan-to-value (LTV) cap	Low administrative burden	Ineffective during rapid housing boom
	Debt-to-income (DTI) cap	Ties loan growth to wage growth	High administrative capacity needed for data on income
	Loan-to-deposit caps	Low administrative burden	Distorts bank funding Not applicable to foreign banks
	Reserve requirement	Low administrative burden	Ineffective with low interest rates, burdens central bank
Liabilities-side tools[b]	Levy on noncore bank liabilities	Price-based measure Acts on broad liability aggregates	Needs legislation. Cannot narrowly target FX vulnerability
	Levy on FX-denominated bank liabilities	Price-based measure Enhances monetary policy Counters FX risk	Needs legislation Narrow base of levy
Bank capital-oriented tools[c]	Countercyclical capital requirements	Conforms to Basel III	Difficulty in calibration Level playing field issues
	Forward-looking provisioning	Modifies bank incentives	Objections from accounting standard setters
	Leverage cap	Modifies bank incentives	Not price based Open to circumvention Vulnerable to bank FDI

a. Asset-side tools limit bank loan growth directly.
b. Liabilities-side tools limit vulnerability to liquidity crises and limit loan growth indirectly.
c. Bank capital-oriented tools limit loan growth primarily through altering incentives of banks.

Dealing with the Challenges of Macro Financial Linkages in Emerging Markets
http://dx.doi.org/10.1596/978-1-4648-0002-3

Table 1.3 Summary of Policy Priorities

Monetary policy autonomy	Financial liberalization/openness	
	Medium/low	*High*
None	• **Asset-side tools**	• **Asset-side tools**
	• (LTV, DTI, loan-to-deposit caps)	• (LTV, DTI)
		• **Bank capital-oriented policies** (dynamic provisioning, leverage caps, countercyclical capital requirements)
Low/medium	• **Asset-side tools** (LTV, DTI, loan-to-deposit cap)	• **Asset-side tools** (LTV, DTI, loan-to-deposit cap)
	• Monetary policy	• Monetary policy
	combined with	**combined with**
	• Liabilities-side tools	• Liabilities-side tools (**noncore liabilities levy**)
	• **(noncore liabilities levy)**	• **Bank capital-oriented tools** (leverage cap)
High	• Monetary policy	• Monetary policy
	• Reserve requirements	• **Bank capital-oriented tools** (dynamic provisioning, leverage caps, countercyclical capital requirements)
	• **Bank capital-oriented tools** (dynamic provisioning, leverage caps, countercyclical capital requirements)	

severe forms of (1) credit booms and (2) FX borrowing, on the other (Ostry and others 2011, 21).

In reference to the recent global financial crisis, the authors regard it as a natural experiment for the effectiveness of capital controls, and note that the evidence is "suggestive of greater growth resilience in countries that had either capital controls (especially on debt liabilities) or prudential measures in place in the years prior to the crisis" (Ostry and others 2011, 23).

There are also important implications for monetary policy autonomy. De Gregorio and others (2000) found that capital controls allowed Chile's central bank to target a higher domestic interest rate over 6–12 months. Capital controls likely have their financial stability effects through their effect on the *composition* of capital flows, rather than on the total amount of the flows. De Gregorio and others (2000) and Cardenas and Barrera (1997) show that capital controls are likely to have shifted the composition of inflows away from short-term claims and debt claims toward longer-term claims that have more benign financial stability implications. Magud, Reinhart, and Rogoff (2011) conducted a meta-analysis of existing survey literature on the effects of capital controls. After analyzing 37 empirical studies, they found that capital controls on inflows (1) make monetary policy more independent, (2) alter the composition of capital flows, and (3) reduce real exchange rate pressures (although the evidence on this is more controversial); however, they (4) do not reduce the volume of net flows (and hence the current-account balance).

To the extent that capital controls have an effect on the composition of capital flows and the likely pace of currency appreciation that gives some additional autonomy to monetary policy, they seem to have a role within the broader macro prudential policy framework.

Concluding Remarks

In this chapter we have given an overview of the policy options that can complement traditional tools of bank regulation and monetary policy in reining in the excesses in the financial system. Table 1.2 provides a taxonomy of macro prudential tools while Table 1.3 summarizes the policy framework within which they may be implemented.

Macro prudential policies aim to lean against excessive asset growth during booms, and thereby achieve more sustainable long-term loan growth. The mirror image of moderating asset growth is the mitigation of vulnerabilities on the liabilities side. The policy debate on macro prudential policies on the Financial Stability Board and the Basel Committee on Banking Supervision has taken place with the focus largely on the developed financial systems that were at the eye of the storm in the recent financial crisis of 2007–09. However, we have seen in this chapter that the financial stability challenges facing emerging and developing economies are perhaps even more acute because of the susceptibility of these economies to the conjuncture ruling in global capital markets and on the relatively early stage of their financial systems.

To the extent that the current global conjuncture with permissive global liquidity conditions is driven by expansive monetary policies pursued by advanced economy central banks, macro prudential policies aimed at achieving financial stability have many points of contact with capital control tools, or to use the more neutral terminology currently in fashion, capital flow management tools.

Because capital flow management tools often have broader macro objectives, such as leaning against the overly rapid appreciation of domestic currency, the dividing line between tools for financial stability and tools for macroeconomic management can be fuzzy. The same is true for the dividing line between monetary policy and policies toward financial stability. Contrary to the textbook division between the two, monetary policy has financial stability implications through changes in the size and composition of bank balance sheets, whereas prudential policies will have direct implications for credit growth and aggregate demand.

Although the study of macro prudential policy frameworks is in its infancy, there is a rapidly accumulating body of work on the subject. Based on existing literature and recent insights, this chapter has provided an analytical framework regarding the motivations for and effects of macro prudential rules on financial institutions that can be considered among a range of policy proposals.

An assessment of macro prudential policies must build on the further development of analytical tools that are better adapted to studying the interactions between institutions and markets in the broader financial system. Further experience with the use of macro prudential tools can be expected to contribute to the subsequent refinements of the framework discussed in this chapter.

Dealing with the Challenges of Macro Financial Linkages in Emerging Markets
http://dx.doi.org/10.1596/978-1-4648-0002-3

Notes

1. The discussion in this subsection is taken from Adrian and Shin (2011), which presents a more detailed analysis of how banking balance sheet management relates to corporate finance principles.
2. The monetary base, one of several standard measures of the money supply, is the sum of currency in circulation and reserve balances. M1 is the sum of currency held by the public and transaction deposits at depository institutions (which are financial institutions that obtain their funds mainly through deposits from the public, such as commercial banks, savings and loan associations, savings banks, and credit unions). M2 is defined as M1 plus savings deposits, small-denomination time deposits (those issued in amounts of less than $100,000), and retail money market mutual fund shares.
3. The inclusion of CDs in noncore liabilities is motivated by the fact that CDs are often held by financial institutions engaged in the carry trade, and who use CDs as an alternative to holding Korean government securities in their carry trade.
4. For example, see Kashayp and Stein (2004) and Adrian and Shin (2010).
5. IMF 2012, 50, http://www.imf.org/external/np/pp/eng/2013/012713.pdf.

References

Adrian, Tobias, and Markus Brunnermeier. 2009. "CoVaR." Staff Report 348, Federal Reserve Bank of New York. http://newyorkfed.org/research/staff_reports/sr348.html.

Adrian, Tobias, and Hyun Song Shin. 2009. "Procyclical Leverage and Value-at-Risk." Staff Report 338, Federal Reserve Bank of New York. http://www.newyorkfed.org/research/staff_reports/sr338.html.

———. 2010. "Liquidity and Leverage." *Journal of Financial Intermediation* 19 (3): 418–37.

———. 2011. "Financial Intermediary Balance Sheet Management." *Annual Reviews in Financial Economics*. http://www.princeton.edu/~hsshin/www/ARFE_2011.pdf.

Assenmacher-Wesche, Katrin, and Stefan Gerlach. 2010. "Financial Structure and the Impact of Monetary Policy on Property Prices." Working Paper, Goethe University, Frankfurt. http://www.stefangerlach.com/Asset%20prices%20(21%20Apr%202010).pdf.

Bank of England. 2009. "The Role of Macroprudential Policy." A Discussion Paper. http://www.bankofengland.co.uk/publications/other/financialstability/roleofmacroprudentialpolicy091121.pdf.

BCBS (Basel Committee on Banking Supervison). 2009. "Strengthening the Resilience of the Banking Sector." December. Bank for International Settlements, Basel, Switzerland. http://www.bis.org/publ/bcbs164.pdf.

———. 2010. "International Regulatory Framework for Banks (Basel III)." Working Paper 127, original version published December 2010 with revised rules June 2011. Bank for International Settlements, Basel, Switzerland. http://www.bis.org/publ/bcbs189_dec2010.htm.

BIS (Bank for International Settlements). 2010a. "Macroprudential Instruments and Fameworks: A Stocktaking of Issues and Experiences." Discussion Paper 38, Committee on the Global Financial System, May. http://www.bis.org/publ/cgfs38.htm.

———. 2010b. "Funding Patterns and Liquidity Management of Internationally Active Banks." Discussion Paper 39, Committee on the Global Financial System, May. http://www.bis.org/publ/cgfs39.htm.

Borio, Claudio, and Philip Lowe. 2002. "Asset Prices, Financial and Monetary Stability: Exploring the Nexus." Working Paper 114, Bank for International Settlements, Basel, Switzerland, July.

———. 2004. "Securing Sustainable Price Stability: Should Credit Come Back from the Wilderness?" Working Paper 157, Bank for International Settlements, Basel, Switzerland, July.

Bruno, Valentina, and H. S. Shin. 2011. "Capital Flows, Cross-Border Banking and Global Liquidity." Working Paper, Princeton University.

———. 2013. "Assessing Macroprudential Policies: Case of Korea." Working Paper, Princeton University.

Cardenas, Mauricio, and Felipe Barrera. 1997. "On the Effectiveness of Capital Controls: The Experience of Colombia during the 1990s." *Journal of Development Economics* 54 (1): 27–57.

De Gregorio, José, Sebastian Edwards, and Rodrigo Valdes. 2000. "Controls on Capital Inflows: Do They Work?" *Journal of Development Economics* 63 (1): 59–83.

Gurley, John G., and Edward S. Shaw. 1960. *Money in a Theory of Finance.* Washington, DC: Brookings Institution.

Hahm, Joon-Ho., Frederic S. Mishkin, Hyun Song Shin, and Kwanho Shin. 2010. "Macroprudential Policies and the Role of the Central Bank." Study commissioned by the Bank of Korea.

Hattori, Masazumi, Hyun Song Shin, and Wataru Takahashi. 2009. "A Financial System Perspective on Japan's Experience in the Late 1980s." Paper presented at the 16th Bank of Japan International Conference, Bank of Japan, Institute for Monetary and Economic Studies, May. http://www.imes.boj.or.jp/english/publication/edps/2009/09-E-19.pdf.

Kashayp, Anil, and Jeremy Stein. 2004. "Cyclical Implications of the Basel II Capital Standards." *Federal Reserve Bank of Chicago Economic Perspectives* 28 (1): 18–31.

Magud, Nicolas, Carmen M. Reinhart, and Kenneth S. Rogoff. 2011. "Capital Controls: Myth and Reality—A Portfolio Balance Approach." Working Paper 16805, National Bureau of Economic Research, Cambridge, MA, February.

Morris, Stephen, and Hyun Song Shin. 2008. "Financial Regulation in a System Context." *Brookings Papers on Economic Activity* Fall: 229–74.

Ostry, J., A. Ghosh, K. Habermeier, M. Chamon, M. Qureshi, and D. Reinhardt. "Capital Inflows: The Role of Controls, 2010." Staff Position Note 10/04, International Monetary Fund, Washington, DC.

———. 2011. "Capital Inflows: The Role of Controls." Staff Discussion Note 10/06, International Monetary Fund, Washington, DC.

Shin, Hyun Song. 2009. "Reflections on Northern Rock: The Bank Run that Heralded the Global Financial Crisis." *Journal of Economic Perspectives* 23 (1): 101–19.

———. 2011. "Macroprudential Policies Beyond Basel III." Macroprudential Regulation and Policy Paper 60, Bank for International Settlements, Basel, Switzerland, June. http://www.princeton.edu/~hsshin/www/MacroprudentialMemo.pdf.

Shin, Hyun Song, and Kwanho Shin. 2010. "Procyclicality and Monetary Aggregates." Discussion Paper w16836, National Bureau of Economic Research, Cambridge, MA. http://www.nber.org/papers/w16836.

CHAPTER 2

Adapting Micro Prudential Regulation for Emerging Markets

Viral V. Acharya*

Introduction

Current financial regulations and bank supervision are essentially *micro pruden-tial* in nature, in that they seek to limit each institution's risk. Many rationales exist for focusing on institution-level risk in this way. First, traditional banking is funded by dispersed creditors who are more likely to respond to warning signals about bank health via disruptive "runs" (demand of immediacy) rather than ensure ex ante that banks remain healthy. Regulators can represent depositors and get around their collective action problem in monitoring and supervising banks by placing some constraints on risk taking. Second, because the govern-ment insures deposits up to a threshold amount to reduce the incidence of dis-ruptive runs, it becomes the effective creditor of financial firms and thus has an interest in minimizing its downside risk from bank failures. Third, in many coun-tries—especially in emerging markets—banks are state owned, making the gov-ernment a direct stakeholder in the financial sector. Government-sponsored enterprises (such as Fannie Mae and Freddie Mac in the United States, or the *Landesbanken* in Germany) and state-owned banks (which play an important role in the banking sector of many Asian countries, including India and China) are primary examples.[1] In such cases, micro prudential regulation is a part of the overall governance structure of individual financial firms.

Yet, increasingly the concern for economies is not the failure of an individual financial firm but a systemwide collapse that threatens to result in loss of inter-mediation and impairment of growth. Such "systemic risk" can result in the failure of a significant part of the financial sector, leading to a reduction in credit

* **Viral V. Achary** is C. V. Starr Professor of Economics and Professor of Finance at the New York University Stern School of Business. He is also with the Center for Economic Policy Research (CEPR) and the National Bureau of Economic Research (NBER). The author is grateful to Hanh Le for valuable research assistance and to Swati R. Ghosh of the World Bank and Stijn Claessens of the International Monetary Fund for use-ful feedback and suggestions.

availability that has the potential to adversely affect the real economy. Given the interconnectedness of various financial elements, the contemporary market-based financial sector should be thought of as not just the deposit-taking, loan-making activities of commercial banks, but also as, including investment banks, money-market funds, insurance firms, and potentially even hedge funds and private equity funds.[2] Even though the financial sectors of emerging economies primarily consist of traditional commercial banks, recent evidence from China and India shows that when commercial banks are restricted in risk-taking and leverage, emerging economies tend to have an outgrowth of "shadow banking," that is, nonbank financial intermediaries (money market funds and nonbank finance corporations) that often remain outside of regulatory scope.

Several types of systemic risks can be generated from the failure of financial institutions, including counterparty risk, especially in interbank markets; spillover risk due to forced asset sales in asset- or market-based economies; the risk of "runs" on the shadow-banking system; or simply the inability to resolve failed banks by selling them to other better-capitalized firms (given their dearth in a systemic crisis) leading to a credit crunch or regulatory forbearance and creation of "zombie" institutions that do not allocate resources effectively in the economy given their debt overhang problems.[3] A financial crisis only serves to exacerbate these risks.

Unless the external costs of such systemic risks imposed on the rest of the financial sector, as well as on the rest of the economy, are internalized by each financial institution, an incentive to take risks that are borne by others will remain. A financial institution's risk is a negative externality on the system.[4] Thus, *financial regulation should be not only micro prudential but also macro prudential in nature*, focused on limiting systemic risk. Absent such macro prudential regulation, economies run the risk of excessively large amplifiers over and above normal cyclical macroeconomic fluctuation. This risk occurs because moral hazard due to regulatory forbearance during systemic crises is particularly severe;[5] even if the regulator would like to commit ex ante to not bail out failed institutions, it is not credible ex post.

The costs of such bailouts tend to be significant, often a nontrivial fraction of the gross domestic product (GDP) of the economies involved. Caprio and Klingebiel (1996) argue that the bailout of the thrift industry cost 3.2 percent of GDP in the United States in the late 1980s. They document that the estimated cost of bailouts were 16.8 percent for Spain, 6.4 percent for Sweden, and 8 percent for Finland. Honohan and Klingebiel (2000) find that countries spent 12.8 percent of their GDP to clean up their banking systems, whereas Claessens, Djankov, and Klingebiel (1999) set the cost at 15–50 percent of GDP. Using longer time-series data, Laeven and Valencia (2008, 2010) and Reinhart and Rogoff (2009a, 2009b) also document that the costs of these crises—assessed over decades and centuries, respectively—appear to be substantial, often amounting to more than 50 percent of GDP, wiping out several years of growth and resulting in "lost decades."

The large potential cost to the economy warrants macro prudential regulation focused on systemic risk, rather than micro prudential regulation focused on an individual institution's risk of failure. Importantly, micro prudential regulation can be readily adapted to incorporate macro prudential concerns.

The next section (Regulatory Distortions and Systemic Risk in Emerging Markets) lays out why systemic risk concerns are as important, if not more important, in emerging markets as in advanced economies. That section also considers, most notably, the pervasive and distortive role played by government guarantees in these countries and the need to charge upfront for the systemic risk of financial firms, which is presently largely government guaranteed. As the role of emerging markets in the global economy rises, the importance of risk spillovers across these markets has grown. Thus, it is important to look for emerging pockets of macro prudential risk, not just inside economies but also outside. Finally, the section discusses in greater detail the possible spillovers and global linkages, and provides a potential blueprint for achieving better international coordination of macro prudential regulation.

The third section (Basel Capital Requirements) takes the Basel capital requirements (Basel III in particular) as a case in which micro prudential regulation largely ignores macro prudential concerns, and in many cases, aggravates macro prudential outcomes. How should micro prudential regulation be adapted to incorporate macro prudential concerns? In the same way that firms are often regulated to limit their pollution or are taxed based on the externalities they cause, macro prudential regulation should consider a "tax" on firms' contribution to systemic risk. To the extent market-based signals are available to assess the risk of institutions and the correlation of this risk with aggregate risks of the economy, systemic risk contributions of financial firms can be measured, as outlined in the next section.

The fourth section (Measuring Systemic Risk) also entertains the possibility that regulators can generate their own valuable information to supplement or substitute for market data, where it is either unavailable or unreliable, as in some emerging markets. In particular, "stress tests" that subject financial firms to a common set of aggregate shocks can assess whether the firms would be adequately capitalized in such scenarios. Thus, rather than limiting the stress scenarios to effects on individual firms, micro prudential stress tests can be given an important macro prudential dimension. Capital shortfalls of firms in such stress tests could be an alternative measure of their systemic risk.

Depending on the availability of market data to assess and measure systemic risk, the fifth section (Regulating systemic risks) proposes regulation of systemic risk. There are three alternatives: capital requirements based on systemic risk contributions; tax or premiums along the lines of deposit insurance premiums; and leverage restrictions as well as adjustments of sector risk weights in (Basel-style) capital calculations, based on outcomes of stress tests.

Whereas all these alternatives may be implementable in an emerging market context, they may serve different purposes in practice. Capital requirements, for instance, may be more easily gamed than premiums (which require upfront cash payments) but also provide a buffer against future losses. Importantly, in many emerging markets and for nonpublicly traded financial firms, market availability of data and risk indicators is a challenge (even though financial firms are increasingly being publicly traded in emerging markets, given the size and growth of capital markets).[6] To the extent systemic risk contributions are not perfectly assessable, direct leverage restrictions (for example, no loan-to-value ratios that exceed 80 percent, or no leverage for financial firms based on overall assets that exceed 15:1) can lend macro prudential regulation a certain amount of robustness to regulators' own "model risk" in assessing systemic risk. Finally, sector risk-weight adjustments (for example, increased risk-weight of mortgages if the entire financial sector is found in a stress test to be increasing exposure to them) recognize that regulation can get outdated and the financial sector can "cherry pick" the cheapest risk-weight classes, once again lending robustness to macro prudential regulation.

The fifth section on regulating risk also touches briefly on issues related to "shadow banking," namely, the propensity of the financial sector to exit the regulatory perimeter and operate in a manner that enables certain concentrations of leverage and aggregate risks to develop risking the macro prudential health of economies. Some measures to integrate the regulation of shadow-banking institutions with traditional banking and financial sectors are discussed. Although this issue may not be paramount for emerging markets at present, it is bound to grow in importance as the financial sector grows and regulations are strengthened. The section closes with a focus on the emerging market context of a proposed policy toolkit.

Regulatory Distortions and Systemic Risk in Emerging Markets

In this section, we discuss market and regulatory failures that lead to financial instability in emerging markets, focusing on three issues: (1) government guarantees, mostly in the form of deposit insurance, (2) the implications of these guarantees in the current crisis, and (3) the transmission of systemic risk. [7]

Government Guarantees

Government guarantees, such as deposit insurance and too-big-to-fail designations, can generate significant moral hazard in the form of risk-taking incentives. Even absent other market failures, this moral hazard can lead to excessive systemic risk and financial fragility. Consider our analysis of the lessons learned from the current crisis in the United States. Deposit insurance enacted in the 1930s in the wake of the Great Depression had long-term success only because significant protections were put in place in terms of insurance charges, regulation (mostly in the form of capital requirements and wind-down provisions), and restrictions on bank activity. As these protections began to erode, the moral hazard problem resurfaced.

To some degree, researchers already knew this. Demirguc-Kunt and Kane (2002), for instance, noted that the number of countries offering explicit deposit insurance increased multifold from 12 to 71 in the 30-year period starting in the 1970s. They argue that the key feature of a successful deposit insurance scheme is the financial and regulatory environment in which it functions, including coverage limits of deposit insurance, the degree to which depositors take coinsurance of their balances, restrictions on certain deposit accounts, and whether the program is funded publicly or privately.

Demirguc-Kunt and Detragiache (2002) look at a large cross-section of countries in the post-1980 period and conclude that deposit insurance increases the likelihood of a banking crisis.[8] Moreover, the likelihood and severity of the crisis are greater for countries that have weaker institutional and regulatory environments and that offer greater coverage to depositors. The authors conclude that the incentive problems associated with the moral hazard from deposit insurance can be partially offset by effective prudential regulation and loss-control features of deposit insurance.

Laeven (2002) finds that in many countries deposit insurance is sharply underpriced, contributing to both the likelihood of a financial crisis and the cost of one if it occurs. Of course, deposit insurance premiums were not collected for most banks in the United States from 1996 to 2005 because the fund was well capitalized.

Government Guarantees and Emerging Markets

It is common practice to provide government guarantees during a crisis. Demirguc-Kunt and Kane (2002) cite the examples of Sweden (1992), Japan (1996), Thailand (1997), the Republic of Korea (1997), Malaysia (1998), and Indonesia (1998). In the current crisis, the United States guaranteed money-market funds after the fall of Lehman Brothers, and made explicit the previous implicit guarantees of the government-sponsored enterprises (GSEs) and the too-big-to-fail institutions.

What is the impact of such guarantees? Honohan and Klingebiel (2003) find that unlimited depositor guarantees and regulatory forbearance increase the fiscal costs of financial crises.[9] Moreover, these actions increase the expectation that the government will use the same solution for future crises, thus killing market discipline and increasing the chances of risk shifting among financial institutions. The lesson is that the problems that plagued the United States are similar to those that have afflicted emerging markets.

Of course, many analysts might point to the apparent "success" of the guarantees employed in the United States in the recent financial crisis and, even more so, to the banks in India and China and the government backing they received. Let us analyze these cases as examples in emerging markets.

Consider India. A significant part of the Indian banking system is still state-owned. Although they are generally considered less efficient and sophisticated than private-sector banks, public-sector banks in India grew in importance during the financial crisis starting in 2008. The reason for their growth is somewhat perverse: there was a "flight to safety" away from private-sector banks, which have limited deposit insurance, to public-sector banks, which are fully guaranteed by the government as outlined in India's Bank Nationalization Act.

Thus, as the financial crisis unfolded in India (particularly in the fall of 2008, by which time the Indian stock market had lost more than half its value and corporate withdrawals from money market funds threatened a chain of liquidations from the financial sector), there was a flight of deposits to state-owned banks.[10] Between January 2008 and February 2009, public-sector banks' market capitalization fell by 20 percent less than that of private-sector banks. This decline was despite the fact that public-sector banks were substantially more likely to lose market capitalization during a marketwide downturn than private-sector banks on the basis of the "marginal expected shortfall" measure, a precrisis measure of systemic risk developed in detail in the final section of this chapter. In addition, private-sector banks with higher systemic risk suffered more during the economy-wide crisis of 2008 (as the systemic risk measure would predict), whereas public-sector banks with higher systemic risk, in fact, performed better! This divergence in behavior of public- and private-sector banks is telling and strongly suggests a role of government guarantees in boosting weak public-sector banks at the expense of similar-risk private-sector banks.

Such support to state-owned enterprises continues. Loan growth at public-sector banks, for instance, was as much as 10 percent, compared with dismally low levels for private-sector banks in 2009. Government guarantees have distorted the level playing field, which is destabilizing for two reasons. First, it has weakened institutions that are, in fact, subject to market discipline. Second, it has raised prospects that "handicapped" private-sector banks may have to lend—or take on other risks—more aggressively to maintain market share and generate comparable returns to shareholders. Bank regulation in India tends to be on the conservative side, often reining in risk-taking with overly stringent restrictions. However, the debilitating effects of government guarantees can travel quickly to the corporate sector and other financial firms reliant on banks, which are not directly under bank regulators' scrutiny or legal mandate.

Let us turn to China. As part of its fiscal stimulus, the Chinese government employed its almost entirely state-owned banking sector to lend at large to the economy. Between July 2008 and July 2009, lending by the Chinese banking sector grew by 34 percent. Although this increase in lending has clearly helped the Chinese economy recover quickly from the effect of the financial crisis in the United States—and its consequent effects on global trade—much of the growth in banking-sector loans mirrors the growth in corporate deposits, that is, loans are often sitting idle on corporate balance sheets, a phenomenon generally associated with severe agency problems in the form of excessive investments.

Although some of the "excess" may be desirable as part of the stimulus, especially if it is in public goods such as infrastructure projects, estimates suggest that excess liquidity is also finding its way into stock market and real estate speculation. It is not inconceivable that such lending through state-owned banks would be reckless and sow the seeds of asset-pricing booms and, perhaps, the next financial crisis. The moral hazard is clear: China has bailed out its entire banking system more than once, and in far greater magnitudes than the United States has in this crisis.

The examples of India and China highlight the classic risks that arise from government guarantees. First, government guarantees create an uneven playing field in banking sectors where some banks enjoy greater subsidies than others. This unevenness invariably leads to excessive leverage and risks by less-subsidized players to compensate for a weak subsidy, and worse lending decisions by more-subsidized players, given the guarantees. Second, government-guaranteed institutions are often employed to disburse credit at large to the economy, but this situation ends up creating distortions because the costs of the guarantees are rarely commensurate with the risks taken. The situation in India partly mirrors that in the United States, where commercial banks enjoyed greater deposit insurance than investment banks; over time, investment banks expanded their leverage significantly, leading to greater systemic risks. The situation in China is comparable to the massive credit expansion and risky betting that occurred on the balance sheets of GSEs like Fannie Mae and Freddie Mac in the United States.

Both of these problems festered because of government guarantees and contributed to the financial crisis of 2007–09. Government guarantees do not just weaken the banks that are guaranteed, but they also create systemic risk by weakening competing banks, subsidizing corporations, and fueling excessive asset speculation.

Systemic Risk and Emerging Markets

As discussed earlier, when it fails, a financial institution can produce systemic risk in several ways: counterparty risk, fire sales, and "runs." One of the principal conclusions from the earlier analysis was that systemic risk is a negative externality on the system and, therefore, cannot be corrected through market forces. In other words, there is a role for regulation to force the financial institution to internalize the external costs of systemic risk. This conclusion applies to financial institutions operating within a domestic market as well as in international markets, and is especially critical for emerging markets.

Even if a domestic regulator penalized a multinational financial firm for producing systemic risk locally, the impact of this penalty may not carry through to all the international markets in which the firm operates. Thus, one can make a case for more severe penalties for firms whose actions can lead to systemic consequences elsewhere. The issue is further complicated by financial institutions' propensity to conduct regulatory arbitrage across national jurisdictions, that is, if institutions are more strictly regulated in one jurisdiction, they may move their base for financial intermediation services to jurisdictions that are more lightly regulated. However, given their interconnected nature, such institutions nevertheless expose all jurisdictions to their risk-taking. Individually, jurisdictions may prefer to be regulation "lite" to attract more institutions and, thereby, jobs.

This crisis' poster child for being internationally interconnected is Iceland.[11] Iceland allowed its banking sector to grow almost tenfold in terms of foreign assets compared with its GDP. Its huge leverage aside, its survival was completely dependent on conditions abroad; the systemic risk of the three largest Icelandic banks (Kaupthing, Landsbanki, and Glitnir) went beyond its own borders. Because these banks had fully exploited internal expansion within Iceland, they opened branches abroad (in particular, in the United Kingdom and the Netherlands) by offering higher interest rates than comparable local banks. When

Icelandic banks began to run aground and faced massive liquidity problems, in a now somewhat infamous event, U.K. authorities invoked an antiterrorism act to freeze their assets. The Icelandic economy essentially shut down.

Although it is generally accepted that capital inflows are critical for emerging markets, there are numerous examples of capital flowing into new, emerging markets only to have the flow reverse when a crisis occurs. These "runs" can seriously harm the corporate and banking sector of developing economies, especially if there are currency, liquidity, or maturity mismatches between assets and foreign liabilities. For example, net private capital flows to emerging Europe fell from approximately US$250 billion in 2008 to US$30 billion in 2009. Unsurprisingly, emerging Europe has been one of the hardest hit in terms of the impact of the crisis on GDP and internal institutions.

The current crisis was severe both for its financial effects (for example, spikes in risk aversion of investors) and for its economic impacts (for example, the largest drop in global trade since World War II).[12] It is, thus, remarkable that emerging markets weathered this financial storm relatively well compared with past experiences. This resilience can be partly attributed to better internal planning (a substantial stock of international reserves) and partly to the availability of liquidity funding from international organizations, such as the International Monetary Fund (IMF) and World Bank. Both elements suggest an approach to international coordination that mirrors how one might regulate systemic risk domestically.

We now turn to a critical assessment of Basel capital requirements: why they need to be fundamentally rethought, in what ways they may be modified, and which of these are particularly suitable in an emerging market context.

Basel Capital Requirements: When Micro Prudential Puts Macro Prudential at Risk

In response to the systemic impact of the failure of the relatively small German bank Herstatt in 1974, the central bank governors of the G-10 established the Basel Committee on Banking Supervision (BCBS). Although it had no statutory authority, the Basel Committee has emerged over the past 40 years as the go-to group to formulate international standards for banking supervision, and especially capital adequacy requirements. The Basel process started with the 1988 Basel Accord (Basel I), which imposed the now infamous minimum ratio of capital-to-risk-weighted-assets of 8 percent. The committee produced a revised framework in June 1999, which culminated in the implementation of a new capital adequacy framework in June 2004 (Basel II). Basel II expanded Basel I's capital requirement rules and introduced internal risk assessment processes. As a result of the financial crisis, the Basel Committee is once again developing and refining proposals for capital adequacy and liquidity requirements, denoted Basel III.

Before outlining the broad strokes of the Basel III agreement, it is helpful to briefly review the earlier Accords because Basel III works iteratively off them.

The purpose of the Basel Accords is to provide a common risk-based assessment of bank assets and required capital levels. Basel I separated assets into categories and gave risk-weights ranging from 0 to 100 percent to each category. Risk-weighted assets are calculated by multiplying the sum of the assets in each category by these risk-weights. Banks then should hold a minimum ratio of 8 percent of capital-to-risk-weighted-assets.

Basel II refined the relatively crude analysis of Basel I by (1) adding further gradation of risk categories; (2) allowing for internal, and more sophisticated, risk models; and (3) incorporating value-at-risk-based capital charges for trading books. Even with the apparent improvements of Basel II, large complex financial institutions (LCFIs), armed with their too-big-to-fail funding advantage, easily exploited the conflict of interests of rating agencies and played off external versus internal risk models, while minimizing value-at-risk, though not systemic risk. Because the Basel II approach measured individual bank risk but ignored systemic risk (the primary rationale for bank regulation) and did not address the fragility that was developing on the bank liability side in the form of uninsured wholesale deposit funding, the financial sector had a race to the bottom in risk-taking and economic leverage and ended up in the poor shape it was in during the crisis.

Basel III recognizes that there are two types of risks that can cause a financial firm to fail:

- *Solvency* or *capital risk*, that is, the market value of the firm's assets falls below its obligations; and
- *Liquidity risk*, that is, the firm cannot convert assets into cash to pay off its obligations because asset markets have become illiquid; or its close cousin, *funding liquidity risk*, that is, the firm is unable to roll over its maturing debt obligations with immediacy at some point in the future.

These risks can spread quickly through fire sales, defaults, and contagious runs, and systemic risk can engulf the financial sector in no time. To the extent that Basel I and II focused almost exclusively on solvency risk, Basel III constitutes an improvement. However, the absence in Basel III of any effort to identify when an institution's solvency or liquidity risk can lead to systemic risk is disappointing. By not differentiating these risks, it directly subsidizes those solvency and liquidity risks that contribute to systemwide instability.

Although Basel III tries to correct some of these areas, its basic approach to regulation is essentially a follow-up to Basel II. Specifically, Basel III is stricter on what constitutes capital; introduces a minimum leverage ratio and, to be determined, higher capital requirements (possibly countercyclical in nature); and creates liquidity ratios that banks will eventually have to abide by. But with respect to systemic risk—the real issue at hand—the July 2010 Basel Committee report states that the committee will "undertake further development of the 'guided discretion' approach as one possible mechanism for integrating the capital surcharge into the Financial Stability Board's initiative for addressing systematically important financial institutions." This statement is somewhat surprising because one would think systemic risk *should* have been the primary focus of the regulatory guidelines.

Dealing with the Challenges of Macro Financial Linkages in Emerging Markets
http://dx.doi.org/10.1596/978-1-4648-0002-3

Capital Requirements

The Basel III rules, as far as capital holdings of banks are concerned, endorsed by the G-20 can be summarized as shown in table 2.1.

In particular, several hybrid instruments are being eliminated as eligible forms of capital, and Tier 3 capital[13] is eliminated altogether, inducing a significant shift in bank liability structure away from hybrid capital, whose growth (especially in Europe) had been substantial pre-2007.

The rules, in response to the severe criticism received by the risk-weighted approach, put a floor under the buildup of leverage in the banking sector by requiring that the ratio of capital to (unweighted) assets be at least 3 percent. In addition, the plan is to introduce additional safeguards against model risk and measurement error by supplementing the risk-weighted assets approach with a simpler measure based on gross exposures.

Other more specific but not yet fully spelled-out changes focus on strengthening the risk coverage of the capital framework by requiring that the reforms:

- Strengthen the capital requirements for counterparty credit exposures arising from banks' derivatives, repo, and securities financing transactions; raise the capital buffers backing these exposures; provide additional incentives to move over-the-counter (OTC) derivative contracts to central counterparties (probably clearinghouses); and, provide incentives to strengthen the risk management of counterparty credit exposures.
- Introduce a series of measures to promote the buildup of capital buffers in good times that can be drawn on in periods of stress by addressing procyclicality; achieve the broader macro prudential goal of protecting the banking sector from periods of excess credit growth; and promote stronger provisioning practices (forward-looking provisioning) and advocate a change in the accounting standards toward an expected loss (EL) approach.

Liquidity Requirements

As discussed earlier, financial distress arises not just from capital risk but also from liquidity risk, and the recent financial crisis shows that liquidity risk deserves

Table 2.1 Capital Adequacy Standards, Basel III

	Year to abide by rule	
Capital type	2013	2019
Minimum equity capital ratio (pure stock)	3.5 percent of risk-weighted assets (RWA)	4.5 percent of RWA
Minimum Tier 1 capital (equity and other instruments, including hybrid bonds)	4.5 percent of RWA	6 percent of RWA
Minimum total capital plus new "capital conservation buffer"	8 percent of RWA	10.5 percent of RWA

Source: Basel Committee on Banking Supervision 2010. Annex 4.

equal footing. The problem arises because regulated institutions, as well as their unregulated siblings, have fragile capital structures in that they hold long-term assets with aggregate risk and low liquidity, but face highly short-term liabilities.

One solution to address this mismatch is to impose liquidity requirements on financial institutions (similar in spirit to imposed capital requirements) with the intention of reducing runs. These would require that a proportion of the short-term funding must be in liquid assets, that is, assets that can be sold immediately in quantity at current prices. This requirement might be sufficient to prevent runs, as it will, in effect, increase the cost of financial institutions taking on carry trades and holding long-term asset-backed securities.

The original December 2009 proposal in Basel III outlined two new ratios that financial institutions would be subject to the following:

- A *liquidity coverage ratio (LCR)*: the ratio of a bank's high-quality liquid assets (for example, cash, government securities) to its net cash outflows over a 30-day period (for example, outflows in retail deposits or wholesale funding) during a severe systemwide shock. This ratio should exceed 100 percent.
- A *net stable funding ratio (NSFR)*: the ratio of the bank's available amount of stable funding (that is, its capital, longer-term liabilities and stable short-term deposits) over its required amount of stable funding (that is, value of assets held multiplied by a factor representing the asset's liquidity). This ratio should also exceed 100 percent.

The introduction of LCR and NSFR as prudential standards has merit. Consider the example of the super senior AAA-rated tranches of collateralized debt obligations (CDOs) relative to a more standard AAA-rated marketable security (say, a corporate bond). Specifically, assume that the probability and magnitude of losses (that is, the expected mean and variance) associated with default are similar between the two classes of securities. What are the implications of LCR and NSFR on these holdings?

"Liquidity risk" refers to the ability of the holder to convert the security or asset into cash. Even before the crisis started, the super senior tranches were considered to be less liquid than standard marketable securities. The fact that these securities offered a spread should not be surprising, given that there are numerous documentations of a price to illiquidity. The LCR would most likely count the AAA-rated CDO less favorably in terms of satisfying liquidity risk.

"Funding risk" refers to the mismatch in the maturity of the assets and liabilities. Financial institutions tend to hold long-term assets using cheap, short-term funding—a type of "carry trade." But this practice exposes the institution to greater risk of a run if short-term funding evaporates during a crisis. These two points suggest that it would be useful to know the "liquid" assets the financial institution holds against its short-term funding. The higher the ratio, the less an institution is subject to a liquidity shock, and, therefore, the less risky it is. The NSFR would help answer this question.

Basel Capital Requirements: An Assessment

From a conceptual standpoint, the Basel capital requirements are a flawed tool for overall financial stability as they are *not* macro prudential in nature. First and foremost, a macro prudential tool should be concerned with—and attempt to address—systemic risk contributions of financial firms. Basel requirements, for the most part, are focused instead *only* on the micro prudential risks of financial firms.

Second, the very act of reducing individual financial firms' risk can, in principle, aggravate systemic risk. For instance, if institutions cannot diversify perfectly but are encouraged to do so at all costs, they can all be left holding the same aggregate risk as they diversify away all idiosyncratic risk. If the costs to bank failures are nonlinearly increasing in number of failures, such diversification could, in fact, be welfare reducing. A good analogy is banks holding AAA-rated tranches to ensure a diversified bet on the housing market. Such a diversified bet was rewarded by Basel requirements in terms of capital regulations relative to holding the underlying mortgages on banking books.

Third, even if one ignores the possibility of individual financial firms becoming more correlated as they reduce their own risks, Basel requirements ignore the *endogenous* or *dynamic* evolution of risks of the underlying assets. Consider again the case of AAA-backed residential mortgage-backed securities (MBS). By providing a relative advantage to this asset class, the Basel requirements explicitly encourage greater lending to residential mortgages. As banks lent down the quality curve, they made worse mortgages (that is, in terms of loan-to-value ratios). Even though residential mortgages as an asset class had historically been stable, a static risk-weight that favored this asset class made it endogenously riskier.

Finally, just as Basel requirements ignore that they increase correlated investments and endogenously produce deteriorating asset quality on a risk-favored asset class, they also ignore that when the risk of this asset class does materialize, financial firms face an endogenous liquidity risk since they are overleveraged in a correlated manner on this asset class. For instance, as each financial firm attempts to deleverage by selling its AAA-backed MBS, so does every other financial firm. Because there is not enough capital in the system to deal with the deleveraging, systemic risk is created, not only ex ante but also ex post. Basel requirements, thus, induce procyclicality over and above the fact that risks are inherently procyclical.

In economic parlance, the Basel risk-weights approach is an attempt to target relative prices for lending and investments by banks, rather than restrict quantities or asset risks directly. In the absence of the price discovery provided by markets, regulators have little hope of achieving relative price efficiency that is sufficiently dynamic and reflective not only of underlying risks but also of the fact that that these risks will evolve. In contrast, concentration limits on asset class exposure for the economy as a whole, or simple leverage restrictions (assets-to-equity ratio not greater than 15:1 for each firm, for instance), or an asset-risk restriction (loan-to-value of mortgages not to exceed 80 percent, for instance) are more likely to be robust and countercyclical macro prudential tools. These tools do not directly address systemic risk but at least offer hope of limiting the risks of individual financial firms and asset classes.

To understand the grave limitations of the current Basel approach to capital requirements, consider the following analysis of financial firms and their risk-taking in the context of the crisis of 2007–09.

Table 2.2 shows the 12 largest write-downs (and credit losses) of U.S. financial institutions from June 2007 (the beginning of the crisis) until March 2010. The top six firms combined saw a total of US$696 billion in losses. Five of these six firms received the largest bailouts (Wachovia was acquired by Wells Fargo). Although prior to their failure, most of these financial institutions were still considered "well capitalized" by regulatory agencies, the market clearly thought differently. The middle column in table 2.2 shows that between June 2007 and December 2008 the market values of the six firms (the first six firms listed in the table) dropped by an average of 88.71 percent, a precipitous decline. Moreover, during this period, any part of the financial sector in which major institutions fell short of capital—special purpose vehicles, such as conduits and structured investment vehicles (in August 2007), independent broker-dealers (in March and September of 2008), money market funds (in September 2008), and hedge funds—faced massive runs on their short-term liabilities. By the fall of 2008 and the winter of 2009, systemic risk had fully emerged and the real economy was suffering the consequences.

This finding begs the obvious question, and one with which regulators must grapple: Why, under the Basel core capital requirement of capital-to-risk-weighted-assets ratio of 8 percent, did the top 20 U.S. banks look "safe" averaging a ratio of 11.7 percent? And perhaps more striking, why did the five largest LCFIs that were subject to Basel rules and effectively failed during the crisis (Bear Stearns, Washington Mutual, Lehman Brothers, Wachovia, and Merrill Lynch) all have

Table 2.2 Largest Write-Downs for U.S. Financial Firms, 2007–10

Firm	Write-downs and credit losses, June 2007–March 2010 (US$ billions)	Equity return, June 2007–December 2008 (percent)	Equity return, June 2007–September 2008 (percent)
Fannie Mae	151.4	−98.14	−99.23
Citigroup	130.4	−82.46	−67.20
Freddie Mac	118.1	−97.98	−99.56
Wachovia	101.9	−88.34	−73.18
Bank of America	97.6	−67.79	−34.35
A.I.G.	97.0	−97.57	−94.50
JP Morgan	69.0	−31.51	−12.13
Merrill Lynch	55.9	−85.16	−72.45
Wells Fargo	47.4	−10.77	4.47
Washington Mutual	45.3	−99.95	−90.07
National City	25.2	−94.29	−86.61
Morgan Stanley	23.4	−75.99	−57.65

Source: Bloomberg.

Dealing with the Challenges of Macro Financial Linkages in Emerging Markets
http://dx.doi.org/10.1596/978-1-4648-0002-3

capital ratios between 12.3 and 16.1 percent, based on their last quarterly disclosure documents? Something was clearly amiss.

To understand what went wrong from a *regulatory* point of view, note that the LCFIs took their leveraged bet as a regulatory arbitrage response to Basel I and II. First, they funded portfolios of risky loans via off-balance-sheet vehicles (conduits and structured investment vehicles [SIVs]). These loans, however, were guaranteed by sponsoring LCFIs through liquidity enhancements that had lower capital requirements under Basel. Thus, the loans were effectively recourse but had a lower capital charge, even though the credit risk never left the sponsoring LCFIs. Second, they made outright purchases of AAA-rated tranches of nonprime securities, which were treated as having low credit risk and zero liquidity and funding risks. Third, they enjoyed full capital relief on AAA-rated tranches if they bought "underpriced" protection on securitized products from monoline insurers (which insure only one type of bond) and A.I.G., both of which were not subject to similar prudential standards. Fourth, in August 2004, investment banks successfully lobbied the Securities and Exchange Commission (SEC) to amend the net capital rule of the Securities Exchange Act of 1934, which effectively allowed for leverage to increase in return for greater supervision. This lobbying was in direct response to the internal risk management rules of Basel II.

Let us consider a few of these observations in greater detail. One of the two principal means for "regulatory arbitrage" under the Basel Accords was the creation of off-balance-sheet vehicles, which held onto many of the asset-backed securities they helped issue in the market. With securitized loans placed in these vehicles rather than on a bank's balance sheet, the bank did not need to maintain any significant capital against them. However, the conduits funded the asset-backed securities with asset-backed commercial paper (ABCP)—short-term, typically less than one-week maturity, debt instruments sold in the financial markets, notably to investors in money market instruments. To be able to sell ABCP, a bank would have to provide the buyers, that is, the banks' "counterparties," with *guarantees* on the underlying credit—essentially bringing the risk back to the banks themselves, even though that risk was not shown on their balance sheets.[14]

These guarantees had two important effects. First, guaranteeing the risk to banks' counterparties was essential in moving these assets off the banks' balance sheets. Designing the guarantees as "liquidity enhancements" with maturities of less than one year (to be rolled over each year) allowed the banks to exploit a loophole in Basel capital requirements. In fact, almost all of these loans had 364-day maturities. The design effectively eliminated the "capital charge" from retaining the risk of these loans, so that banks achieved a tenfold increase in leverage for a given pool of loans. Second, the guarantees ensured the highest ratings for the off-balance-sheet vehicles from the rating agencies. Indeed, the AAA ratings made it possible for banks to sell ABCP to money market funds, which are required by law to invest mainly in short-term, highest-rated paper. This allowed banks to fund the ABCP at low interest rates, similar to that paid on deposit accounts.

Acharya, Schnabl, and Suarez (2009) document an increase in the ABCP market from US$600 billion in 2004 to US$1.2 trillion in the second quarter of 2007. When the collapse occurred in the next quarter, the cost of issuing ABCP rose from just 15 basis points over the federal funds rate to over 100 basis points (peaking at close to 150 basis points). Consequently, the ABCP could no longer be rolled over, and banks had to return the loans to their balance sheets. Acharya, Schnabl, and Suarez (2009) show that when the crisis hit, of the US$1.25 trillion in asset-backed securitized vehicles, only 4.3 percent of the loss was structured to remain with investors. The remaining loss wiped out significant portions of bank capital and threatened banks' solvency.

Off-balance-sheet financing was not the only way banks performed "regulatory arbitrage" against the Basel rules. In the second approach, a bank would still make loans and move them from its balance sheet by securitizing them. The bank then turned around and reinvested in AAA-rated tranches of the same securitized products they (or other banks) had created. Because of their AAA ratings, these securities had a significantly lower capital requirement under the Basel II arrangement. For commercial banks, the Basel Accord weighted the risk of AAA-rated securities at less than half of the risk of ordinary commercial or mortgage loans, and thus required an even lower capital reserve for them (a 20 percent risk-weight, compared with 50 percent for mortgages and 100 percent for corporate bonds). In 2004, the SEC granted stand-alone investment banks the ability to employ internal models to assess credit risk and the corresponding capital charge. This rule change allowed the investment banks to take on even higher leverage than commercial banks, with leverage duly skyrocketing from a 22:1 debt-to-equity ratio to 33:1 within just three years.

In fact, as a Lehman Brothers' report from April 2008 shows (see table 2.3), banks and thrifts, GSEs, and broker-dealers held US$789 billion of the AAA-rated CDO tranches that were backed by nonprime loans in 2007, or approximately

Table 2.3 Distribution of the U.S. Real Estate Exposures
US$, billions

	Loans	HELOC	Agency MBS	Nonagency AAA	CDO subord	Non-CDO subord	Total	
Banks & thrifts	2,020	869	852	383	90		4,212	39%
GSEs & FHLB	444		741	308			1,493	14%
Brokers/dealers			49	100	130	24	303	3%
Financial guarantors		62			100		162	2%
Insurance companies			856	125	65	24	1,070	10%
Overseas			689	413	45	24	1,172	11%
Other	461	185	1,175	307	46	49	2,268	21%
Total	2,925	1,116	4,362	1,636	476	121	10,680	
	27%	10%	41%	15%	4%	1%		

Source: Mago, Sabarwal, and Iyer 2008.
Note: HELOC = home equity line of credit; MBS = mortgage-backed security; AAA = prime bond credit rating; CDO = collateralized debt obligation.

Figure 2.1 Growth in Total Assets and Risk-Weighted Assets
trillions of euros

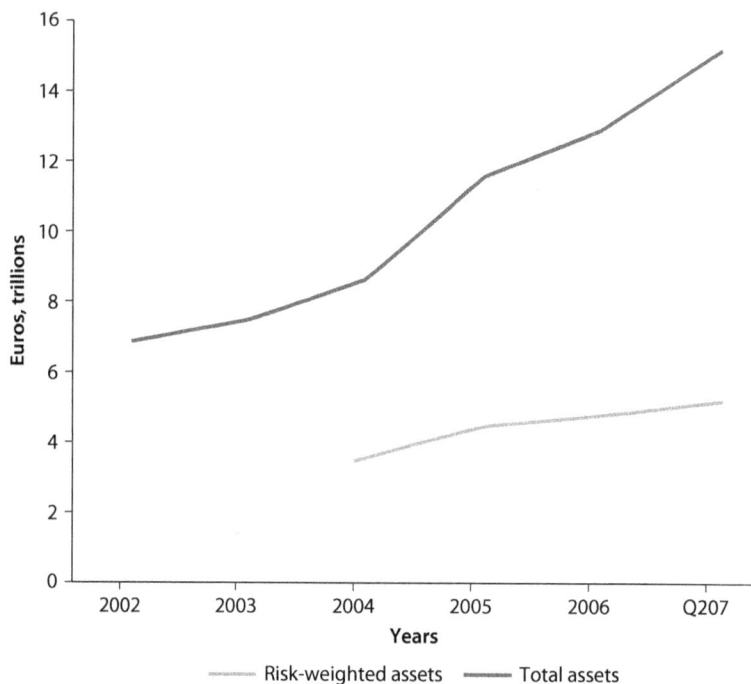

Source: IMF 2008, based on balance sheets of 10 largest global financial institutions.

50 percent of the volume outstanding at the time. Moreover, banks, broker/dealers, and monoline insurers also held the majority of the subordinated tranches of the CDOs. They collectively held US$320 billion of the US$476 billion total outstanding.

Arbitraging Basel's capital requirements resulted in a doubling of global banking balance sheets between 2004 and 2007 with only a minor increase in Basel-implied risk (figure 2.1). This fact alone should have been a red flag to regulators, but combined with the growth in short-term shadow-banking liabilities from US$10 trillion to US$20 trillion between 2000 and 2007 (compared with US$5.5 trillion to US$11 trillion in traditional bank liabilities), it is clear in hindsight that the focus of Basel capital requirements over the prior 30 years has been misplaced.

In fact, as illustrated in table 2.2 and figure 2.2, financial firms with the best regulatory capital ratios (effectively, caused by substantial regulatory arbitrage) fared the worst in terms of market capitalization declines during the crisis. In other words, their high regulatory capital ratios, that is, low unweighted-assets-to-risk-weighted-assets ratio in figure 2.2, were not a sign of their financial stability, but ironically a sign of their propensity to hold onto systemically risky assets with maximum economic leverage.

It is thus somewhat surprising that Basel III, in many ways, mirrored the Basel Committee's previous two attempts. While the Basel III process focuses on using

Figure 2.2 Bank Equity Price Changes and Balance Sheet Leverage
percent

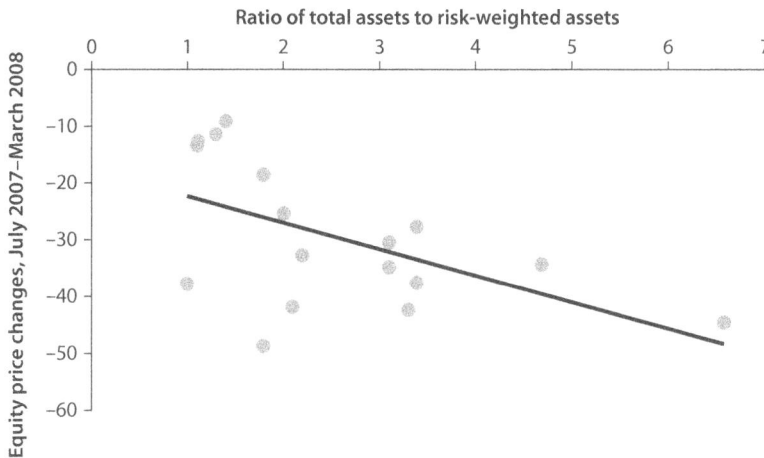

Source: IMF 2008.

more stringent capital requirements to get around some of these issues, it ignores the crucial market and regulatory failures of the financial system:

- Although recognizing the systemic risk of financial firms, the Basel approach remains focused on the risk of the individual institution and not the system as a whole. In other words, the level of a firm's capital requirements in Basel I, II, or III does not depend on its interaction with other financial firms.
- Whatever capital or liquidity requirements are placed on one set of financial institutions, it is highly likely that the financial activities affected by these requirements will simply move elsewhere in the shadow-banking system. Without an understanding that the entire financial system must be looked at and treated in unison, Basel III will run into the same shadow-banking issues that arose with Basel I and II.
- There seems to be no recognition of the role government guarantees play in the allocation of capital. *Ceteris paribus*, the more guarantees a firm receives, the lower its costs of debt funding. This artificially increases the relative cost of nonguaranteed funding like equity, preferred stock, and possibly subordinated debt (under a credible resolution authority).

Also problematic is that the Basel process retains old definitions of capital and leverage not entirely suitable for reducing excessive systemic risk brought on by modern financial firms. It is certainly true that Basel III has tightened the treatment of off-balance-sheet financing. Moreover, the fact that liquidity risk is now at the forefront of Basel III, and presumably future financial regulation in the United States as a result of the Dodd-Frank Act, is clearly a step forward. The LCR and NSFR liquidity adequacy standards are reasonable approaches toward the regulation of liquidity risk. But their focus is still not on measures that actually reflect broad systemic risk, and the approach is eerily similar to that of Basel I and II for setting capital requirements. All the adjustment factors and weights used in calculating the LCR and NSFR have their counterparts in the risk-weights of capital ratios. It is very likely that implementation of the liquidity ratios will push banks toward regulatory arbitrage of the liquidity weights, in particular, to the *best-treated* illiquid securities and systemically risky funding. Of course, the unintended consequence will be a concentration into these activities. Regulators should be acutely aware of this problem and be prepared ex ante to adapt in an expedited way.

The other problem is that the liquidity rules do not seem to take into account the impact a liquidity crisis at one bank has on the financial sector as a whole, especially in a crisis. In other words, banks that contribute more to systemwide liquidity events (in a crisis) should be charged for this negative externality.

Finally, a significantly problematic issue with Basel III's specific implementation of liquidity risk management is whether the risk-weights on government bonds are suitably calibrated for the emerging sovereign credit risk in European zone countries, which implies that many securities that would traditionally have been both liquid and safe, are now liquid (because of central bank collateral qualification) but significantly credit risky.

In summary, although Basel III does make indirect attempts to address systemic risk by considering a capital surcharge for global systemically important financial institutions (G-SIFIs) and requiring countercyclical capital surcharges, it is useful to ask: How should micro prudential regulation be adapted to incorporate macro prudential concerns? In the same way that firms are often regulated to limit their pollution or are taxed based on the externality they cause, macro prudential regulation should consider a "tax" on firms' contribution to systemic risk. To the extent market-based signals are available to assess the risk of institutions and the correlation of this risk with aggregate risks of the economy, systemic risk contributions of financial firms can be measured. We discuss this measurement issue in the next section and then present some specific forms that regulation incorporating systemic risk could take in the final section of the chapter where we entertain the possibility that in some emerging markets, market-based assessments may as of now be infeasible, though with the growing size and nature of capital markets in these countries, they may become more feasible in the future.

Measuring Systemic Risk

Macro prudential regulation needs to ascertain which institutions are, in fact, systemically important. Indeed, the systemic risk of an individual institution has not yet been measured or quantified by regulators in an organized manner, even though systemic risk has always been one of the main justifications for our regulatory apparatus.[15]

Institutions that follow highly procyclical activities are heavily correlated with aggregate economic conditions. If these institutions are also highly levered, especially with short-term debt, they face "runs" in the event of sufficiently adverse news about their condition making them more prone to failure and liquidation. If their failure were unrelated to aggregate conditions, their liquidation would be straightforward; healthy players in the financial sector would acquire their assets. However, when institutions' asset risk is correlated with that of the economy, they are likely to fail when the rest of the financial sector is also under stress, and their liquidation is difficult and potentially destabilizing for other players if fire-sale asset prices lead to externalities. In this case, systemic risk propagates through firm failures on asset prices. The markdowns in prices of illiquid "toxic" assets during the crisis of 2007–09 may be attributed (at least partly) to several, highly levered financial firms having taken a one-way bet on the housing price in the economy—a bet that went bad and produced difficult funding conditions for less levered financial institutions that were holding similar assets.

Interconnection among financial firms can also lead to systemic risk under crisis conditions. Financial institutions are interconnected in a variety of networks in bilateral and multilateral relations and contracts, as well as through markets. Under normal conditions, these interconnections are highly beneficial to the financial system and its constituents. For example, they can be used by financial institutions to diversify risk as well as to accumulate capital for specific functions. Under crisis conditions, this is not the case: first, these interconnections (including markets) may fail to function in the normal way, resulting in particular institutions facing excessive and unexpected risks. Second, many interconnections and commitments cannot be altered quickly and, therefore, may transfer risk and losses across financial firms in a crisis, resulting in cascading failures.

Third, certain institutions are central to key financial networks, and their failure can result in widespread failures. These institutions may either be "too large" (to fail) or may be highly interconnected, or both. The failures of Bear Stearns, Lehman Brothers, and A.I.G. all contributed to systemic risk in the form of uncertainty about which interconnections would transmit default risk. In the case of Bear Stearns, the risk was stemmed through government support. But in the case of Lehman Brothers, the risk spread as losses on Lehman bonds caused the Reserve Primary Fund, a money market fund, to "break the buck,"[16] causing a run on it and several other money market funds. In the case of A.I.G., its counterparty position was so large (in terms of exposures of other potentially systemic institutions and municipalities in the United States as well as in Europe) that it could not be allowed to fail.

Finally, although size by itself need not lead to systemic effects of failures, it may do so if large-scale liquidations are feared and lead to markets disruptions, interconnections, and the loss of intermediation functions. The failure of Continental Illinois Bank in 1984, the near collapse of Long-Term Capital Management in 1998, and that of Citigroup in the autumn of 2008 are appropriate examples. Of course, these examples bring with them the curse of "too-big-to-fail" expectations and the attendant moral hazard problems.

The discussion to follow is centered on the following themes: (1) the criteria for determining systemic institutions can be supplemented with market-based continuous measures of systemic risk; (2) the need to assess systemic risk is linked to the interconnectedness of institutions and the role centralized data repositories could play in such assessment; (3) employing stress tests and aggregated risk exposure reports to assess the risk of the system as a whole (not just during crises but on a regular basis); and (4) whether the list of systemic institutions should be made public.

Market-Based Measures of Systemic Risk

By way of example, the U.S. Dodd-Frank Act of 2010 proposes that systemically important financial institutions (SIFIs) be identified. In partial departure from the Act, we do not recommend a pure reliance on classification-based criteria with specific thresholds. Suppose for example that banks are divided into systemic risk categories by size and that resolution plans applied only to the largest size category. Clearly, there would be tremendous advantage for banks that are near the lower threshold of the largest size category to remain just below that level. Indeed, larger banks may simply break themselves up but still be exposed to a common aggregate risky asset (the housing market, for instance). In this case, the true systemic risk may not be substantially reduced as the comovement in different parts of the financial sector remains, even though it is now contained in many more, smaller institutions. The same regulatory arbitrage rationale applies for a coarse categorization based on leverage. A corollary of this argument is that a group of institutions that are individually small but collectively exposed to the same risk—for example, money market funds—could all experience runs when there is an aggregate crisis. They should be considered as part of a potentially systemic risk pocket of the economy.

An alternative to coarse categorization of systemic risk is to employ market-based measures that are more continuously variable.[17] One possibility is to use market data to estimate which firms are most exposed—and, therefore, would contribute most to the losses incurred—during an economywide downturn. Such measures would be inexpensive and responsive to market conditions. They would also be natural complements to the more detailed investigations envisioned in the act.

These measures are generally based on stock market data because they are most regularly available and least affected by bailout expectations. For instance, the simple marginal expected shortfall (MES) measure estimates the loss that the equity of a given firm can expect if the broad market experiences a large fall. A firm with both a high MES and high leverage will find its capital most depleted in a financial crisis relative to required minimum solvency standards and, therefore, faces high risk of bankruptcy or regulatory intervention. It is such under-capitalization of financial firms that leads to systemic risk.[18]

Overall, the two approaches—relying on simple systemic risk criteria (such as size, leverage, and interconnectedness) and relying on market-based estimates of systemic risk—are complementary. The first is more transparent, likely to flag obvious candidates, and may be the only option available if a large part of the financial sector is not publicly traded or stock price data are unreliable; the second cross-checks whether some candidates have been missed altogether (or some obvious ones are less systemic than they seem) based on market perceptions. For instance, securities broker-dealers show up as being most systemic in every year since 1963, based on stock market data (the MES measure), even though they have remained essentially unregulated. By contrast, A.I.G. is a natural one-way insurance provider of large quantities that was not identified by stock market data as being significantly systemic until six months into the crisis. Whereas systemic risk categories can be "arbitraged" by market participants, market-based systemic risk measures are more difficult to evade until the firm's true systemic risk has diminished.

Interconnectedness

A key issue that arises in measuring systemic risk is that interconnections of financial institutions are somewhat opaque, and their precise nature may be different in a stressed scenario than under normal conditions. For instance, counterparty exposures can reverse signs when conditions change. There is no simple answer to these questions, but important steps can be taken.

To assess the interconnectedness of a financial institution, detailed information about exposures to other institutions through derivative contracts and interbank liabilities is essential. Obtaining this information requires legislation that compels reporting, such that all connections are registered in a repository immediately after they are formed or when they are extinguished, along with information on the extent and form of the collateralization as well as the risk of collateral calls when credit quality deteriorates. These reports could be aggregated by risk and maturity types to obtain an overall map of network connections. What is important from the standpoint of systemic risk assessment is that such reports, and the underlying data, be rich enough to help estimate *potential exposures* to counterparties under infrequent but socially costly marketwide or economywide stress scenarios. For each systematically important institution, for instance, knowing the following is relevant: (1) what are the most dominant risk factors in terms of losses and liquidity risk (for example, collateral calls) likely to be realized in stress scenarios; and, (2) what are its most important counterparties in terms of potential exposures in stress scenarios. A transparency standard that encompasses such requirements is needed with ready access to information for purposes of macro prudential regulation.

The often international nature of such networks further complicates the picture. Because many counterparties may be foreign entities, the data to follow the stress event may not be available. As subsidiaries of the firm under examination may be registered internationally, the flow of funds may also be exceedingly difficult to follow. The Lehman bankruptcy illustrates many of these issues.

On the bright side, however, many clearing and settlement businesses are already international, providing information to the public and confidential data to regulators. Such global organizations will be natural components of the regulatory environment and their contributions should be warmly welcomed. One recommendation for improving the functioning of the over-the-counter (OTC) derivatives market is to move the public utility function out of private financial firms (for example, clearinghouses) wherever possible and to subject the public utility to sufficiently high capital standards, so as to eliminate most of the systemic risk associated with the performance of this function. Going forward, as many OTC derivatives start being centrally cleared, clearinghouses would be important "utilities" that should be included in the set of systemically important institutions and, thus, be subject to prudential risk standards.

Stress Tests

To understand the behavior of financial institutions and project their likely behavior into infrequent future scenarios, one needs to be able to model such scenarios in the first place. An attractive way of dealing with such projection is to conduct "stress tests" along the lines of the Supervisory Capital Assessment Program (SCAP) exercise conducted by the Federal Reserve and other regulators in the United States in 2009. SCAP reported:[19]

> From the macro prudential perspective, the SCAP was a top-down analysis of the largest bank holding companies (BHCs), representing a majority of the U.S. banking system, with an explicit goal to facilitate aggregate lending. The SCAP applied a common, probabilistic scenario analysis for all participating BHCs and looked beyond the traditional accounting-based measures to determine the needed capital buffer. The macro prudential goal was to credibly reduce the probability of the tail outcome, but the analysis began at the micro prudential level with detailed and idiosyncratic data on the risks and exposures of each participating BHC. This firm-specific, granular data allowed tailored analysis that led to differentiation and BHC-specific policy actions, for example, a positive identified SCAP buffer for ten BHCs and no need for a buffer for the remaining nine.

We believe stress tests should be a regular part of the macro prudential toolkit to determine the risk of institutions in stressed systemic scenarios, as well as to assess the overall systemic risk of the financial sector in such scenarios. Valuable knowledge and experience was developed in the 2009 SCAP exercise that could be built upon by regulators all over the world.[20]

Acharya and others (2010a) have found that market-based measures of systemic risk (such as MES and leverage) help shed more light on the outcomes of the SCAP exercise. Thus, the historical data-based systemic risk measures and the projected systemic risk measures through stress tests are complementary. Regulators should embrace both as useful cross checks and independent pieces of valuable intelligence for assessment of systemic risk of financial firms.

Transparency

We recommend a fully transparent approach to systemic risk measurement and categorization. A key benefit of transparency is that releasing valuable capitalization and counterparty exposure information can allow market participants to price risk in contracts with each other more accurately, and to employ suitable risk controls. The primary objection to the public disclosure of systemically important institutions is that it implicitly confers too-big-to-fail or too-interconnected-to-fail guarantees on such institutions. The problem of implicit guarantees, however, is best resolved by the creation of a resolution authority and a process that limits the fallout from failure. Unfortunately, forces against transparency gather momentum when a credit resolution mechanism or recapitalization plan is not in place. To wit, absent the ability to deal with potentially insolvent firms once they have been detected, regulators would shy away from releasing this information and instead let such institutions fester and potentially risk the rest of the financial sector. However, the evidence presented so far suggests that the information released by the SCAP exercise of 2009 on relative strengths and weaknesses of banks in the United States was perceived as welcome news in the marketplace, since it was followed by a credible plan to get them to recapitalize.

Another key benefit of requiring regulators to produce transparent systemic risk reports that are based on information aggregated across institutions and markets is that they help address another risk *within* an institution—the so-called operational risk—which can also lead to systemic risk concerns if it brings down a sufficiently large and systemically important firm. Operational risk is typically attributed to deficiencies in corporate processes (a firm's risk management systems), in its people (caused by incompetence, fraud or unauthorized behavior), and in its technology (its information systems, quality of its data, its mathematical modeling). Risk management systems benefit considerably from information transparency (intrafirm as well as interfirm), while satisfying all corporate, regulatory, and privacy constraints. Within a company, there have to be rules for daily aggregation of positions that are reported to senior management, ideally in conjunction with matching aggregate information received from important counterparties to reduce probabilities of errors and fraud. At the corporate level, the net positions of the separate divisions of the company have to be compiled and analyzed (including dependencies and risk correlation analyses). Thus, it is beneficial if a top-down structure for risk reports required by the systemic risk regulator is in place, whereby minimum standards are imposed on individual firms to gather and aggregate such information on their own exposures. At regular intervals, the aggregate information would be shared with the regulator and other counterparties.

To facilitate such transparency, high-quality data must be collected from the financial sector, in a timely manner, and be subject to both data integrity standards and analysis for purposes of building and disseminating adequate systemic risk measures and reports. A model is the newly proposed Office of Financial Research (OFR) in the United States, which could over time provide "financial stability reports" of the type produced by central banks in a number of economies.[21]

Regulating Systemic Risk: Adapting the Micro Prudential for the Macro Prudential

Two challenges exist in the regulation of systemic risk. First, systemic risk must be measured as we have discussed so far. Second, economic theory suggests that the tightness of regulation should be based on the extent to which a given firm is likely to contribute to a general crisis, so that the correct price can be charged to each firm for its contributions to systemic risk. We propose a framework to achieve this goal that is advantageous for a number of reasons: it forces regulators and financial firms to deal explicitly with systemic risk; it reduces moral hazard, in that it provides incentives for regulated firms not to take on excessive systemic risk; it reduces the procyclicality of risk taking; and it is based on tools tested and well understood by the private sector.

Three regulations based on this overall approach are presented.[22]

Capital Requirements: An Alternative to Basel III

Under this scheme, a systemic risk regulator would first measure each firm's systemic risk contribution, as discussed earlier. Then, the regulator would impose requirements or costs depending on each firm's contribution. One natural way to do this consistent with current regulation is to impose capital requirements, that is, the regulator would impose a capital requirement that depends explicitly on systemic risk contributions. This method adjusts the incentives of firms to limit their contributions to aggregate risk since keeping capital reserves is costly and, additionally, it gives the firm an appropriate safety buffer in systemic crises.[23]

For instance, the "systemic capital charge" would be

$$SCC = s \cdot MES\% \cdot A$$

where s is the systemic factor chosen by the regulator to achieve a given degree of aggregate safety and soundness; $MES\%$, the marginal expected shortfall expressed in percent of assets, would measure the aggregate tail risk on the firm; and A would be the assets of the firm.

This equation is, in effect, Basel II with systemic risk. The focus on systemic risk would be a clear improvement over existing regulations, but it must be enforced efficiently. Two key points must be insisted upon. First, there must be a limit on the ability to decrease apparent leverage by moving assets off the balance sheet.[24] Second, the measurement of systemic risk must be either acyclical (or even countercyclical) to avoid fire sales induced by violations during crises. In particular, the MES measure could, in principle, be replaced by the capital shortfall estimated for a financial firm in a stress test conducted by the regulators under some extreme aggregate outcomes.[25]

"Taxing" the Externality: A FDIC-Style Premium

A second possibility is to "tax" the activity that imposes a negative externality on the system, that is, to tax activity leading to systemic risk. The tax has two benefits. First, it discourages behavior that leads to systemic risk, and, second, the generated levies could potentially go toward a general "systemic crisis fund," to be used in the future by the regulators to inject capital into the system at their discretion. Of course, in equilibrium, some institutions will still find it optimal to engage in risky behavior and, therefore, pay the higher taxes, while others will reduce their risky behavior.

Financial institutions that pose systemic threats have three characteristics: excessive leverage, highly illiquid securities, and concentration of aggregate risk. Given these characteristics, the tax can take various forms.

One possibility is to approach this issue the same way that deposit insurance is implemented. Institutions that take deposits are governed by sequential servicing rules in terms of deposit withdrawals, that is, first come, first served. This method increases the probability of a run on the financial institution's assets. The probability of a run imposes discipline on the financial institution but, in a world of balance-sheet opacity, runs on poorly performing institutions can also lead to runs on disciplined institutions and, thus, to systemic risk. As a result, the government offers guarantee programs by insuring the deposits of participating institutions up to a certain amount.

For instance, in recognition of the fact that insurance is not free, the U.S. Federal Deposit Insurance Corporation (FDIC) imposes a fee on financial institutions. Until 1993, this fee was based only on the size of the institution's deposits and not on its risk. This method of assessing the fee created a severe moral hazard problem because these institutions could borrow at artificially low rates and undertake risky investments. As FDIC losses rose during the 1980s, FDIC contracts were redesigned.[26] That being said, while the new contracts do lead to premiums increasing in the risk characteristics of financial institutions, no systemic measure is incorporated into the assessment rate formula.[27]

We propose to charge an additional *systemic risk fee* to each financial institution based not only on the amount of assets it holds, but also on its contribution to systemic risk (based on its MES, as described earlier); its individual risk characteristics, including the ones under current FDIC rules; and on measures of complexity and interconnectedness. The majority of financial firms contribute only marginally to systemic risk, so presumably their fee would be close to zero.

Leverage Restrictions and Sectoral Risk-Weight Adjustments

One concern often raised with market measures is that they may not be readily available in emerging markets, at least not with high reliability or frequency. Another concern is that regulators might lack sophistication or expertise to price deposit insurance premiums in a way that would sufficiently counteract incentives to build up systemic risk in good times. Ongoing research shows that the former is not necessarily the case, and utilizing somewhat simpler but coarser approaches can be a way around the latter.

The most popular of these simpler approaches is a direct leverage restriction, a variant of which can be imposed at the level of each institution. No risk-weights are attached so that (perhaps with the exception of the highest-rated government debt) all assets are treated equally in terms of their potential risks. The leverage restriction, then, is simply that the institution's unweighted assets not exceed its equity value by more than a set threshold, say 15:1. Alternately, leverage restrictions can be imposed at the level of each asset class (limiting mortgages to loan-to-value ratios less than 80 percent, for instance).

Although apparently simple, these restrictions, in fact, require a fair bit of regulatory oversight and sophistication. If enforcement is weak, the financial sector can evolve a "shadow- banking" system, as was the primary problem in the United States in the buildup to the financial crisis. The regulation must now ensure that all assets—on and off the balance sheet—are suitably accounted for in leverage calculations. Similarly, if regulators have to use coarse leverage measurements on complicated securities and derivatives, regulatory arbitrage would push the financial sector toward innovation of such products. Again, this would call for sufficiently broad-scoped asset-level leverage requirements. Although it is conceivable that it would be useful to "ban" outright certain derivatives and innovation, there is no evidence that this approach has worked. Regulators are often playing catch-up to the financial sector. Hence, more prudent enforcement would ensure that the regulatory perimeter is irrefutably enforced, so that *all* risks of the financial sector are dealt with adequately while limiting system leverage.

Another macro prudential tool that is less market dependent—and one that is employed by some emerging markets, such as India—is the sector-weight adjustment approach. This approach requires horizontal aggregation of financial institutions' balance sheets and risk exposures to identify over time, say, annually, which asset classes are being "crowded in" as far as systemic risk concentrations are concerned. For instance, if mortgages or mortgage-backed securities are increasingly picking up the lion's share of all risks on bank balance sheets, then regulators could proactively react by limiting any further buildup. This limit could be achieved by increasing the risk-weights on future exposures to this asset class. In principle, stress tests could also be employed to glean such information about emerging pockets of risk concentrations.

One advantage of the dynamic sector risk-weight adjustment approach is that if it is consistently implemented by regulators and anticipated by the financial sector, then it can act as a valuable countercyclical incentive. Financial firms, anticipating the future risk in risk-weights, may stop adding exposure to an asset class once it is sufficiently crowded in. One disadvantage is that it may create a race to "get in first." The approach relies heavily on regulatory discretion being prescient in identifying risk pockets and on regulators having sufficient will in good times to lean against the wind of fast-growing asset classes.

Of course, there is no reason why these approaches could not be used in conjunction. Good regulation should look for robustness or resilience, both to its own potential errors as well as to the arbitrage of regulation by the financial sector. Rule-based approaches, such as in the capital requirements or in tax and premium schemes described earlier exonerate the regulators from relying too much on discretion and, therefore, from the lobbying influence of the industry; whereas discretionary-based approaches counterbalance the rule-based approach by creating sufficient dynamic and constructive ambiguity in the minds of the industry about increasing correlated risks and leverage. Our recommendation, however, is that discretionary approaches such as sector-based risk adjustments should also be sufficiently rule-based, to the extent possible, in terms of the framework guiding the adjustments.

Dealing with Shadow Banking
Shadow banking refers to a system of financial institutions that mostly look like banks. These financial institutions borrow short-term funds in rollover debt markets, leverage significantly, and lend and invest in longer-term and illiquid assets.

This part of the financial system includes asset-backed commercial paper (ABCP), money market funds, securities lending and collateralized repos (at broker-dealers).[28] Although shadow banks may not be paramount for emerging markets at present, the issue could grow in importance as financial sectors expand and regulators strengthen regulation. Indeed, nonbank finance corporations and money-market-fund-style activities are already on the rise in fast-growing economies such as China and India even as regulators employ deposit rate ceilings and interest rate rises to contain commercial-bank loan growth. Lessons from the impact of the recent crisis on how to regulate shadow banking are, therefore, important for emerging markets so that shadow-banking risks can be contained proactively rather than postcrisis.

Important differences exist the in current regulatory treatment of the shadow-banking and banking sectors. The shadow-banking system is, for the most part, unregulated. It is also unprotected from banklike runs (that is, there are no explicit guarantees provided by the government). The financial crisis of 2007–09 showed that much of the shadow-banking system (investment banks and money market funds, in particular) ended up being bailed out. This part of the financial system, considered in whole, was too big to fail.

As the housing market deteriorated in 2007 and prices fell in the credit market, the value of assets held by shadow banks fell significantly and put into question their solvency. Given the opaque nature of these institutions, uncertainty about which institutions were solvent led to a run on the sector. For instance, when Lehman Brothers failed in September 2008, the Prime Reserve Fund, a large money market fund, was exposed to its short-term debt. The losses on Lehman caused the fund to "break the buck." Not knowing what other non-Treasury money market funds were holding, investors immediately pulled their funding from these funds, causing a run on the money market sector and, thereby, the collapse of the commercial paper market for financial institutions. To restore confidence, the government had to guarantee the money market sector. There are numerous other such examples from the recent crisis, and their systemic impacts cannot be understated.

Uncertainty and lack of information in the financial sector are not novel concepts. The Panic of 1907 and the various banking crises during 1930–32, in the wake of the Great Depression, are just some examples of how uncertainty about the solvency of financial institutions can lead to systemwide bank runs. The Federal Reserve (as a lender of last resort), the FDIC, and deposit insurance were created in response to these systemic runs. Arguably, the most important aspect of this system is that depositors no longer had to run on the bank because the government now guaranteed their funds. To counteract the moral hazard such safety nets invariable induced, policy makers set up a system of countervailing barriers: (1) banks would have to pay to be a part of the deposit insurance system, so, at least, on an ex ante basis, regulators took into account the cost of the insurance; (2) the risk-taking activities of banks were ring fenced to the extent that there was a separation between commercial and more risky investment banking activities; and (3) enhanced supervision and winding-down provisions of individual banks in the form of capital requirements and prompt corrective action were established.

The initial success of these Depression-era measures in stabilizing the financial sector (until shadow banking eventually outgrew them) offers two lessons to reduce the buildup of systemic risk in the shadow-banking system today.

The first lesson is to explicitly guarantee the short-term liabilities of the shadow-banking sector in a systemic crisis. In return, institutions like broker-dealers, ABCP conduits and money market funds would (1) be charged a fee akin to the FDIC premium; (2) have their risk-taking activities restricted; (3) be forced to hold a capital buffer; and (4) be subject to wind-down provisions to avoid excessive risk shifting in distress.

The second is to leave the shadow-banking institutions unprotected, but set up an airtight mechanism for dealing with these firms in a systemic crisis. Specifically, if there is a run on an institution's liabilities, then, with the approval of a systemic risk regulator (or the central bank), the institution may suspend redemptions. This action would not in itself either initiate bankruptcy proceedings or force the firm into receivership. The collateral underlying these liabilities would be sold off in a slow orderly fashion (or, alternatively, pledged back to the lenders). But since most of the lenders in the shadow-banking system participate in this sector to access liquidity, the government would, at a significant haircut and for a fee, lend against the collateral. This way the lenders would have access to some funds during a systemic crisis, thus allaying any fears that all their funds would be frozen for a prolonged period. Most importantly, however, any losses in the collateral would eventually be borne by these creditors and not by taxpayers.[29]

The Emerging Market Context

Although the three approaches proposed earlier for marrying micro prudential and macro prudential objectives may be potentially implementable in an emerging markets context, they may serve different purposes in practice.

First, capital requirements, for instance, may be more easily gamed than premiums (which require upfront cash payments) but also provide a buffer against future losses. Tax premiums, conversely, deplete such a buffer. When financial firms are not publicly traded, their ability to tap into market equity capital may be limited and a push for tax premiums can cause a severe reduction in asset growth, that is, an induced credit crunch.

Second, in many emerging markets and for nonpublicly traded financial firms, market availability of data and risk indicators is a challenge (even though financial firms are increasingly being publicly traded in emerging markets, given their size and growth of capital markets). Some of the data limitations are as follows: rating agencies are generally less available and thus ratings less used for loan classifications; data series are shorter so that through-the-business-cycles classification of loans to assess their risks gets harder; and, until recently, emerging markets have been far more volatile in growth and risk terms than the developed markets of the West.

Taking account of these limitations, micro prudential regulation of financial sectors in emerging markets could provide the required macro prudential slant by adopting a number of tools. Direct leverage restrictions (for example, no loan-to-value ratios that exceed 80 percent, or no leverage for financial firms based on overall assets that exceeds 15:1) can lend micro prudential regulation a certain amount of robustness in additional to regulators' own "model risk" in assessing risks. Sector risk-weight adjustments (for example, increased risk-weight of mortgages if the entire financial sector is found to be increasing exposure to mortgages in a stress test) recognize that regulation can get outdated and the financial sector can "cherry pick" the cheapest risk-weight classes, once again lending robustness to macro prudential regulation. Lastly, transparency and disclosure for financial firm assets and liabilities could be improved to build longer datasets over time and, thus, better through-the-cycle assessments of risks. Many emerging markets already have credit bureaus and more research could be conducted using them to assess the key historical macro- and micro-drivers of credit crunches.

Notes

1. Acharya and others (2011) paint a compelling picture that Fannie Mae and Freddie Mac, the government-sponsored enterprises in the United States to securitize mortgages, effectively participated in a substantial race to the bottom in risk-taking with private-sector financial institutions, in which both their government mandates for lending for affordable housing and their poor regulatory capital requirements (given their deteriorating portfolios since 1991) played a crucial role.

2. The scope of macro prudential regulation is the financial industry, rather than any cyclical sector in the economy, because of the financial industry's intermediation role. Financial institutions are a unique part of the economy in that they act as intermediaries between parties that need to borrow and parties willing to lend. Indeed, poor performance of the financial industry will impose additional losses to the rest of the economy, from entrepreneurs to retirees.

3. Goodhart (2010) also considers asymmetric information, which can be a significant contributor to markets freezing up, as are issues concerning the governance structure of banks that, because of shareholders versus creditor/taxpayer conflicts, can lead to socially inefficient outcomes.

4. An analogy can be made to an industrial company that produces emissions that lower its own costs but pollute the environment.

5. See Acharya (2001) and Acharya and Yorulmazer (2007) for a discussion

6. Some of the data limitations are: rating agencies are generally less available and thus ratings less used for loan classifications; data series are shorter so that through-the-business-cycles classification of loans to assess their risks gets harder; and, until recently, emerging markets have been far more volatile in growth and risk terms than developed markets of the West.

7. The discussion of this section is partly based on Acharya, Cooley, Richardson, and Walter (2010).

8. See also Hovakimian, Kane, and Laeven (2003).

9. See also Claessens, Klingebiel, and Leaven (2004) and Kane and Klingebiel (2004) for further analysis and discussion of the costs of providing guarantees during a banking crisis.

10. In a notable incident, Infosys, the bellwether of Indian technology and a NASDAQ-listed company, moves its cash in hand from ICICI Bank, one of the largest private-sector banks, to State Bank of India, the largest public-sector bank.

11. See Buiter and Sibert (2008).

12. http://www.wto.org/english/news_e/pres10_e/pr598_e.htm.

13. Tier 1 capital—also called "core capital" or "basic equity"—includes equity capital and disclosed reserves. Tier 2 capital—also called "supplementary capital"—includes undisclosed reserves; revaluation reserves; general provisions or general loan-loss reserves; hybrid debt capital instruments; and subordinated term debt. Tier 2 capital cannot exceed Tier 1 capital, which means that effectively at least half of a bank's capital base should consist of Tier 1 capital. Tier 1 capital is the most stable and reliable source of funding for a bank's operations. Tier 3 capital to cover market risks may be used only at the discretion of the national authorities, and includes only short-term subordinated debt that satisfies certain conditions. Tier 3 capital is limited to 250 percent of a bank's Tier 1 capital that is required to support market risks. See http://www.bis.org/publ/bcbs128.pdf - p14.

14. See Acharya, Schnabl, and Suarez (2009).

15. The discussion of financial architecture in this section draws in part from Acharya and others (2010).

16. "Breaking the buck" occurs when a money market mutual fund's net asset value (NAV) drops below US$1 per share. Money market funds are not federally insured like bank deposits; therefore, fund assets have an implied promise to preserve capital at all costs and preserve the US$1 floor on share prices.

17. The use of market-based measures has recently been studied by Acharya and others (2010a) and (2010b), Adrian and Brunnermeier (2009); Brownlees and Engle (2010); De Jonghe (2010); Gray and Jobst (2009); Huang, Zhou, and Zhu (2009), and Lehar (2005), among others.

18. An implementation of this idea is now available at the New York University Stern School of Business volatility laboratory (Vlab). Rankings are updated regularly and posted on Vlab at: http://vlab.stern.nyu.edu/. Over time, these rankings will be extended to European and Australasian financial firms.

19. See the Federal Reserve Bank of New York report on the SCAP exercise (Hirtle, Schuermann, and Stiroh 2009)

20. The Dodd-Frank Act of 2010 in the United States calls for systemic institutions to be subject to periodic stress tests: "The Board of Governors, in coordination with the appropriate primary financial regulatory agencies and the Federal Insurance Office, shall conduct annual analyses in which nonbank financial companies supervised by the Board of Governors and bank holding companies described in subsection (a) are subject to evaluation of whether such companies have the capital, on a total consolidated basis, necessary to absorb losses as a result of adverse economic conditions." Moreover, systemically important financial institutions are required to perform semi-annual tests. Such assessments may be done more frequently in a crisis and may complement the firm's own test.

21. Christensson, Spong, and Wilkinson (2010) document, for instance, how financial stability reports in five countries (United Kingdom, Sweden, the Netherlands, Spain,

and Norway) describe identification of risks to the system (low interest rates, rising asset prices, increasing debt levels and trade imbalances, risks from the United States) and exploit market-price data and balance sheet data as well as regulatory intelligence (supervision and stress-test data).

22. This discussion is based on Acharya and others (2009).

23. Purely idiosyncratic risk would require less capital and firms might occasionally fail if they took significant risk, but an isolated failure can generally be resolved by the private sector and would not cause externalities (deposit insurance creates the need for additional regulations, but this is not our focus here).

24. The recent crisis has shown that firms such as Bear Stearns and Citigroup looked extremely well-capitalized even at points when it became clear that because of erosion of their equity's market values, they had limited funding capacity (if any) to perform day-to-day operations and manage their liquidity in an orderly fashion.

25. Greenlaw and others (2011) argue that the amount of capital required of a financial firm should depend on a stress test not just on the firm's own direct losses, but also on indirect loss contributions if these losses lead to deadweight losses through fire sales and contagion risks. Elliott (2011) provides a discussion of how bank capital requirements could be designed in a countercyclical manner to contain the boom and bust cycle of credit.

26. The Federal Deposit Insurance Corporation (FDIC) was created in the wake of the Great Depression to address the massive number of bank runs that took place from 1930 to 1933. The contracts went through several iterations ending with the Federal Deposit Reform Act of 2005 which instituted a pricing scheme for deposit premiums that attempted to capture risk by combining examination ratings, financial ratios, and, for large banks, long-term debt issuer ratings. Institutions are divided into four risk categories: I through IV. The lowest risk category contains institutions considered healthy by the examiners that are well capitalized, with total-risk-based ratios of 10 percent, tier 1 risk-based ratio of 6 percent, and tier 1 leverage ratio of 5 percent. Within risk category I, a premium between 5 and 7 cents per US$100 of deposits would be assessed, depending on formula, which takes into account tier 1 leverage ratios, loans past due 30–89 days/gross assets, nonperforming assets/gross assets, net loan charge-offs/gross assets, and net income before taxes/risk-weighted assets. As health and capitalization weakens for the firm, the risk category increases, eventually leading to premiums as high as 43 cents per US$100 of deposits.

27. The historical mandate that the FDIC must return premiums to the sector if losses are low is a very poor idea. It is paramount to returning fire insurance if there has been no fire yet.

28. The size of this market is roughly US$8 trillion in the Unites States (and even larger by some estimates) and matches the size of deposits, both insured and uninsured, held at depository institutions. The growth of shadow banking over the last 25 years has been extraordinary relative to the growth in deposits.

29. Finally, at least a part of the shadow-banking system such as money market funds and ABCP vehicles appear to have evolved largely as an end run around regulations on commercial banks. The loopholes involving different accounting and regulatory capital treatments of on- and off-balance sheet assets should be removed because they facilitate leverage buildup in the shadow-banking world in opaque forms. Money market funds are also generally an end run around taxes or restrictions on banks to offer high interest rates on deposits or any interest rates on corporate deposits. Such distortions could also be eliminated.

Dealing with the Challenges of Macro Financial Linkages in Emerging Markets
http://dx.doi.org/10.1596/978-1-4648-0002-3

References

Acharya, Viral V. 2001. "A Theory of Systemic Risk and Design of Prudential Bank Regulation." Working Paper, Stern School of Business, New York University, New York.

Acharya, Viral V., Christian Brownlees, Robert Engle, Farhang Farazmand, and Matthew Richardson. 2010. "Measuring Systemic Risk." In *Regulating Wall Street: The Dodd-Frank Act and the New Architecture of Global Finance*, edited by Viral V. Acharya, Thomas Cooley, and Matthew Richardson. Hoboken, NJ: John Wiley & Sons.

Acharya, Viral V., Lasse Pedersen, Thomas Philippon, and Matthew Richardson. 2009. "Regulating Systemic Risk." In *Restoring Financial Stability: How to Repair a Failed System*, edited by Viral V. Acharya and Matthew Richardson, chapter 13. John Wiley & Sons.

———. 2010a. "Measuring Systemic Risk." Working Paper, Stern School of Business, New York University, New York.

———. 2010b. "A Tax on Systemic Risk." In *Quantifying Systemic Risk*, edited by Joseph Haubrich and Andrew Lo. Cambridge, MA: National Bureau of Economic Research.

Acharya, Viral V., Philipp Schnabl, and Gustavo Suarez. 2009. "Securitization without Risk Transfer." Working Paper, Stern School of Business, New York University, New York.

Acharya, Viral V., and Tanju Yorulmazer. 2007. "Too Many to Fail—An Analysis of Time-Inconsistency in Bank Closure Policies." *Journal of Financial Intermediation* 16 (1): 1–31.

Acharya, Viral. V, Stijn van Nieuwerburgh, Matthew Richardson, and Lawrence White. 2011. *Guaranteed to Fail: Fannie Mae, Freddie Mac and the Debacle of Mortgage Finance*. Princeton, NJ: Princeton University Press.

Adrian, T., and Markus Brunnermeier. 2009. "CoVar." Staff Report, Federal Reserve Bank of New York, New York.

Basel Committee on Banking Supervision. 2010 (revised June 2011). "Basel III: A Global Regulatory Framework for More Resilient Banks and Banking Systems." Bank for International Settlements, Basel, Switzerland. http://www.bis.org/publ/bcbs189.pdf.

Brownlees, Christian T., and Robert Engle. 2010. "Volatility, Correlation and Tails for Systemic Risk Measurement." Technical Report, Department of Finance, New York University, New York.

Buiter, William, and Anne Sibert. 2008. "The Collapse of Iceland's Banks: The Predictable End of a Non-Viable Business Model." In *The First Global Financial Crisis of the 21st Century Part II*, edited by Andrew Felton and Carmen Reinhart. Centre for Economic Policy Research (CEPR), VoxEU online information policy portal.

Caprio, Gerard, and Daniela Klingebiel. 1996. "Bank Insolvencies: Cross Country Experience." Policy Research Working Paper 1620, World Bank, Washington, DC.

Christensson, Jon, Kenneth Spong, and Jim Wilkinson. 2010. "What Can Financial Stability Reports Tell Us About Macroprudential Supervision?" Federal Reserve Bank of Kansas City. Presentation at the Research Conference, "Government Intervention and Moral Hazard in the Financial Sector," at Norges Bank, September 2.

Claessens, Stijn, Simeon Djankov, and Daniela Klingebiel. 1999. "Financial Restructuring in East Asia: Halfway There?" Financial Sector Discussion Paper 3, World Bank, Washington, DC.

Claessens, Stijn, Daniela Klingebiel, and Luc Leaven. 2004. "Resolving Systemic Financial Crises: Policies and Institutions." Policy Research Paper 33, World Bank, Washington, DC.

De Jonghe, Olivier. 2010. "Back to the Basics in Banking? A Micro-Analysis of Banking System Stability." *Journal of Financial Intermediation* 19 (3): 387–417.

Demirgüç-Kunt, Alsi, and Enrica Detragiache. 2002. "Does Deposit Insurance Increase Banking System Stability? An Empirical Investigation." *Journal of Monetary Economics* 49 (7): 1373–406.

Demirgüç-Kunt, Alsi, and Edward J. Kane. 2002. "Deposit Insurance around the Globe: Where Does It Work?" *Perpsectives* 16 (2): 175–95.

Elliott, Douglas. 2011. "Exploring Counter-Cyclical Bank Capital Requirements." Working Paper, the Brookings Institution, Washington. DC.

Goodhart, Charles. 2010. "How Should We Regulate the Financial Sector?" In *The Future of Finance—The LSE Report*, edited by Richard Layard and Paul Woolley. London: London School of Economics and Political Science.

Gray, Dale, and Andreas A. Jobst. 2009. "Tail Dependence Measures of Systemic Risk Using Equity Options Data—Implications for Financial Stability." Working Paper, International Monetary Fund, Washington, DC.

Greenlaw, David, Anil Kashyap, Kermit Schoenholtz, and Hyun Song Shin. 2011. "Stressed Out: Macroprudential Principles for Stress Testing." Chicago Booth Research Paper No. 12-08, Fama-Miller Working Paper, Princeton University, Princeton, NJ.

Hirtle, Beverly J., Til Schuermann, and Kevin J. Stiroh. 2009. "Macroprudential Supervision of Financial Institutions: Lessons from the SCAP." Working Paper, Federal Reserve Bank of New York, New York.

Honohan, Patrick, and Daniela Klingebiel. 2000. "Controlling Fiscal Costs of Bank Crises." Working Paper 2441, World Bank, Washington, DC.

———. 2003. "The Fiscal Cost Implications of an Accommodating Approach to Banking Crises." *Journal of Banking & Sector* 27 (8): 1539–60.

Hovakimian, Armen, Edward J. Kane, and Luc Laeven. 2003. "How Country and Safety-Net Characteristics Affect Bank Risk-Shifting." *Journal of Financial Services Research* 23 (3): 177–204.

Huang, Xin, Hao Zhou, and Haibin Zhu. 2009. "A Framework for Assessing the Systemic Risk of Major Financial Institutions." *Journal of Banking & Finance* 33 (11): 2036–49.

IMF (International Monetary Fund). 2008. "Global Financial Stability Report." International Monetary Fund, Washington, DC, April.

Kane, Edward J., and Daniela Klingebiel. 2004. "Alternatives to Blanket Guarantees for Containing a Systemic Crisis." *Journal of Financial Stability* 1 (1): 31–63.

Laeven, Luc. 2002. "Pricing of Deposit Insurance." Policy Research Working Paper 2871, World Bank, Washington, DC.

Laeven, Luc, and Fabian Valencia. 2008. "Systemic Banking Crises: A New Database." Working Paper WP/08/224, International Monetary Fund, Washington, DC.

———. 2010. "Resolution of Banking Crises: The Good, the Bad, and the Ugly." Working Paper 10/146, International Monetary Fund, Washington, DC.

Lehar, Alfred. 2005. "Measuring Systemic Risk: A Risk Management Approach." *Journal of Banking and Finance* 29: 2577–603.

Mago, Akhil, Rahul Sabarwal, and Madhuri Iyer. 2008. "Residential Credit Losses—Going into Extra Innings?" U.S. Securitized Products, Lehman Brothers, New York, April 11.

Reinhart, Carmen M., and Kenneth S. Rogoff. 2009a. *This Time Is Different: Eight Centuries of Financial Folly*. Princeton, NJ: Princeton University Press.

———. 2009b. "The Aftermath of Financial Crises," *American Economic Review, American Economic Association* 99 (2): 466–72.

CHAPTER 3

Capital Flow Volatility and Systemic Risk in Emerging Markets: The Policy Toolkit

Stijn Claessens and Swati R. Ghosh*

Introduction

As the global financial crisis has shown, reaping the benefits of financial develop-ment and international financial integration without incurring large risks remains a key challenge for many countries around the world. The financial system is inherently procyclical, that is, it tends to amplify the business cycle. Faced with a positive shock, financial institutions and markets can behave in the same man-ner, fuelling asset price and credit booms, and leading to a generalized expansion of economic activity. When the cycle turns, asset prices decline, credit gets reduced, and the economy can slow down. In the extreme, disturbances can lead to financial crises with major real sector dislocations and large fiscal costs. This procyclicality and risk of financial crises importantly relates to various aspects of international financial integration, with capital flows often being quite volatile.

In advanced countries (ACs), the buildup in banking systems' vulnerabilities prior to the recent crisis took place through complex chains of credit intermedia-tion and involved large gross capital flows. Global banks (particularly European banks) were key players in this process, raising funds on U.S. wholesale markets and then lending these funds back to U.S. residents through purchases of securi-tized claims on U.S. borrowers, mostly related to residential mortgages (Shin 2012). Although net capital inflows—that is, the net of gross inflows and out-flows—were relatively small, gross exposures ended up very large.[1] The shock

* **Stijn Claessens** is an Assistant Director with the Research Department of the International Monetary Fund (IMF). **Swati R. Ghosh** is an Adviser with the Poverty Reduction and Economic Management Vice Presidency, World Bank. The authors are grateful to Roxana Mihet, Lindsay Mollineaux, and Ezgi Ozturk for excellent research assistance and to Amar Bhattacharya for extensive discussions and suggestions on an earlier version of this chapter. The views expressed here are those of the authors and should not be attributed to the IMF or the World Bank, or their respective executive directors or management.

that originated in the U.S. subprime market quickly affected many financial systems around the world. Because banks were vulnerable on their funding side to wholesale markets and developments in the U.S. dollar shadow-banking system, liquidity shortages spread quickly. These disturbances led to major real sector dislocations as the tightening of funding spurred a downward cycle of balance sheet contractions and deleveraging, declining asset prices, sharp curtailment in global trade, and declining economic activity.

In the wake of the crisis, countries are undertaking many efforts to improve their financial systems, strengthen resilience to shocks (including to those originating internationally), and reduce the natural tendency for financial systems to display procyclical behavior. The international financial architecture is also being modified to help reduce spillovers. Although not yet finished, this agenda has already shown some results (see FSB 2012 for an overview of achievements and areas of remaining needed reforms). Emerging markets (EMs), however, face even greater challenges in dealing with international financial integration and cross-border flows, for several reasons.

First, EMs tend to receive capital flows that, even in net terms, are large relative to their domestic economies and overall absorptive capacity—especially relative to the size and depth of their financial systems.[2] On average, net private capital flows relative to M2 over 2000–10, for example, have been many times larger for EMs than for ACs. Similarly, financial flows are much larger as a share of their domestic capital markets for EMs than for ACs. Second, EMs are more prone to (larger) shocks, in part because their economies are smaller and less diversified, and because they have less domestic economic and political stability. In addition, shocks of any kind—positive or negative, external or domestic in origin—are exacerbated and propagated more easily in EMs because of structural and institutional characteristics (such as weak enforcement of property rights and poor information infrastructures). In particular, large capital inflows—much of which are intermediated through banking systems—tend to interact with and amplify the domestic financial and real business cycles to a greater extent than in ACs.

Unless managed properly, international financial integration thus poses serious challenges to economic and financial sector stability in EMs. This chapter examines these challenges. It first empirically investigates the interactions of capital flow surges and stops, domestic financial cycles and financial crises in EMs with their real sector (business) cycles, and compares these to those in ACs. These findings build on earlier work (Claessens, Kose, and Terrones 2011; Claessens and Ghosh 2012) which showed that business cycles and financial cycles are much more volatile in EMs than in ACs. That work highlighted how adverse financial cycles combined with recessions, although not necessarily more frequent or longer, tend to lead to worse and deeper losses in EMs than in ACs. Conversely, recoveries combined with favorable financial cycles tend to be stronger (and faster) in EMs than in ACs. We expand on those insights by also considering cycles in capital flows and financial crises, which allow us to compare the implications of various types of financial events for the real economy and across the two groups of countries. Our data indicate that capital flow surges and sudden capital outflows are the financial events associated with the greatest amplification in business cycles in EMs.

Because the comparison of financial events in relation to the behavior of business cycles highlights the importance of capital flows in EMs, we analyze the macroeconomic challenges and buildups of domestic financial sector vulnerability during large surges of capital inflows. These vulnerabilities can generate systemic risks that manifest themselves in the face of shocks (domestic or external in origin) that can trigger capital outflows or "sudden stops" and downturns in financial and economic cycles. We then examine the broad policy toolkit available to EMs, including macro prudential measures, taking into account the characteristics of EMs. We conclude that EMs are likely to have to use a more heterodox mix of policy tools, notably including macro prudential policies, but also capital flows management (CFM) tools.[3]

The chapter is organized as follows. The first section analyzes the nature of the links between various financial cycles—domestic financial (credit) and asset prices cycles, and capital-flow movements—and crises and domestic business cycles, comparing across types of financial events and between EMs and ACs. As this analysis highlights the important role of capital flows in affecting the business cycles in emerging markets, the next section focuses on the determinants and behavior of capital flows and the role that domestic banking sectors play in intermediating such capital flows. It documents in particular the dimensions of increased macro and financial sector vulnerability associated with large surges in capital inflows. The third section discusses the broad policy toolkit available to deal with these vulnerabilities, including macroeconomic management and macro prudential and capital flow management policies. The last section concludes the chapter.

The Interplay between Domestic Financial Capital Flows and Business Cycles

This section reviews the empirical record of how financial events and business cycles interact in a large sample of countries and compares these interactions for EMs with those for ACs.

Samples and Methodology

We studied business cycles and financial events in 61 countries (23 ACs and 38 EMs) using as much as possible quarterly data. The methodology we employed to identify the business and domestic financial cycles focused on changes in the levels of variables. A recession (expansion) begins just after the economy reaches a peak (trough) and ends as the economy reaches a trough (peak).[4] Recoveries can be measured either by the time it takes to reach the level of the previous peak (duration) or by the output increase in the first four quarters (amplitude). The methodology for determining financial cycles is the same as for business cycles, that is, we identified downturns and upturns in (real) financial variables. Phases of cycles can be characterized according to their intensity (amplitude), duration, cost (cumulative loss, but only in case of recessions), and severity (slope). For business cycles we used output, whereas for domestic financial cycles we used credit, equity prices, and house prices. All variables are in real terms. The period we covered is from the first quarter of 1960 to the fourth quarter of 2011, with differences in data coverage between ACs and EMs (often only more recent data was available for EMs).

For capital flows, we used the methodology of Ghosh and others (2012), where "surges," that is, large capital inflows relative to the recipient economies, are defined as those that fall in the top 30 percent of the country-specific distribution of net capital inflows to GDP for the country *as well as* in the top 30 percent of the overall distribution of net capital inflows to GDP for the whole samples, or the subsamples of ACs or EMs.[5] Conversely, large capital outflows (as a share of GDP) are defined as capital outflows that fall in the top 30 percent outflows for the country *and* the top 30 percent overall for the whole or the two subsamples. We used annual data, given the large intrayear volatility in capital flows and data availability.

Note though that there is much overlap among these financial events, with the overlaps somewhat greater for EMs, especially as regards to capital flows. For example, of the 31 large capital outflows events for ACs, 3 are also credit crunches, whereas for EMs, of the 46 outflow episodes, 15 are also credit crunches. For ACs, the domestic financial events tend to overlap more among each other. For example, of the 35 house-price busts for ACs, 17 were also credit crunches (of which 11 were also equity busts) and an additional 7 were also equity busts. Conversely for EMs, of the 16 house-price busts, only 3 were also credit crunches (of which none were also equity busts), yet an additional 7 were also equity busts (note that this might be due to more limited house-price data for EMs).

In addition, we looked at extreme adverse financial events, that is, banking, currency, and sovereign debt crises, for which we used the definitions and data from Laeven and Valencia (2012), and "sudden stops," for which we use the data from Forbes and Warnock (2012), where the latter partly overlap with our large capital outflow events. Altogether, we considered five types of adverse financial events: credit crunches, equity and house-price busts, large capital outflows, and financial crises; and four types of favorable financial events: credit, equity prices, house-price booms, and large capital inflows.

We then considered the overlap between business cycles and the various financial events.[6] Table 3.1 shows the overlap of recessions with the five adverse financial events and of the recoveries with the four favorable events. The coincidence of adverse business phases with adverse financial events is, not surprisingly, quite large. We see that of the 292 recessions, 160, 43, 36, 107, and 52 overlap with financial crises, large capital outflows, credit crunches, equity prices, and house-prices busts, respectively. The coincidence of favorable business phases with favorable financial cycles is somewhat less. Of the 257 recoveries, 53, 23, 60, and 17 overlap with large capital inflows and credit, equity prices, and house-price booms, respectively. Note that all of these financial events are relatively extreme, since we did not consider "normal" credit expansions and contractions,

Table 3.1 Number of Recessions and Recoveries Associated with Financial Events

	World	Advanced	Emerging
Total number of recessions	292	156	136
Recessions associated with			
Financial crises	160	70	90
Net high capital outflows	43	19	22
Credit crunches	36	22	22
Equity price busts	107	61	42
House price busts	52	42	13
Total number of recoveries	257	134	116
Recoveries associated with			
Surges	53	21	36
Credit booms	23	11	15
Equity booms	60	30	32
House price booms	17	9	8

Notes: For crunches, busts, booms, surges, and outflows the events are identified separately for each country group and total of advanced and emerging is not equal to the world.

asset prices increases or decreases, or small capital inflows or outflows relative to GDP, which can be expected to accompany business cycles.

There was a relatively higher overlap between financial crises and recessions for EMs (90 out of 136 recessions were related to a financial crisis) than there was for ACs (70 out of 156). Equity price busts overlapped relatively more with recessions in ACs (61) than in EMs (42). Recoveries tended to overlap with favorable financial events, especially with capital flows surges, relatively more for EMs than for ACs (36 out for 116 for EMs compared with 21 out of 134 for ACs).[7]

The overlap among the various types of financial crises was also large (figure 3.1), and again somewhat stronger for EMs than for ACs. For example, of the 26 debt crises, 21 were also currency crises, and of these, 13 were also banking crises. Of the 203 sudden stops, 30 were also currency crises and 44 were also banking crises. As such, it is can be harder to isolate the relationships between individual financial events and business cycles.

Financial Events and Business Cycles: Empirical Evidence

We next studied the implications of various types of financial events for the real economy, that is, the behavior of output, and how these implications compared between ACs and EMs. This comparison allowed us to investigate what financial events may be most affecting the real economy in each group of countries. Table 3.2 provides an overview of the main results (for related findings on the effects of overlaps between business and financial cycles and differences between EMs and ACs, see Claessens and others (2011).

We started with reviewing the impact of the overlap of financial disruptions with a recession on the depth of the recession (table 3.2a). Not surprisingly, output declines in recessions associated with an adverse financial event are large,

Figure 3.1 Number of Financial Crises

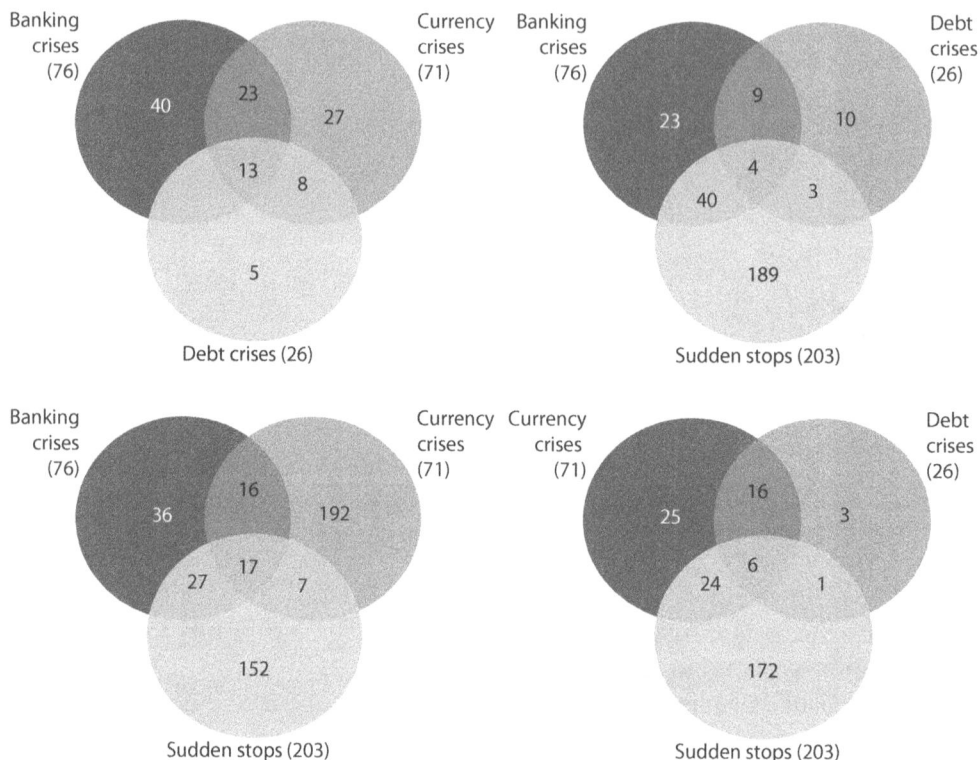

Banking crises (76)   40   23   27   Currency crises (71)

13   8

5

Debt crises (26)

Banking crises (76)   23   9   10   Debt crises (26)

4

40   3

189

Sudden stops (203)

Banking crises (76)   36   16   192   Currency crises (71)

17

27   7

152

Sudden stops (203)

Currency crises (71)   25   16   3   Debt crises (26)

6

24   1

172

Sudden stops (203)

Sources: The dates of banking, currency, and debt crises are from Laeven and Valencia (2012) and the dates of sudden stops are from Forbes and Warnock (2012).

Notes: A financial crisis starting at time T coincides with another financial crisis if the latter starts at any time between $T-3$ and $T+3$. A financial crisis starting at time T coincides with two other financial crisis if the latter two start at any time between $T-3$ and $T+3$. The sample consists of 38 emerging market and 23 advanced countries.

especially in EMs. In case of credit crunches, equity price, and house-price busts, output declined in EMs by 5.4, 7.1, and 5.5 percent, respectively, with cumulative losses of some 10, 13, and 14 percent, respectively. These outcomes were more adverse than those in ACs where recessions with such crunches or price busts tended to have drops in output of "only" 2.2–2.8 percent. The much stronger link is probably because gyrations in domestic financial markets in EMs are often associated with large swings in the direction and volume of capital flows, as noted earlier. The worst outcomes in EMs were indeed for sudden capital outflows, where output declined by some 9.5 percent, whereas large capital outflows in ACs only meant a 2.8 percent drop in output (with cumulative output losses of 19.4 percent and 5.8 percent for EMs and ACs, respectively). Declines and losses were also large in recessions associated with financial crises, with output losses of some 2.4 percent for ACs and 6.4 percent for EMs. These losses, however, were still far less than those for recessions associated with large capital outflows, especially for EMs and, overall, volatility in capital flows thus appears to be a very important "driver" of recessions in EMs.

Table 3.2 Recessions and Recoveries Associated with Financial Events

A. Recessions associated with...

	Financial crises	Capital outflows	Credit crunches	Equity price busts	House price busts
All countries					
Duration	4.16	5.02	3.78	4.16	4.46
Amplitude	−4.18	−4.88	−4.77	−4.39	−2.64
Cumulative loss	−7.58	−11.98	−9.76	−8.58	−5.86
Slope	−1.07	−1.06	−1.15	−1.14	−0.62
Advanced countries					
Duration	4.40	6.11	3.95	4.30	4.62
Amplitude	−2.43	−2.76	−2.78	−2.76	−2.18
Cumulative loss	−4.92	−5.85	−6.19	−5.23	−4.75
Slope	−0.55	−0.56	−0.88	−0.79	−0.48
Emerging market countries					
Duration	3.98	4.09	3.41	4.17	4.23
Amplitude	−6.38	−9.48	−5.43	−7.09	−5.49
Cumulative loss	−9.90	−19.39	−9.76	−13.49	−13.56
Slope	−1.80	−2.61	−1.41	−1.70	−1.77

B. Recoveries associated with...

	Capital inflows	Credit booms	Equity price booms	House price booms
All countries				
Duration	5.21	6.00	5.34	4.13
Amplitude	4.94	7.89	5.52	6.65
Slope	1.13	1.74	1.39	2.02
Advanced countries				
Duration	3.71	3.45	4.52	5.75
Amplitude	2.53	6.25	3.13	4.43
Slope	0.67	1.59	0.81	1.16
Emerging market countries				
Duration	5.08	5.54	6.14	3.00
Amplitude	6.16	8.84	7.77	8.85
Slope	1.49	2.21	2.08	2.93

Notes: Financial crises include four events: banking, debt, currency crises defined as in Laeven and Valencia (2008) and sudden stops defined as in Forbes and Warnock (2012). Outflows are the highest 30 percent of net capital outflows in the country-specific distribution, and they are in the 30th percentile of the overall distribution of net capital flows to GDP. Credit crunches are the worst 25 percent of all credit downturns calculated by the amplitude in credit. Equity price (house price) busts are the worst 25 percent of all equity price (house price) downturns calculated by the amplitude in equity prices (house prices). Inflows are the net capital flows to GDP in the top 30th percentile of the country-specific distribution, as well as in the top 30th percentile of the overall distribution of net capital flows to GDP. Credit (equity price, house price) booms are the top 25 percent of the credit (equity price, house price) upturns calculated by amplitude in credit (equity price, house price). A recession is associated with a financial crisis (outflows) if the financial crisis (outflows) starts at the same time of the recession or one year before or two years after the peak of the recession. A recession is associated with a crunch (bust) if the crunch (bust) starts at the same time of the recession or one quarter before the start of the recession. A recovery is associated with an inflow (boom) if the inflow (boom) starts at the same time of the receovery or one year before or two years after (one year before or two quarters after) the start of the recovery.

Dealing with the Challenges of Macro Financial Linkages in Emerging Markets
http://dx.doi.org/10.1596/978-1-4648-0002-3

Conversely, output increases were much greater in recoveries associated with favorable financial events, and more so in EMs than in ACs (table 3.2b). Recoveries associated with asset price booms meant an 8 to 9 percent increase in output in EMs versus 3 to 4 percent in ACs. Similarly, in recoveries associated with credit booms, output increases were 1.5 percentage points larger in EMs than in ACs: 8.8 percent versus 6.3 percent. The smaller difference between EMs and ACs with respect to the relationship between credit booms and output likely reflects, in part, the similar importance of banking systems in both groups of countries (the non-bank part of the financial system tends to be less developed in most EMs). In ACs, output increased the most in recoveries associated with credit booms while asset prices were less important for output increases, whereas in EMs all types of domestic financial booms had similarly large relationships with the size of the recoveries. Large capital inflows were not the most important "driver" of upswings in the business cycle for EMs. Nevertheless, recoveries associated with capital inflows experienced twice as large an output increase in EMs than in ACs: 6 versus 2.5 percent.

A Closer Look at Capital Inflows and Their Implications

The previous section established that in general, but especially for EMs, capital flows interact very strongly with real sector developments. It also noted that, compared with the experiences in ACs, capital flow cycles in EMs overlap to a greater degree with domestic financial cycles and financial crises. What causes these two facts? We discuss two explanations: "surges" or large capital flows to and from EMs are more volatile and often driven by global (financial) factors, rather than by domestic developments; and capital flows interact in a more intense way with the domestic financial systems and consequently real economy in EMs. For the first explanation, we review the literature on the determinants of capital flows to EMs. For the second, we discuss the mechanisms through which such financial-real interactions take place, focusing in particular on flows intermediated through the banking sector (which forms the bulk of cross-border flows), and how this can lead to both larger macroeconomic and domestic financial cycles. Finally, we review how this can lead to a buildup of vulnerability during surges of capital inflows to EMs and document dimensions of such increased observed vulnerabilities—both macroeconomic and financial—that validate the channels leading to the buildup discussed earlier.

The Nature of Private Capital Flows to ACs and EMs

The amounts of gross private capital flows to and from both ACs and EMs have increased sharply over the last decades. Flows have also been highly volatile, especially in the past few years. There are differences, however, in the behavior of net capital flows to ACs versus those to EMs. For ACs, capital flows are more about risk-sharing and the benefits of diversification, with, as noted, gross outflows generally offsetting gross inflows, generating relatively small and smoother movements in net capital flows. By contrast, for EMs, because international financial integration is as much about risk-sharing as about having access to more external financing, both gross and net capital flows have been sizable (figure 3.2).[8]

Figure 3.2 Gross and Net Capital Flows

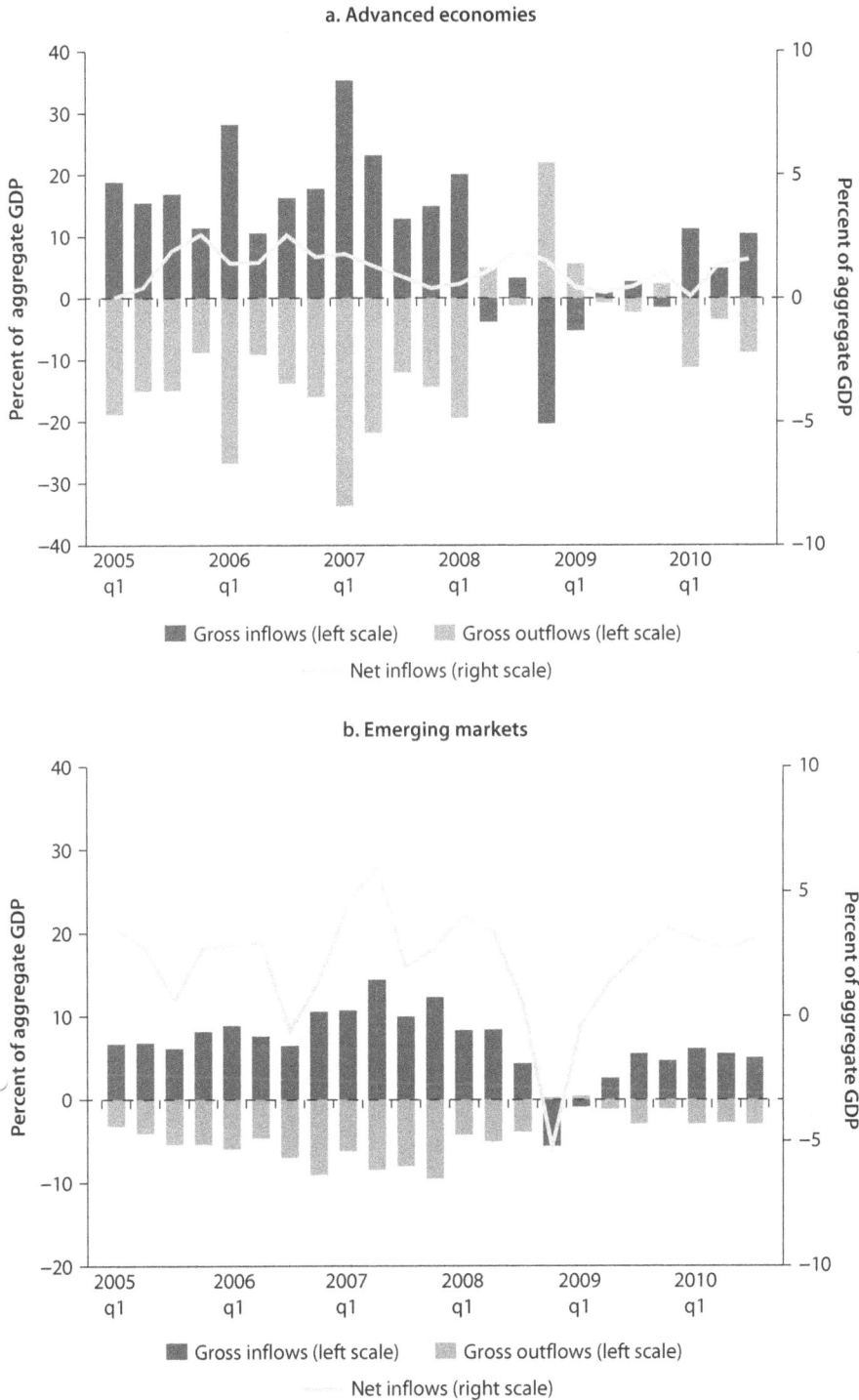

a. Advanced economies

b. Emerging markets

Source: Based on data from IMF World Economic Outlook April 2011.
Note: GDP = gross domestic product.

Moreover, these net flows have been much more volatile (figure 3.3), increasing steadily in the decade before the crisis, falling dramatically during the global financial crisis, and then rebounding sharply again, with some falling off more recently (see figure 3.2).

Figure 3.3 Volatility of Net Private Capital Inflows

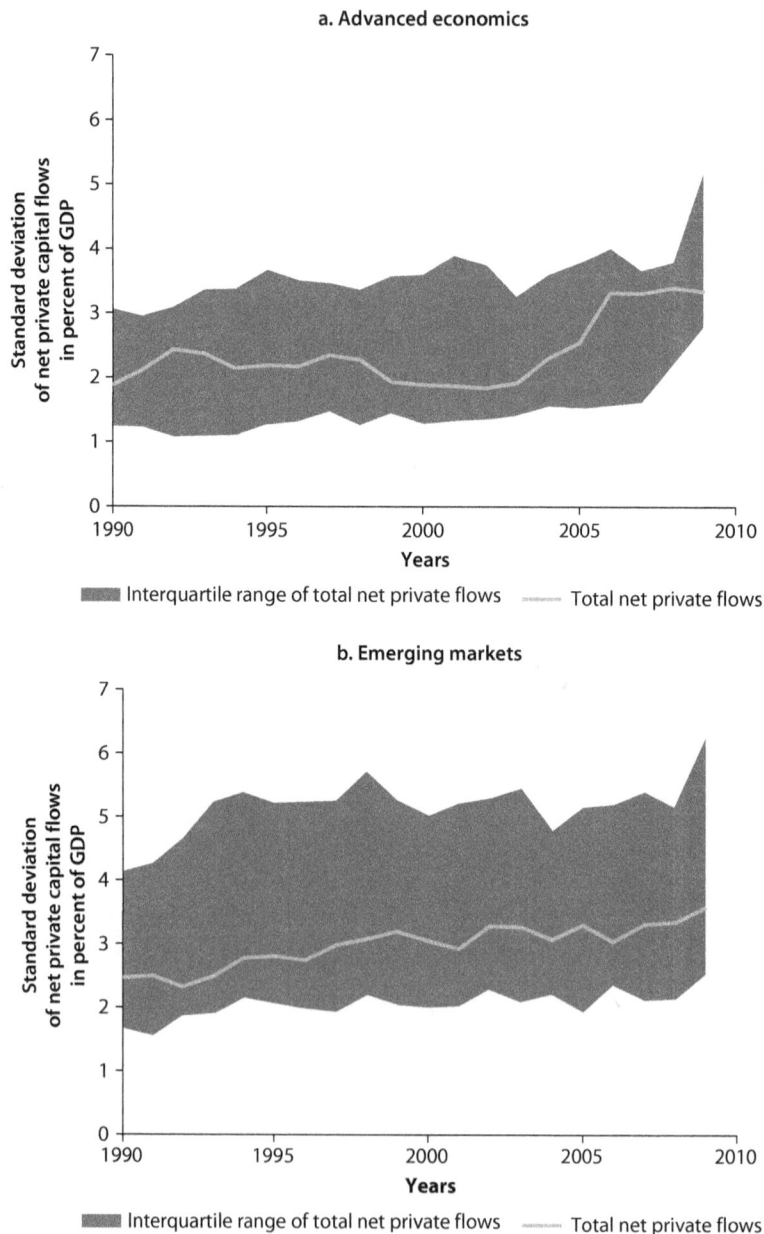

a. Advanced economics

b. Emerging markets

Source: Based on data from IMF World Economic Outlook April 2011.
Note: GDP = gross domestic product.

There are also differences in the volatility of the various types of capital flows, with bank flows especially volatile for both EMs and ACs and portfolio debt flows debt very volatile for ACs in particular (figure 3.4). FDI and portfolio equity flows tend to display less volatility for both EMs and ACs. Because the

Figure 3.4 Volatility of Different Types of Net Private Capital Inflows

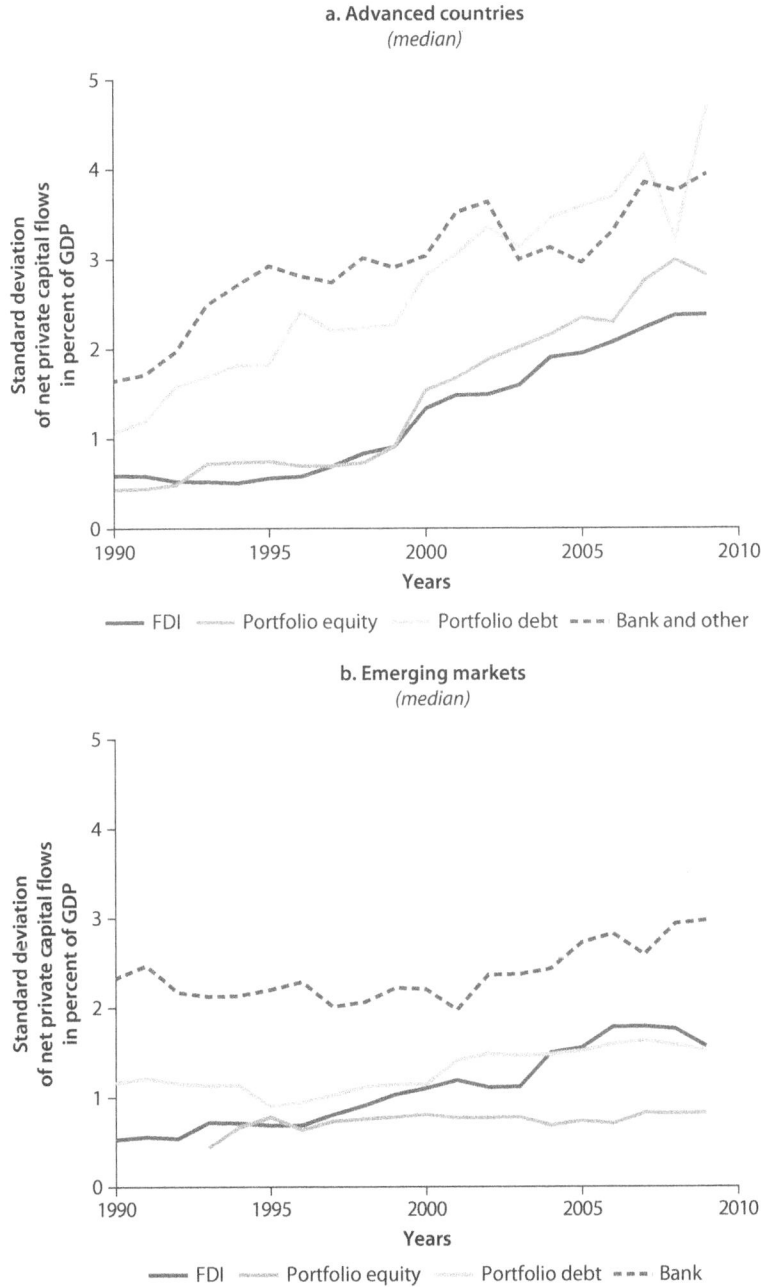

a. Advanced countries
(median)

b. Emerging markets
(median)

Source: Based on data from IMF World Economic Outlook April 2011.
Note: FDI = foreign directive investment; GDP = gross domestic product.

Dealing with the Challenges of Macro Financial Linkages in Emerging Markets
http://dx.doi.org/10.1596/978-1-4648-0002-3

volatility of individual capital flows is not higher in EMs compared with ACs, much of the higher volatility of overall net private flows to EM reflects the fact that the different types of flows have tended to be positively correlated with each other. By contrast, in the case of ACs, the various types of flows act as broad substitutes within the capital account (negatively correlated with each other) and have thus helped to dampen the volatility of total net flows (figure 3.5). The persistence (and, hence, predictability) of net capital inflows is also generally low, and is, moreover, lower in EMs than in ACs.

A large literature exists on what drives capital flows and the role of "push" (global) versus "pull" (country-specific) factors. In equilibrium, capital flows to a country must reflect both push and pull factors. Perhaps a more relevant question is the relative importance, that is, what factors determine how much of the changes in net capital inflows. Recent research (IMF 2011) using a global factor model found that a growing share of the total variation of net flows to EMs is explained by common factors. In particular, although the model underscores the dominance of economy-specific factors, it showed that the share explained by common factors increased from about 15 percent in the 1980s to about 23 percent in the 1990s and to more than 30 percent in the 2000s. This increase implies that capital flows are increasingly determined by factors outside the domestic economy.

Even more important for EMs is that recent research (Ghosh and others 2012) found that surges of capital inflows (large capital inflows) to EMs are

Figure 3.5 Correlations between Different Types of Net Flows and the Rest of the Financial Account

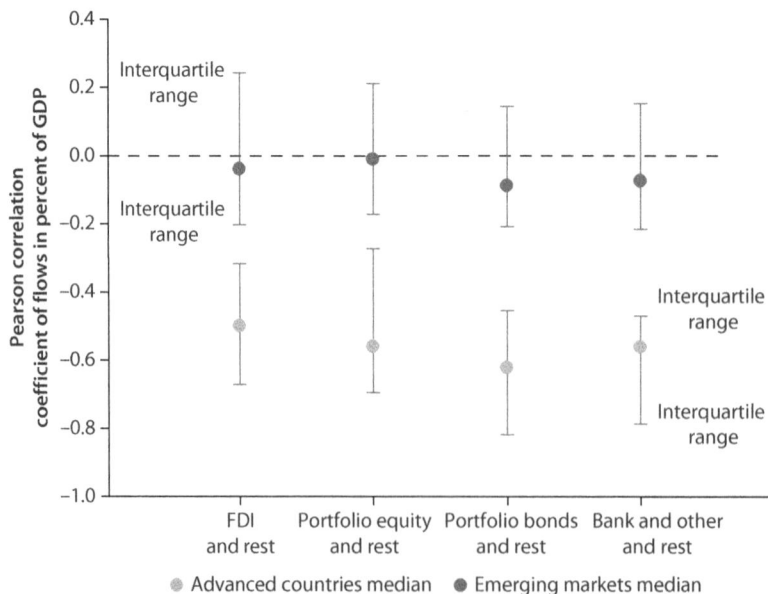

Source: Based on data from IMF World Economic Outlook April 2011.
Note: FDI = foreign directive investment; GDP = gross domestic product.

synchronized across countries, and that such surges are strongly influenced by global factors, namely global liquidity conditions and global uncertainty.[9] However, while global conditions dictate the likelihood of capital flows of significant magnitudes to EMs as a whole, individual country conditions still matter. *Conditional* on a surge occurring, whether a particular country receives a portion of a generalized surge of capital flows, depends on prevailing macroeconomic and other country circumstances. Moreover they found that the magnitude of the surge of capital to a particular country depends on country-specific factors. Economic growth, external financing needs, financial openness and interconnectedness, and institutional quality appear to be significant factors in explaining the likelihood and the magnitude of the surge. Capital inflow surges end up therefore being procyclical with respect to domestic economic conditions.[10]

Ghosh and others (2012) also found that the share of surges in net capital inflows (that is, very large inflows) to EMs increased over time, rising from 10 percent in the 1980s to 20 percent in the 1990s, and to almost 30 percent in the last decade (figure 3.6). During surges, the composition of flows also tended to be more skewed towards bank and portfolio debt, away from the more stable direct and portfolio equity investment flows (figure 3.7). This relationship is presumably because such debt flows are the most responsive to changes in global environment and relative rates of return (figure 3.8). For the same reasons, debt flows are also more volatile and exhibit the lowest persistence.

Figure 3.6 Share of Surges in Capital Inflows

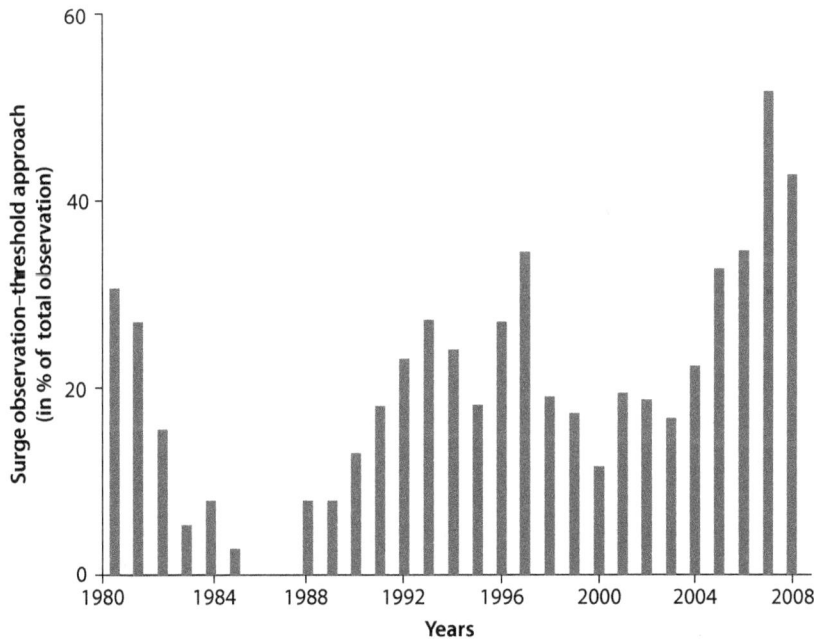

Source: Ghosh and others 2012.

Dealing with the Challenges of Macro Financial Linkages in Emerging Markets
http://dx.doi.org/10.1596/978-1-4648-0002-3

Figure 3.7 Size and Composition of Flows during Surge Periods

a. Emerging Asia

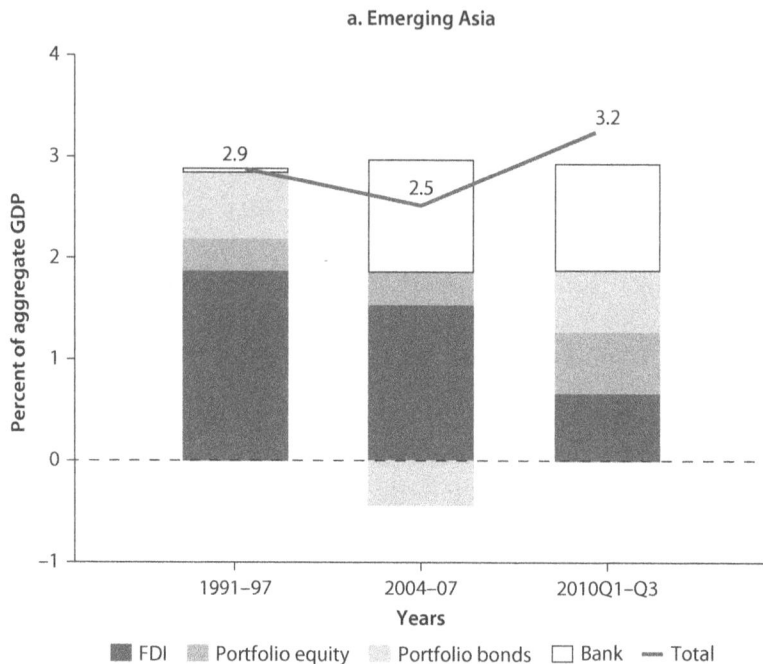

b. Emerging Latin America

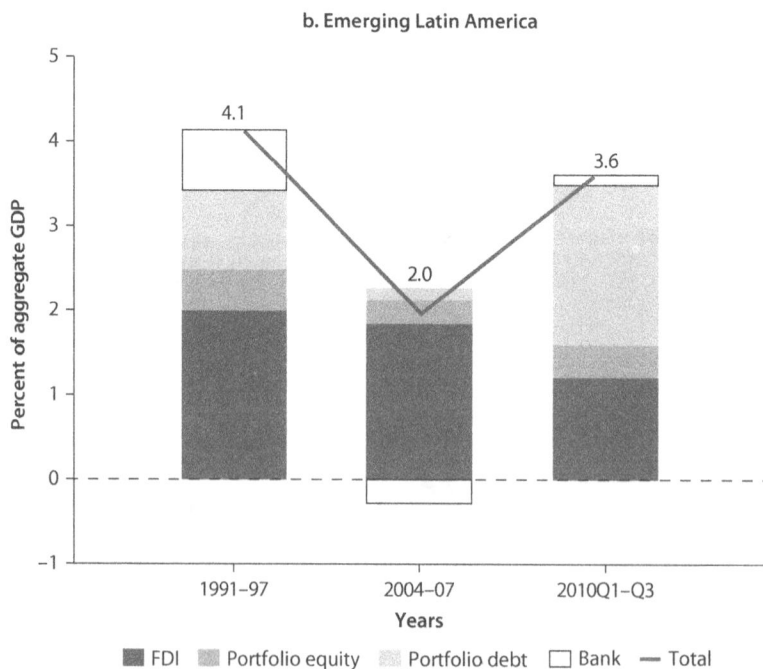

Figure continues next page

Figure 3.7 Size and Composition of Flows during Surge Periods *(continued)*

c. Emerging Europe

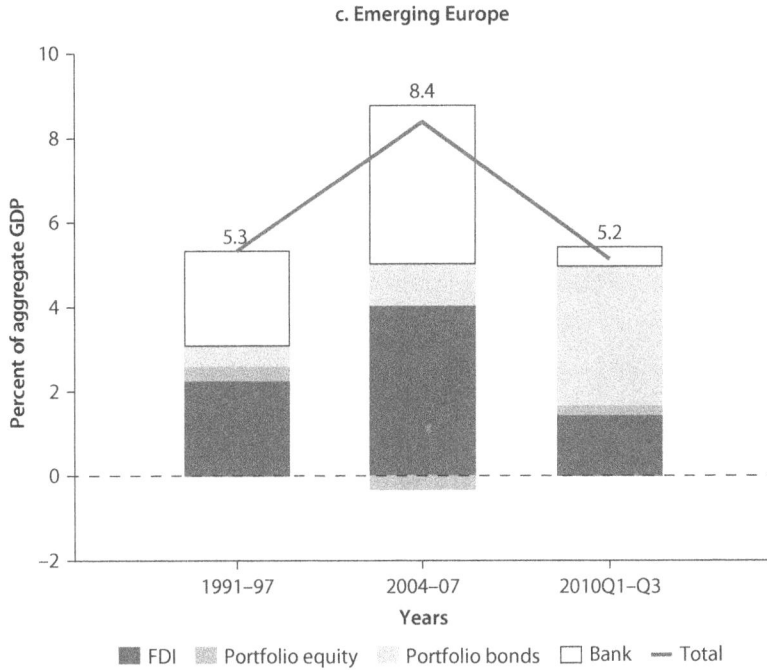

Source: Based on data from World Economic Outlook, April 2011, IMF.
Note: FDI = foreign directive investment; GDP = gross domestic product.

Figure 3.8 Responsiveness of Different Flows to Global Factors

a. Low global interest rates 1987, 1991–94, 2001–10: Q3

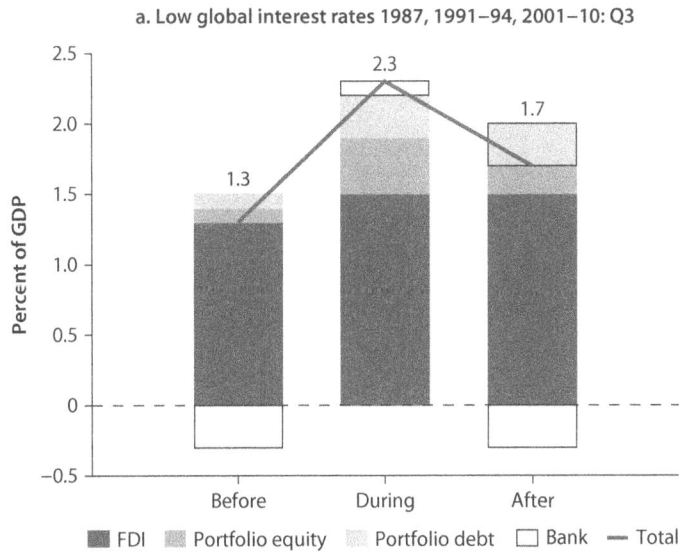

Figure continues next page

Dealing with the Challenges of Macro Financial Linkages in Emerging Markets
http://dx.doi.org/10.1596/978-1-4648-0002-3

Figure 3.8 Responsiveness of Different Flows to Global Factors *(continued)*

b. Low global risk aversion (VIX) 1989, 1991−96, 2004−07

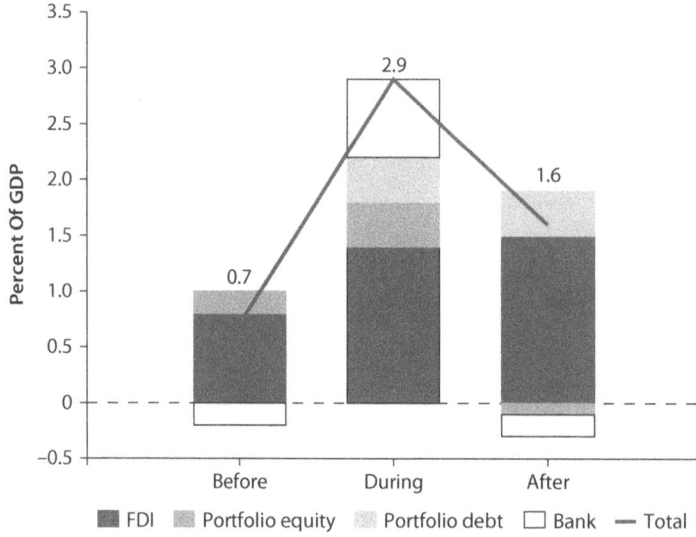

c. Low interest rates, low VIX,
high growth differential
1991-93, 1996, 2004-07

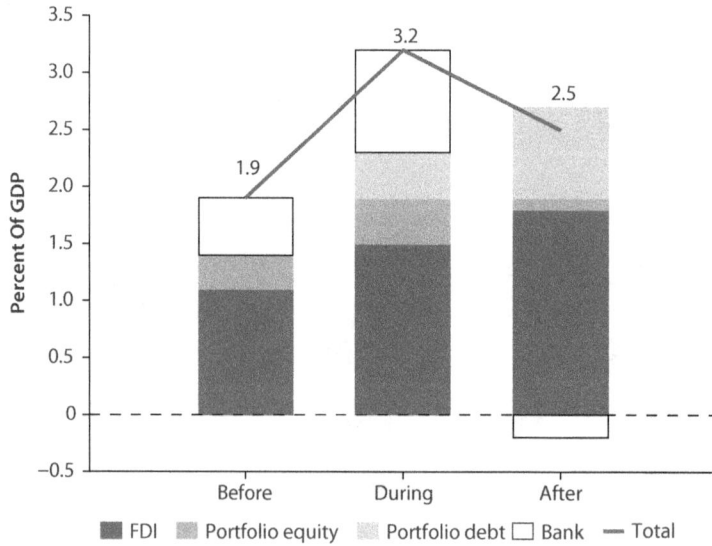

Source: Based on data from World Economic Outlook, April 2011, IMF.
Note: FDI = foreign directive investment; GDP = gross domestic product.

In summary, net capital inflows to EMs tend to be volatile, and recent years have seen several periods of sharp rises in large net capital inflows to EMs, followed by slowdowns or reversals. Large capital inflows are often initiated by global conditions, with the bulk of the flows during such periods being debt-creating flows, of which bank flows are an important component. Although EMs do not appear to experience a higher incidence of capital flow surges than ACs, the magnitude and pace of capital flow surges for EMs have tended to be larger in relative terms, especially with respect to domestic financial variables (see also Agosin and Huaita 2012).

These findings help explain why in EMs large capital inflows can generate macroeconomic challenges and can heighten systemic risks in the financial sector (particularly when intermediated through the domestic banking sector) that materialize when these capital flows slow down or reverse.

Mechanisms Underlying the Interactions between Capital Flows, Domestic Financial Cycles, and Business Cycles

What are the mechanics or channels through which the observed interactions among capital flows, and domestic business, and financial cycles arise for EMs? The starting point is that because of financial frictions, finance—be it in ACs or EMs—is inherently procyclical, that is, it tends to amplify the business cycle (see Brunnermeier and others 2009 for a review). This procyclicality can originate from the behavior of financial institutions or markets (supply side) or from changes in borrowers' balance sheets and income statements (demand side).[11] Further, because of externalities (spillovers) and other factors (some aspects of micro prudential regulation, for instance), this natural procyclicality is amplified for the sector as a whole. Thus, faced with a positive shock, financial institutions tend to behave in the same manner, expanding their balance sheets and increasing their demand for assets, which raises asset prices, fuelling a cycle and leading to a generalized expansion of credit and economic activity.

This procyclicality in domestic bank lending can interact with capital flows. When credit is expanding rapidly, outstripping the pool of locally available funds, banks will turn to international sources of funding (as mentioned earlier, the bulk of capital flows in surges is composed of bank and other lending). The ability of banks to raise funds internationally fluctuates, in turn, with global credit market conditions (see Bruno and Shin 2011; and Avdjiev, McCauley, and McGuire 2012). The presence of foreign-owned banks can further accentuate these credit cycles, given their easier access to both international financial markets and the internal capital markets of their parent banks.

As such, ample global liquidity and low investor risk aversion—and EMs' good growth prospects—can mean a surge of capital to EMs. These capital inflows can place upward pressures on the exchange rate. They provide domestic banks both the means to increase lending and the incentives to do so, because there is an expansion of demand and activity, especially in the nontradable sectors, coming from the asset price booms. In turn, as the value of banks' net worth rises and measured risks fall, their balance sheet capacity expands. Banks then increase their lending again, which further fuels the domestic financial cycle, with again (more) capital inflows. Of course, these mechanisms can also play out in reverse.

These interactions between financial and real sectors may be more driven by capital flows in EMs than in ACs for a number of reasons. First, as noted, EMs tend to receive not only relatively large capital flows, but flows that are largely intermediated through their financial systems. This intermediation alone would make capital flows tend to interact with and amplify domestic financial and real business cycles in EMs to a greater extent than in ACs. The relatively large presence of foreign-owned banks in many EMs—market shares are often more than 70 percent (Claessens and van Horen 2012)—can further accentuate this amplification. Importantly, the stronger interactions also reflect EMs' structural and institutional characteristics. A key structural characteristic is that EMs' financial sectors are still largely bank dominated, most often relying on collateral (between 72 and 85 percent of loans require collateral, higher than in ACs). This characteristic naturally creates more procyclicality when asset prices and collateral values change. Given more limited alternative sources of financing, changes in bank lending are likely to have a greater impact on the real economy.

Institutional and other weaknesses can also increase the impact of capital flows, especially in the face of negative shocks. Although EMs have made substantial progress, they still lag behind ACs in measures of overall quality of institutions, have weaker legal regimes and enforcement, and have less of a track record. Market discipline of financial institutions does not work as well in EMs, given lower information disclosure and transparency, and greater prevalence of insider-type corporate governance arrangements, including nonfinancial corporations often linked to financial institutions. These weaknesses can serve to heighten investor nervousness or even lead to a loss of investor confidence in the face of minor shocks.[12] EMs can then be subject to sudden stops and reversals of capital flows. If cumulative inflows were large and occurred through the banking system, such reversals could have very significant impacts on the domestic economy.

The Buildup of Vulnerability through Capital Inflows

The same interactions imply that large capital inflows can increase vulnerabilities at the macroeconomic level and exacerbate systemic risks in the financial sector (figure 3.9). At the macro level, large inflows in net terms are the financial counterpart to the savings and investment decisions in the country and affect the exchange rate, inflation, and current account positions. Surges of capital inflows can put upward pressures on the exchange rate (in countries with floating rates) or lead to an expansion of the money supply in countries with fixed exchange rates (unless sterilized). They can generate widening current account deficits, inflationary pressures, asset booms, and higher debt ratios. To the extent that short-term debt flows are more sensitive to interest rate differentials, the composition of capital inflows will skew toward short-term debt flows.

Figure 3.9 Capital Inflows and the Potential Buildup of Vulnerability

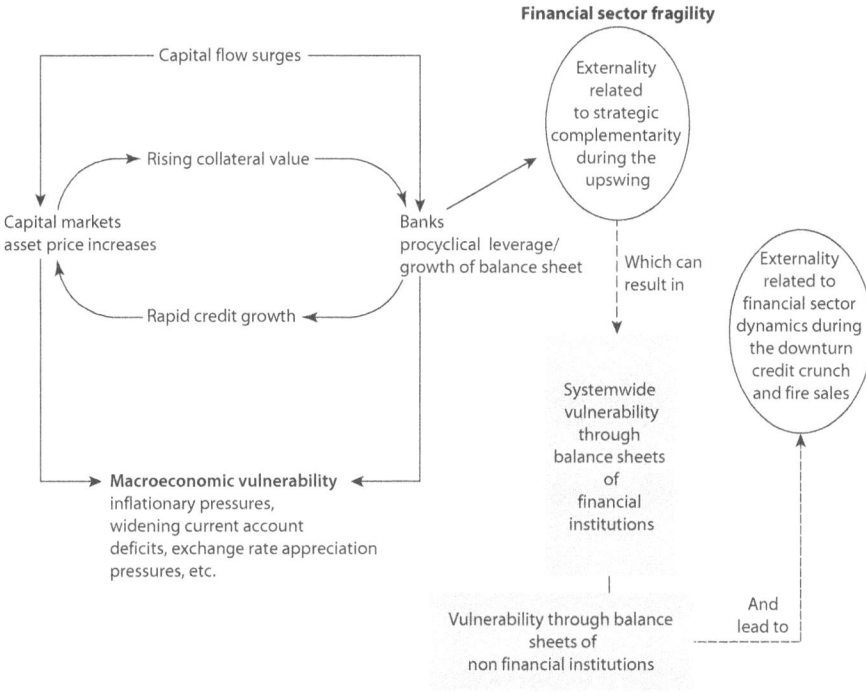

Figure 3.10 shows movements in key macroeconomic variables—current account positions, fiscal position, debt structure, output growth, real effective exchange rate, and inflation—for EMs and some developing countries that received surges in capital inflows. It compares the period before and during the surge in capital inflows and shows that there was a deterioration of the current account (or increases in current account deficits), some widening of fiscal deficits, a slowdown in growth rates, an appreciation of the real effective exchange rate, and an increase in inflation. Capital flows, thus, amplify domestic cycles and contribute to overheating pressures (manifested in inflation, exchange rate appreciation, and current account deficits), leading to macroeconomic vulnerabilities.

Capital flows—the bulk of which are typically bank flows—can lead to increased financial sector vulnerabilities as mismatches in banks' balance sheets arise, and as lending standards often deteriorate during phases of rapid credit extension. As noted by Shin (2013), retail deposits mostly grow in line with the size of the economy and wealth of the household sector. When credit grows faster than the pool of these "core" deposits, banks will turn to wholesale funding (noncore liabilities), some of it foreign funds. As banks' balance sheets increase, not only noncore-to-core-liabilities but also leverage ratios and loan-to-deposit ratios will rise. With many financial institutions likely to respond in the same manner, the cycle of increased asset prices and credit will be fuelled further, increasing the vulnerability of the financial system as a whole.

Dealing with the Challenges of Macro Financial Linkages in Emerging Markets
http://dx.doi.org/10.1596/978-1-4648-0002-3

Figure 3.10 Capital Inflow Surges and Indicators of Macroeconomic Vulnerability

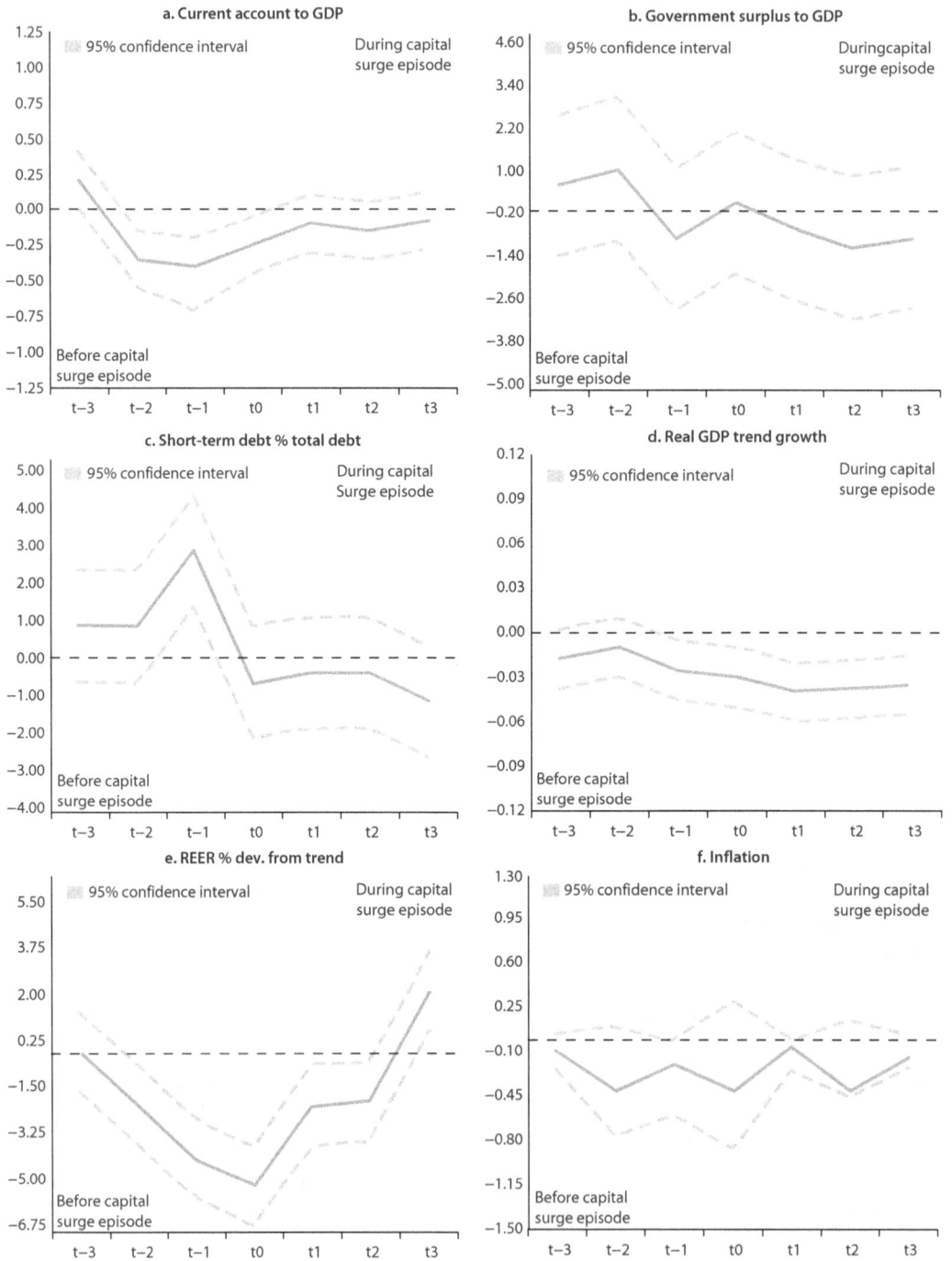

Source: Calculations using International Monetary Fund data.

Figure 3.11 shows how capital flows can pose challenges to financial stability. It shows a pronounced trend increase in banks' noncore-to-core-liabilities during surge periods. Bank loan-to-deposit growth also increases sizably and other indicators of potential financial sector vulnerability (bank asset growth, growth in banks' leverage ratios and overall credit growth) show some upward trend during the surge compared with the presurge period.

While there can be strong buildups of both macroeconomic and financial sector vulnerabilities during the upturn of domestic cycles, these vulnerabilities

Figure 3.11 Capital Inflow Surges and Indicators of Financial Sector Vulnerability

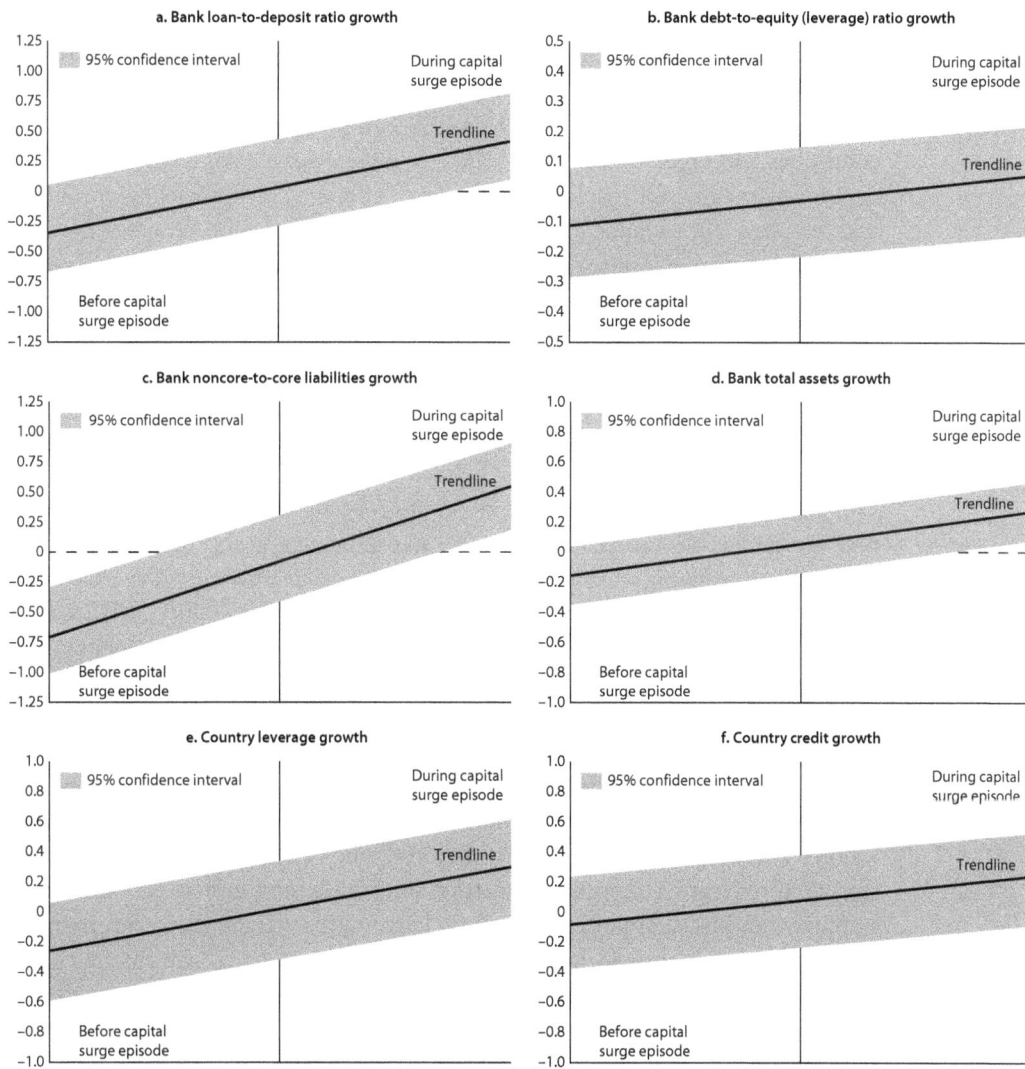

Source: Calculations using data from International Monetary Fund's Bankscope database.

manifest themselves most clearly in the face of a negative shock or during cyclical downturns. As risks have been built up, negative shocks—a domestic cyclical downturn, or a global shock, leading to capital outflows—can then easily lead to domestic economic and financial downturns.

Dealing with Capital Inflows Surges and Vulnerability Buildup

Given the trends and potential risks arising from volatile capital flows, what policy tools are available to EMs, besides diligent application of micro prudential regulations and tight supervision? A significant literature exists on the macroeconomic challenges of managing capital inflows and appropriate macroeconomic, macro prudential and capital flow management policies (see Korinek 2011 for a review of academic work and IMF 2012 for policy-related analyses). Not surprisingly, the appropriate policy options depend on the (global) causes of the capital flows and their temporary or permanent nature, and on prevailing domestic conditions and objectives. Some of these studies suggest a somewhat sequential, decision-tree-type approach, with choices depending on prevailing conditions and concerns (for instance, Ostry and others 2011). Generally, however, for most EMs receiving large inflows, it is likely that a sequential approach will not suffice and that a combination of macroeconomic, macro prudential policies and capital flow management policies is needed to avoid tradeoffs and limitations associated with each individual policy instrument (Ghosh 2010). This combination is sketched in figure 3.12.

Country differences will, therefore, be key in determining the optimal combination of policies. For example, in the face of large capital inflows, allowing the exchange rate to appreciate would be an appropriate response for countries running current account surpluses; however, an exchange rate appreciation in economies already running current account deficits would only serve to exacerbate competitiveness concerns. Frequently, as documented in figure 3.10, capital inflows lead to domestic overheating pressures. Thus for countries where competitiveness or current account deficits and domestic inflationary pressures are concerns, sterilized foreign exchange intervention might be an option. However, sterilized intervention may prove fiscally too costly and ineffective, especially if capital flows are largely driven by global liquidity and short-term interest differentials, since higher domestic interest rates would only serve to attract more inflows. Although tightening fiscal policy could be beneficial under such circumstances, it may prove difficult in practice since EMs tend to have few automatic stabilizers and fiscal policy operates with lags. Using several policy instruments as a package may then help minimize the limitations of each instrument and be more effective overall.

What about the vulnerabilities in the financial sector? The observed increase in average banking system vulnerabilities during surges of capital inflows to EMs argue for the use of macro prudential policies (MaPPs), together with supportive macroeconomic policies. The premise for the use of MaPPs rests on the existence of externalities and spillovers from the actions of individual agents/financial

Figure 3.12 Macroeconomic Policies and Macro Prudential Policies to Deal with Challenges of Capital Inflows

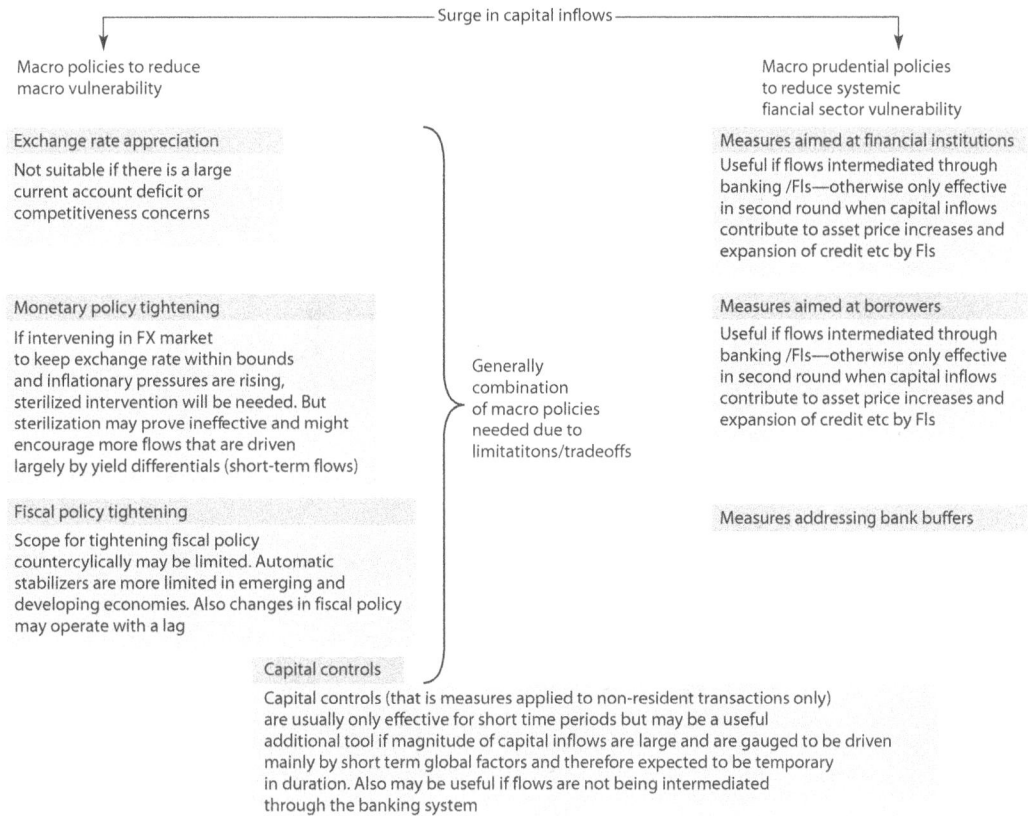

Note: FX = foreign exchange; FI = financial institution.

institutions (see De Nicolò, Favara, and Ratnovski 2012 for a review). When private and social costs and benefits of actions of individual financial institutions or agents diverge, micro prudential measures, which focus on individual financial institutions' actions and their stability, are not sufficient alone since they do not take account of the externalities that can lead to a buildup of systemic risk. Furthermore, some policies, including micro prudential regulations, although important to address other public policy objectives at the individual institution's level, can lead to behavior that creates systemic risks.

Indeed, as noted earlier, the links among capital flows, financial and real cycles appear to be even stronger in EMs than in ACs, which would *a priori* provide an even stronger argument for EMs to use MaPPs. Moreover, inasmuch as the use of certain MaPP measures are effective in reducing banks' borrowing abroad, MaPPs can also serve in helping to mitigate some of the macroeconomic pressures arising from surges in capital inflows. Not surprisingly, EMs have been using MaPPs to a greater extent than ACs have, even prior to the global crisis (figure 3.13).

Figure 3.13 Use of MaPPs in Emerging Markets versus Advanced Countries

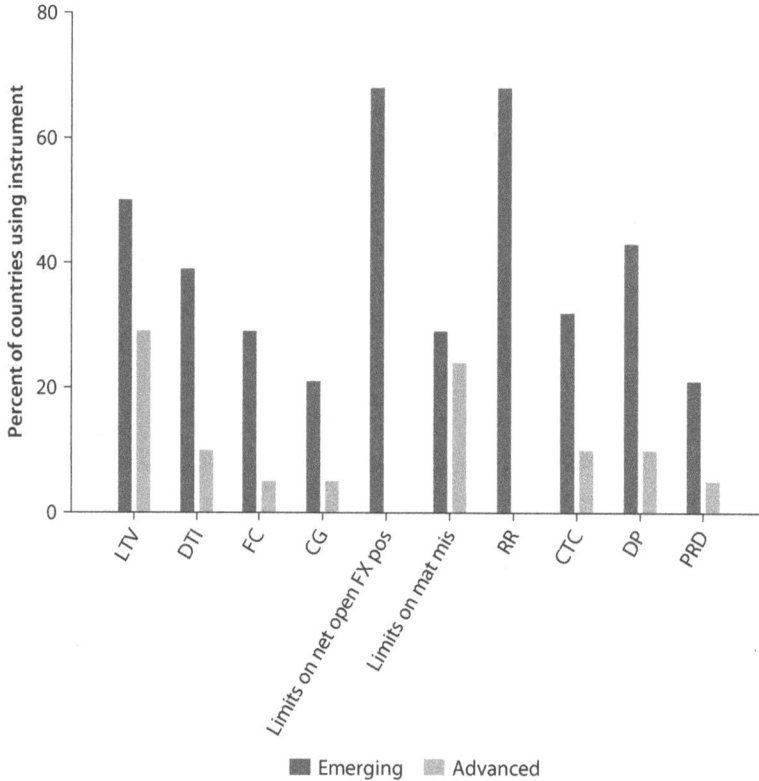

Source: International Monetary Fund internal survey of country desk economists for 48 countries, both ACs and EMs. (See Lim and others 2011, referenced in chapter 5, as well as Table 5.2 for the exact coverage and definitions of terms).

Although theory supports the use of MaPPs, the empirical evidence is still at early stages (see chapter 5). Important outstanding questions include the effectiveness of MaPPs in reducing financial sector vulnerabilities; whether some MaPPs are more suited to reducing the buildup of vulnerabilities, while others are more geared toward building up buffers; the calibration of MaPPs to circumstances and available indicators of risks to financial stability; how MaPPs need to be adapted to individual country characteristics; and the robustness of MaPPs in light of political economy constraints (see chapters 1 and 2 for views on how to adapt MaPPs to EMs and developing countries).

Conclusions

More so than ACs, EMs remain exposed in many ways to various external risks. Aggravating EMs' large exposures (particularly in regard to capital flows), large foreign bank presence, and significant degree of dollarization are their weaker institutional environments. EMs are also subject to more serious constraints on fiscal and monetary policies, and relatedly, more limited headroom than are ACs.

To manage these risks, we argue that EMs should continue to use a different and broad set of policies, including MaPP tools in addition to monetary, fiscal, and micro prudential policies.

At the same time, concerns in EMs are becoming similar to those of ACs given their rapidly changing financial sectors. Changes in financial systems raise—as they did for ACs before the global crisis—challenges of supervisory oversight, where to draw the perimeter, how to address emerging developments (such as shadow banking), and how to regulate and supervise foreign banks. Also, as banks in EMs increase in size and complexity, cross-sectional risks (for example, arising from "too big to fail" and contagion) are increasing. Importantly, domestic financial cycles in EMs are becoming more important in driving economic outcomes—indeed many are already experiencing concerns about credit booms, including real estate, and their attendant risks.

Overall, EMs are therefore likely to benefit by continuing their general pragmatic approach of supporting the use of traditional macroeconomic management tools with both MaPPs and CFM tools as needed. What constitutes the best mix of policies though, can benefit from further research, including investigations into what are the most effective and efficient MaPP approaches.

Notes

1. "Gross inflows" and "gross outflows" are also "net" items since capital flows can involve transactions by foreigners (nonresidents) and domestic agents (residents). Gross inflows refer to the *net of foreigners' purchases of domestic securities* and *domestic residents' sales* of foreign securities. Gross outflows refer to the net of *foreigners' sales of domestic securities* and *domestic residents' purchases of foreign securities*. Net inflows are the net of the two—that is gross inflows minus gross outflows. For a resident vs. nonresident and inflows vs. outflows, four-way-based classification of gross capital flows, see Forbes and Warnock (2012).

2. In the case of EMs, net capital inflows generally reflect changes in their external liabilities or gross inflows since EMs' gross outflows (or changes in their asset positions) tend to be much smaller in magnitude as their holdings of foreign assets are still relatively small.

3. Analytically, a distinction can be made between macro prudential measures, which are motivated by systemic financial risk concerns and which aim to limit the financial sector's contribution to overall risks or strengthen its ability to cope with risks, and CFM measures, which are motivated by overall macroeconomic risks and which aim to affect the rights or ability of nonresidents or residents to enter into capital account transactions. In practice, the two categories have a sizable overlap (for example, limits on banks' foreign exchange positions driven by systemic financial risk considerations can be considered both a macro prudential and a CFM tool). The overlap is not complete, however. For instance, a tax imposed on equity flows motivated by macro vulnerability concerns (such as excessive exchange rate appreciation) could be classified as a CFM tool but not as a macro prudential tool. Or a loan-to-value limit motivated by systemic considerations imposed on banks could be considered a macro prudential, but not a CFM, tool.

4. The methodology determined the peaks and troughs of any given series by first searching for maxima and minima over a given period of time. It then selected pairs

of adjacent, locally absolute maxima and minima that met certain censoring rules requiring a certain minimal duration of cycles and phases. For further details on the methodology see Claessens, Kose, and Terrones (2011),

5. We used the samples of ACs and EMs separately to determine the 30 percent cutoffs as capital flow volatility is much larger for EMs than for ACs (using a combined sample would show very few surges or stops in ACs).

6. The overlap was defined for credit, equity, and house-price cycles as financial events that start at the same time as the recessions (or recoveries) or one quarter before the start of the recessions (or recovery). Capital flows events and financial crises, which are only dated on an annual basis, are considered to overlap with the business cycle if the financial event started at the same time as the recession (or recovery) or one year before or two years after the peak (trough) of the business cycles.

7. Note that the latter is partly because of the differences in data coverage between ACs and EMs. For instance, for most EMs, data on credit developments start later than for ACs and house-price data are still not available for all EMs. At the same time, capital flows data are generally available for the whole sample period. This means that we are more likely to document large movements in capital flows than large domestic financial cycles during business cycles in EMs.

8. Indeed, inflow surges to EMs are mainly liability driven, that is, reflect nonresident purchases of domestic assets (Ghosh and others 2012).

9. Ghosh and others found that the unconditional probability of a surge is 22 percent. Against this probablility, a 100 basis-point fall in U.S. real interest rates—at mean values—increases the probability of a surge by 3 percentage points; and a 1 standard deviation reduction in volatility of S&P500 index by 3 percentage points.

10. Ghosh and others suggest, therefore, that global factors act largely as "gatekeepers"— capital surges toward EMs only when conditions are ripe, but once a hurdle is passed, the volume of capital flows is largely independent of the conditions.

11. The latter amplification mechanisms are collectively known as "the financial accelerator." These models show how small shocks, real or financial, can be propagated and amplified across the real economy as they lead to changes in access to finance for corporations and households. Here the financial system is less a cause of, but more accommodates, procyclicality. Obviously, there are many interactions between the demand and supply sides causes. See Brunnermeier, Eisenbach, and Sannikov 2012, for a review of analytical models of both demand and supply side factors.

12. Moreover, capital outflows from an EM can sometimes originate in response to developments unrelated to that particular EM. This could arise from "pure" contagion whereby adverse developments/shocks in one EM cause investors to withdraw from other EMs even though the economic fundamentals may be dissimilar because of more fragile investor confidence. Or in some cases it can occur for more structural reasons. For instance, as foreign bank presence is greater in EMs than in ACs, more than double, shocks to foreign banks' operations (including those originating from headquarters) can have significant impacts on EMs' domestic financial and real sectors.

References

Agosin, Manuel R., and Franklin Huaita. 2012. "Overreaction in Capital Flows to Emerging Markets: Booms and Sudden Sops." *Journal of International Money and Finance* 31 (5): 1140–55.

Avdjiev, Stefan, Robert N. McCauley, and Patrick McGuire. 2012. "Rapid Credit Growth and International Credit: Challenges for Asia." Working Paper 377, Bank for International Settlements, Basel, Switzerland, April.

Brunnermeier, Markus K., Thomas Eisenbach, and Yuliy Sannikov. 2012. "Macroeconomics with Financial Frictions: A Survey." NBER Working Paper No. 18102, National Bureau of Economic Research, Cambridge, MA.

Brunnermeier, Markus K., Charles Goodhart, Andrew Crocket, Avinash Persaud, and Hyun Shin. 2009. "The Fundamental Principles of Financial Regulation." 11th Geneva Report on the World Economy, International Center for Monetary and Banking Studies, Geneva

Bruno, Valentina, and Hyun Song Shin. 2013. "Capital Flows, Cross-Border Banking and Global Liquidity." NBER Working Paper No. 19038, National Bureau of Economic Research, Cambridge, MA.

Claessens, Stijn, and Swati R. Ghosh. 2012. "Financial Regulations on International Capital Flows and Exchange Rates." EWC/KDI Conference on Financial Regulations on International Capital Flows and Exchange Rates. The East-West Center and the Korea Development Institute, Honolulu, Hawaii.

Claessens, Stijn, M. Ayhan Kose, and Marco E. Terrones. 2011. "How Do Business and Financial Cycles Interact?" Working Paper 11/88, International Monetary Fund, Washington, DC. http://www.imf.org/external/pubs/ft/wp/2011/wp1188.pdf (shorter version published in *Journal of International Economics* 87 (1): 178–90.

Claessens, Stijn and Neeltje van Horen. 2012. "Foreign Banks: Trends and Impact." IMF Working Paper No. 12/10, International Monetary Fund, Washington, DC.

De Nicolò, Gianni, Giovanni Favara, and Lev Ratnovski. 2012. "Externalities and Macroprudential Policy." Staff Discussion Notes12/05, International Monetary Fund, Washington, DC.

FSB (Financial Stability Board). 2012. "Financial Stability Board Reports to G20 on Progress of Financial Regulatory Reforms." Financial Stability Board, Press Release, November 5. http://www.financialstabilityboard.org/press/pr_121105.pdf.

Forbes, Kristin, and Frank Warnock. 2012. "Capital Flow Waves: Surges, Stops, Flight and Retrenchment." *Journal of International Economics* 88 (2): 235–51.

Ghosh, Swati R. 2010. "Dealing with the Challenges of Capital Inflows in the Context of MacroFinancial Links." Economic Premise Note 19, World Bank, Washington, DC.

Ghosh, Atish R., Jun Kim, Mahvash S. Qureshi, and Juan Zalduendo. 2012. "Surges." Working Paper 12/22, International Monetary Fund, Washington, DC.

IMF (International Monetary Fund). 2011. "World Economic Outlook—Tensions from the Two-Speed Recovery: Unemployment, Commodities, and Capital Flows." International Monetary Fund, April. http://www.imf.org/external/pubs/ft/weo/2011/01/.

———. 2012. *The Liberalization and Management of Capital Flows—An Institutional View.* Washington, DC: International Monetary Fund.

Korinek, Anton. 2011. "The New Economics of Prudential Capital Controls: A Research Agenda." *IMF Economic Review* 59 (November 7): 523–61.

Laeven, Luc, and Fabian Valencia. 2008. "Systemic Banking Crises: A NewDatabase." Working Paper WP/08/224, International Monetary Fund, Washington, DC.

———. 2012. "Systemic Banking Crises Database: An Update." Working Paper 12/163, International Monetary Fund, Washington, DC.

Lim, C. H., F. Columba, A. Costa, P. Kongsamut, A. Otani, M. Saiyid, T. Wezel, and X. Wu. 2011. "Macroprudential Policy: What Instruments and How to Use Them? Lessons from Country Experiences." Working Paper 11/238, International Monetary Fund, Washington, DC.

Ostry, Jonathan David, Atish R. Ghosh, Karl Friedrich Habermeier, Luc Laeven, Marcos Chamon, Mahvash Saeed Qureshi, and Annamaria Kokenyne. 2011. "Managing Capital Inflows: What Tools to Use?" Staff Discussion Note 11/06, International Monetary Fund, Washington, DC.

Shin, Hyun Song. 2012. "Global Banking Glut and Loan Risk Premium. 2011 Mundell-Fleming Lecture, *IMF Economic Review* 60 (July): 155–92.

———. 2013. "Adapting Macro Prudential Approaches to Emerging and Developing Economies." In *Dealing with the Challenges of Macro Financial Linkages in Emerging Markets*, edited by Otaviano Canuto and Swati R. Ghosh. Washington, DC: World Bank.

CHAPTER 4

Monetary Policy and Macro Prudential Regulation: Whither Emerging Markets

Otaviano Canuto and Matheus Cavallari*

Introduction

Until the onset of the global financial crisis, there was convergence in thinking toward a set of blueprints for monetary and exchange-rate regimes. An increasing number of central banks, both in advanced and emerging markets, had adopted a combination of inflation-targeting regimes and exchange-rate flexibility. Alternatively, small, integrated economies had the option of virtually abdicating the exercise of monetary policy by fixing their exchange rates. Confidence was rising in the effectiveness of this approach to deliver macroeconomic stability, and implicitly, to achieve smooth international monetary cooperation, provided that there was no major fiscal imbalance in national economies.

The close relationship between inflation targeting and macroeconomic stability led to the belief that financial stability should be solely pursued by micro prudential regulatory and supervisory measures. Monetary policy would take care of inflation by acting upon expectations of future interest rates and, thus, the yield curve and long-term interest rates that affect aggregate demand. Flexible exchange rates would ensure smoother balance-of-payments adjustments. Micro prudential regulation of bank capital and banking supervision would, in turn, prevent excessive risk-taking.

Confidence in such a combination of an inflation-targeting-cum-flexible-exchange-rates regime and independent financial regulation and supervision has been shattered by the scale and synchronization of asset price booms and busts that led to the current global financial crisis. It is now increasingly accepted that,

***Otaviano Canuto** is the Senior Advisor on BRICS Economies in the Development Economics Department at the World Bank. He previously served as the Bank's Vice President and Head of the Poverty Reduction (PREM) Network at the World Bank. **Matheus Cavallari** is a consultant for the PREM Network. The authors would like to thank, without implicating them in any way, Alain Ize, Augusto de la Torre, Bernard Hoekman, Jeff Chelsky, Luis Serven, and Pierre-Richard Agénor for helpful comments on a preliminary draft. The views herein are entirely those of the authors and should not be attributed to the World Bank, its Executive Board of Directors, or any of the governments they represent.

to some extent, the interdependence between macroeconomic and financial stability calls for coordination between monetary policy and macro prudential regulation. Additionally, the magnitude of cross-border spillovers of asset price booms and busts, as well as corresponding country policy responses in the case of large countries, have undermined the belief in the sufficiency of flexible exchange rates as a shock absorber.

The purpose of this chapter is twofold. First, we take stock of where monetary and exchange-rate policies are heading as a consequence of recent practical experiences, and revisit theoretical monetary policy tenets. After outlining the received wisdom, we address the implications of monetary policy's neglect of asset price booms and busts. We then approach the challenges faced by any attempt to consider asset price booms and busts and spillovers from abroad, as well as to integrate macro prudential policy into monetary policy.

The second purpose is to point out some of the challenges faced particularly by monetary authorities in emerging markets under the new monetary policy paradigm (see "New Challenges Faced by Central Banking in Emerging Markets," the fourth section). On a perennial basis, like their counterparts in advanced economies, they face the challenges of adjusting their blueprints for decision making after the revealed insufficiencies of the received wisdom. Besides analytical and empirical knowledge gaps, the issues of time consistency, central bank independence, and international policy coordination are becoming more complex. Furthermore, over a (hopefully) more temporary horizon, emerging market monetary authorities are having to deal with an additional set of challenges, given that the current scenario of debt overhang and unconventional monetary policies in advanced economies is likely to last, and a global low-growth environment tends to exacerbate economic losses derived from exchange-rate misalignments.

Flexible Inflation Targeting and Micro Prudential Regulation: What Was Missing?

This section looks at some of the elements that were missing or underappreciated in the policy framework that prevailed prior to the crisis in the areas of prudential regulation, asset price booms and busts, cross-border spillovers from these booms and busts, and the policy responses of large countries.

Flexible Inflation Targeting Regimes and Isolated Prudential Regulation

Before the global financial crisis, a set of core principles for monetary policy had reached a high degree of acceptance. As a consequence, an increasing number of countries—both advanced countries and emerging markets—had converged toward a combination of inflation-targeting regimes and floating exchange rates.[1] In that context, provided that monetary and macroeconomic stability could be taken for granted, responsibility for the stability of the financial system belonged to another policy realm, namely that of micro prudential tools, concerned with ensuring the soundness of individual institutions and the protection of depositors (Canuto 2011a).

Mishkin (2011) proposed a set of monetary policy principles around which a degree of consensus had emerged before the crisis. First, the classic "inflation is always and everywhere a monetary phenomenon" principle gave the central bank the responsibility to manage the inflation rate. This principle did not mean that all economists agreed that money growth determines the pace of price evolution. As both supply and demand sides of the money market are prone to continuous change, managing monetary aggregates had come to be seen as inefficient, contrary to what early monetarists once argued (Friedman and Meiselman 1963; Friedman and Schwartz 1963). The short-term interest rate appeared as the main instrument to be wielded, at least in normal situations, while other instruments were available to deal with stress situations. However, the majority of economists believed that the source of sustained inflation is an overexpansionary monetary phenomenon.

Second, stable inflation at low levels should be pursued. Substantial costs of high inflation could be identified as distortions in resource allocation, regressive redistribution of wealth, taxes on cash holdings, and nominal illusion, among others.[2]

Third, there should be no long-term trade-off between unemployment and inflation. The augmented Phillips curve (Friedman 1968; Phelps 1968) was to be part of the toolkit of almost every central banker, as monetary policy could be used to shift the level of inflation in the short run, but with no free lunch in the long run as people will adapt their expectations. In this sense, only inflation surprises could have an impact on the real economy. In other words, the money illusion could be generated only temporarily.[3]

Fourth, the role of expectations is fundamental in macroeconomics. The rational expectations revolution had won the case in favor of the importance of market expectations regarding policy measures, as people would react and incorporate their systematic component. In this sense, managing expectations about future policies becomes a central component of monetary policy making (Svensson 2005; Woodford 2003). In other words, "the radical element is the implication that central bank secrecy ought to be replaced by central bank transparency" (Wyplosz 2009, 9).

Fifth, central bankers would need to increase (reduce) nominal interest rates by more than the rise (decline) in inflation to keep inflation under control. Intuitively, ex ante real interest rates must increase (lower) after a positive (negative) inflationary shock to bring down (up) inflation to its target, as the output gap widens (becomes negative). This corollary is known as the Taylor Principle (Taylor 1993; Woodford 2003). In a world with more than one policy instrument, the full set needs to be considered. Intuitively, the net impact of the manipulation of all monetary tools on the economy after an inflationary (deflationary) shock should be contractionary (expansionary).

Sixth, the time-inconsistency problem is highly relevant, as agents would recognize if policy makers tried to exploit the short-run Phillips curve to obtain short-run political goals.[4] Private agents learn about the inconsistency of policy makers and adapt their decisions. This notion "has led to a number of important insights regarding central bank behavior—such as the importance of reputation (formalized in the concept of reputational equilibria) and institutional design" (Mishkin 2011, 8).

Seventh, since people recognize inconsistent policy makers and adapt their expectations, a central bank should have a credible commitment to its targets. A nominal anchor, determined by the government, would help coordinate those expectations, making it harder to bend to a temptation of adopting time-inconsistent behavior. Additionally, an independent monetary authority would help make this process more credible, and avoid possible political interventions (Mishkin and Westelius 2008). To improve efficiency, clear and consistent objectives with respect to monetary policy transparency are desirable.

By following this list of principles, the consensus view was that economies could achieve the best macroeconomic outcome possible. Controlled monetary expansion, low inflation to keep output in line with its potential, no temptation to overexploit the short-run trade-off between inflation and employment, and anchored inflation expectations managed without inconsistency by an independent central bank were necessary and sufficient conditions to sustain macroeconomic stability. Even in the presence of asset bubbles, the best option would be to intervene to address the subsequent impact on the output gap and inflation.

Accordingly, the move toward a policy framework of flexible inflation targeting, if widely adopted, would ensure macroeconomic stability at both national and international levels. Large nominal exchange-rate adjustments and overshooting should become a rarer phenomenon. By fostering exchange-rate variability, the adjustment of international positions would become faster and smoother, with demand shocks dealt with through interest- and exchange-rate changes. Global demand would remain at appropriate levels as a corollary to widespread and successful application of such a monetary regime. On top of that, the necessity for costly self-insurance in the form of international foreign-exchange reserves could be minimized, as intervention on exchange rates would be necessary only for short-lived market disruptions.

Prior to the global financial crisis, financial stability was also taken as assured by individual financial institutions adopting sound micro prudential rules, maintaining adequate levels of capital commensurate with the risks they faced. Competition in financial markets under an appropriate set of micro prudential rules would ensure financial stability. Low and stable inflation achieved through flexible inflation targeting would reduce the inflation-risk premium and financial regulation and supervision could be provided as an independent function. The "Great Moderation" in developed economies, with relatively low inflation rates and small output fluctuations from the mid-1980s onward, seemed to vindicate that confidence (Canuto 2011a).

As we now know, this world of presumed stable monetary and financial conditions was severely shaken by the global financial crisis. Asset price booms and busts were acknowledged as both pervasive and harmful: real estate and stock-market bubbles contributed to excess U.S. household debt and to fragile asset-liability structures; the interconnectedness of financial firms' balance sheets became too deep; and the danger of too-big-to-fail institutions dramatically rose. The rapid global transmission of an asset price bust pushed the world economy to the edge of quasi collapse in 2008.

Many economists hold the view that nothing substantial was missing from the framework just outlined. The global financial crisis could be attributed to deviations from the blueprint, either on the monetary policy or financial supervision and regulation sides. For some, like Taylor (2009), it was lax monetary policy that led to the creation of asset bubbles and then to financial instability and its impact on growth and macroeconomic stability. For others, like Svensson (2010), the financial crisis was caused by factors other than monetary policy; monetary policy and financial stability policy are distinct and it was the latter that failed. Financial stability policy failed due to distorted incentives for excessive leverage, lack of due diligence, lax regulation and supervision, rapid growth of securitization, myopic and asymmetric remuneration contracts, idiosyncratic features of the U.S. housing policy (such as government-sponsored enterprises), information problems, hidden risks in complex securities, and underestimation of correlated systemic risks. These causes should not be associated with any shortcomings of monetary policy.

Conversely, many economists pointed out missing dimensions in the analytical underpinnings of the received wisdom on both monetary and prudential policies. Asset price booms and busts, in particular, seemed to be too pervasive and too severe to be dismissed as an anomaly. As well put by Frankel (2009), it became harder to sustain the orthodox view according to which "central banks should essentially pay no attention to asset prices, the exchange rate, or export prices, except to the extent that they are harbingers of inflation."

Asset Price Booms and Busts as a Missing Dimension

The blueprint of basic principles for a monetary policy framework, outlined earlier, did not give due attention to how financial markets and their channels of interconnectivity are relevant for macroeconomic stability. It had been long held that asymmetric information and market failures played a significant role in financial systems and in business cycles. Nonetheless, the mainstream view remained that markets and private institutions could self-adjust in an efficient way and manage their own market and liquidity risks properly. Microregulation and supervision of individual entities would sufficiently discipline the behavior of private agents.

Even when the frequent appearance of bubbles started to be acknowledged, the belief was that attempts to detect and prick them at an early stage would be impossible to accomplish and potentially harmful. If necessary, resorting to interest rate cuts to safeguard the economy after bubble bursts would be the optimum procedure, conditional on subsequent impact on inflation and output gap (Bernanke and Gertler 2000).

In fact, the issue was the object of an intensive debate for sometime before the crisis—the so-called "lean versus clean" debate (Mishkin 2009). Although many argued in favor of monetary policy "leaning against the wind" from financial developments, the prevalent opinion was that difficulties in detecting bubbles would outweigh the advantages of doing so. Furthermore, monetary policy tools would be too a blunt way to curb the rise of bubbles, as correspondingly sharp interest rate hikes would have harmful unintended consequences on output growth and volatility. The best approach would then be to have monetary policy react only if and when "mopping up" or "cleaning up" the financial mess after bubble bursts was necessary.

As the evidence on the significant presence of real estate and stock-market asset price busts over the past 40 years became clear—see, for example, IMF (2009)—the pendulum swung toward arguments in favor of some "leaning against the wind." The experience with widespread busting of both house and stock price bubbles beginning in 2007 is indeed singular in the past 40 years (figure 4.1). However, one can observe not only the frequency of previous episodes, but also that those "asset price busts are relatively evenly distributed before and after 1985—a year that broadly marks the beginning of the Great Moderation" (IMF 2009, 95).

As Borio and Shim (2007, 7) have stated: "The establishment of credible anti-inflation regimes and the globalization of the real side of the economy may have been to make it more likely that, occasionally, financial imbalances build up against the background of low and stable inflation. These imbalances can have potentially serious implications for the macroeconomy and financial stability to the extent that they unwind in a disruptive way. By financial imbalances we mean overextensions in private sector balance sheets, characterized by joint credit and asset price booms that 'go too far,' sowing the seeds of the subsequent bust. In other words, changes in the economic environment may have increased the 'elasticity' of the economy or, put differently, its potential *procyclicality*." It has now become clear that if monetary policy makers and prudential regulators are to succeed in their stabilization missions, complacency with respect to asset price cycles will have to be left behind.

The pervasiveness and magnitude of asset price booms and busts led to the acknowledgment of a distinction between *micro financial risks*, which arise due to specific problems in individual financial institutions, and *macro financial risks*,

Figure 4.1 Asset Price Busts

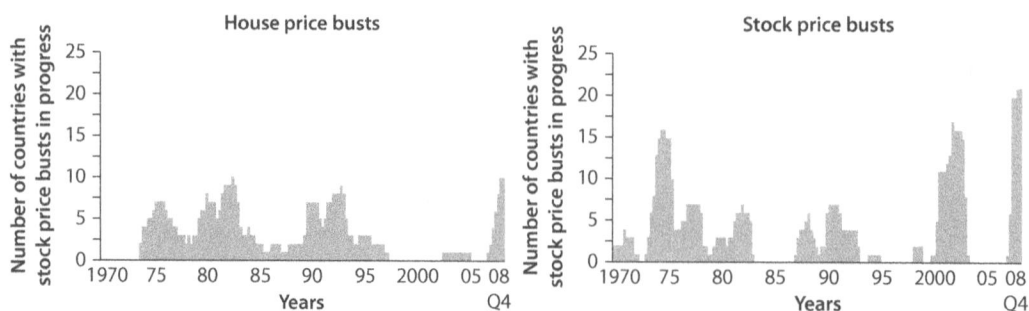

Source: World Economic Outlook, 2009, 96.

which affect the financial system as a whole because of the interconnectedness of the institutions within the system. The conceptual innovation from the past five years is that micro prudential tools—concerned with ensuring the soundness of individual institutions and the protection of depositors—are not sufficient for financial stability and the avoidance of financial crises. Sound risk management of individual financial institutions is not enough to guarantee sound management of systemwide risk.

Despite well-designed micro prudential rules, there might be spillovers and externalities across institutions that affect the financial system as a whole (for example, bank panics, fire sale of assets, and credit crunches). Either because of interlinkages among balance sheets of financial institutions or because of contagion in terms of confidence, risks taken by a single financial institution can affect the entire financial system.

For example, a financial system composed of large, interconnected firms is likely to produce moral hazard in the face of the (now) standard too-big-to-fail dilemma for policy makers. Even if all firms are soundly regulated, the possibility of one failure in this interconnected system creates contagion and negative externalities to the whole system. But this can also happen in a system composed of small, perfectly regulated firms without direct links among financial firms' balance sheets. It suffices that all firms use the same identical risk-assessment model, one not considering a specific tail event. If this event materializes, the whole system could be at risk, regardless of its apparent robustness and lack of connectedness.[5]

Asset price booms and busts may well establish a feedback loop with procyclical risk assessments present in traditional micro prudential rules. Suppose, for example, that there is an increase in house prices due to a demand shock. The rise in the value of real estate used as collateral raises the probability of repayment for housing loans and lowers the risk premium. Additionally, if financial institutions follow their own assessment of risks when estimating appropriate ratios between capital and risk-weighted assets to be held, capital costs associated with such credits decline. Reduced borrowing costs then stimulate borrowing for other purposes, potentially leading to further increases in real estate prices. If bubbles develop, the whole network of larger interlinked balance sheets may look sound, despite its dependence on overvalued collateral.

By the same token, the importance of financial intermediation and market segmentation to monetary policy decisions was underestimated before the financial crisis (Blanchard, Dell'Ariccia, and Mauro 2010). Most of the time, the connection among specialized investors is done by arbitrage (for example, securities lending, repo markets and commercial mortgage back securities). However, this link among markets can stop working during moments of acute lack of confidence or information. As a consequence, the transmission of monetary policy through short-term interest rates to other credit assets may become obstructed. In extreme situations, the central bank has to step in, despite moral hazard risks, to avoid downward spirals of destruction of liquidity.

Dealing with the Challenges of Macro Financial Linkages in Emerging Markets
http://dx.doi.org/10.1596/978-1-4648-0002-3

Wholesale funding, which is often outside the perimeter of conventional micro prudential regulation, can carry similar risks to deposits, and can pose systemic risks beyond the banking sector. It represented 40 percent of total liabilities of the Euro area banking system and 25 percent in the United States, the United Kingdom, and Japan as of mid-2010 (GSFR 2010). The literature on bank runs can illustrate the importance of aggregate liquidity risk management and how high the costs of countervailing such runs can end up in taxpayers' pockets (Goodhart and Perotti 2012).

The so-called shadow-banking system had an important role in the creation of liquidity during the "Great Leveraging," absorbing assets in the process of maturity and liquidity transformation and search for leverage and higher yields. Some benefits from nonbank financial intermediation include (1) increasing efficiency, innovation, and specialization; (2) enabling investors to diversify and mitigate risks; (3) providing greater flexibility and investment opportunities; and (4) supplying liquidity and funding (IIF 2012b; Ghosh, del Mazo, and Ötker-Robe 2012). Conversely, as market participants generally try to minimize the impact of regulation and its associated costs, the interconnection of regulated banks and these institutions highlighted the narrowness of previously defined micro prudential rules.

With the benefit of hindsight, it has become clear that "inflation and output do not typically display unusual behavior ahead of asset price busts" (IMF 2009, 93). In other words, well- behaved inflation and output performance provide few if any assurances that asset prices will not acquire a life of their own, with potentially high costs in terms of output foregone during the moments of bust. Besides noting the typical economic costs associated with asset price busts, IMF (2009) detects and points out some leading indicators of busts, namely, rapidly expanding credit, deteriorating current account balances, and large shifts into residential investment.

Therefore, the framework of flexible inflation targeting regime and micro prudential regulation is not necessarily sufficient to avoid asset price booms and busts because of *macro financial risks* that may develop beyond the scope of the framework. Given the high costs associated with asset price busts—including the possibility of protracted negative feedback loops between unsound private balance sheets, public sector imbalances, and/or foregone employments and gross domestic product (GDP)—the negligence must be addressed.

Cross-border Spillovers from Asset Price Booms and Busts and Large-Country Policy Responses as a Missing Dimension

The neglect of asset price booms and busts by the received wisdom regarding inflation targeting and micro prudential regulation acquires an additional dimension in the case of capital-receiving countries, such as most emerging markets. Even if these countries succeed in avoiding domestic generation of *macro financial risks*, they may experience asset price booms and busts caused by net capital-flow ebbs and tides derived from asset price cycles abroad. Because those countries are incorporated into the network of interlinked balance sheets of international financial institutions, they are vulnerable to spillovers and externalities, including contagion in terms of confidence, as risks taken procyclically in large countries end up affecting the entire global system. By the same token, policy responses taken at the countries where asset price booms and busts unfold affect capital-receiving countries.

The framework of flexible inflation targeting and micro prudential regulation does not address cross-border spillovers of asset price booms and busts and policy responses, although these are often of first-order relevance. The neglect of asset price booms and busts, in particular, has a counterpart in the neglect of cross-border capital flows and macroeconomic policy spillovers. Both types of over-flows and spillovers bring implications in terms of higher volatility of activity on the real side, more complicated monetary policy management, and augmented financial-sector risks (CIEPR 2011).

Positive or negative feedback loops between domestic balance sheets and liquidity in other countries may outweigh by far the mitigating effects coming from exchange-rate fluctuations in such situations. Furthermore, flexible exchange rates lose their ability to smooth balance-of-payment adjustments under prolonged situations of extraordinary liquidity inflows or outflows, as their persistent disequilibrium may have long-lasting effects on the domestic allocation of resources.

In what follows, we try to sketch some of the frontiers along which the flexible inflation targeting regime will need to evolve to integrate neglected macro financial risks.

Challenges to Integrate Macro Financial Linkages and Macro Prudential Regulation into Monetary Policy

Challenges to integrating macro financial linkages and macro prudential regulation into monetary policy include: integration of asset prices into monetary policy reaction functions, integration with macro prudential regulation, discretion versus rules, and dealing with cross-country spillovers.

Integration of Asset Prices into Monetary Policy Reaction Functions
Asset price booms and busts are now considered too important to be left in financial supervisors' hands. As mentioned, the pendulum of opinions has moved in favor of those arguing for monetary policy "leaning against the wind" to prevent asset price bubbles, rather than the "mop-up-afterwards" approach.

Evidence suggests that financial cycles are more pronounced in emerging market economies than in developed economies (Calderon and Serven 2011; Claessens and Ghosh 2012). Whereas there is no significant difference between those two groups of economies in the duration of recessions or recoveries during financial cycles, downturns in activity are larger and more intense in emerging markets. The same observation can be seen for asset price cycles—durations are similar, but the median peak-to-trough amplitudes for stock prices, housing prices, and real exchange rates are larger for emerging markets.

Dealing with the Challenges of Macro Financial Linkages in Emerging Markets
http://dx.doi.org/10.1596/978-1-4648-0002-3

Although most financial upturns do not lead to crashes, large-scale financial booms are a meaningful predictor of crises. Also, because synchronization of economic activity, credit growth, and asset prices are material (and real economic losses are usually higher) it is even more important that emerging economies integrate these aspects into monetary policy.

One question comes to the fore: Should central banks incorporate indicators of financial stability into their reaction function in a kind of "augmented Taylor rule"? Should they react automatically to variations in asset prices—or some associated variable, such as credit expansion—as they do under inflation-targeting regimes in the case of variations in output gaps and inflation?

An intermediary position in the "lean versus clean" spectrum has been offered by Blinder (2010), who argues that "a distinction should be drawn between credit-fueled bubbles (such as the house price bubble) and equity-type bubbles in which credit plays only a minor role (such as the tech stock bubble)." In this view, the "mop-up-afterwards" approach would still be appropriate for equity bubbles not fueled by borrowing, but the central bank should try to limit credit-based bubbles—though probably combining regulatory instruments and interest rates. This view may eventually become the new consensus on how to deal with asset price bubbles; indeed, Bernanke (2010) came close to endorsing it.

Yet it remains advisable not to treat asset prices on the same footing as the common components of "Taylor rules." After all, "even the best leading indicators of asset price busts are imperfect—in the process of trying to reduce the probability of a dangerous bust, central banks may raise costly false alarms. Also, rigid reactions to indicators and inflexible use of policy tools will likely lead to policy mistakes. *Discretion is required* [emphasis added]" (IMF 2009, 116).

Such a cautious approach does not mean complacency. On the contrary, signs of rising macro financial risks may demand a response from monetary policy makers. But first it is necessary to properly identify the reasons behind the evolution of rising asset prices and credit—a task that is far from simple, as one can conclude after examining the challenges to integrate financial frictions into forecast models (annex 4A) and to identify financial instability risks (annex 4B).

Integration with Macro Prudential Regulation

One takeaway of the above discussion is the relevance for both macroeconomic and financial stability of macro prudential regulation commensurate with the acknowledged macro financial risks. As a complement to micro prudential regulation, macro prudential regulation should be concerned with the stability of the financial system as a whole and the mitigation of risks to the real economy, that is, strengthening financial stability vis-à-vis endogenous propagation and exogenous shocks. It should aim to make the overall incentive structure for individual firms coherent and consistent so that externalities are internalized. The idea is to design a set of principles and rules that can reduce each institution's contribution to systemic risk and thus smooth the financial cycle (that is, reducing the systemic risk that inherently builds up in booms and has damaging consequences in slumps since leverage, risk-taking, credit, and asset prices are procyclical and crises typically follow booms).

The objective of macro prudential regulation is not to eliminate the financial cycle but to reduce its amplitude and associated systemic risk. Procyclicality is linked to all business cycles and goes *pari passu* with most fundamentals and behaviors (for example, investments and "animal spirits"). What macro prudential rules can do is reduce procyclicality and control the externalities that amplify fluctuations. By doing this, they can ensure that the financial system operates with less systemic risk and can enhance the resilience of the system in downturns.

Potential gains from macro prudential policy have been discussed long before the recent financial crisis. However, despite an overall convergence around a definition, there is no consensus about which macro prudential policy targets and instruments should be prioritized. In terms of specific targets for macro prudential policies, one may attempt to countervail measured risks during business cycles (Brunnermeier and Sannikov 2009); to stabilize the provision of financial intermediation services (Bank of England 2009); or to avoid bubble creation processes. One could also highlight options to limit macroeconomic costs of system distress, to address interlinkages and exposures of financial institutions and the procyclicality of the system (Caruana 2010); to discourage individual institutions to generate systemic risk and negative externalities (Perotti and Suarez 2009); to control social costs of a generalized drop in asset prices caused by credit crunches and/or fire-sales (Hanson, Kashyap, and Stein 2010); or to enhance financial system resilience (CGFS 2010). There are many ways to approach the objective, and policy makers have a range of macro prudential tools to cope with each angle.

One of the main ideas that emerged as suitable for implementation after the 2008 crisis was to enhance capital and liquidity regulations since both problems were at the origin of the quasi meltdown of the global financial system after the Lehman Brothers collapse. A more robust banking system (in terms of capital and liquidity) would be less subject to crises (or, at the very least, not require the magnitude of transfers from taxpayers that was observed). Tighter regulatory standards might also contribute to smaller output fluctuations and to higher welfare gains even apart from banking crises. There are a number of studies (for example, BCBS 2010) that point out that better capitalization and higher liquidity of banks reduce the likelihood and the severity of crises; and that regulatory reforms can reduce the amplitude of business cycles, especially using countercyclical capital buffers.

The Bank for International Settlements (BIS) and the Basel Committee on Banking Supervision (BCBS) have been advocating the adoption of countercyclical capital standards. Buffers need not be part of the prudential minimum capital requirement and would be capital in excess of that minimum, so that it is available to absorb losses in bad times. Countercyclical capital buffers would limit (1) the risk of large-scale accidents in the banking system and (2) the amplification of macroeconomic fluctuations during crises.[6] The macro prudential rationale is the time-inconsistency argument that risks tend to build up in good times, but their negative consequences materialize only with a lag. This feature reveals the limitations of current risk measurement practices as well as distortions in the micro prudential incentives of individual firms.

There is a perception that risk-sensitive minimum capital requirements embedded in Basel II could lead to excessive procyclicality.[7] Conversely, some have argued that by raising capital requirements in a countercyclical way, regulators could help choke off asset price bubbles—such as the one that developed in the U.S. housing market—before a crisis develops. The Turner Review (see Financial Services Authority 2009), for instance, favored countercyclical capital requirements, as did Brunnermeier and Sannikov (2009), who propose to adjust capital adequacy requirements over the cycle by two multiples—the first related to above-average growth of credit expansion and leverage, the second related to the mismatch in the maturity of assets and liabilities.

At the international level, there has been progress toward establishing new standards in this area; the BCBS developed a countercyclical framework that involves adjusting bank capital in response to excess growth in credit to the private sector, which it views as a good indicator of systemic risk. In a proposal released in September 2010, the Basel Committee suggested the implementation of a countercyclical capital buffer ranging from 0 to 2.5 percent of risk-weighted assets. Overall, total capital requirements would rise from a minimum of 8 percent of risk-weighted assets today under Basel II up to 13 percent when the maximum value for the countercyclical capital buffer is taken into account (BCBS 2011).

Macro prudential instruments can be discussed in a time-series dimension or in cross section (Borio 2011), mirroring the types of macro financial risks mentioned previously. When systemic behavior over time is considered, the key issue is how risks can be amplified by interactions within the financial system and between the financial system and the real economy. As discussed, such feedback loops are a crucial component of endogenously generated business cycles. In its turn, the cross-section dimension relates to the common exposure of institutions at each point of time. Correlated assets, or even counterparty interrelations, create such a link among financial institutions.

Table 4.1 shows a typology of macro prudential instruments offered by Galati and Moessner (2011). Whether macro prudential instruments are expected to tackle time-series or cross-section dimensions, they overlap with micro prudential ones.

Can we reduce financial instability without using monetary policy, relying only on prudential and regulatory rules incorporating macro financial risks? Would that guarantee both financial and macroeconomic stability? Most practitioners have expressed the view that a combined (articulate) use of both monetary and macro prudential policies and rules is superior to a standalone implementation of either (Canuto 2011a). Instead of "a corner solution where one instrument is devoted entirely to one objective, the macro-stabilization exercise must be viewed as a joint optimization problem where monetary and regulatory policies

Table 4.1 Macro Prudential Tools

	Examples
1. Risk measurement methodologies	
By banks	Risk measures calibrated through the cycle or to the cyclical trough
By supervisors	Cyclical conditionality in supervisory ratings of firms; Develop measures of systemic vulnerability (for example commonality of exposures and risk profiles. intensity of inter-firm linkages) as basis for calibration of prudential tools; Communication of official assessments of systemic vulnerability and outcomes of macro stress tests;
2. Financial reporting	
Accounting standards	Use of less procyclical accounting standards; dynamic provisions
Prudential filters	Adjust accounting figures as a basis for calibration of prudential tools: Prudential provisions as add-on to capital: smoothing via moving averages of such measures; time-varying target for provisions or for maximum provision rate
Disclosures	Disclosures of various types of risk (for example credit, liquidity), and of uncertainty about risk estimates and valuations in financial reports or disclosures
3. Regulatory capital	
Pillar 1	Systemic capital surcharge; Reduce sensitivity of regulatory capital requirements to current point in the cycle and with respect to movements in measured risk; Introduce cycle-dependent multiplier to the point-in-time capital figure; Increased regulatory capital requirements for particular exposure types (higher risk weights than on the basis of Basel II, for macroprudential reasons)
Pillar 2	Link of supervisory review to state of the cycle
4. Funding liquidity standards	Cyclically-dependent funding liquidity requirements; Concentration limits; FX lending restrictions: FX reserve requirements; currency mismatch limits; open FX position limits
5. Collateral arrangements	Time-varying Loan-to-value (LTV) ratios; Conservative maximum loan-to-value ratios and valuation methodologies for collateral; Limit extension of credit based on increases in asset values; Through-the-cycle margining
6. Risk concentration limits	Quantitative limits to growth of individual types of exposures; (Time-varying) interest rate surcharges to particular types of loans
7. Compensation schemes	Guidelines linking performance-related pay to ex ante longer-horizon measures of risk; back-loading of pay-offs; Use of supervisory review process for enforcement
8. Profit distribution restrictions	Limit dividend payments in good times to help build up capital buffers in bad times
9. Insurance mechanisms	Contingent capital infusions; Pre-funded systemic risk insurance schemes financed by levy related to bank asset growth beyond certain allowance; Pre-funded deposit insurance with premia sensitive to macro (systemic risk) in addition to micro (institution specific) parameters
10. Managing failure and resolution	Exit management policy conditional on systemic strength; Trigger points for supervisory intervention stricter in booms than in periods of systemic distress

Source: Galati and Moessner 2011, 10.
Note: FX = foreign exchange.

are used in concert in pursuit of both objectives" (CIEPR 2011, 7). Prudential rules and monetary policy are parameters to each other, as their standalone stances affect the evolution of asset prices. Therefore, a joint optimization pursuit is likely superior to isolated "corner solutions."

In the time-series dimension of macro prudential issues, monetary policy and macro prudential tools can clearly be complementary in reducing procyclicality. For example, during simultaneous asset price and macroeconomic booms, one could combine higher contingent capital requirements and additional liquidity surcharges with interest rate hikes. Because of the imperfect substitutability between these measures, the greatest effectiveness should be considered when calibrating jointly their intensities.[8]

Additionally, when the short-term interest rate reaches a lower bound, macro prudential policies can be used to cope with specific financial vulnerabilities, or even to increase traction of monetary policy. As mentioned, the nominal zero bound is now taken more seriously as an issue than it was before the crisis, as witnessed by the recent use of "quantitative easing" and other unconventional monetary policies (Brahmbhatt, Canuto, and Ghosh 2010). In such situations, Goodhart (2011) argued that the first macro prudential tool to be used should be the central bank's own balance sheet. This issue has not been as relevant for most emerging markets, as average inflation has been higher, the crisis's collateral effects milder, and fiscal policy more available.

In fact, we have witnessed major central banks using balance sheets in the last few years when other tools—like lower capital requirements in order to alleviate banks' capital burden and compress credit spreads to the final borrower—are out of reach because of generalized fears of bank insolvency. As many emerging economies have held historically higher capital ratios, this instrument can be used in parallel with interest rate cuts as China, Brazil, and Turkey have recently done.

The scope for joint calibration may be less obvious in the case of cross-sectional macro prudential regulation, in which the calibration of the latter must be done top down. The calibration must also consider that diverse institutions have different contributions to systemic risk, with institutions with greater systemic relevance receiving tighter macro prudential requirements. Estimating the individual contribution to systemic risk is always a challenge. In any case, from the cross-section perspective, it is clearly easier to cope with vulnerabilities through macro prudential tools than with short-term interest rate instruments. Policy makers can go directly to their area of concern (for example, real estate credit, leveraged loans or currency mismatches) and tighten or loosen the respective rules, whereas the alternative of containing high growth of real estate credit just by hiking interest rates reaches every credit line and is probably not the most efficient option.

Discretion versus Rules

How effective are the macro prudential instruments just described? A recent study of country experiences found that they can be effective in mitigating systemic risk (Lim and others 2011). Some instruments were shown to be particularly effective in reducing procyclicality (for example, caps on loan-to-value or on debt-to-income ratios, ceilings on credit or credit growth, reserve requirements). The evidence of effectiveness did not depend on the exchange-rate regime or the size of the financial sector, but differed according to types of shock.

The huge variety of macro prudential tools makes it necessary to tailor policy designs to specific purposes. However, too much uncertainty about changes implemented by the government may be counterproductive and costly in terms of less credit provided if rules and regulations change very often. The trade-off is on the one hand, more discretionary, time-varying macro prudential policies and on the other hand, less uncertainty from stable and general macro prudential rules. Moreover, too many ad-hoc changes make it harder to assess interactions among different macro prudential tools, and between them and monetary transmission mechanism.

The issue of how best to calibrate tools to avoid excessive procyclicality of the financial system involves a trade-off between discretion and rules (Borio and Shim 2007). Take, for instance, the case of *dynamic provisioning* rules (that is, capital requirements of financial institutions that rise/fall faster than leverage) versus a discretionary setting of required reserves, in both cases reinforcing—and reducing the burden of—the direction taken by monetary policies. There is no consensus on whether its calibration should be discretionary or in the form of built-in stabilizers, like reaction functions used in monetary policy. Because imbalances are infrequent and specific to each period, discretionary measures may be more useful to fine tune or target specificities. The system may also become too rigid vis-à-vis nonfinancial shocks—such as real-side productivity shocks—in the presence of automatic rules. As with discretionary monetary policy, discretionary calibration may be more subject to policy error or public or political pressures, in addition to increasing regulatory uncertainty and encouraging financial disintermediation. In practice, a combination of both macro prudential built-in stabilizers and discretionary measures are used.

A rule of thumb for integrating monetary policy and macro prudential regulation may be to retain some division of labor, even if their combination is considered the best way to go. Fine tuning via monetary policy should be favored when stability issues are of a homogeneous and reversible nature, like those associated with generalized waves of market euphoria or panic. Changes in automatic macro prudential rules, in turn, are to be made in cases of permanent, structural shocks. More ad-hoc discretionary prudential policies should be used for specific but systemically significant disturbances from a cross section perspective. Countercyclical tools should be used with parsimony and caution, as distinguishing between transitory and permanent shocks in real time is always challenging.

Such division of labor may also be justified by the fact that macro prudential instruments tend to be more demanding in terms of implementation lags and transaction costs to financial institutions, whereas movements in short-term interest rates are faster, simpler to carry out and easier to communicate to the general public.

It is worth highlighting the departure from the rule-based world of policy making of the conventional framework described at the beginning of this paper.

Even if the flexible inflation targeting maintains its basic rationale and principles, the consideration of asset prices and the complementarity with macro prudential regulation in monetary policy decisions introduces a degree of discretion. This is a flipside of the discovery that the relevant dimension of asset price cycles was ignored by the earlier paradigm. With discretion, though, all those policy and political risks expected to be precluded via rules, return.

Dealing with Cross-Country Spillovers

Cross-border capital flows and the potential transmission of asset price booms and busts via interconnected balance sheets imply additional layers of complexity as compared to purely domestic asset price cycles. As surges in capital inflows can have collateral macroeconomic effects, potentially increasing financial vulnerabilities, macroeconomic and/or macro prudential policies could be adopted as a response to those surges. As discussed, asset and credit bubbles may originate from abroad and dwarf a prevailing macro prudential regulation designed to tame purely domestic asset price booms. Furthermore, if capital inflow surges lead to prolonged far-from-equilibrium real exchange rates, they may have distortive and long-lasting effects on the domestic allocation of resources.[9]

Magud and Reinhart (2006) pointed out four fears that motivate policy makers to be proactive in managing capital flows: fear of exchange-rate appreciation, of hot money, of large inflows, and of loss of monetary autonomy. Higher levels of the exchange rate could damage the competiveness of domestic industries. Sudden inflows of hot money pose risks of sudden reversals, increasing the volatility of exchange rates. "If capital controls and related macro prudential measures are seen not as instruments of exchange rate management but as part of a package of policies targeted at financial stability, then it is the *composition* of capital flows that takes center stage rather than their volume" (CIEPR 2011, 11). However, sometimes the problem is not one of an undesirable composition of inflows, but rather their size. A surge in foreign capital poses risks of asset price or credit bubbles if the economy has limited capacity to absorb.[10] At the same time, cash-rich agents could be encouraged to excessive risk-taking and herd behavior, which suggests that some restrictions or taxes on capital flows could be useful—including as a way to gain additional freedom in setting short-term interest rates.

A sequential approach to cope with surges of capital inflows is offered by Ostry and others (2010). As per macroeconomic concerns, policy makers should ask themselves whether the exchange rate is undervalued and should be allowed to float upwards, as a first step. If it is not the case, the country could start with a policy of accumulation of reserves, provided that increasing their levels is desirable. But if there is an inflationary concern, policy makers should sterilize these interventions.[11] If inflation is under control, another option would be simply to cut interest rates. As costs are incurred by the sterilization process, there are limits beyond which it is no longer attractive to keep buying foreign currency. In this case, fiscal tightening may be an option to attenuate the external stimulus. If the scope for fiscal contraction is limited, then capital controls could be useful to deal with the situation.

In parallel, if capital inflows cause prudential concerns, the macro prudential toolkit may be more efficient and should be used before capital controls. If policy makers are able to identify the source of concern, a macro prudential measure could be better targeted than is the case for a broader restriction. As an illustration, if the concern is excessive borrowing from abroad or its impact on domestic credit growth, increasing capital requirements for these activities may be more transparent, efficient, and easier to implement than taxing all foreign sources of funding. Additionally, if the country's capital account is too open and financial markets too deep, it could be very difficult to implement effective capital controls, given circumvention strategies.

A substantial controversy about effectiveness of interventions in foreign exchange markets exists in the literature. As such interventions often become inevitable, at least in situations like one of significant temporary inflows, it is worth reviewing their channels of influence.

Interventions in exchange markets can be sterilized or not sterilized. The latter has an impact on the nominal exchange rate. At least until recently, the conventional wisdom was in favor of the sterilization option, so that monetary policy could deal with inflationary issues separately.

How does a sterilized intervention work? Two channels can be mentioned: the portfolio balance channel and the expectation—or signaling—channel (Mussa 1981). By the portfolio balance channel, government interventions change the composition of agents' portfolios, altering the relative price of foreign assets relative to domestic assets. The impact on the exchange rate depends on whether those assets are perfect substitutes, in which case there would be no impact on the exchange rate, or otherwise there is an impact as agents try to rebalance their portfolios. Additionally, if Ricardian equivalence does not hold, even if the assets are perfectly substitutable, interventions should have a net effect on the level of exchange rate through this channel because of tax issues (Sarno and Taylor 2001).

The signaling channel is based on the possibility that agents can see interventions (sterilized or not) as a signal about future economic policy. Different expectations about policies in the future affect present variables in a forward-looking perspective. This perception could occur because agents change their view about future actions by monetary authorities or because they change their assessment about the impact of interventions. It suggests that hidden interventions should tend to be less effective than the public and transparent ones.

In theory, exchange interventions can be effective, but what about the practical evidence? The conventional wisdom of ineffectiveness has been challenged. A review of empirical evidence led "to conclude cautiously that official intervention can be effective, especially if the intervention is publicly announced and concerted and provided that it is consistent with the underlying stance of monetary and fiscal policy" (Sarno and Taylor 2001, 862).

The effectiveness of capital controls is also an important issue because it is one of the ultimate options to address potential risks to financial and macroeconomic stabilities derived from capital inflow surges. As an illustration, large capital inflows could encourage domestic overborrowing and excessive exchange-rate exposure. The usual objectives to establish capital controls are to reduce the volume of these flows, to modify their composition toward a longer maturity profile, to diminish real exchange-rate pressures, to strengthen the autonomy of monetary policy, or to use a combination of these objectives.

Magud and Reinhart (2006) made an effort to find common ground among noncomparable results in the empirical literature. They suggest that capital controls on inflows have been successful in altering the composition of flows in favor of longer maturity and to increase monetary policy independence, but there is no clear evidence for the other objectives. However, by doing their own exercise, they not only confirmed those two influences, but also found some evidence of reducing exchange-rate pressure. In any case, capital controls seem not to lower the volume of net flows (Ostry and others 2010). In sum, there is evidence in favor of the effectiveness of capital controls depending on country-specific needs and the availability of options.[12]

For our purposes, capital controls and exchange-rate interventions can be seen as options to be combined with monetary and macro prudential policies, options that can even increase, or at least help, the effectiveness of the latter. Depending on the vulnerability identified, policy makers could choose those measures that can be most efficient and appropriate to circumstances. Consideration has to be given, though, to costs associated with curbing capital inflows in the case of countries with low saving rates.

In any case, it is fundamental to keep in sight the differences in managing capital inflows that are expected to be temporary or permanent. The former calls for policies aiming at ring-fencing the economy from volatility. However, even if inflow surges are permanent, some action may be implemented to postpone adjustments in the economy and/or smooth transitional effects. For example, an important discovery of natural resources could change the fundamentals of an economy toward higher current account surplus, which in turn would lead to more appreciated exchange rates in the near future. Notwithstanding the fact that a resource reallocation is hard to avoid at the end—or at least not without increasing difficulties—some measures could be in place to check the pace of transfers. In the same sense, a consolidation of better fundamentals in emerging markets tends to attract abnormally high inflows of capital for some time, during the transition, as investors adjust their portfolio (stock) exposure to the new reality. Furthermore, the inevitable sluggishness to adjust on the side of the supply of new assets may lead to a price overshooting of existing assets, with some negative side-effects (Canuto 2011b).

In sum, once asset price cycles and spillovers are acknowledged as a fact of life, capital flow management policies become one—highly or lowly effective—item of the toolkit of combined monetary-cum-macro-prudential policies used to address macroeconomic and financial instability risks. This is particularly the case in economies subject to significant spillovers from asset price cycles and policies from abroad, and in which the scale and duration of spillovers turn a narrow set of prudential and monetary policies insufficient to ring-fence the economy. Nevertheless, one has to take into account the shorter life of capital-control effectiveness, as volatility will migrate and show up elsewhere, given the ultimately fungible character of capital flows and its creativity to design circumvention strategies.

New Challenges Faced by Central Banking in Emerging Markets

The significant number of emerging markets economies whose central banks adopted flexible inflation targeting prior to the crisis reflected a perception that such a regime could work well despite distinctive differences with advanced economies. To what extent would differences in stages of financial development and asset price cycles change that perception? What would be the implications of the current situation with many large advanced economies facing a protracted public debt overhang and adopting unconventional monetary policies? Given the incomplete global adoption of flexible exchange rates, what are the risks associated with widespread exchange-rate interventions with global growth lower than prior to the crisis? As we leave behind the hypothesis of a world of fully rule-based monetary and prudential policies, what are the political economy challenges faced by emerging markets' policy makers?

How Different Are Emerging Markets' Asset Price Booms and Busts?

Agénor and Pereira da Silva (2012) highlighted four features of financial systems in most emerging markets (or "middle-income countries") that differentiate them from advanced economies. First, commercial banking is still by far predominant in financial intermediation. Despite deepening local capital markets in recent years, nonbank financial intermediation (hedge funds, commodities funds, private equity groups, and money market funds) is not yet a full-fledged alternative.[13]

Second, as a flipside of the absence of diversification, bank credit has strong impacts on the supply side of the economy. This situation creates a complication for the transmission of monetary policy since interest-rate variations aiming at controlling aggregate demand also have a supply-side effect in a countervailing direction, given that firms borrow short term to finance working capital needs.

Third, the financial system is "often highly vulnerable to small domestic or external disturbances, even more so to global financial cycles, as a result of increased financial integration. Abrupt reversals in short-term capital movements tend to exacerbate financial volatility, particularly in countries with relatively fragile financial systems, weak regulatory and supervision structures, and policy regimes that lack flexibility" (Agénor and Pereira da Silva, 2012, 4).

Finally, the experience with costly banking crises over the last decades was marked by highly asymmetric effects among output drops, depth and duration of credit crunches, and impacts on unemployment and poverty. In any case, as a result of the harshness of lessons learned, banking supervision and regulation has since strengthened substantially in many emerging markets (Canuto 2010).

Notwithstanding the size and higher degree of sophistication that financial systems have acquired in large emerging markets, one may expect spillovers from abroad to acquire an importance as a generator of domestic asset price booms and

busts that outweighs domestically generated asset price movements. This is particularly the case when, like recently, the global context of excess liquidity makes
most emerging economies potential recipients of massive inflows of foreign capital. In effect, such inflows have ebbed and flowed following the adoption of
unconventional monetary policies in advanced economies (Canuto, Garcia-Kilroy,
and Silva 2012a). These flows have had a structural component: they have been
related to the perception of improvement (and, later, relative disappointment) of
emerging markets' growth prospects. However, these flows also have had a temporary component: portfolio investments and short-term deposits. In a context of
high liquidity in international markets and an uncertain outlook for mature
economies, many have seen this component as excessive and mostly reflective of
"push" factors in its origins, rather than of "pull" factors on the absorptive side.

Part of this large inflow to many emerging markets has been absorbed by the
accumulation of central bank reserves. Reserve accumulation policies have usually been implemented together with a policy of sterilization, in order to maintain an independent monetary policy. However, the intensity and magnitude of
present inflows can make it difficult to sterilize them fully and resources that
remain available to market participants may end up contributing to a significant
expansion in credit. Net private capital inflow into emerging countries rose from
less than US$200 billion in 2002 to just under US$1 trillion in 2012. In 2007,
this amount reached almost 9 percent of emerging markets' GDP (figure 4.2).
Low-cost external funding creates incentives to increase risk-taking and can
result in asset price distortions, including of the exchange rate. Hence, excessive
capital inflows have often contributed to a brisk pace of domestic credit growth
in emerging markets, which potentially fuels inflationary pressures and aggravates
financial instability.

Figure 4.2 Emerging Market Private Capital Inflow, Net

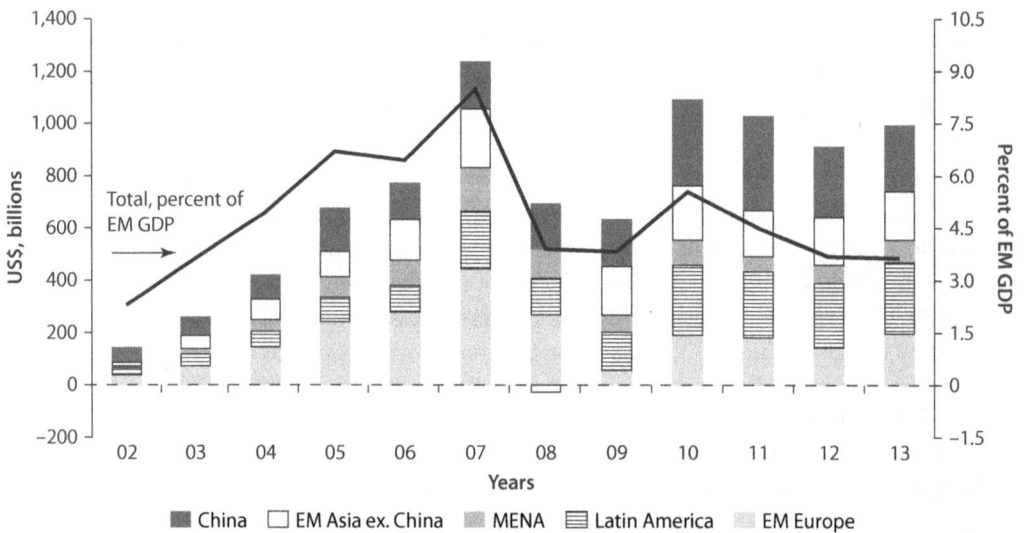

Source: IIF 2012a, 1.

Unconventional Monetary Policies and the "Politicization of Finance" in Advanced Economies

High (and unsustainable) levels of public debt in several large advanced economies—as well as debt overhangs in the financial sector and/or households—are not likely to be fully reversed in the near future (Canuto 2010). Difficulties in rapidly tackling the issue through flow adjustments (fiscal consolidation, bank deleveraging, household savings) sizable enough to matter are immense and would lead to deeper growth slowdown and unemployment. Therefore, policies and credit events leading to asset/liability adjustments (public or interstate absorption of debts, or debt restructuring) have taken place and are likely to continue in the near future (Canuto, Garcia-Kilroy, and Silva 2012a).

One now sees the hands of governments and central banks all over the place in finance, sustaining markets with their maneuvers on quantities and prices of available assets. One might view such a process as "politicization of finance," in the sense that market fundamentals are not weighing in as they would under normal conditions, and decisions on whether to hold assets and institutions are intertwined with political factors:

1. Central banks' balance sheets in countries at the core of the crisis have expanded dramatically because of purchases of domestic assets to ease monetary conditions and contain asset fire sales.
2. Yield curves have flattened to maintain long-term yields close to historically low levels.
3. Support to banks via bailouts or broad liquidity facilities has avoided the collapse that funding costs imposed by private creditors would lead to.
4. Regulatory requirements of liquidity have been tweaked, and in practice, have created a captive demand for government bonds, pushing down yields.
5. Currency markets have been subject to systematic interventions by heretofore hands-off governments, no longer comfortable with free floating under current conditions.

An open "politicization" of finance has occurred in the sense that the dynamics of financial asset prices are now influenced by the political sphere. Consider the Euro zone in the first half of 2012. Policy makers in those member countries under financial stress held the view that the chances of success would rise with the support of supplementary creation of public money by the European Central Bank (ECB). Conversely, the ECB's actions were constrained by, among other factors, the political view predominant in other Euro-zone countries according to which such a support could only go to a certain level before undermining the political willingness to reform. Until mid-2012, financial markets moved between the poles of collapse and stability, in accordance with signals of the balance of those political views—backing or pushing back ECB's debt purchases. Risk premiums moved down only after the ECB's pledge to do "what it takes" to save the euro, during the summer, reflecting an apparent political support of such attitude.

Dealing with the Challenges of Macro Financial Linkages in Emerging Markets
http://dx.doi.org/10.1596/978-1-4648-0002-3

Consider the U.S. fiscal retrenchment—the so-called fiscal cliff—poised to be reached in 2013 in case an agreement between government and Congress is not definitely reached. The possibility of a "cliff" has been created by the battle between political views in Congress, instead of private investors requiring higher yields to buy U.S. Treasuries. As additional distortion, the Federal Reserve has conducted Operation Twist since late 2011 aiming to compress long-term interest rates by buying long-term Treasuries and simultaneously sterilizing with short-term debt. As monetary easing can be less effective without a concurrent fiscal stimulus from now on, a precocious fiscal adjustment may well harm the prospects of economic and financial recovery.

In such context, emerging-market central bankers face a double challenge, in addition to normal ones: (1) the likelihood of large capital flow swings in the future will remain high, with corresponding spillovers on domestic financial and asset price dynamics; and (2) domestic political pressure undermining central bank autonomy may rise substantially, as a mirror of what is happening in advanced economies.

Unwinding of Global Imbalances and Interventions on Exchange Rate Markets

Another source of departure from the flexible inflation-targeting blueprint is associated with the unwinding of global imbalances poised to take place—either virtuously or not. Given prospects for global economic growth lower than before the crisis, policy attempts to interfere with the evolution of exchange rates are more likely to be undertaken making it even harder for other central banks to adhere to the conventional blueprint.

With the benefit of hindsight, we are now better informed of the fragilities of the global growth prior to the crisis (Canuto 2010). High levels of domestic absorption (consumption and investment) in some large countries were accompanied by overindebtedness of households, banks and/or governments, which was in turn backed by correspondingly appreciated assets (house prices, acquisition of low-risk status by integration to the Euro zone and others). Other countries grew substantially by exporting goods to attend that appetite contributing to substantial current-account imbalances (figure 4.3). Such a combined pattern of current-account deficits-surpluses also materialized within the Euro area.

The flipside of such a high and prolonged current-account pattern was the resistance to exchange-rate appreciation by surplus countries, compounded by the fact that many surplus countries also became poles attracting foreign capital. Some countries resorted to stringent capital controls and other barriers to capital entry, whereas most piled up huge foreign reserves. These reserves were in turn put back as liquid assets acquired from deficit countries, which became one of the factors sustaining persistent current-account imbalances.

The global financial crisis has essentially been the unfolding of the unsoundness of balance sheets once the widespread asset price overvaluation came to a halt (as previously discussed). Debt-deleveraging dynamics and macroeconomic

Figure 4.3 Current Account Balances, 2012

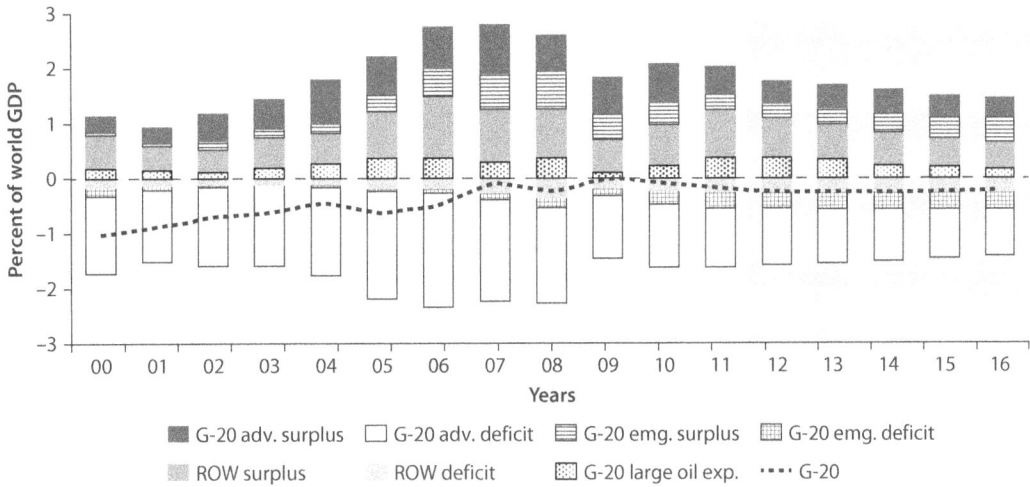

Source: IMF staff estimates.

slowdown in deficit countries explain the shrinkage of imbalances in the wake of the crisis (figure 4.3). It is still to be seen whether surplus countries will increase their domestic absorption with intensity and speed enough to compensate for the retrenchment of absorption in heretofore deficit countries, and thus settle the forecast of unwinding global imbalances on a global growth path higher than the current one.

One may guess is that as "fear of floating (upward)" tends to rise in the next few years, an environment much less benign than that prevailing before the crisis is likely to manifest itself. Some exchange rate "floaters" will become more like "fixers," which will affect not only monetary policy in those countries but also the dynamics of cross-border movement of liquidity and asset trade.[14] For instance, in combination with the unconventional monetary policies pursued in several large advanced economies, more frequent tinkering with exchange rates will set the stage for potential "currency wars."

Waning Rule-Based Policy Making and Political Economy Pressures on Central Banks

As we have argued earlier, the acknowledgment that asset price cycles and cross-border spillovers lead to weakening the belief that monetary policy making and prudential regulation could eventually become entirely based on rules. Without denying the benefits accrued by rules and clear communication, we remarked the inevitability of some discretionary policy choices even under normal conditions.

We have added several reasons why discretion and off-the-rule central banking decisions in emerging countries may become more frequent. In this case, gains derived from central bank credibility will inevitably risk erosion, which will substantially increase the requirement in terms of communication and justification of measures taken. In addition to the analytical and implementation challenges not fully realized by the "flexible-inflation-targeting-*cum*-isolated-prudential-regulation" framework, discretionary policy decisions may open a venue for political economy pressures against central bank autonomy.

Concluding Remarks

Until the outbreak of the global financial crisis, there was some convergence of thinking toward flexible inflation targeting. Controlled monetary expansion, low inflation with output being kept in line with its potential, defenses against the temptation to overexploit the short-run trade-off between inflation and employment, inflation expectations anchored and managed without inconsistency by an independent central bank, and a central bank that manipulates ex ante real interest rates to pursue a nominal target would be necessary and sufficient conditions to sustain macroeconomic stability. Flexible exchange rates and micro prudential tools would complement this framework to safeguard macroeconomic and financial system stabilities.

Monetary policy tools are too blunt to curb asset price bubbles, as correspondingly sharp interest rate hikes would have harmful unintended consequences on output growth and volatility. For some time, the prevailing opinion became that the best approach would be to use monetary policy only to "clean up" the financial mess after bubble bursts. As the debate evolved, an intermediary position gained prominence: the "mop-up-afterwards" approach would be appropriate for equity bubbles not fueled by overborrowing, whereas the central bank should try to limit credit-based bubbles—though probably combining microregulatory instruments and interest rates.

We also remarked how the crisis has undermined the belief in the sufficiency of the conventional framework. Even if implemented in accordance with those blueprints, the framework would not necessarily be capable of avoiding significant asset price booms and busts because of macro financial risks that may develop beyond its scope. And given the high costs associated with significant asset price busts—including the possibility of protracted negative feedback loops between overleveraged private balance sheets, public sector imbalances, and/or foregone employment and GDP—that negligence must be corrected. Additionally, cross-border capital flows and macroeconomic policy spillovers were disregarded. And both types of overflows and spillovers may bring implications in terms of higher volatility of activity on the real side, more complicated monetary policy management and augmented financial-sector risks.

How could we adjust the framework to take into account asset price booms and busts and spillovers? First of all, acknowledge that signs of rising macro financial risks may demand a particular response from monetary policy makers. However, it is necessary to properly identify the reasons behind rising asset prices and credit—a task that is far from simple.

As a complement to micro prudential regulation, macro prudential regulation should be concerned with ensuring the stability of the financial system as a whole and the mitigation of risks to the real economy. It should aim to make the overall incentive structure for financial firms coherent and consistent so that externalities are internalized by the system.

In fact, most practitioners have expressed a belief that a combined use of monetary and macro prudential policies and rules tends to be superior to a stand-alone implementation of either. Therefore, a joint optimization pursuit is likely superior to isolated "corner solutions."

Clearly, over time, monetary policy and macro prudential tools can be complementary in the pursuit of less procyclicality. For example, during simultaneous asset price and macroeconomic booms, one could combine higher contingent capital requirements and additional liquidity surcharges with interest rate hikes. There is imperfect substitutability between these measures, so best effectiveness should be considered when calibrating jointly their intensities.

The scope for joint calibration may be less obvious in the case of cross-sectional macro prudential regulation, in which the calibration of the latter must be done top down. In this case, it is clearly easier to cope with vulnerabilities through macro prudential tools than with short-term interest-rate instruments. Policy makers can focus directly on their concern, for example, real estate credit or leveraged loans or currency mismatches, and tighten or loosen the respective rules. One may wonder about the alternative of containing high growth of real estate credit just by hiking interest rates, but this measure reaches every credit line and most often will not be the most efficient option.

The huge variety of macro prudential tools makes possible policy designs tailored for specific purposes. But too much uncertainty may be counterproductive and costly if rules and regulations change often. There is thus a trade-off between, on the one hand, more discretionary, time-varying macro prudential policies, as more effective tools to cope with specific types of shocks and, on the other hand, less uncertainty associated with stable and general macro prudential rules. Moreover, too many ad hoc changes make it harder to assess interactions among different macro prudential tools, and between them and the monetary transmission mechanism.

A rule of thumb for integrating monetary policy and macro prudential regulation may be to retain some labor division, even if their articulated combination is now considered to be the best way to go. Fine-tuning via monetary policy should be favored when stability issues are of a homogeneous and reversible nature, like those associated with generalized waves of market euphoria or panic. Changes to automatic macro prudential rules, in turn, are to be made in cases of permanent shocks that alter major parameters of the economic system. More discretionary prudential policies should be resorted to in cases of specific, but systemically significant, disturbances from a cross section perspective. Lasting countercyclical tools should be used with parsimony and caution, as distinguishing between transitory and permanent shocks in real time is always challenging.

Such division of labor may also be justified by the fact that macro prudential instruments tend to be more demanding in terms of implementation lags and transaction costs to financial institutions. Conversely, movements in short-term interest rates are faster, simpler to carry out and easier to communicate to the general public. Likewise, managing expectations about policy makers' intentions is essential to improving policy effectiveness.

Once asset price booms and busts and cross-country spillovers are acknowledged as a fact of life, capital flow management policies become one item of the toolkit of combined monetary-cum-macro prudential policies to address macroeconomic and financial instability risks. This is particularly the case in economies subject to significant spillovers from asset price dynamics and policies from abroad, and in which the scale and duration of spillovers turn a narrow set of prudential and monetary policies insufficient to ring-fence the economy. Capital controls and exchange-rate interventions can be seen as options to be combined with fiscal, monetary, and macro prudential policies in the face of spillovers. The former can even increase, or at least help, the effectiveness of the latter. Consideration has to be given, though, to costs associated with curbing capital inflows in the case of countries with low saving rates. One must also take into account the short shelf life of capital-control effectiveness, as volatility will migrate and show up elsewhere, given the ultimately fungible character of capital flows and the creativity of agents to design circumvention strategies.

To approach the current set of challenges faced by central banks in emerging markets, we highlighted two aspects. First, four features make financial systems in most emerging market economies different than in advanced economies: (1) commercial banking is still by far predominant in financial intermediation; (2) as a flipside of the absence of diversification, bank credit has strong impacts on the supply side of the economy; (3) the financial system is frequently vulnerable to small domestic or external disturbances—even more so than to global financial cycles—as a result of increased financial integration; and (4) as a result of the harshness of lessons learned, banking supervision and regulation has strengthened substantially in emerging markets. Notwithstanding the size and higher degree of sophistication that financial systems have acquired in large emerging markets, domestically generated asset price dynamics tend to be dominated by those associated with spillovers from abroad.

A second trait of the current global environment worth highlighting is the "politicization of finance." One now sees the hands of governments and central banks all over the place in finance, sustaining markets with maneuvers upon quantities and prices of assets. Market fundamentals are not weighing in as under normal conditions, and decisions to support assets and institutions are intertwined with political factors.

In such a context, emerging-market central bankers face a double challenge: (1) the likelihood that large capital-flow swings in the future will remain high, with corresponding spillovers on domestic financial and asset price dynamics; and (2) domestic political pressure undermining central bank autonomy, as a mirror of what is happening in advanced economies.

Asset price booms and busts and cross-border spillovers lead to some weakening of the belief that monetary policy and prudential regulation could eventually become entirely based on rules. Without denying the benefits accrued by rules and clear communication, we remarked on the inevitability of some discretionary policy even under normal conditions. Central bank discretion in emerging countries may become more frequent. In addition to the analytical and implementation challenges not fully realized at the time of the "flexible-inflation-targeting-cum-separate-prudential-regulation" framework, discretionary policy decisions may also open a venue for political economy pressures against central bank autonomy.

Annex 4A: Integration of Financial Frictions into Forecast Models

Inflation targeting is a forecast-based framework for monetary policy decisions and thus strongly dependent on the quality of economic modeling, and therefore on the interpretation of underlying trends in the economy. A functionally useful model should not be overly complex and must draw on both empirical evidence and macroeconomic intuition about the transmission channels of shocks.

This chapter stressed the importance of adequately incorporating financial frictions into the conduct of monetary policy. A vast literature considering the importance of market failures as generators of financial frictions existed well before the crisis (Bernanke 1983; Calomiris 1993; Stiglitz and Weiss 1981; Bernanke, Gertler, and Gilchrist 1999, among many others). However, its integration into monetary policy remained fragmented in the Dynamic Stochastic General Equilibrium (DSGE) models that comprise the workhorses of central banks, including the Federal Reserve Bank (Mishkin 2011).

Take the case of macroeconometric models used for simulating stress test conditions, where the treatment of macro financial linkages is undertaken in three sequential phases. The first step is to forecast key macro variables in one scenario and, second, assess the impact of financial risks in banks' asset quality with other independent models (satellite models). Finally, the impacts on banks' balance sheets, earnings, and levels of capital necessary to cope with the stress simulated are estimated (Cihak 2007; Schmieder, Puhr, and Hasan 2011).

What is missing is an assessment of the feedback loops from the third step (financial institutions) to the first scenario (macroeconomy). Additionally, there is no consideration of the interconnectedness among financial institutions (for example, network effects).[15]

Some advances have been made in this area. One can mention quantile regression methods to model extreme stress (Koenker and Hallock 2001), which use more granular data to improve the details of the banking analysis, change focus from credit risk exclusively to incorporate more about liquidity risk, and consider banks' income nonlinearities or credit migration and comovement of bank profits (BCBS 2012). However, the most challenging aspect remains how to model the feedback loop and shock contagion within financial institutions, as well as between them and the real economy. Such contagion is key to understanding the depth of the recent global financial shocks.

In their turn, DSGE models are constructed using microeconomic-consistent foundations in a general equilibrium framework, assuming rational forward-looking optimizing behavior. Some numerical calibrations are used to mimic the dynamics observed in the real economy. Then one can assess the impact of exogenous shocks, or compare the outcomes of different policy designs. Some imperfections can be introduced in the decision making of consumers, firms, and policy makers. Recent efforts incorporate financial frictions in DSGE models (BCSB 2012). Notwithstanding such developments, by construction it is hard to incorporate any kind of irrational behavior, inefficient markets, or formation of asset price bubbles in those models.[16] All these elements could generate endogenous mechanisms of crisis propagation, as they were decisive in the recent period.

Many challenges remain for future use of DSGE models. We can highlight the need to incorporate welfare cost/benefit analyses between different economic agents, transitions and impacts in reducing the volatility of the business cycle. The interaction and tradeoff of different mixes of stabilization policies is not also sufficiently explored.[17] The maturity mismatch between assets and liabilities and the effects of market valuation are not satisfactorily incorporated. Furthermore, different degrees of borrower riskiness and sector diversification should be important to analyze interactions among heterogeneous agents (BCBS 2012).

Because DSGE are linearly approximated around a unique model's steady state, they pose additional challenges to deal with tail events. In these cases, one can argue in favor of multiple equilibriums and nonlinearity. "Because economic downturns typically result in even greater uncertainty about asset values, such episodes may involve an adverse feedback loop whereby financial disruptions cause investment and consumer spending to decline, which in turn, causes economic activity to contract." (Mishkin 2011, 22). Such circularity generates nonlinearities, as new rounds of uncertainty make financial disruptions even worse. The implied domino effect can generate different equilibriums depending on, among other factors, the government's capacity to stabilize private expectations in the middle of a perverse cycle.

Tail events could result from a complete coordination failure in private confidence, for example, this is one of the main explanations for the recent financial crisis pointed out by Akerlof and Shiller (2010). Methods for complex systems developed in areas such as physics, engineering, and biology may provide new ways to cope with collective behavior and nonlinear interconnections between the financial sector and the real economy. Some researchers have recognized the dynamic behavior in the economy as producing nonlinearities as responses to specific shocks, but this complexity is far from incorporated in the toolkit of central bankers.

Annex 4B: Identification of Financial Instability Risks

Many different approaches have been developed to identify and better understand potential vulnerabilities and systemic risks. Part of the literature focus on early indicator models, while other studies search for the main stylized economic patterns associated with past precrisis periods. Both may be useful as tools to identify fragilities and motivate preemptive action before crises.

Qualitative and quantitative intelligence can be very useful to better advise and improve policy making, but determining timing and triggers is more difficult. In general, quantitative indicators are based on aggregate or sectors/institutions data. One set of measures commonly used is the estimates of deviations of variables from their long-term trends, for example, credit-to-GDP, housing prices, and equity prices. Intuitively, as an economy moves away from its trend, the probability of building up imbalances increases, and consequently the chances of a crisis also rise. However, there are doubts about the capacity of these models to produce valid out-of-sample forecasts (BCBS 2012)—among other reasons because structural changes may explain the apparent deviation from the trend. Another group of indicators uses micro data, for example, balance sheet data, banks' capital and liquidity positions, and distance-to-default ratios. These indicators are constructed from medians, means, or correlations.

The IMF's early warning exercise (EWE) is a systematic effort to combine quantitative analysis of vulnerabilities and transmission channels with feedback from financial professionals, academics, and policy makers (IMF 2010). The models and indicators are grouped in three blocks: sectoral and market vulnerabilities, country risk, and systemic implications. The first block assesses external-sector risks (for example, cross-border capital flows, external imbalances, and exchange-rate misalignments), fiscal risks (for example, rollover and financing risks, market perception of sovereign risk, and sensitivity of the public sector to shocks), corporate sector risks (for example, leverage and liquidity, and profitability), asset price and market valuation (for example, real estate and equity market bubbles), and financial market risk attitudes (for example, asset and market volatility and the global financial stability map). The second block of models intends to empirically quantify macro tail risks and worst outcomes, attributing probabilities. Finally, in the third block, systemic implications from models of cross-border bank contagion and distress dependence framework are drawn from financial market data. Large complex financial institutions and different global scenario simulations are also considered in this block.

Another initiative is the financial stress index (FSI), which aggregates five indicators: the spread of the three-month interbank rate over government bills for the same maturity, negative quarterly equity returns multiplied by minus one, realized volatility on the equity index, the same indicator for nominal exchange rate, and the volatility of the yield in the three-month government bill. Duca and Peltonen (2011) did a "quartile" standardization to create an indicator between zero and three, in which higher values mean deeper stress. Then, optimal thresholds for policy interventions were calculated for standalone indicators and probabilities of systemic events. Their results showed that asset price misalignments and credit booms are useful leading indicators for systemic events and that models outperform standalone indicators because they consider domestic and global macro financial vulnerabilities.

The Self-Organizing Financial Stability Map (SOFSM) is another tool to identify vulnerabilities. The changing nature of the numerical forecasts motivated this initiative. The effort was the "development of tools with clear visual capabilities

Dealing with the Challenges of Macro Financial Linkages in Emerging Markets
http://dx.doi.org/10.1596/978-1-4648-0002-3

to complement numerical predictions." (ECB 2010, 1). SOFSM allows a two-dimensional representation of a multidimensional financial stability space in colorful maps. The systemic financial crisis metrics is based on a financial stress index from Duca and Peltonen (2011), as mentioned earlier.

Another example of a visual instrument is illustrated in IMF (2010), as the early-warning exercise results are aggregated depending on the number of flags in each sector, considering the distance of the current situation in standard deviations from the models' forecast. Then each sector assessments are aggregated with equal weights to an overall rating. Colors (red, orange, or green) are attributed to different levels of vulnerabilities. In the case of missing data and/or models, judgment and qualitative feedback are used to provide a final country rating.

Notes

1. The concept of *flexible inflation targeting* refers to a credible central bank committed to stabilize inflation at an explicit or implicit target in the long run, but that may also be pursued to stabilize output around its natural rate level in the short run, as per Svensson (1997) and Mishkin (2011). Very recently, Woodford (2011) proposed an extension of this concept, arguing that objectives for financial stability, inflation, and output gap may be balanced jointly when setting short-term interest rates.

2. Some debate about exactly how low low inflation should be emerged after the onset of the current financial crisis (Blanchard, Dell'Ariccia, and Mauro 2010). Many central bankers have worked with inflation targets around 2 percent as an optimum (Romer and Romer 2002). However, in deflationary recessions, a *lower bound for nominal interest rates* could become an additional constraint to stimulate the economy, as nominal interest target rates cannot go below zero. A liquidity trap may likely emerge in the context of severe financial crises, as the effectiveness of monetary policy through short-term interest rate manipulation becomes limited when a lower bound is reached. Although no central banker would advocate in favor of high inflation, it is difficult to assess the marginal cost of 1 or 2 percent higher inflation relative to the benefit of having an additional buffer for extreme crises. In emerging markets, where credibility is often a work in progress and inflation targets are often higher, the potential cost of permanently higher inflation should overcome the flexibility gains in situations of extreme crisis.

3. It is worth noticing however the dissent already expressed by behavioral economists who were then putting some doubts in people's capacity to correctly assess money illusion, arguing that monetary policy could have an even more significant effectiveness by exploring this friction, as later systematized by Akerlof and Shiller (2010).

4. A time-inconsistency problem appears when policy makers prefer one policy in advance but a different one when the time comes to it. In the context of monetary policy, policy makers may want to announce their commitment to low-inflation targets years ahead. However, once in a high-inflation environment today, policy makers move away from incurring costs of disinflation. Because private decision makers would recognize this inconsistent conduct, the announcement would be worthless.

5. de la Torre and Ize (2009) offer a three-pronged approach to factors underlying the global financial boom-bust cycle: "(i) managers of financial institutions understood the risks they were taking but made the bet because they thought they could capture the upside windfalls and leave the downside risks to others (*the agency paradigm*);

(ii) managers understood the risks they were taking, yet went ahead because they did not internalize the social risks and costs of their actions (*the externalities paradigm*); and (iii) managers did not fully understand the risks they were running into; instead, they reacted emotionally to a constantly evolving, uncertain world of rapid financial innovation, with an excess of optimism on the way up and, once unexpected icebergs were spotted on the path, a gripping fear of the unknown on the way down (*the mood swings paradigm*)" (de la Torre and Ize 2009, 2).

6. "Any effective scheme would need to have a number of features. First, it would identify the correct timing for the accumulation and release of the capital buffer. This means correctly identifying good and bad times. Second, it would ensure that the size of the buffer built up in good times is sufficiently large to absorb losses without triggering serious strains. Third, it would be robust to regulatory arbitrage, including manipulation. Fourth, it would be enforceable internationally. Fifth, it would be as rule-based as possible, acting as an automatic stabilizer. In particular, this would ease the pressure on prudential authorities to refrain from taking restrictive measures in good times. Sixth, it should have a low cost of implementation. Finally, it would be simple and transparent." Drehmann and others (2010, 1).

7. A series of quantitative exercises conducted by the BCBS has assessed the impact of the cyclicality of capital requirements regimes taking risk-sensitivity into account. One of the methodologies used adjusted for the compression of probability of default (PD) estimates in the internal ratings based approach during benign credit conditions by using PD estimates for a bank's portfolios in downturns. Using higher PD (for risk) during upturns would provide—by subtraction with actual data—an estimate of cyclical effects.

8. Appropriate models that account for how macro prudential tools affect monetary policy transmission are fundamental to such coordinated policies. Bean and others (2010) show that variations on incentives to banks' capital offer better outcomes than the stand-alone use of monetary policy to lean against bubbles. Agénor, Koray, and Pereira da Silva (2011) develop a general-equilibrium framework for analyzing a similar issue. They conclude that if monetary policy can react strongly to deviations of inflation from target, the best policy is an aggressive augmented interest rate rule—regardless of the degree of persistence in the policy rate. If monetary policy cannot react sufficiently strongly (because the central bank fears destabilizing markets by raising interest rates sharply while inflation remains subdued, for instance), combining a credit-augmented interest rate rule and a countercyclical capital regulatory rule is optimal for promoting economic stability.

9. Asset price booms and busts may be transmitted without actual capital flows, not only indirectly through synthetic operations that may not require cash transfers, but also through pure contagion of expectations and risk behavior. In the latter case, macro and micro prudential tools as well as macroeconomic policies are obviously the means to deal with them.

10. Recently, for example, "because the creation of new assets in developing countries will be slower than the increase in demand for them, the price of existing assets in those markets—equities, bonds, real estate, and human capital—are likely to overshoot their long-term equilibrium value. Recent history is full of examples of the negative side-effects that can arise" (Canuto 2011b, 1).

11. Garcia (2011) shows how sterilized interventions by the central bank in an inflation-targeting regime tend to have an expansionary effect on aggregate demand. This is, for example, the case when capital inflows correspond to a strong demand for domestic

private assets. This means that full sterilization of domestic monetary impacts may ultimately need a local-currency bond purchase larger than the size of the original foreign exchange acquisition. See more on sterilization later in this section.

12. Klein (2012, 2) has found a distinction of effects between "long-standing controls on a wide range of assets and episodic controls that are imposed and removed." The former contribute to lower values of variables related to financial vulnerability, while that is not the case with the latter. Furthermore, "neither long-standing nor episodic controls significantly affect exchange rates." These results are consistent with findings that show decreasing effectiveness of controls with higher degrees of domestic financial sophistication and international integration. These features make easier the development of circumvent strategies, which anyway tend to appear as time elapses.

13. See Ghosh, del Mazo, and Ötker-Robe (2012) on recent developments of "shadow banking" in some emerging markets, although with forms and nature very different than the case of advanced economies.

14. "(…) there is an element of externality in capital controls in that one country's success in evading capital inflows only increases the difficulty of other countries doing the same. This is certainly a problem at the level of emerging markets as a group." (CIEPR 2011, 27).

15. Alfaro and Drehmann (2009) investigated the reasons for the poor performance of macro stress tests by comparing the outcomes of these tests with actual events for a large sample of historical banking crises.

16. See for instance Gelain, Lansing, and Mendicino (2012), as an alternative approach to the standard DSGE with fully rational expectations, intended to capture the links between asset prices, credit expansion, and real economic activity in a more realistic model.

17. Angelini, Neri, and Paneta (2012) discussed the interactions between monetary and macro prudential policies and also potential gains to jointly manage them.

References

Agénor, P. R., A. Koray, and L. Pereira da Silva. 2011. "Capital Regulation, Monetary Policy and Financial Stability." Working Paper 237, Central Bank of Brazil, April.

Agénor, P. R., and L. Pereira da Silva. 2012. "Macroeconomic Stability, Financial Stability, and Monetary Policy Rules." *International Finance* 15-2: 205–24.

Akerlof, G., and R. Shiller. 2010. *Animal Spirits: How Human Psychology Drives the Economy, and Why It Matters for Global Capitalism*. Princeton, NJ: Princeton University Press.

Alfaro, R., and M. Drehmann. 2009. "Macro Stress Tests and Crises: What Can We Learn?" *Bank for International Settlements Quarterly Review* December: 29–41.

Angelini, P., S. Neri, and F. Paneta. 2012. "Monetary and Macroprudential Polices." Working Paper Series 1449, European Central Bank, July.

BCBS (Basel Committee on Banking Supervision). 2010. *An Assessment of the Long-Term Impact of Stronger Capital and Liquidity Requirements*. Basel, Switzerland: Bank for International Settlements.

———. 2011. *Basel III: A Global Regulatory Framework for More Resilient Banks and Banking Systems*. Basel, Switzerland: Bank for International Settlements.

———. 2012. "Models and Tools for Macroprudential Analysis." Working Paper 21, Bank for International Settlements, Basel, Switzerland.

Bank of England. 2009. "The Role of Macroprudential Policy." Discussion Paper, Bank of England, London.

Bean, C., M. Paustian, A. Penalver, and T. Taylor. 2010. "Monetary Policy after the Fall." Federal Reserve Bank of Kansas City, Jackson Hole Symposium, August 28.

Bernanke, B. 1983. "Nonmonetary Effects of the Financial Crisis in Propagation of the Great Depression." *American Economic Review* 73 (3): 257–76.

———. 2010. "Monetary Policy and the Housing Bubble." Remarks at the American Economic Association Meetings, Atlanta, GA, January.

Bernanke, B., and M. Gertler. 2000. "Monetary Policy and Asset Price Volatility." Working Paper 7559, National Bureau of Economic Research, Cambridge, MA.

Bernanke, B., M. Gertler, and S. Gilchrist. 1999. "The Financial Accelerator in a Quantitative Business Cycle Framework." In *Handbook of Macroeconomics*, vol. 1, part 3, edited by edited by John B. Taylor and Michael Woodford, 1341–93. Amsterdam: North-Holland.

Blanchard, O., G. Della'Ariccia, and P. Mauro. 2010. "Rethinking Macroeconomic Policy." Staff Position Note 10/03, International Monetary Fund, Washington, DC.

Blinder, A. 2010. "How Central Should the Central Bank Be?" *Journal of Economic Literature* 48 (1): 123–33.

Borio, C. 2011. "Implementing a Macroprudential Framework: Blending Boldness and Realism." *Capitalism and Society* 6 (1): article 1.

Borio, C., and I. Shim. 2007. "What Can (Macro-)Prudential Policy do to Support Monetary Policy?" Working Paper 242, Bank for International Settlements, Basel, Switzerland.

Brahmbhatt, M., O. Canuto, and S. Ghosh. 2010. "Currency Wars Yesterday and Today." Economic Premise 43, World Bank, Washington, DC, December. www.worldbank. org/economicpremise.

Brunnermeier, M., and Y. Sannikov. 2009. "A Macroeconomic Model with a Financial Sector." Princeton University. http://www.princeton.edu/~markus/research/papers/ macro_finance.pdf.

Calderon, C., and L. Serven. 2011. "Macro-Prudential Policies over the Cycle in Latin America." Paper presented at the Latin American and Caribbean Economic Association and Latin American Meeting of the Econometric Society—2012 Annual Meetings, Lima, Peru, November 1–3.

Calomiris, C. 1993. "Financial Factors in the Great Depression." *Journal of Economic Perspectives* 7: 61–85.

Canuto, O. 2010. "Recoupling or Switchover? Developing Economies in the Global Economy." In *The Day after Tomorrow: A Handbook on the Future of Economic Policy in the Developing World*, edited by edited by O. Canuto and M. Giugale, 29–49. Washington, DC: World Bank.

Canuto, O. 2011a. "How Complementary Are Monetary Policy and Prudential Regulation?" Economic Premise 60, World Bank, Washington, DC, June. www.worldbank.org/ economicpremise.

Canuto, O. 2011b. "Risky Growth Engines." Project Syndicate, January 21.

Canuto, O., C. Garcia-Kilroy, and A. C. Silva. 2012a. "The New Financial Landscape: What It Means for Emerging Market Economies." Economic Premise 87, August, World Bank, Washington, DC. www.worldbank.org/economicpremise.

Caruana, J. 2010. "Macroprudential Policy: Working towards a New Consensus." Remarks presented at the high-level meeting, "The Emerging Framework for Financial Regulation and Monetary Policy," jointly organized by the Bank for International Settlements's Financial Stability Institute and the International Monetary Fund Institute, Washington, DC, April 23.

CGFS (Committee on the Global Financial System). 2010. "Macroprudential Instruments and Frameworks: A Stocktaking of Issues and Experiences." CGFS Paper 38, Bank for International Settlements, Basel, Switzerland.

CIEPR (Committee on International Economic Policy and Reform). 2011. *Rethinking Central Banking.* Washington, DC: Brookings Institution.

Cihak, M. 2007. "Introduction to Applied Stress Testing." Working Paper 07/59, International Monetary Fund, Washington, DC.

Claessens, Stijn, and Swati R. Ghosh. 2012. "Financial Regulations on International Capital Flows and Exchange Rates." EWC/KDI Conference on Financial Regulations on International Capital Flows and Exchange Rates. The East-West Center and the Korea Development Institute, Honolulu, Hawaii.

de la Torre, A., and A. Ize. 2009. "Regulatory Reform: Integrating Paradigm." Policy Research Working Paper Series 4842, World Bank, Washington, DC.

Drehmann, M., C. Borio, L. Gambacorta, G. Jimenez, and C. Trucharte. 2010. "Countercyclical Capital Buffers: Exploring Options." Working Paper 317, Bank for International Settlements, Basel, Switzerland.

Duca, M., and P. Peltonen. 2011. "Macro-Financial Vulnerabilities and Future Financial Stress: Assessing Systemic Risks and Predicting Systemic Events." Working Paper Series 1311, European Central Bank.

ECB (European Central Bank). 2010. "Financial Stability Review." Frankfurt, December.

Financial Services Authority. 2009. "The Turner Review: A Regulatory Response to the Global Banking Crisis." International Swaps and Derivatives Association, Inc., London.

Frankel, J. A. 2009. "What's In and Out in Global Money." Finance and Development, International Monetary Fund, September.

Friedman, M. 1968. "The Role of Monetary Policy." *American Economic Review* 58: 1–17.

Friedman, M., and D. Meiselman. 1963. "The Relative Stability of Monetary Velocity and the Investment Multiplier in the United States, 1897–1958." In *Stabilization Policies,* edited by a Series of Research Studies Prepared for the Commission on Money and Credit, 165–268. Englewood Cliffs, NJ: Prentice-Hall.

Friedman, M., and A. Schwartz. 1963. *A Monetary History of the United States, 1867–1960.* Cambridge, MA: National Bureau of Economic Research.

Galati, G., and R. Moessner. 2011. "Macroprudential Policy—A Literature Review." Working Paper 337, Bank for International Settlements, Basel, Switzerland.

Garcia, Marcio G. P. 2011. "Can Sterilized FX Purchases under Inflation Targeting Be Expansionary?" Department of Economics, Pontificia Universidade Catolica do Rio de Janeiro, April.

Gelain, P. K. Lansing, and C. Mendicino. 2012. "House Prices, Credit Growth, and Excess Volatility: Implications for Monetary and Macroprudential Policy." Working Paper 2012–11, Federal Reserve Bank of San Francisco.

GFSR (Global Financial Stability Report). 2010. *International Monetary Fund—World Economic and Financial Surveys, October.* Washington, DC: International Monetary Fund.

Ghosh, S., I. Gonzalez del Mazo, and I. Ötker-Robe. 2012. "Chasing the Shadows: How Significant Is Shadow Banking in Emerging Markets?" Economic Premise 88, World Bank, Washington, DC, September.

Goodhart, C. 2011. "The Macro-Prudential Authority: Powers, Scope and Accountability." *OECD Journal: Financial Market Trends* 2011 (2): 1–26.

Goodhart, C., and E. Perotti. 2012. "Preventive Macroprudential Policy." *VoxEu* (blog). http://www.voxeu.org/article/preventive-macroprudential-policy.

Hanson, S., A. Kashyap, and J. Stein. 2011. "A Macroprudential Approach to Financial Regulation." *Journal of Economic Perspectives* 25 (1): 3–28.

IIF (Institute of International Finance). 2012a. "Capital Flows to Emerging Economies." Research Note, June.

———. 2012b. "'Shadow Banking': A Forward-Looking Framework for Effective Policy." Research Paper, June.

IMF (International Monetary Fund). 2009. "Lessons for Monetary Policy from Asset Price Fluctuations." World Economic Outlook, October.

———. 2010. "The IMF FSB Early Warning Exercise: Design and Methodological Toolkit." International Monetary Fund. www.imf.org/external/np/exr/facts/ewe.htm

Klein, M. W. 2012. "Capital Controls: Gates and Walls." Paper presented at the Fall 2012 Brookings Panel on Economic Activity, Washington, DC, September 13–14.

Koenker, R., and K. Hallock. 2001. "Quantile Regression." *Journal of Economic Perspectives* 15 (4): 143–56.

Lim, C., F. Columba, A. Costa, P. Kongsamut, A. Otani, M. Saiyid, T. Wezel, and X. Wu. "Macroprudential Policy: What Instruments and How to Use Them?" Working Paper 11/238, International Monetary Fund, Washington, DC.

Magud, N., and C. Reinhart. 2006. "Capital Controls: An Evaluation." Working Paper 11973, National Bureau of Economic Research, Cambridge, MA.

Mishkin, F. 2009. "Will Monetary Policy Become More of a Science? " In *Monetary Policy Over Fifty Years: Experiences and Lessons*, edited by D. Bundesbank, 81–107. London: Routledge.

———. 2011. "Monetary Policy Strategy: Lessons from the Crisis." Working Paper 16755, National Bureau of Economic Research, Cambridge, MA.

Mishkin, F., and N. Westelius. 2008. "Inflation Band Targeting and Optimal Inflation Contracts." *Journal of Money, Credit and Banking* 40 (4): 557–82.

Mussa, M. 1981. *The Role of Official Intervention*. New York: Group of Thirty.

Ostry, J., A. Ghosh, K. Habermeier, M. Chamon, M. Qureshi, and D. Reinhardt. "Capital Inflows: The Role of Controls, 2010." Staff Position Note 10/04, International Monetary Fund, Washington, DC.

Perotti, E., and J. Suarez. 2009. "Liquidity Risk Charges as a Macroprudential Tool." Policy Insight 40, November, Center for Economic Policy Research, London.

Phelps, E. 1968. "Money-Wage Dynamics and Labor Market Equilibrium." *Journal of Political Economy* 76 (S4): 678–711.

Romer, C., and D. Romer. 2002. "The Evolution of Economic Understanding and Postwar Stabilization Policy." Rethinking Stabilization Policy. Proceedings, Federal Reserve Bank of Kansas City, 11–78.

Sarno, L., and M. Taylor. 2001. "Official Intervention in the Foreign Exchange Market: Is It Effective and, If So, How Does It Work?" *Journal of Economic Literature* 39 (3): 839–68.

Schmieder, C., C. Puhr, and M. Hasan. 2011. "Next Generation Balance Sheet Stress Testing." Working Paper 11/83, International Monetary Fund, Washington, DC.

Stiglitz, E., and A. Weiss. 1981. "Credit Rationing in Markets with Imperfect Information." *American Economic Review* 71 (3): 393–410.

Svensson, L. 1997. "Optimal Inflation Targets, 'Conservative' Central Banks, and Linear Inflation Contracts." *American Economic Review* 87 (March): 98–114.

———. 2005. "Monetary Policy with Judgement: Forecast Targeting." Discussion Paper 5072, Center for Economic Policy Research, London.

———. 2010. "Inflation Targeting and Financial Stability." Policy Lecture at the Center for Economic Policy Research/European Summer Institute 14th Annual Conference, "How Has Our View of Central Banking Changed with the Recent Financial Crisis?" Central Bank of Turkey, Izmir, October 28–29.

Taylor, J. B. 1993. "Discretion versus Policy Rules in Practice." *Carnegie-Rochester Conference Series on Public Policy* 39: 195–214.

———. 2009. *Getting Off Track: How Government Actions and Interventions Caused, Prolonged and Worsened the Financial Crisis.* Stanford: Hoover Institution Press.

Woodford, M. 2003. *Interest and Prices: Foundations of a Theory of Monetary Policy.* Princeton, NJ: Princeton University Press.

———. 2011. "Inflation Targeting and Financial Stability." Speech at Einaudi Institute for Economics and Finance, Rome.

Wyplosz, C. 2009. "What Do We Know about Monetary Policy that Friedman Did Not Know?" Working Paper 63, Commission on Growth and Development, Washington, DC.

CHAPTER 5

Macro Prudential Policies to Mitigate Financial Vulnerabilities in Emerging Markets

Stijn Claessens, Swati R. Ghosh, and Roxana Mihet*

Introduction

This chapter analyzes the use of macro prudential policies (MaPPs) aimed at reducing vulnerabilities in banking systems, with a special focus on their use in and for emerging markets (EMs). Recent events have highlighted the high costs of financial crises. More generally, the potential for instability arising from the financial system—whether from excessiveness in cycles or from spillovers through interconnectedness—is increasingly being recognized. Accordingly, there is a growing interest in the potential for MaPPs to complement micro prudential regulations and traditional macroeconomic management policies, notably monetary policy and fiscal policy, to help contain (the buildup of) systemic risks and achieve greater financial stability, and in this way reduce adverse consequences of financial volatility—including from crises—for the real economy.

Whereas many analyses have been motivated by the (ongoing) crisis in advanced countries (ACs), EMs have had much greater experience with MaPPs in recent years, in part because they have had more pronounced business and financial cycles, partly because of their greater exposures to volatile international capital flows, commodity price shocks, and other risks. In this context, there is much for ACs to learn from EMs about the effectiveness of MaPPs. And there are, of course, lessons for EMs themselves.

* **Stijn Claessens** is Assistant Director with the Research Department at the International Monetary Fund. **Swati R. Ghosh** is an Adviser with the Poverty Reduction and Economic Management Vice Presidency, World Bank. **Roxana Mihet** is at Oxford University. The analysis in this chapter is based in part on a paper prepared for the National Institute of Public Finance and Policy-Department of Economic Affairs-Journal of International Money and Finance conference, Rajasthan, India, December 12–13, 2012. The authors are grateful to Lindsay Mollineaux for research assistance. The views expressed here are those of the authors and should not be attributed to the International Monetary Fund or the World Bank, or their respective Executive Directors or Management.

The chapter, therefore, asks the following questions. What are the specific market failures and externalities that can motivate the use of MaPPs to reduce systemic risks? What are the key MaPPs available to countries to reduce systemic risks? Which MaPPs have countries actually used and what is the evidence to date on the effectiveness of different MaPPs to reduce financial system vulnerabilities?

Most studies on the use and effectiveness of MaPPs take an aggregate perspective, that is, they investigate the effects of MaPPs either at the overall economic or at the financial sector level, for example, on leverage or credit growth or the occurrence of a financial crisis, or at the level of a subsector, such as real estate. We review empirical evidence on the role of MaPPs in limiting vulnerabilities in individual banks (and thereby overall banking systems) over the past decade. Because this work uses a large sample of countries, it allows for analysis of differences in country circumstances and conditions, including between ACs and EMs, and between relatively open and closed capital account economies. It is able to differentiate by type of MaPP and by the phase of the financial cycle—upswings or downswings.

This work finds that macro prudential policies aimed at the borrowers—caps on debt-to-income (DTI) and loan-to-value (LTV) ratios—are quite effective in (indirectly) reducing banking system vulnerabilities. Also, limits on foreign currency lending are effective in reducing vulnerabilities in boom times. Although countercyclical buffers (such as reserve requirements, restrictions on profit distribution, and dynamic provisioning) also help mitigate increases in bank leverage and asset growth (dimensions of financial sector vulnerability), few macro prudential tools help stop declines in these bank variables in adverse times.

We interpret the fact that demand-oriented measures aimed at the real estate markets are consistently effective in addressing financial-sector vulnerabilities as indicative of two facts: one, real estate cycles are an important aspect of overall financial cycles that often trigger major concerns about systemic banking risks, thus making these measures important; and two, addressing demand for credit directly can be effective in reducing banking system vulnerabilities because it faces fewer problems of implementation, including circumventions.

The results suggest that macro prudential tools are best used as ex ante tools, that is, for reducing the buildup in bank risks in boom periods, rather than for mitigating declines when the cycle turns. Although macro prudential policies can help lessen a systemic crunch by providing buffers so that banks do not (need to) reduce leverage, assets, and noncore liabilities as much during bad times, in practice these effects are absent, or not very strong. We also conjecture that some macro prudential policies aimed at mitigating the buildup of financial vulnerabilities (including caps on LTV and DTI) can work perversely during financial downturns if not sufficiently lowered because they make adjustments more difficult. As such, macro prudential policies need to be properly calibrated and adjusted.

We conclude that MaPPs can be important elements of the policy toolkit aimed at overall systemic risk mitigation, especially for EMs exposed to international shocks. However, we note that in as much as MaPPs affect resource allocations, they can also entail costs. Poorly designed or wrongly implemented, MaPP tools can be circumvented and imply further distortions. We therefore argue that to provide their full benefits, MaPPs need to be properly chosen and carefully calibrated depending on country and financial system characteristics, including capital account openness, and adjusted as circumstances change.

This chapter is structured as follows. Motivated by the case of EMs, the first section discusses the conceptual rationale for MaPPs in general, as well as the various MaPPs that can be used to deal with specific risks and shocks, depending on a country's structural features and macroeconomic and financial sector conditions. The next section reviews empirical evidence on the use of MaPPs and the effectiveness of different instruments in reducing banking system vulnerabilities. The final section concludes, with reference to EMs' current situations, prospects and vulnerabilities, on whether and how MaPPs can best be used.

Why Macro Prudential Regulations May Be Needed and the Actual Toolkit

The global financial crisis has highlighted that, even with macroeconomic stability, using a judicious mix of micro prudential regulation, supervision, and market discipline to address potential risks at the level of individual financial institutions—even if well-designed and implemented—does not ensure financial stability. Because of externalities, private costs and benefits of the actions of individual financial institutions and agents can diverge from their social values. Measures that focus on individuals' actions and institutions' stability alone do not suffice to limit a buildup of systemic risk. Furthermore, some policies, including micro prudential regulations, although important for public policy objectives at the individual institution's level, can lead to behavior that creates systemic risks. Neither is traditional macroeconomic management, notably monetary policy and fiscal policy, necessarily able nor the most effective to contain (the buildup of) systemic risks, especially not for EMs (see Ghosh 2010; Claessens and Ghosh forthcoming).

Although the benefits of a broader approach has been recognized by some, notably at the Bank for International Settlements (BIS),[1] it is only recently that policy makers and academics have started to acknowledge the need to use policy instruments that target the soundness of the financial system as a whole. In this context, MaPPs are promising in principle, as academic research has also highlighted (for an early analytical review of the need for MaPPs, see Brunnermeier and others 2009; see also Hanson, Kayshap, and Stein 2011, and De Nicolò, Favara, and Ratnovski 2012).

Their use, however, requires a clear identification of the aspects of systemic risks that need to be addressed and their fundamental causes. Systemic risk can be cyclical—whereby financial institutions and markets overexpose themselves to risks in the upswing of the financial cycle and then become overly risk averse in the downswing, rendering the entire financial system and economy vulnerable to booms and busts. Or it can be cross sectional—whereby the actions and problems of individuals or financial institutions can have spillover effects on the overall financial system. Although both types of risks can arise from externalities and market failures, the appropriate policy tools differ between the two (Allen and Carletti 2011; Bank of England 2011; De Nicolò, Favara, and Ratnovski 2012; and Schoenmaker and Wierts 2011 provide similar classifications of sources of systemic risks and related policy measures).

The use of MaPPs will also depend on the availability and efficacy of other policy instruments—notably monetary, fiscal, micro prudential and capital flow management (CFM) policies ("capital controls") that can help address these risks.

Research has made less progress in developing robust advice to help choose the proper MaPP and calibrate its design (for example, the level of a capital surcharge or loan-to-value limit). Whereas recent work on capital account liberalization (IMF 2011b; Ostry and others 2011) has helped clarify in which types of countries and circumstances CFM tools can be useful, equivalent analysis and framing are yet to happen for MaPPs.

Procyclicality

The financial sector is inherently procyclical, that is, it amplifies the business cycle.[2] The two-way interactions between the financial sector and real sector "causing" this procyclicality largely operate through changes in the values of assets and leverage. A positive shock (such as a productivity shock) increases the value of a bank's assets (for example, loans and securities), and if the bank targets a desired leverage ratio, it will increase its asset holdings in response to the increase in asset value. Faced with a common shock, if all financial institutions do the same thing, the increased demand for assets raises their prices, further fuelling the cycle and leading to a generalized expansion of credit.

In the process, banks' balance sheet structure can become more vulnerable to shocks (or a downturn in the economy) through a range of balance sheet mismatches and weaknesses. These mismatches include rising leverage ratios, maturity mismatches and, especially in the case of EMs and developing countries, foreign exchange (FX) mismatches. On the liability side, the ratio of noncore-to-core funding tends to rise. As banks seek to expand their balance sheets, they generally turn to noncore funding since the more stable core (mainly deposits) liabilities tend to be more sluggish (see Hahm, Shin, and Shin 2012 for a model and empirical analysis of how an increase in noncore-to-core funding is often a precursor to financial crises).

Once the financial system as a whole becomes more leveraged, it becomes vulnerable to shocks such as sudden withdrawals of funds, stops in capital inflows, or changes in asset prices. Indeed, even small shocks such as slight increases in borrower defaults or small declines in collateral values during a downturn can trigger systemwide problems. If equity buffers are insufficient to absorb losses, for example, banks may be forced to deleverage, in turn creating systemwide declines in the supply of external financing. Or a negative shock that shakes depositors' confidence can expose banks to the risk of runs, forcing them to hoard liquidity or sell assets at depressed market prices to meet withdrawals, if the systemwide maturity transformation (lending long and borrowing short) or reliance on wholesale funds is high. Negative externalities related to fire sales can then come into play because a generalized sell off of financial assets causes a decline in asset prices, which in turn further impairs the balance sheets of intermediaries amplifying the contractionary phase of the cycle.

It is also possible that instead of, or in addition to, selling financial assets to regain liquidity and improve capital ratios, banks may reduce new credit extension, ration credit via higher margins/haircuts or raise interest rates or other costs to borrowers (externalities related to credit crunches). Such deleveraging via reduced credit extension will have general effects because the economic slowdown adversely affects borrowers by lowering output and prices. This situation raises the probability of default for all other borrowers and can set off a cycle of adverse effects on the real economy, again further amplifying banking-sector losses.

Positive (negative) exogenous shocks, which can be one trigger of a financial sector upturn (or downturn), can then get amplified through financial-sector frictions and the factors discussed earlier. There is also increasing recognition in the literature of the possible role of collective cognition, in which the dynamics are endogenous to the financial development process itself and get amplified by experience-based expectations. Thus, faced with the new and unknown (say, following a financial innovation and improving economy), market participants can be subject to waves of optimism and exuberance. At some point, however, a significant dissonance initiates a mood swing fueled on the downturn by acute uncertainty aversion (de la Torre, Ize, and Schmukler 2012).

Although the financial sector, thus, naturally exhibits procyclicality, several factors can amplify the buildup and heighten vulnerability by accentuating procyclical behavior, encouraging greater risk taking, or inducing correlated behavior (figure 5.1).[3]

Some aspects of micro prudential regulation, although intended to enhance stability at the level of the individual financial institutions, can actually increase the system's procyclicality. This situation is the case, for instance, with the Basel capital requirements and other micro prudential regulations designed to ease agency problems or frictions by providing some "skin in the game" (and buffers against unexpected shocks).[4] Even under the essentially flat capital requirements of Basel I, bank capital regulation had the potential to be procyclical because bank profits may turn negative during recessions, impairing banks' lending capacity. Additionally, the internal ratings-based approach of Basel II makes capital requirements an increasing function of banks' estimates of their loans' probability of default and loss given default, which are both likely to decrease (increase) during upturns (downturns). This approach thus creates procyclicality, especially in downturns when the rules can substantially exacerbate the negative impact of recessions on banks' supply of credit and, thereby, on the economy as whole. Hence, there are many concerns about the procyclicality introduced by rules such as Basel II.[5] Micro prudential regulations may also encourage correlated asset choices across financial institutions—since these regulations assigned similar risk-weights to certain asset classes, thereby favoring preferences of some asset classes over others and encouraging financial institutions to make the same asset choices.

Dealing with the Challenges of Macro Financial Linkages in Emerging Markets
http://dx.doi.org/10.1596/978-1-4648-0002-3

Figure 5.1 Factors That Can Lead to Systemic Risks and the Need for MaPPs

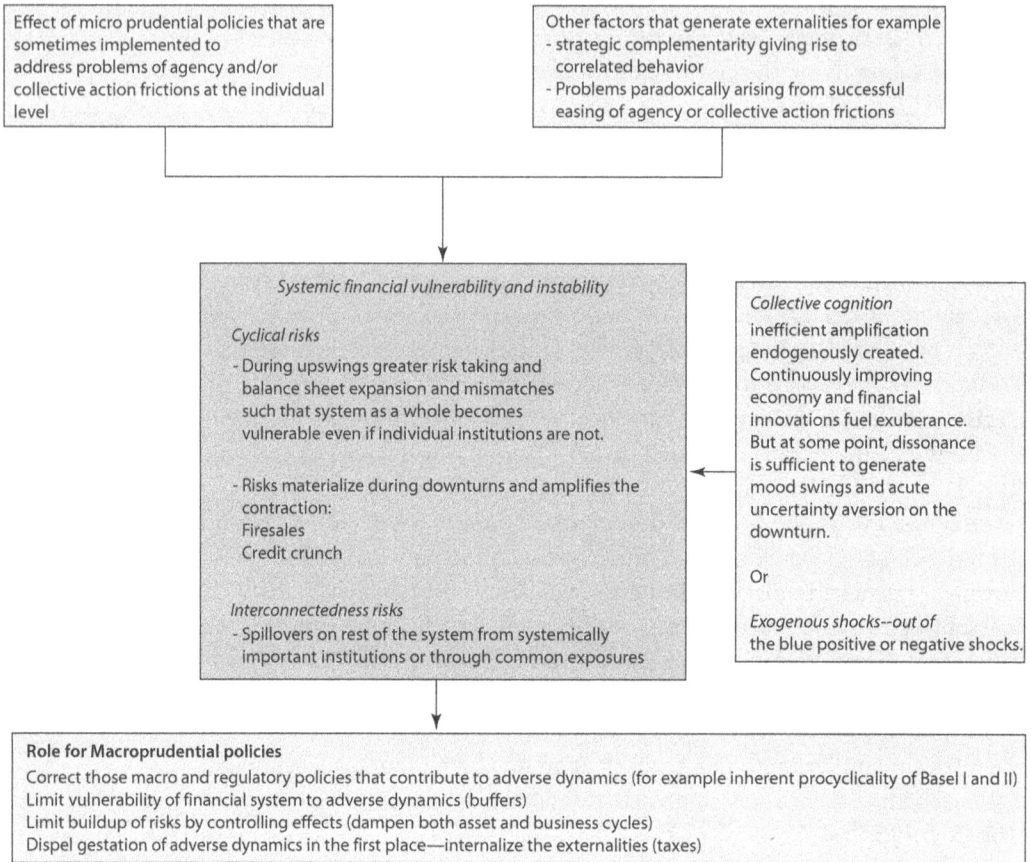

Some (nonprudential) policies or practices aimed at reducing agency and/or participation frictions can also increase risk-taking and procyclicality.[6] For instance, remuneration contracts of managers commonly include a variable, performance-related component to better align the incentives between managers (agents) and shareholders (principals). However, the asymmetry of such schemes—whereby managers are highly paid if they make profits, but are not penalized for losses—can result in greater risk-taking on their part. Similarly, limited liability, which applies to bank shareholders, as it does for any other corporate shareholder, and is designed to foster entrepreneurism (and in the case of the financial sector, participation in financial markets) can encourage greater risk-taking. In particular, limited liability can encourage the use of value-at-risk (VaR) models. Shareholders do not care about tail risks—for an equity holder protected by limited liability, it does not matter whether the firm goes bust marginally or whether it goes bust spectacularly (Shin 2008).[7] Since empirically measured risk (for example, volatility, which directly influences VaR) is low during booms and high during busts, banks expand their balance sheets and increase leverage during upturns and contract their balance sheets and reduce leverage during downturns. Thus adopting VaR encourages procyclical behavior.

Similarly, margins or haircuts that adjust over the cycle can also lead to greater procyclicality, especially in down cycles when margin/haircut spirals can occur.[8]

Some of these practices or policies generate strategic complementarities that lead to or actively encourage correlated behavior among financial institutions and markets and hence increase systemic vulnerability.[9] For instance, correlated behavior can arise as a result of reputational concerns and the incentive structures for bank managers. When bank managers care about market perceptions of their ability, their credit policies are influenced by those of other banks (Rajan 1994). Peer benchmarking can also give rise to correlated behavior because a bank reporting poor performance due to losses will be evaluated harshly unless many other banks suffer losses at the same time. Banks therefore have incentives to roll over bad loans to hide the loans until the buildup of bad loans forces them to coordinate a strategy of loss recognition and credit contraction. The prospect of a government bailout in the event of financial distress can also lead banks to engage in correlated asset choice ex ante. As financial institutions try to mimic each other's strategy—knowing there is safety in numbers—there is an increase in the systemic vulnerabilities of the financial system (De Nicolò, Favara, and Ratnovski 2012).

Attempts at reducing agency, collective action, or participation frictions that, on the one hand, are associated with successful financial development can, on the other hand, paradoxically, exacerbate systemic vulnerability. An example from de La Torre, Ize, and Schmukler (2012) relates to the availability of public information. More public information can reduce the ability to appropriate rents from private information, which eases agency frictions. At the same time, though, it can encourage investors to free ride (leading to a collective action problem). Rather than investing in analysis and monitoring, and staying committed investors may invest short and rely on market liquidity to exit at the first sign of trouble.

Risks from Interconnectedness

The cross sectional dimension of systemic risk arises from the interconnectedness of financial institutions and markets. This interconnectedness can result in a specific shock to an institution or market at a point in time being amplified as it is propagated throughout the system (see Allen and Gale 2007; Diamond and Rajan 2001; Bebchukand Goldstein 2011). The shock may spread through the network of interconnected balance sheets of financial institutions when one systemically important financial institutions (SIFI) is hit, or it can spread because of direct actual or anticipated common exposures of financial institutions to a particular asset class (for example, commercial real estate, or foreign exchange risks) through financial markets and asset prices. Spillovers can also arise because of feedback from the real economy.

Financial institutions can reduce but not entirely eliminate these externalities since the shape of interconnectedness in the financial system is beyond the individual bank's control. Externalities stemming from interconnectedness are particularly strong for SIFIs. Unlike smaller institutions, distressed SIFIs cannot be easily wound down, since they are large and complex, operate internationally, and play a role as backbones of the financial infrastructure. These institutions can then become too important to fail or too big to fail, leading to government subsidies ex ante (because they can attract financing at lower costs) and ex post (because they get bailed out when they run into distress).

Cyclical and interconnectedness risks can interact to exacerbate vulnerabilities. Although links among financial institutions can help them manage risk and distribute funds to where they can be deployed effectively, intrafinancial system activity can also increase the tendency for lending to become excessive during the upswing of a business cycle as discussed earlier. For instance, the dispersion of risks and the increased complexity in the financial system associated with securitization before the financial crisis reduced incentives to screen and monitor lending. This impairment in underwriting standards, in turn, exacerbated the extent of overborrowing in the real economy. Also, funding chains between banks and other financial intermediaries can mean that systemwide maturity transformation may be high, even though maturity transformation at any individual level may appear small.

Linkages within financial systems can also tend to exhibit procyclicality and contribute to time-varying risk in its own right by increasing the potential for contagion during exuberant periods, and increased risk aversion during times of financial turmoil. In particular, for a given level of lending to the real economy, a system that has longer, larger, or more opaque chains of intrafinancial system claims is more prone to amplifying shocks through counterparty risk. Excessive intrafinancial system activity also poses liquidity risks. Because of greater sensitivity to individual firm characteristics and marketwide sentiment, wholesale funding may be particularly flighty and shocks to one or more institutions can propagate withdrawals of funding in interbank and other wholesale markets during times of stress. Most of these risks appear in all types of countries, but with some variation. For ACs, besides domestic financial cycles often related to real estate booms and busts, interconnections among large SIFIs and through financial markets are important drivers of systemic risks. For EMs, with still less developed financial systems with smaller, less systemic banks and fewer interconnections, cyclical risks often related to global financial cycles and capital flows (especially in the form of bank flows) are important drivers of overall risk (see also Shin 2012). For further differences between EMs and ACs in terms of the typical behavior of business and financial cycles, refer to Claessens, Kose, and Terrones (2011a, 2011b).

The Macro Prudential Toolkit

To mitigate these causes of systemic risk, a number of MaPP instruments have been proposed and some have been used, even before the global financial crisis.[10] Table 5.1 categorizes these measures in a matrix (for other classifications of MaPPs, see Bank of England 2011 and IMF 2011a). The matrix's columns show the goals of five groups of MaPP policies and the rows show whether the instruments are

Table 5.1 The Macro Prudential Toolkit

	Policy tool group				
	1	*2*	*3*	*4*	*5*
	Capital requirements, provisioning, surcharges	*Restrictions on financial sector balance sheet (assets, liabilities)*	*Restrictions related to borrower, instrument, or activity*	*Taxation, levies*	*Other measures (including institutional infrastructure)*
Expansionary phase	Countercyclical capital requirements, leverage restrictions, general (dynamic) provisioning	Time varying caps/ limits on: - mismatches (FX, interest rate) - reserve requirements	Time varying caps/ limits/rules on: - DTI, LTI, LTV - margins, hair-cuts - lending to sectors - credit growth	**Levy/tax on specific assets and/or liabilities**	- Accounting (for example, varying rules on mark to market) - Changes to compensation, market discipline, governance
Contractionary phase: fire sales, credit crunch	Countercyclical capital requirements, general (dynamic) provisioning	Liquidity limits (for examples, Net stable funding ratio, Liquidity coverage ratio)	Adjustment to specific loan-loss provisioning, margins or hair-cuts (for example, through the cycle, dynamic)	**Levy/tax (for example, on noncore liabilities)**	- Standardized products - OTC vs. on exchange - Safety net (central bank/ treasury liquidity, fiscal support)
Contagion, or shock propagation from SIFIs or networks	Capital surcharges linked to systemic risk	Institution- specific limits on (bilateral) financial exposures, other balance sheet measures	Varying restrictions on asset composition, activities (e.g., Volcker, Vickers)	Tax/levy varying by externality (size, network)	- Institutional infrastructure (for examle, CCPs) - Resolution (for example, living wills) - Varying information, disclosure

Enhancing resilience

Dampening the cycle

Dispelling gestation of cycle

applied to address cyclical systemic risks (and if so whether on the expansionary or contractionary phase) or systemic risks arising from interconnectedness.

Table 5.1 classifies macro prudential policies by intended target and method in five groups: (1) capital and provisioning requirements; (2) quantitative restrictions on financial institutions' balance sheets; (3) quantitative restrictions on borrowers, instruments, or activities; (4) taxation/levies on activities or balance sheet composition; and (5) other, more institutionally oriented measures, such as accounting changes and changes to compensation. Categories 1, 2, 4, and 5 can be seen as affecting the supply side of financing, whereas category 3 aims to affect the demand for financing. Although this overlap is less precise, tools shaded in dark grey are more aimed at enhancing resilience, those in light grey are more aimed at dampening the cycle, and those in the striped cells are aimed at dispelling the gestation of the cycle

Specific measures under each of the 15 combinations include those correcting or compensating for fundamental factors that can give rise to externalities and market failures and those that compensate for policy factors that can contribute to adverse financial dynamics (such as the procyclicality introduced by micro prudential capital requirements).

The measures in the first four columns are meant to be time-, institution-, or state-varying, while the ones in the fifth column are meant to be more structural. Some measures fall into more than one combination depending on how they are used. As noted, many of the measures are tools traditionally used for micro pru-dential objectives; however, by making them vary by time, institution, or state of the world, they can be used to achieve macro prudential objectives, such as dampening the amplitude of the cycle. We will discuss the more important ones.

Capital requirements, provisioning, surcharges. Capital and provisioning require-ments, in the first column, can have an impact on reducing the amplitude of the upswing of the cycle (first row), but are primarily considered tools for building more resilience in the financial sector (second row). Under Basel III, for example, a countercyclical capital buffer ranging between 0–2.5 percent of risk-weighted capital is to be introduced on top of the capital conservation buffer, when aggre-gate credit and other indicators are judged to signal a buildup of systemic risk.[11] General dynamic provisioning is also a countercyclical tool that builds up a cushion against expected losses in boom times (first row) that can be reversed during the downswing (second row).[12] Both countercyclical requirements could help dampen the effects of externalities associated with strategic complementari-ties in the upswing as well as with externalities related to fire sales and credit contraction in the downswing. A few countries have already used some variant of these measures, allowing for analyses of their effectiveness (see Jimenez and others 2012, for the case of Spain). A capital surcharge on SIFIs (too big to fail) (third row), also proposed under Basel III, is geared toward mitigating the exter-nalities associated with financial institutions' interconnectedness.

Restrictions on financial sector balance sheet. Restrictions on banks' balance sheets, in the second column, are often considered for micro prudential purposes. They can also be used to achieve macro prudential objectives such as dampening the amplitude of the cycle (first and second rows). Measures range from (time varying) restrictions on balance sheet mismatches, such as on foreign exchange mismatches, and maturity mismatches. Reserve requirements that require bank-ing institutions to hold a fraction of their deposits/liabilities as liquid reserves normally held at the central bank in the form of cash or other forms such as government securities, have been used as a liquidity and credit policy tool, that is, as a monetary policy tool. They can, however, also be used as a macro pruden-tial tool to affect asset composition and dampen procyclicality.[13] Reserve require-ments appear to be used that way in EMs and developing countries. Federico, Vegh, and Vuletin (2012), for example, found that in a sample of 52 developing countries 74 percent have used reserve requirements countercyclically. RRs can be applied on liabilities and on assets (the latter would entail holding reserves against different asset classes, with the regulator setting adjustable reserve requirements on the basis of its concern with each asset class, Palley, 2004).

Given the potential risks arising from a liquidity shortage during the contractionary phase, as evidenced during the global financial crisis, the Basel III discussion includes a proposed set of liquidity requirements (second row): the liquidity coverage ratio (LCR) and the net stable funding ratio (NSFR).[14] To reduce buildup of systemic risks and externalities that can arise during the contractionary phase, restrictions on balance sheets can also include countercyclical requirements on noncore-to-core funding, leverage, or other ratios.

Additional measures aim at enhancing the resilience of banking system to reduce risks of spillovers (third row). Here measures can be micro prudential in nature as well, like restrictions on financial institutions' bilateral exposures or other balance sheet limits, but be designed and used with the macro prudential objectives of reducing interconnectedness.

Restrictions related to borrower, instrument, or activity. Measures related to borrowers (third column) in the expansionary phase of the cycle (first row) are typically designed to limit the leverage of borrowers to manage financial institutions' credit risk and include (time varying) caps on LTV ratios (which can also be applied differentially to loans of different characteristics (such as mortgages or central versus peripheral locations) and (time varying) caps on debt-to-income ratios. And caps on credit growth directly address asset growth and the potential risks during the upswing of the financial cycle. These measures can act as a brake on banks' asset growth, but also help to reduce leverage and the impact of declines in asset prices and economic prospects during downturns (second row). Structural measures limiting banks' activities (third row), such as the Volcker rule in the United States and the Vickers rule in the United Kingdom, can limit the risks of spillovers due to interconnections.

Taxation, levies. As proposed by Shin (2010) among others and discussed by IMF (2010), a tax or levy (fourth column) applied to some balance sheets concept can serve to mitigate the externalities that lead to excessive asset growth during the upswing, for example, by limiting risky funding (first and second row). For bank and nonbank financial institutions engaged in market-based activities, macro prudential regulations can take the form of procyclical margin requirements (see, for example, Geanakoplos 2009; Gorton 2009; and Gorton and Metrick 2010). Requiring through-the-cycle margins or haircuts can help mitigate the externalities arising during the expansionary and contractionary phase because it would mean margins remain higher (lower) during upswings (downswings). Also levies on noncore liabilities can help reduce the probability that financial institutions would run into aggregate funding problems in the first instance. Similar to a capital surcharge, a tax can be levied on SIFIs to encourage them to reduce their externalities (third row).

Other measures (including institutional infrastructure). Finally, a wide set of institutional infrastructure changes can serve a macro prudential role (fifth column) as either they limit the frictions or deeper distortions that give rise to financial cycles in the first place (first and second) row or they help reduce the spillovers by building stronger protections (third row). For further discussion of these more institutionally oriented measures, refer to Andritzky et al. (2009).

What MaPPs Have Countries Used and How Effective Have They Been?

The previous two sections discussed the analytical reasons for MaPPs and the specific tools countries can use in principle. The preferred use will vary depending on the country's exposure to shocks and risks, and its structural, institutional, and financial market characteristics that affect the amplification of financial and real sector cycles. The country's financial structure, that is the importance of banks versus capital markets in external financing, is likely to be an important factor in the choice of policy. For example, financial institution-based measures are likely to be of greater importance when much of the external financing comes from the regulated financial system. Such financial structures can differ vastly across countries.

The use and effectiveness of policies could also vary depending on the availability and effectiveness of fiscal, monetary, and micro prudential policies. For example, some countries can use monetary policy to affect the financial cycle, but for others, such as those in a currency union with a pegged exchange rate, this policy is not available (even when available, the effectiveness of monetary policy is not clear). Others may have less room to conduct countercyclical fiscal policy. The degree of financial openness will matter for the choice of policies because it affects the degree to which some policies can be implemented and, more generally, because it determines exposures (for instance, there are strong links between the behavior of capital flows and bank vulnerabilities, as outlined by Hahm, Shin, and Shin 2012 Claessens and Ghosh 2013). Institutional environment constraints (for example, lack of data or expertise), political economy, and other factors may lead countries to adopt MaPPs in ways different from what is preferable. A major issue is that little is known about the actual effectiveness of various MaPPs, thus their use has proceeded on an experimental basis.

This section first reviews the use of MaPPs in a large sample of countries, and then reviews studies on their effectiveness, examining in detail the tools and approaches used to reduce financial vulnerabilities in banking systems.

Use of MaPPs

Data on the use of macro prudential policies in recent years were collected through a survey of country authorities as well as from an internal IMF survey of country desk economists for 48 countries, both ACs and EMs (see Lim and others 2011 for the exact coverage and definitions). Based on these data, 35 countries (10 ACs and 25 EMs) have implemented at least one MaPP instrument during the period 2000–10. The eight specific instruments used were categorized as: caps on loan-to-value (LTV) and debt-to-income (DTI), limits on credit growth (CG), limits on foreign currency (FC), that is, lending limits; reserve requirements (RR), dynamic provisioning (DP), countercyclical requirements (CTC), limits on profit redistribution (PRD), and a residual category (other).[15]

Table 5.2 Overall Use of Macro Prudential Instruments

Type of instrument	Total countries	Frequency of use (percent)	Emerging markets	Advanced economies	Closed capital account	Open capital account	Frequency of EMs-year (5)	Frequency of ACs-year (percent)
	(1)	(2)	(3)	(4)	(5)	(6)	(7)	(8)
Loan-to-value limits (LTV)	24	44	15	9	11	13	35	74
Debt-to-income limits (DTI)	7	9	5	2	4	3	8	11
Credit growth limits (CG)	6	8	5	1	4	2	10	1
Limits on foreign currency lending (FC)	8	8	7	1	4	4	10	3
Reserve requirements (RR)	5	5	5	0	5	0	7	0
Dynamic provisioning (DP)	9	9	8	1	5	4	9	11
Countercyclical capital requirements (CTC)	2	1	2	0	2	0	2	0
Regulations on profit redistribution (PRD)	6	3	6	0	4	2	4	0
Other	13	12	12	1	6	7	15	1
Total by classification	35	100	25	10	15	20	100	100

Note: There were 35 countries using a macro prudential policy at any point during the period 2000–10. Countries are classified into emerging versus advanced economies (IMF 2013) and open versus closed capital account countries (Chin and Ito 2008). A country was defined as an open capital account country if its Chinn-Ito index was larger than the global mean in 2005 and a closed capital account country if its Chinn-Ito index was smaller than the global mean in 2005. The frequency of use is the ratio of country pairs using a particular instrument to the total number of country-year pairs using a macro prudential policy (for example, during 2000–10, 44 percent of the time, countries used caps on LTV ratios compared with only 9 percent of the time using DTI ceilings).

Overall, countries used LTVs the most (table 5.2, column 1): 24 countries used them in at least one year during this period. Next was DPs (9 countries), FCs (8 countries), DTIs (7 countries), and CG caps and PRDs (6 countries); RRs (5 countries); and CTCs (2 countries).

Weighting by the length of time over which the macro prudential policies are used (column 2 in table 5.2), the most often-used policy in the sample of countries was by far the LTV, which was used in about 44 percent of the country-year combinations when a policy was used. Next, besides "other," were four categories used about equally frequently (in about 8 percent of the cases each): DTI, CG caps, FC lending limits, and DP. These policies were followed by RRs (5 percent), PDRs (3 percent), and finally CTCs (1 percent). Note that some countries used more than one policy at a time, making these comparisons relative to the overall use of macro prudential policies.

Use of a specific policy can be expected to vary between advanced countries and emerging markets and between open versus closed capital account countries in part due to the variation in source of systemic risks. In advanced countries, LTVs are used the most (table 5.2, columns 3 and 4). Advanced countries using LTVs over this period were Canada, France, Hong Kong SAR, Italy, the Republic of Korea, Norway, Singapore, Spain, and Sweden. Use of other macro prudential policies by advanced countries is rarer: only Hong Kong SAR and Korea use DTIs; Singapore uses CG limits; Austria, FCs; Spain, DPs; and Norway and

Korea, "other" tools. Whereas LTV caps and foreign currency limits are used almost equally in both open and closed economies, reserve requirements were only used in relatively closed capital account countries (table 5.2, columns 5 and 6). This use of policy tools likely reflects differences in both risk exposures and financial system structures, and possibly the degree of financial liberalization. Otherwise, the differences in use between open and closed economies are not as stark as those between emerging markets and advanced countries.

Differences between emerging markets' and advanced countries' use of specific policies are starker when considering the length of time over which the policies were used (columns 7 and 8 of table 5.2, which report usage percentages by country-year observations for each group). Emerging markets used a much broader set of policies over a longer period than advanced countries did. Perhaps because emerging markets tend to be more concerned with large and volatile capital inflows and with related systemic liquidity risk, they tended to favor capital flow- and liquidity-related policies (FC and RR). But they also used limits on credit growth more often, possibly in part because they tend to have less liberalized financial systems. They also tend to place more limits on profit distributions. Conversely, as noted, advanced countries tend to prefer LTVs (74 percent of their usage by country-year observations). They also used DTI and dynamic provisioning relatively more than emerging markets. This usage suggests that advanced countries are relatively more concerned with risks arising from excessive leverage, and the consequent deleveraging.

Effectiveness of MaPPs

A number of papers have analyzed the effects of MaPPs on various measures of financial vulnerability and stability and documented the effectiveness of some MaPPs. Lim and others (2011) using cross-country regressions, found MaPPs to be effective in reducing the procyclicality of credit and leverage. Specifically, tools, such as LTV and DTI caps, ceilings on credit growth, reserve requirements, and dynamic provisioning rules, can mitigate the "procyclicality" of credit. Crowe and others (2011) found that MaPPs linked to the real estate cycle, such as maximum LTV, appear to have the best chance to curb a real estate boom. They argue that the narrower focus of such tools reduces their costs. Regarding measures aimed at strengthening the banking system (such as dynamic provisioning), they argue that such tools may help to cope with a bust, even if they fail to stop a boom. Vandenbussche, Vogel, and Detragiache (2012), covering countries in Central, Eastern, and southeastern Europe, find that measures like capital ratio requirements and nonstandard liquidity measures (marginal reserve requirements on foreign funding or marginal reserve requirements linked to credit growth) helped slow down housing price inflation.

Dell'Ariccia and others (2012) found that MaPPs can reduce the incidence of general credit booms and decrease the probability that booms end up badly.[16] Consistent with MaPPs' focus on financial vulnerabilities, they found a lower probability of a bad boom, primarily for booms that end in a crisis, with the effect on the probability of economic underperformance not very different. They concluded that MaPPs can reduce the risk of a bust while simultaneously reducing the vulnerability of the rest of the economy to troubles in the financial system.

Some case studies focused on specific risks or market segments. Jiménez and others (2012) found that in Spain countercyclical macro prudential policies, such as dynamic provisioning, were useful in taming credit supply cycles. More importantly, during bad times, dynamic provisioning helps smooth the downturn, upholding firm credit availability and performance during recessions. Igan and Kang (2011) found evidence of LTV and DTI limiting mortgage credit growth in Korea.

Most of these studies investigated the effects of MaPPs either at the macroeconomic or overall financial sector level, such as leverage or credit growth or the occurrence of a financial crisis, or at the level of subsector, such as real estate.

Our recent analysis (Claessens, Ghosh, and Mihet 2013) investigates how MaPPs may affect certain channels by which vulnerabilities and externalities can arise at *the microeconomic* level. Specifically, we explore the role of MaPPs in limiting vulnerabilities in individual banks (and thereby banking systems) in 48 ACs and EMs. Using data for 2,800 banks, three vulnerability measures were calculated: increase in leverage, growth in assets, and increase in noncore-to-core liabilities. These measures differ across countries. The typical expansionary phase is stronger in EMs than in ACs, and entails much larger leverage, asset, and noncore-to-core liabilities growth than in ACs, while the typical contractionary phase is deeper in EMs than in ACs. Similarly, open capital account countries have more volatility than closed capital account countries. Importantly, these measures of vulnerability also differ across countries that have adopted MaPPs and those that have not, with the median change in risk variables being higher for those that adopted some MaPPs.

Using the panel data, the various MaPPs were related to the vulnerabilities measures. Regressions controlled for whether the country was in an expansionary or contractionary phase of the business cycle, and whether other macroeconomic policies were used that complemented MaPPs in limiting vulnerabilities. The work also explored differences between ACs and EMs and between closed and open capital account countries.

The regression results, summarized stylistically through different shadings in table 5.3, suggest that many MaPPs can help in controlling banking system vulnerabilities, with at times complementary relationships among MaPPs. Thus, those instruments shaded in black were found to be statistically significant in limiting the increase in vulnerability (as measured by an increase in leverage ratio, asset growth, or noncore-to-core liabilities) through the cycle. Specifically:

- *Measures aimed at borrowers:* Loan-to-value and debt-to-income caps can reduce bank leverage growth, asset booms, and noncore-to-core liabilities growth, especially when there is more procyclicality in these variables (that is, when the cycles are more intense).
- *Measures aimed at financial institutions (addressing asset side):* Limits on credit growth help reduce asset growth. Foreign currency lending limits are also effective, with (statistically) significant coefficients for all three bank vulnerability indicators.

Dealing with the Challenges of Macro Financial Linkages in Emerging Markets
http://dx.doi.org/10.1596/978-1-4648-0002-3

- *Measures aimed at financial institutions (addressing liabilities side):* Reserve requirements reduce asset growth. They are not found to affect the leverage cycle. Neither do they reduce the noncore-to-core liabilities growth, rather the opposite, perhaps because higher reserve requirements induce the banks to seek additional funds to finance the reserve requirements, which at the margin means more noncore liabilities (see chapter 1).
- *Measures addressing bank buffers:* Dynamic provisioning appears to be a robust instrument in reducing growth in all three measures. Countercyclical capital requirements are effective in reducing growth in leverage and assets. Restrictions on profit distribution seem to be effective in reducing leverage and asset growth but not in reducing growth in noncore-to-core liabilities.

When the analysis was conducted differentiating upswings from downswings, the results show that macro prudential policies are much more effective in booms than in busts, with many coefficients statistically significant in expansionary periods and many fewer coefficients significant in contractionary periods. Again, the instruments that were shown to have a statistically significant effect (and of the correct sign) are shown shaded in black (table 5.3). Specifically we found that in booms, caps on loan-to-value and debt-to-income ratios, limits on foreign currency lending, dynamic provisioning, and limits on profit redistribution helped limit leverage growth; all macro prudential policies except for limits on credit growth and limits on profit redistribution helped limit asset growth;

Table 5.3 Summary of Effectiveness of Macro Prudential Policies in Reducing Leverage, Asset, and Noncore-to-Core Ratios

	Through the cycle			Upturns			Downturns			Open economies relative to Closed economies			Emerging markets relative to Advanced countries		
	Lev	Asset	NCC	Lev	Asset	NCC	Lev	Asset	NCC	Lev	Asset	NCC	Lev	Asset	NCC
LTV															
DTI															
CG															
FC															
RR															
DP															
CTC															
PRD															

Source: Claessens and others 2013.

Note: Lev = leverage growth; NCC = noncore-to-core liabilities. A country is defined as an open capital account country if its Chinn-Ito index is larger than the global mean in 2005 and a closed capital account country if its Chinn-Ito index is smaller than the global mean in 2005.

Effective
Perverse effect
More effective
Less effective

and limits on foreign currency lending and dynamic provisioning helped limit noncore-to-core liabilities growth.

In principle, tools such as reserve requirements could provide liquidity cushions, while dynamic provisioning could help build capital buffers during upturns, supporting lending during downturns. Other tools such as limits on profit redistribution could also have countercyclical, buffer effects, helping banks' willingness to maintain (or at least reduce less) balance sheets in bad times. In our regressions, however, very few policies affect in a statistically significant way the speed of decline when the credit cycle reverses. The only ones that are significant and positive are DTI ratios, which help maintain overall leverage growth during downturns, limits on foreign currency lending, and "other," which help maintain overall bank asset growth. DTI ratios also help limit the decline in noncore-to-core liabilities. Some negative signs, that is, policies that actually worsen the declines, were seen. These perverse effects are shaded in light grey in table 5.3. Specifically, caps on LTV ratios and caps on credit growth appear to lower asset growth during downturns, and caps on LTV ratios and limits on foreign currency borrowing seem to worsen declines in noncore-to-core liabilities.

That macro prudential policies are mostly effective in the expansionary times only may not be surprising because most macro prudential policies are not designed to mitigate contractionary periods as such. It could even be that tools like LTV limits actually act perversely during periods of credit contractions and asset price declines. As borrowers' net worth and income decline, for example, strict LTV limits make it even harder for lenders to extend loans, possibly leading to further declines in house prices and setting of a perverse cycle of even tighter LTV ratios. Unless the limits are adjusted quickly in a rightly calibrated manner—that is, without unduly increasing systemic risks—their effects may be perverse.

To investigate whether there are differences between the effectiveness of macro prudential policies depending on country characteristics, we also ran regressions interacting macro prudential policies with group dummies, where emerging markets and open economies are the dummies (coefficients without interactions, therefore, refer to the general effects and coefficients for the interactions refer to the additional effects for emerging markets and open economies). The results show that only a few policies affect risks in the groups differently as only a limited number of interaction coefficients are found to be statistically significant. This finding is largely because macro prudential policies tend to be used more by emerging markets and closed economies, making direct comparisons limited (no results are then reported).

Policies found to be more effective (statistically significant) for open economies (relative to close capital account economies) and for emerging markets (relative to advanced countries) are shown in vertically stripped cells in table 5.3. Policies found to be less effective in the same contexts are shown as gridded cells. The results suggest that caps on LTV ratios are less effective in reducing asset growth in open economies and caps on DTI ratios are less effective in reducing leverage growth in emerging markets and open economies. Caps on credit growth affect asset growth more for closed than open economies and limits on foreign currency borrowing help reduce asset growth somewhat more in emerging markets and open economies, and noncore-to-core growth in open economies. Dynamic provisioning seem to work better in closed economies for controlling leverage and asset growth and "other" limits seem of more value in emerging markets and closed economies for reducing leverage and asset growth. Otherwise, regression results suggest no statistically significant differences between instruments in limiting some of the risk buildups in emerging markets' (or closed countries') banking systems versus those in advanced countries' (or open countries') systems.

Conclusions

Recent theoretical advances support a role for macro prudential policies in safeguarding financial stability. Such policies can reduce the buildup of vulnerabilities and can help mitigate the impact of adverse cycles by encouraging a greater buildup of buffers. Indeed, empirical analyses confirm that countries stand to benefit from greater use of MaPPs to reduce systemic risk.

Some macro prudential policies are better suited to reducing the buildup of vulnerabilities, whereas others are geared toward building up buffers. Macro prudential policies thought to be more effective in reducing vulnerabilities help reduce risks during upswings. In contraction phases, though, some of these tools seem to prevent a rebound in financial variables, suggesting that they may be ineffective in fostering a restoration of financial intermediation during adverse conditions. However, tools that help build buffers in good times generally not only reduce the level and the growth of bank risk measures during upswings, but also help provide cushions that alleviate more severe crunches during downswings. As such, these tools may be more promising.

There are large differences across countries in the use of macro prudential policies, with emerging markets and countries with closed capital accounts using them more than advanced countries and open capital account countries. We find evidence that some of the macro prudential policies are more effective in reducing banking sector vulnerabilities (as measured by increase in leverage, growth in assets, and increase in noncore-to-core liabilities) in emerging markets than in advanced economies.

This is not surprising, given both their more frequent use in these countries and the fact that these countries' financial systems are often simpler, making it more likely that macro prudential policies are effective. We also find the effects of macro prudential policies to be quantitatively greater in open capital account countries, even though they are used relatively less in these economies.

As documented, emerging markets have been at the forefront of using macro prudential policies. Advanced countries' ongoing financial crises and weak economic performance in contrast to emerging markets' stable financial systems and continued solid performance, however, leads one to question the view that emerging markets are more exposed to risks and in need of macro prudential policies. In principle, all types of countries can experience the externalities and market failures that macro prudential policies aim to address. In practice, the choice of which macro prudential policies, if any, to use will be country and circumstance specific. Indeed, our findings suggest that the use and effects of macro prudential policies depend on country-specific circumstances. Although in some respects, concerns in emerging markets about systemic risks are becoming similar to those of advanced countries, emerging markets are likely to need a different and broad set of policies, including macro prudential policy tools in addition to fiscal and micro prudential policies. At the same time, their pragmatic approaches to date in using these tools can benefit from further research regarding which approaches are the most effective and efficient given country- and circumstance-specific conditions (see also Acharya 2013, and Shin 2011 for suggestions on how to adapt macro prudential policies to emerging markets and developing countries).

Notes

1. In particular, the many works by Borio and White, including Borio and White (2003) and White (2006), highlighted the boom and bust patterns in financial markets and the need for broader tools. See Clement (2010) on the origins of the term "macro prudential," whose first recorded use at the BIS was in 1979.

2. Procyclicality can arise from the behavior of financial intermediaries (supply side) and from changes in borrowers' balance sheets and income statements. The latter amplification mechanisms, collectively known as "the financial accelerator," operate through the demand side of financial transactions. Models show how small shocks, real or financial, can be propagated and amplified across the real economy as they lead to changes in access to finance for corporations and households. Here the financial system is less a cause of procyclicality, but rather accommodates it. Obviously, there are many interactions between the demand and supply side causes of procyclicality. See Brunnermeier, Eisenbach, and Sannikov (2012) for a review of models of macro financial linkages and Angelini and others (2009) for a general review of financial sector procyclicality.

3. These factors all result in externalities of one form or other. In the case of factors that exacerbate procyclicality, this externality takes place through the impact of individual financial institutions' actions on asset prices, which indirectly leads to correlated outcomes (expansion of balance sheets and balance sheet vulnerabilities). In the case of factors that give rise to strategic complementarity, the externality arises directly through correlated behavior.

4. Agency frictions refer to frictions that limit the capacity of individuals to delegate and contract bilaterally—and hence hinder financial development—due to (1) asymmetric information frictions (which lead to a misalignment of incentives between the principal (for example, depositors) and the agent (for example, the banker), because the agent, who has more information on his or her actions, can use this informational advantage to act in ways that are not in the interests of the principal; or (2) contract enforcement costs.

5. However, for capital requirements to have contractionary effects, some banks must find it difficult to respond to the accumulation of losses or higher capital requirements by issuing new equity and the borrowers of the constrained banks must be unable to switch to other sources of finance.

6. Participation frictions or collective frictions refer to frictions that constrain economic agents' participation in financial markets or financial inclusion broadly defined. Much of the gains from financial activity relate to a reduction in transactions costs, and the increase in liquidity and risk diversification benefits that come with greater participation

in financial markets. Hence, limited participation can constrain financial development (de la Torre, Ize, and Schmukler 2012).

7. Moreover, during the upswing, in a situation in which the best borrowers may already have access to the loans they want/or the list of sound projects are limited, banks' drive to expand their balance sheets may be associated with their moving down the quality ladder to lend to increasingly riskier borrowers/projects.

8. When cash lent on repo trades (short-term borrowed money) is lower than the market value of the collateral security, the applicable discount is referred to as a "haircut." In securities lending, the market value of the collateral to be posted always has to be higher than that of the securities, and the overcollateralization is referred to as the margin. The spiral arises because many institutions finance their asset positions with (short-term) borrowed money (repos) and have to put up margins in cash or are imposed a haircut (discount) on the assets they provide as collateral to assure the lender that the loan can be recovered in case the borrower defaults. As margins/haircuts increase in times of price declines—as lenders want more protection—a general tightening of lending results (margins and haircuts implicitly determine the maximum leverage a financial institution can adopt). The margin/haircut spiral then reinforces the capital adequacy and VaR channels in making institutions reduce their leverage. See further Brunnermeier and Pedersen (2009); Adrian and Shin (2010), and Geanakoplos (2009).

9. Strategic complementarity arises when the payoff to a certain strategy rises with the number of financial institutions adopting the same strategy (De Nicolò, Favara, and Ratnovski 2012).

10. Note that many of these instruments can also serve some other policy objectives, including, besides micro prudential objectives, consumer protection, and competition policy.

11. According to the original guidance document (BCBS 2010), intentions to raise the level of the capital buffer would be preannounced by up to one year, but a decision to decrease the buffer would take place immediately.

12. Most of the dynamic provisioning measures are a variation on the following rule: DP = through-the-cycle loss ratio × flow of new loans minus flow of specific provisions (where specific provisions correspond to realized losses). Thus, the formula implies that during boom times dynamic provisions are positive and contribute to the increase in loss provisions as realized losses are below the-through-the cycle loss ratio. The requirement for extra buildup of loan-loss provisioning could act as a brake during boom times. The reverse is true during downswings, with the drawdown serving as an additional cushion.

13. When applied to deposits, regulations usually specify the level of the requirement according to deposit type (for example, demand or time) and its currency denomination (domestic or foreign). Regulations also set a holding period relative to the reserve statement period for which the reserve requirement (RR) is computed and whether they *are* remunerated or nonremunerated. When they apply only to new deposits they are referred to as marginal RRs. In addition RRs can apply to domestic or foreign nondeposit liabilities of banks' balance sheets.

14. The LCR goal is to ensure that banks have liquidity to survive one month of stressed funding conditions. Therefore, the LCR identifies the amount of unencumbered (that is, not pledged and not held as a hedge for any other exposure) high-quality liquid assets that can be employed to offset expected cash outflows over a 30-day horizon. The NSFR is a complement to the LCR with a goal of addressing longer-term

structural maturity liquidity mismatches in banks' balance sheets. It sets a minimum acceptable amount of stable funding based on liquidity characteristics of a bank's assets over one-year horizon. The NSFR is defined as the ratio between available stable funding and required stable funding. Stable funding includes those types and amounts of equity and liability financing expected to be reliable sources of funding over a one-year horizon under stress scenarios. Stable funding is defined as the total amount of capital; preferred stock with maturity greater than one year; and secured and unsecured borrowing and liabilities (including deposits with effective maturities of one year or greater; proportion of stable wholesale funding, nonmaturity deposits, and/or term deposits of less than one year expected to stay with the institution for an extended period of idiosyncratic stress).

15. A dummy variable for each instrument takes the value of 1 for countries and years in which that instrument is used or zero otherwise. Only for some of the MaPP do we also know the level: caps on loan-to-value and debt-to-income ratios, which vary from 0 to 1 and 0 to 0.5, respectively.

16. When estimating regressions using the subcomponents of their macro prudential index, they find that credit and interest controls and open foreign exchange position limits enter significantly in most regressions, although their significance is sensitive to the specific combination of variables included.

References

Acharya, Viral. 2013. "Adapting Micro-Prudential Regulation for the Emerging Markets." In *Dealing with the Challenges of Macro Financial Linkages in Emerging Markets*, edited by Otaviano Canuto and Swati R. Ghosh., Washington, DC: World Bank.

Adrian, Tobias, and Hyun S. Shin. 2010. "Liquidity and Leverage." *Journal of Financial Intermediation* 19 (3): 418–37.

Allen, Franklin, and Elena Carletti. 2011. "Systemic Risk and Macroprudential Regulation." University of Pennsylvania. http://www.iea-world.com/docs/1043.pdf.

Allen, Franklin, and Douglas Gale. 2007. *Understanding Financial Crises.* Clarendon Lectures on Finance Series. New York: Oxford University Press.

Andritzky, Jochen, John Kiff, Laura Kodres, Pamela Madrid, Andrea Maechler, Aditya Narain, Noel Sacasa, and Jodi Scarlata. 2009. "Policies to Mitigate Procyclicality." Staff Position Notes 09/09, International Monetary Fund, Washington, DC.

Angelini, P., U. Albertazzi, F. Columba, W. Cornacchia, A. Di Cesare, F. Panetta, A. Pilati, C. Salleo, and G. Santini. 2009. "Financial Sector Pro-Cyclicality: Lessons from the Crisis," Occasional Paper 44, Banca D'Italia, Rome.

Bank of England. 2011. "Instruments of Macroprudential Policy." Discussion Paper.

BCBS (Basel Committee on Banking Supervision). 2010. *A Global Regulatory Framework for More Resilient Banks and Banking Systems.* Basel, Switzerland: Bank for International Settlements.

Bebchuk, Lucian, and Itay Goldstein. 2011. "Self-Fulfilling Credit Market Freezes." *Review of Financial Studies* 24: 3519–55.

Borio, Claudio E. V., and William R. White. 2003. "Whither Monetary and Financial Stability: The Implications of Evolving Policy Regimes?" Presentation at the symposium, "Monetary Policy and Uncertainty: Adapting to a Changing Economy," sponsored by the Federal Reserve Bank of Kansas City, Jackson Hole, Wyoming. August.

Brunnermeier, Makus K., Thomas Eisenbach, and Yuliy Sannikov. 2012. "Macroeconomics with Financial Frictions: A Survey." Working Paper 18102, National Bureau of Economic Research, Cambridge, MA.

Brunnermeier, Makus K., Charles Goodhart, Andrew Crocket, Avinash Persaud, and Hyun Shin. 2009. "The Fundamental Principles of Financial Regulation: 11th Geneva Report on the World Economy." International Center for Monetary and Banking Studies.

Brunnermeier, Makus K., and L. H. Pedersen. 2009. "Market Liquidity and Funding Liquidity." *Review of Financial Studies* 22 (6): 2201–38.

Chinn, Menzie and Hiro Ito. 2008. "A New Measure of Financial Openness." *Journal of Comparative Policy Analysis* 10 (3): 309–22.

Claessens, Stijn, and Swati R. Ghosh. Forthcoming. "Business and Financial Cycles in Emerging Markets: Lessons for Macro-Prudential Policies." In *Financial Regulations on International Capital Flows and Exchange Rates*, edited by Dongsoo Kang and Hyun Song Shin. Honolulu, Hawaii: East-West Center; Seoul: the Korea Development Institute.

Claessens, Stijn, Swati R. Ghosh, and Roxana Mihet. 2013. "Macro-Prudential Policies to Mitigate Financial System Vulnerabilities." *Journal of International Money and Finance.* http://www.sciencedirect.com/science/article/pii/S026156061300096X

Claessens, S., M. A. Kose, and M. Terrones. 2011a. "Financial Cycles: What? How? When?" In *NBER 2010 International Seminar on Macroeconomics*, edited by Richard H. Clarida and Francesco Giavazzi, 303–43. Chicago: University of Chicago Press.

———. 2011b. "How Do Business and Financial Cycles Interact?" Working Paper 11/88, International Monetary Fund, Washington, DC. (Shorter version published in *Journal of International Economics* 87(1):178–90).

Clement, Piet. 2010. "The Term Macroprudential: Origins and Evolution." *BIS Quarterly Review.* Bank for International Settlements, Basel, Switzerland, March.

Crowe, C. W., G. Dell'Ariccia, D. Igan, and P. Rabanal. 2011. "How to Deal with Real Estate Booms: Lessons from Country Experiences." Working Paper 11/91, International Monetary Fund, Washington, DC.

de la Torre, Augusto, Alain Ize, and Sergio L. Schmukler. 2012. "Financial Development in Latin America and the Caribbean: The Road Ahead." In the World Bank Latin American and Caribbean Studies Series, World Bank. https://openknowledge.world-bank.org/handle/10986/2380.

De Nicolò, G., G. Favara, and L. Ratnovski. 2012. "Externalities and Macroprudential Policy." Staff Discussion Note 12/05, International Monetary Fund, Washington, DC.

Dell'Ariccia, Giovanni, Deniz Igan, Luc Laeven, and Hui Tong. 2012. "Policies for Macrofinancial Stability: Options to Deal with Credit Booms." Staff Discussion Note 12/06, International Monetary Fund, Washington, DC.

Diamond, D. W., and R. G. Rajan. 2001. "Banks, Short-Term Debt and Financial Crises: Theory, Policy Implications and Applications." In *Carnegie-Rochester Conference Series on Public Policy.* Amsterdam: Elsevier.

Federico, Pablo, Carlos Vegh, and Guillermo Vuletin. 2012. "Reserve Requirement Policy Over the Business Cycle." Draft, University of Maryland, College Park, September 10. http://www.cass.city.ac.uk/__data/assets/pdf_file/0016/171106/3.-Federico-v2.pdf.

Geanakoplos, John. 2009. "The Leverage Cycle." *NBER Macroeconomics Annual 2009* 24: 1–65. http://papers.nber.org/books/acem09-1.

Ghosh, Swati. R. 2010. "Dealing with the Challenges of Capital Inflows in the Context of Macro Financial Links." Economic Premise Note 19, World Bank, Washington, DC.

Gorton, Gary. 2009. "Slapped in the Face by the Invisible Hand: Banking and the Panic of 2007." Prepared for the Federal Reserve Bank of Atlanta's 2009 Financial Markets Conference, "Financial Innovation and Crisis," Jekyll Island, GA, May 11–13.

Gorton, Gary, and Andrew Metrick. 2010. "Regulating the Shadow Banking System." *Brookings Papers on Economic Activity* Fall: 261–97.

Hahm, Joon -Ho., Hyun Song Shin, and Kwanho Shin. 2012, "Non-Core Bank Liabilities and Financial Vulnerability." Working Paper 18428, September, National Bureau of Economic Research, Cambridge, MA.

Hanson, Samuel, Anil Kayshap, and Jeremy Stein. 2011. "A Macroprudential Approach to Financial Regulation." *Journal of Economic Perspective* 25 (1): 3–28.

IMF (International Monetary Fund). 2010. *A Fair and Substantial Contribution by the Financial Sector: Report to the G20.* Washington, DC: IMF.

———. 2011a. "Macroprudential Policy: An Organizing Framework." Board Paper, IMF, Washington, DC, April.

———. 2011b. "Recent Experiences in Managing Capital Inflows: Cross-Cutting Themes and Possible Guidelines." Policy Paper, IMF, Washington, DC, April.

———. 2013. "World Economic Outlook, April 2013: Hopes, Realities, Risks." World Economic and Financial Surveys, IMF, Washington, DC, April.

Igan, Deniz, and Heedon Kang. 2011. "Do Loan-to-Value and Debt-to-Income Limits Work? Evidence from Korea." Working Paper 11/297, International Monetary Fund, Washington, DC.

Jiménez, Gabriel, Steven R. G. Ongena, Jose -Luis Peydro, and Jesus Saurina Salas. 2012. "Macroprudential Policy, Countercyclical Bank Capital Buffers and Credit Supply: Evidence from the Spanish Dynamic Provisioning Experiments." Discussion Paper 2012–011, European Banking Center, Tilburg, the Netherlands.

Lim, C. F. Columba, A. Costa, P. Kongsamut, A. Otani, M. Saiyid, T. Wezel, and X. Wu. 2011. "Macroprudential Policy: What Instruments and How to Use Them? Lessons from Country Experiences." Working Paper 11/238, International Monetary Fund, Washington, DC.

Ostry, Jonathan David, Atish R. Ghosh, Karl Friedrich Habermeier, Luc Laeven, Marcos Chamon, Mahvash Saeed Qureshi, and Annamaria Kokenyne. 2011. "Managing Capital Inflows: What Tools to Use?" Staff Discussion Note 11/06, International Monetary Fund, Washington, DC.

Palley, Thomas. 2004. "Asset-Based Reserve Requirements: Reasserting Domestic Monetary Control in an Era of Financial Innovation and Instability." *Review of Political Economy* 16 (1): 43–58.

Rajan, Raghuram G. 1994. "Why Bank Credit Policies Fluctuate: A Theory and Some Evidence." *Quarterly Journal of Economics* 109: 399–441.

Schoenmaker, Dirk, and Peter J. Wierts. 2011. "Macroprudential Policy: The Need for a Coherent Policy Framework." Policy Paper 13, Duisenberg School of Finance, Amsterdam.

Shin, Hyun Song. 2008. *Risk and Liquidity.* Clarendon Lectures in Finance Series. New York: Oxford University Press.

———. 2010. "Non-Core Liabilities Tax as a Tool for Prudential Regulation." Policy Memo, Princeton University. http://www.princeton.edu/~hsshin/www/NonCoreLiabilitiesTax.pdf.

———. 2011. "Adapting Macroprudential Approaches to Emerging and Developing Economies." Report commissioned by the World Bank's Poverty Reduction and Economic Management (PREM) Network, World Bank, Washington, DC, May.

———. 2012. "Global Banking Glut and Loan Risk Premium." 2011 Mundell Fleming Lecture, *IMF Economic Review* 60 (July): 155–92.

Vandenbussche, Jérôme, Ursula Vogel, and Enrica Detragiache. 2012. "Macroprudential Policies and Housing Prices: A New Database and Empirical Evidence for Central, Eastern, and Southeastern Europe." Working Paper, International Monetary Fund, Washington, DC.

White, William R. 2006. "Procyclicality in the Financial System: Do We Need a New Macrofinancial Stabilisation Framework?" Working Paper 193, January, Bank for International Settlements, Basel, Switzerland.

CHAPTER 6

Sailing through the Global Financial Storm

Brazil's Recent Experience with Monetary and Macro Prudential Policies to Lean Against the Financial Cycle and Deal with Systemic Risks

Luiz Awazu Pereira da Silva and Ricardo Eyer Harris*

Introduction

The global financial crisis of 2008–12 prompted a renewal of both analytical thinking and policy practices regarding the interaction and mutual complementarity between monetary and prudential regulatory policies, given the simultaneous objectives of macroeconomic and financial stability.

Many of these issues were present before the global financial crisis but have been thoroughly revisited since, essentially because: (1) overwhelming evidence showed that macro financial linkages allowed for the buildup of significant financial risk in an environment of macroeconomic stability without adequate regulation; (2) analysts realized that the cost of mopping up after crises such as that of 2008 is extraordinarily high, suggesting that prevention is preferred to remedies; and (3) destabilizing side effects resulted from the unprecedented injections of global liquidity by monetary authorities of advanced economies, exacerbating sudden floods of capital into emerging economies.

Going back to where it began, by the end of the 1990s and early 2000s the world economy was enjoying the so-called great moderation, partly due to the progressive—and successful—adoption by central banks of flexible inflation-targeting monetary policy framework. The perceived attraction of inflation

* **Luiz Awazu Pereira da Silva** is Deputy Governor and **Ricardo Eyer Harris** is Advisor at the Central Bank of Brazil. The views expressed are those of the authors and do not necessarily reflect those of the Central Bank of Brazil. We thank participants at the World Bank—Bank Indonesia Conference in Bali, Indonesia, November, 2011 and the International Monetary Fund Article IV Mission in May 2012 for useful interactions and comments.

Box 6.1 The Global Financial Crisis: Origin and Policy Responses in Emerging and Advanced Economies

Long before the crisis—since the mid-1990s—Brazil had adopted standard macroeconomic policies, including an inflation-targeting framework, to control inflation and anchor expectations. Fiscal policies were strengthened to ensure that markets perceived debt dynamics as sustainable. Together with many (though not all) emerging markets, Brazil opted for a flexible exchange rate regime as a first buffer against capital market mood swings and volatility. Last but not least, Brazil did not embark on the fashionable financial deregulation movement of the 1990s, keeping a conservative prudential regulatory framework for its financial sectors, which remained tightly supervised and well capitalized.

Advanced economies did not follow the same path, perhaps because of the absence of emergencies, less pressure—at that time—from markets or rating agencies, and a self-reassuring belief in their own singularity. In those countries, private and public debt increased, sometimes beyond existing institutional fiscal pacts such as the Maastricht treaty in the Euro zone. Financial deregulation was conducted with great confidence on the capacity to dissipate risk using sophisticated derivative products that priced financial instruments very well except under tail events. Last but not least, the monetary policy response to shocks in the United States (for example, the burst of the Internet bubble or the 9/11 attack) managed to produce quick recoveries. However, they relied on prolonged periods of low-interest rates that did not translate into higher inflation because of the concomitant disinflationary pressure of China's exports of durable goods. Nevertheless, financial conditions were eased by enough to conceivably trigger excessive risk-taking behavior by both lenders and borrowers. In that context, in addition to agency problems, classic Minsky problems of financial market behavior were exacerbated, including: procyclicality; very high leverage; deterioration of lending standards; and excessive credit financing increasingly riskier borrowers.

In many advanced economies, excessive credit (including in the housing market) allowed for a pattern of arguably unsustainable consumption financed by debt. Current account deterioration was large enough to trigger the debate about global imbalances. The benign view[a] was that these current account deficits and surpluses were a win-win situation for both developing and developed countries. Surplus developing economies would benefit from deep developed consumer markets to export their goods and services, and deficits could always be financed by a host of new financial instruments. The opposite view[b] was that this was an unstable equilibrium. In addition, lax macro prudential regulation of financial sectors reacted with lags and/or too timidly to the accumulation of risks. And, since many financial institutions were global by definition, risks would cross borders and spread potential financial instability worldwide. The "benign view" prevailed and the crisis eventually struck, beginning in mid-2007 (the subprime debacle in the United States) and continuing until the Lehman Brothers spike in mid-September 2008.

The crisis caught emerging and advanced economies in different positions along the spectrum of macro and financial fragility: the former were ending a cycle of macro policy consolidation and had stronger financial sectors that had been tested through crises; the

box continues next page

Box 6.1 The Global Financial Crisis: Origin and Policy Responses in Emerging and Advanced Economies (*continued*)

latter were at the peak of a cycle of credit-fueled growth and had allowed their financial sectors to become highly vulnerable to shifts in confidence and changes in asset price valuation in their balance sheets. Because policy makers in advanced economies had thoroughly studied the Great Depression, liquidity provision to troubled banks was swift and massive. Together with a first round of fiscal stimulus, that response avoided an even greater collapse of interconnected global markets. Happily, for the first time, many emerging markets—Brazil was a case in point—could also implement countercyclical policies to support activity. But, after a rebound, advanced economies faced a dwindling recovery by the end of 2010. Additional fiscal policy action then met local political economy constraints in the United States and the Euro zone, as well as bond market suspicion of how advanced economies' debt stocks would remain marketable (at sustainable prices) in an environment of prolonged mediocre growth. With all advanced economies at the zero bound of their monetary policy rates, unconventional monetary easing emerged as the option of last resort, first with the United States quantitative easing and (much) later with the European Central Bank's long-term refinancing operations. In that context, global liquidity increased and resulted in significantly higher-than-usual capital inflows into emerging markets. As economic recovery continued to lag in advanced countries, monetary policy remained loose. Global excessive liquidity became a major driving force behind recent capital flows into emerging markets in general and Brazil in particular.

a. For example, Cooper (2007); Dooley, Folkerts-Landau, and Garber (2009); Caballero, Farhi, and Gourinchas (2008)
b. For example, as early as 2005, Roubini and Setser (2005) and then Obstfeld and Rogoff (2009) and Borio and Disyatat (2011).

targeting was to deliver low and stable inflation while minimizing growth fluctuations, relying on a simple policy instrument—namely, a short-term interest rate. At the same time, the framework took advantage of flexible exchange rates to smooth external pressures, thus avoiding the recognized pitfalls of pegged or fixed regimes and turning reserve accumulation into a healthy precaution rather than an absolute necessity. Provided that one's "house was in order," this combination brought credibility and stability to macroeconomic policies and policy makers. The fact that the adoption of inflation targeting with flexible exchange rates was so widespread (despite notable holdouts) seemed to support, on a global as opposed to a merely local scale, a virtuous cycle of aggregate demand growth with low inflation and fewer threats to balance-of-payment positions. Meanwhile, regarding financial stability, a neat separation principle seemed to hold: regulators recommended the use of a set of well-tested and traditional micro prudential instruments to ensure that financial intermediaries performed their function without engaging in practices that could undermine the robustness of the system. Things seemed to be going so well that central banking was becoming a boring business to the point that some countries even chose to convert to

Dealing with the Challenges of Macro Financial Linkages in Emerging Markets
http://dx.doi.org/10.1596/978-1-4648-0002-3

the model of split institutional responsibilities (that is, to separate the two objectives of price stability and financial stability)—and, in so doing, also split into separate entities the regulatory-supervisory and lender-of-last-resort functions.

The only nagging doubt was about how central banks should deal with asset price bubbles. The discussion was motivated by the late-1990s episodes of stock market booms and busts, after Japan's property market problems in the late 1980s. Should central banks react to rapidly rising asset prices, and, if so, how? As usual, the economics profession provided a divided answer, each side with a well-grounded rationale. One side of the divide[1] argued that higher asset prices had the propensity to enhance wealth effects transmitting into consumption and eventually consumer prices; thus it was warranted to "lean against the wind" of asset price surges, acting in a preventive way. They also noted that financial imbalances may very well build up in an environment of stable prices; low and stable rates of inflation may even foster asset price bubbles due to excessively optimistic expectations about future economic prospects or to increased propensity to take on more risk. At a minimum, price stability should not be taken as a sufficient condition for financial stability. The opposite camp[2] claimed that pricking asset price bubbles with monetary policy instruments was bound to impact the base interest to such a degree as to do great damage to macroeconomic stability. They also argued that it is exceedingly hard to determine whether an ongoing rise in asset prices is justified by fundamentals or is a bubble. Therefore, the central banks could compromise their reputation by getting into the muddy business of attempting to identify bubbles ex ante.

In practical terms, the generally adopted protocol was to forsake any attempt to lean with the base policy rate against asset price inflation; but, if it turned out to have been a bubble, as it would prove to be by eventually bursting, the solution was to clean up afterwards. The collateral damage caused by the bursting of the bubble on macroeconomic performance could presumably be remedied with a more accommodative monetary policy stance.

One could arguably detect that a partial departure from this general attitude was present when the Federal Reserve, confronted with more evidence of herd behavior in stock and housing markets, tried to talk markets down[3] by suggesting that they were displaying "irrational exuberance." While that attempt involved a quasi-official verdict about the departure of asset prices from fundamentals, the fact that intervention remained purely verbal ultimately helped to enshrine the notion that conventional monetary policy instruments should not go out chasing asset price inflation.

But other types of nuance were later introduced into the debate, bringing the "clean up after" camp[4] closer to those advocating prevention. One key step in this direction was the realization that bubbles based on credit—as was notably the case of housing bubbles, as opposed to garden-variety stock market bubbles— might more clearly call for preventive intervention, considering the much more deleterious effects of the eventual market downturn on banks' balance sheet as compared to those of households'. The argument was that instead of getting into the tricky issue of whether increases in asset prices faithfully reflect the corresponding fundamentals, central banks should focus on the mutual interaction between asset price and credit dynamics, with one eye on the potential for unstable feedback loops and the other on their joint effect on aggregate demand.

Thus, credit connections rather than asset prices per se moved to center stage as the critical variable to observe in the rethinking of monetary and prudential-regulatory policies. After the full manifestation of the global 2008 crisis, a number of voices[5] started calling on central banks to incorporate explicitly and systematically a financial stability objective into their reaction function, arguing that they should consider the interplay between the objectives of macroeconomic stability and financial stability. This new literature reflected a growing concern that, under lax regulation, the achievement of price stability may have been associated with an increased risk of financial instability.

In parallel, policy makers were also realizing that traditional micro prudential tools had been insufficient to dampen financial risk and reflecting about macro financial policies.[6] A number of proposals started to revisit prudential guidelines and to extend them to a larger macroeconomic dimension, with a view on the buildup of systemic risk. That was the idea behind "macro prudential" regulation, aimed at strengthening the financial system and at encouraging more prudent lending behavior in economic upturns (for example, by raising capital requirements in a countercyclical way, to help choke off credit-related asset price bubbles in their early stages).[7] Macro prudential regulation became, naturally, the favorite candidate to fill this new role of guarding the crossroads between asset price and credit dynamics.[8]

In 2010, a paper by the Committee on the Global Financial System (CGFS) of the Bank for International Settlements (BIS) mapped the available set of macro prudential instruments and frameworks and summarized the experiences in using them. The variety of existing tools is illustrated in table 6.1, which organizes the various instruments according to the vulnerability they address and the financial system component they target.

The underlying idea was to use existing micro prudential instruments in a more comprehensive way (that is, extend them to a macro prudential dimension) to "lean against the financial cycle." That implied a countercyclical calibration of these tools across all financial sector institutions. For example, during upturns in the financial cycle, regulation would increase buffers that could be used in downturns: higher capital and liquidity requirements, more stringent and forward-looking provisioning rules, limits to concentration, loan size, maximum debt-to-income levels, foreign exchange exposure, and so on. The expected result of applying such brakes was that financial institutions would refrain—considering the higher costs of expanding certain components of their assets and the forward guidance provided by these messages—from engaging in excessive expansion of their lending, especially to riskier segments of the market. But the paper only alluded in passing to the possible interaction between monetary policy and macro prudential tools, listing strands of the literature that touched on how changes in the funding cost of banks would affect banks' lending behavior, or how bank capital would affect the transmission of monetary policy.

Dealing with the Challenges of Macro Financial Linkages in Emerging Markets
http://dx.doi.org/10.1596/978-1-4648-0002-3

Table 6.1 Macro Prudential Instruments by Vulnerability and Financial System Component

		Financial system component				
		Bank or deposit-taker		Non-bank investor	Securities market	Financial infrastructure
		Balance sheet[a]	Lending contract			
Vulnerability	**Leverage**	capital ratio risk weights provisioning profit distribution restrictions credit growth cap	LTV cap debt service / income cap maturity cap		margin/ haircut limit	
	Liquidity or market risk	liquidity / reserve requirements FX lending restriction currency mismatch limit open FX position limit	valuation rules (eg. MMMFs)	local currency or FX reserve requirements	central bank balance sheet operations	exchange trading
	Interconnect-edness	concentration limits systemic capital surcharge subsidiarisation				central counterpar-ties (CCP)

Source: BIS 2010.
[a] Capital and other balance sheet requirements also apply to insurers and pension funds, but we restrict our attention here to the types of institutions most relevant for credit intermediation.

At the same time, empirical studies were carried out by the BIS and the International Monetary Fund (IMF), drawing lessons from country experiences in using macro prudential instruments. In particular, the IMF produced a comprehensive account of existing cases[9] showing that these tools were mostly introduced to reduce systemic risk, either in its time dimension and/or its cross-sectional dimension, and that they were quite effective. The study used cross-country comparisons to show that macro prudential tools have helped to dampen procyclicality of financial systems and that they do not seem to depend on the particular policy regime adopted by each country.

The global financial crisis would provide a stressful opportunity for Brazil to put to test these policy and analytical proposals.

The Effects of the Global Financial Crisis on Brazil

Brazil sailed quite well through the first acute phase of the global financial crisis. Nonetheless, the effects of the crisis were severe. After the Lehman Brothers episode, in the last quarter of 2008, trade flows contracted 6.9 percent year-on-year (YOY); industrial production fell by 27 percent quarter-on-quarter (QOQ);

capital outflows rose by 36 percent QOQ causing an exchange-rate depreciation spike of 32 percent YOY; and credit growth fell by 35 percent YOY. In one month (October 2008), trade financing fell by 30 percent and the debt rollover ratio went down from 167 percent to 22 percent. From July to October, liquidity ratios in Brazilian banks fell from 1.73 to 1.43. The Brazilian authorities took immediate action in face of the shock.[10] First, they addressed liquidity problems both in domestic and foreign currencies: bank reserve requirements were lowered, injecting about R$116 billion worth of liquidity (or 4 percent of GDP) into the economy; lines of credit in foreign exchange were provided to the private sector; the central bank offered US$14.5 billion (7 percent of total international reserves at the end of 2008) in spot market auctions. Foreign exchange swap contracts to the tune of US$33 billion were also offered by the central bank, helping an orderly wind-down of large foreign exchange derivatives exposures by domestic corporations (amounting to an estimated US$37 billion at the end of September 2008). The second line of action was to calibrate policy instruments to provide stimulus to economic activity: the monetary policy base rate was lowered by a total of 500 basis points (bps), from 13.75 percent per annum (p.a.) to 8.75 percent p.a.; a number of tax breaks were put in place and the fiscal surplus target was reduced from 3.8 percent in 2008 to 2.5 percent of GDP in 2009; credit extension by public financial institutions rose by R$105 billion (3.3 percent of GDP).

The response of the Brazilian economy was swift, and produced the expected V-shaped recovery pattern. Despite the strong policy-driven rebound throughout 2009, GDP growth was still zero for that calendar year, but in 2010, GDP grew 7.5 percent YOY, domestic demand by 10.3 percent, with private consumption expanding 7.2 percent YOY and investment by 11.1 percent YOY.

Meanwhile, advanced economies were struggling with their own recoveries and that initiated a second phase of the crisis. The crisis had revealed severe problems in the global banking system, which continued despite the unprecedented initial response of governments and central banks, combining fiscal stimulus, monetary expansion (with significant purchases and holding of bank debt, mortgage-backed securities (MBS), and Treasury instruments by central banks) and institutional bailouts. After an initial recovery in the second half of 2009 and early in 2010, the Federal Reserve resumed its balance sheet expansion in August 2010 as it observed that the economy was not growing fast enough. In November 2010, the Federal Reserve announced a second round of quantitative easing. Other central banks, all with policy rates already pressed against the zero lower bound, followed suit.

As a result, in 2010, policy rates were negative in real terms in advanced economies and expansionary monetary policy (including unconventional measures) resulted in provision of ample liquidity that affected international financial markets, contributing to high global liquidity. Although these policies of advanced economies may have been justified from the point of view of their domestic situation, it is now accepted that they created spillovers to emerging markets (EMs). Sluggish recovery in advanced economies and weak financial

Dealing with the Challenges of Macro Financial Linkages in Emerging Markets
http://dx.doi.org/10.1596/978-1-4648-0002-3

accelerators caused liquidity injections to remain largely on the balance sheets of financial institutions. Yield, risk, and growth differentials (low interest rates in advanced economies, narrowing relative risk premia, two-speed growth prospects) led to stronger demand for emerging market assets and put pressure on emerging currencies to appreciate.

Moreover, global liquidity was also affecting EMs through its effects on commodity prices, further contributing to the appreciation of commodity currencies. Expanding global liquidity appears to be correlated with higher commodity prices, although fundamentals (excess long-term demand) may have given crucial support to these price rises. On the real demand side, strong economic growth in EMs, social structure changes in China and India, and more resource-intensive development strategies have put pressure on commodity prices. But, most likely, global excess liquidity also played a role, in addition to fundamentals, in compounding rising trends in commodities and energy prices. Of course, it is far from trivial to attest and quantify causal relationships, as there is limited robust empirical evidence that excess global liquidity favored commodity financialization, and it is even harder to determine to what extent it was the causal factor behind price rises.

Nevertheless, higher commodity prices do improve fundamentals of commodity exporters; and that, in turn, triggers additional capital flows into these economies. Despite policy action in recipient countries, excess inflows contributed to the appreciation of several commodity-based currencies, as for instance in Australia, Canada, Brazil, and Chile, among others. The volume and intensity of capital flows in 2010 posed a challenge to policy makers in these countries because the impact of the overly liquid international environment was inflationary, in spite of the currency appreciation that inevitably took place, at a time when the strong post-crisis V-shaped recovery already gave rise to inflation pressures in EMs.

In a way, strong capital inflows were actually compounding the inflationary pressures already suffered by EMs as a consequence of their expanding domestic demand and globally rising commodity prices. Capital flows added fuel to local inflationary pressures as they exacerbated the procyclicality of local financial sectors in recipient economies: they contributed to an excessive expansion of domestic credit by lowering funding costs and relaxing local credit standards. Not only did the ample foreign funding to local credit markets intensify the impulse to aggregate demand, especially on the consumption side, but it also weakened the transmission of domestic monetary tightening, as conventional monetary policy instruments operate essentially through the funding costs of banks. Finally, excessive capital flows increased the risks of financial instability, since banks increased their foreign currency exposure at the same time as they lowered credit standards in response to higher liquidity. Therefore, "sudden floods," that is, surges in capital inflows, can lead to credit and asset price bubbles, and can impact the exchange rates of commodity exporters.[11]

In the second half of 2010 and early 2011, Brazil was facing exactly those challenges. The economy was showing signs of overheating (see table 6.2), with

Table 6.2 Activity, Credit, Capital Flows, and Prices

	Unit	2009				2010				2011			
		Q1	Q2	Q3	Q4	Q1	Q2	Q3	Q4	Q1	Q2	Q3	Q4
Activity													
GDP	% YOY	2.9	0.7	−1.4	−0.3	2.5	5.4	7.6	7.5	6.3	4.9	3.7	2.7
Domestic demand	% YOY	−0.5	−0.2	1.0	7.6	10.8	9.8	8.4	7.1	5.7	5.3	2.3	2.0
Ind. production	% YOY	−14.6	−12.3	−8.2	5.9	18.2	14.3	8.0	3.3	2.8	0.6	0.0	−2.1
Unemployment	%	8.6	8.6	7.9	7.2	7.4	7.2	6.6	5.7	6.3	6.3	6.0	5.2
Capital Flows (Gross)													
Reserves	USD b	190.4	201.5	221.6	238.5	243.8	253.1	275.2	288.6	317.1	335.8	349.7	352.0
Reserves	% YOY	−2.5	0.3	7.3	23.1	28.0	25.6	24.2	21.0	30.1	32.7	27.1	22.0
Portfolio	USD b	25.1	46.4	55.0	46.9	29.7	30.1	38.7	35.1	24.5	28.6	22.7	25.2
Portfolio % of GDP	%	8.6	13.4	11.9	8.9	5.8	5.6	7.1	6.4	4.1	4.6	3.6	4.0
Bank credit	USD b	2.3	5.2	4.0	8.1	10.3	7.6	12.3	13.2	25.7	15.3	14.4	4.8
Bank credit % of GDP	%	0.8	1.5	0.9	1.5	2.0	1.4	2.2	2.4	4.3	2.5	2.3	0.8
FDI	USD b	6.6	5.0	7.6	11.2	6.7	12.1	11.9	24.7	15.6	16.8	19.1	17.3
FDI % of GDP	%	2.3	1.4	1.6	2.1	1.3	2.3	2.2	4.5	2.6	2.7	3.0	2.7
Total	USD b	72.5	101.2	106.6	127.2	94.8	104.9	119.1	146.4	134.9	139.0	146.8	127.4
Total percent of GDP	%	24.9	29.3	23.0	24.2	18.5	19.5	21.8	26.7	22.5	22.3	23.4	20.2
Credit (Oustanding)													
Consumer	% YOY	18.5	17.0	15.7	17.7	18.4	16.3	17.1	19.1	17.9	18.2	16.9	13.9
Payroll-guaranteed	% YOY	22.6	30.3	33.9	36.1	37.2	29.7	27.8	28.4	21.8	19.5	17.8	12.5
Housing	% YOY	40.3	41.8	43.0	40.8	48.1	50.1	50.7	55.5	49.9	49.4	47.1	44.1
Ear-marked	% YOY	27.2	24.3	32.0	28.9	30.7	34.9	28.6	27.1	25.8	23.8	26.4	26.6
Non-earmaked	% YOY	23.6	17.0	10.4	9.1	10.9	13.2	15.7	17.7	18.0	17.8	15.7	14.7
Total	% YOY	24.7	19.1	16.6	15.0	16.9	19.8	19.9	20.9	20.6	19.9	19.4	18.8
Total percent of GDP	%	40.7	41.5	43.6	43.7	43.1	43.6	44.3	45.2	45.2	46.0	47.4	49.0
Prices / Asset Prices													
CRB metals (USD)	% YOY	−48.1	−39.5	−10.3	48.6	85.2	43.5	17.6	27.8	30.0	35.1	25.9	−6.6
CRB food (USD)	% YOY	−21.9	23.0	−25.4	7.6	20.2	14.0	27.4	26.8	38.2	40.4	27.8	6.9
CRB total (USD)	% YOY	−28.0	−24.7	−16.0	18.9	34.6	23.2	19.8	24.0	30.0	30.8	20.7	−0.4
CPI (IPCA)	% YOY	5.6	4.8	4.3	4.3	5.2	4.8	4.7	5.9	6.3	6.7	7.3	6.5
CPI-food	% YOY	9.3	5.0	4.1	3.2	5.6	5.1	5.4	10.4	8.8	8.9	9.9	7.2
CPI-services	% YOY	6.8	7.2	6.9	6.4	6.9	6.8	6.9	7.6	8.5	8.8	9.0	9.0
WPI (IGP-M)	% YOY	5.6	−0.6	−3.0	−4.4	0.5	5.0	9.3	13.9	13.5	9.7	7.6	4.3
ER nominal	% YOY	30.4	19.0	1.1	−31.3	−25.9	−8.0	−5.7	−3.3	−7.4	−13.0	1.8	8.1
REER	% YOY	13.2	6.5	−6.2	−26.0	−20.0	−13.3	−9.0	−7.9	−6.3	−6.7	0.8	5.2
Real estate (SP)	% YOY	22.8	23.5	23.9	24.2	24.5	25.1	26.2	27.4	24.5	27.4	28.8	27.8
Real estate (RJ)	% YOY	13.9	15.0	17.6	20.6	23.5	29.0	34.7	38.6	41.7	44.0	42.3	37.3
BOVESPA	% YOY	−39.9	−23.4	21.7	60.2	54.2	16.9	12.1	1.0	−2.6	2.4	−28.3	−20.0

Source: Based on data from the Central Bank of Brazil.

domestic demand growing 5.7 percent YOY in the first quarter of 2011, and inflationary pressures resulting from the resulting domestic supply-demand imbalances combined with global pressures on commodity prices. Local supply shocks and idiosyncratic regulated price adjustments also played a role: adjustments in urban transportation fares, which have a relevant weight in the consumer price index (CPI); atypical price hikes on food items, caused by unfavorable weather conditions in some production areas; and a supply shock in ethanol, an important fuel for the passenger car fleet (either used separately or as part of the regular gasoline blend). In addition, Brazil faced inflationary pressures stemming not from cyclical or momentary factors, but rather from structural social transformation, with a growing middle class boosting the demand for nontradables, while their rising incomes also represented a cost shock on labor-intensive sectors. Inflation in services was particularly representative of these latter trends.[12]

The diagnosis of overheating in the economy was conducted *pari passu* with the monitoring of the buildup of potential threats to financial stability. Brazil had been going through an already long cycle of rapid credit expansion—about 22.2 percent p.a. on average between 2005 and 2011—especially for consumer credit. To a large extent, such credit expansion corresponded to a process of natural deepening of financial markets in Brazil, with explanatory factors both structural and cyclical, including institutional improvements to loan contracts and collateral quality, strong fundamentals, in particular in the labor markets, and upward social mobility for about 40 million Brazilians, with new middle-class members now accessing credit. However, the fragility of the recovery in mature economies, combined with favorable perspectives for the Brazilian economy, intensified the inflow of foreign financing, part of which was directed to the local credit market (see table 6.2). The central bank was concerned that excessive volume of inflows could exacerbate the already strong growth in local credit markets by increasing credit multipliers. Lower cost of external funding could also weaken the transmission mechanism of monetary policy through channels related to credit, diminishing its potency as an aggregate demand management instrument, as well as causing distortions in the price of domestic assets.

Credit Market Developments

Since the mid-2000s, the dynamism of the credit market in Brazil has been intense and has translated into a continuous growth in the credit-to-GDP ratio. Greater levels of credit penetration, among other factors, contributed to the amplification of the power of monetary policy in Brazil. In 2010, in particular, credit operations in the Brazilian financial system, having left behind the impact of the 2008–09 crisis, were again expanding briskly and in line with domestic demand growth, which was boosted by a buoyant job market, improvements of income levels, and strong confidence indicators.

Credit growth to households did not change the stability of debt-service-to-income ratios (see table 6.3): higher volumes of debt as a proportion of income were compensated by lower costs and longer tenors. Interest rates and spreads

Table 6.3 Credit Market

	Unit	2009				2010				2011			
		Q1	Q2	Q3	Q4	Q1	Q2	Q3	Q4	Q1	Q2	Q3	Q4
Firms													
Total (growth rate)	%YOY	28.5	19.7	16.0	12.6	14.5	20.4	19.9	19.6	20.1	18.2	17.8	18.4
Average interest rate	%	30.2	28.2	26.4	26.0	26.2	26.8	28.8	28.4	30.4	31.0	30.8	29.3
Spread	p.p.	18.6	18.4	17.8	17.1	17.1	16.8	18.3	17.7	19.0	19.2	19.1	18.7
NPL (90 days overdue)	%	1.94	2.55	2.75	2.43	2.20	1.97	1.80	1.68	1.73	1.84	1.90	1.91
Households—Total Credit													
Total (growth rate)	% YOY	20.1	18.4	17.3	18.3	20.0	19.0	19.9	22.5	21.2	22.0	21.5	19.3
Total percent of GDP	%	17.7	18.5	19.3	19.3	19.3	19.3	19.6	20.2	20.3	20.7	21.4	22.0
Average rate	%	52.6	47.2	44.2	43.3	42.0	41.0	39.9	40.0	44.2	46.6	45.9	45.2
Spread over deposit	p.p.	41.6	37.3	34.3	32.5	30.9	29.2	28.5	28.3	31.7	34.1	34.2	35.0
Total debt to Income	%	32.5	33.3	34.2	35.2	36.1	37.2	38.2	39.0	39.8	40.7	41.8	42.5
Total debt service to income	%	18.8	19.5	19.3	19.5	19.2	19.4	19.1	19.3	19.8	20.3	21.9	22.2
NPL (90 days overdue)	%	7.1	7.0	7.1	6.5	6.1	5.7	5.4	5.0	4.9	5.2	5.3	5.5
Worst risk category/total	%	9.4	9.2	9.1	8.8	8.3	7.9	7.6	7.1	6.9	7.2	7.4	7.6
Households—Consumer Credit													
Total (growth rate)	%YOY	18.5	17.0	15.7	17.7	18.4	16.3	17.1	19.1	17.9	18.2	16.9	13.9
Total percent of GDP	%	13.0	13.7	14.2	14.2	14.0	14.0	14.1	14.5	14.4	14.5	14.8	15.0
Average rate	%	53.9	47.0	44.6	44.6	43.8	42.6	41.9	43.2	47.9	49.5	49.3	49.7
Spread over deposit	p.p.	43.0	37.0	34.6	33.5	32.4	30.6	30.3	31.3	35.2	36.9	37.6	39.5
Average maturity	months	13.0	14.8	15.1	15.2	15.5	15.7	16.1	16.2	16.2	16.3	16.5	17.6
NPL (90 days overdue)	%	8.5	8.5	8.3	7.9	7.3	6.9	6.5	6.2	6.2	6.6	7.0	7.3
Worst risk category/total	%	9.9	9.7	9.7	9.4	8.8	8.4	8.0	7.5	7.4	7.8	8.2	8.5
Households—Car Loans													
Total (growth rate)	%YOY	−3.3	0.6	4.5	17.8	26.5	33.8	43.3	50.7	48.0	45.3	35.7	27.8
Total percent of GDP	%	2.5	2.5	2.7	2.7	2.8	3.0	3.3	3.5	3.6	3.8	4.0	4.1
Average rate	%	32.0	28.6	26.0	25.4	24.3	24.0	23.6	23.8	28.1	30.4	29.1	27.3
Spread over deposit	p.p.	21.0	18.5	15.9	14.2	12.8	12.0	12.0	11.9	15.4	17.8	17.4	17.1
Average maturity	months	n.a.	16.0	17.0	17.0	18.0	19.0	19.0	20.0	20.0	19.0	19.0	19.0
NPL (90 days overdue)	%	6.4	6.9	6.1	5.5	5.0	4.4	3.8	3.2	3.7	4.5	5.2	5.9
Loan-to-Value (average)	%	71.2	72.0	74.7	74.9	77.4	77.9	78.6	77.8	70.6	74.9	73.6	71.9
Worst risk category/total	%	6.3	6.6	6.0	5.5	4.8	4.2	3.6	2.8	3.1	3.6	4.2	4.8

Source: Based on data from the Central Bank of Brazil.
Note: n.a. = not applicable.

for household loans declined, maturities lengthened, and delinquency rates (non-performing loan [NPL] ratios) were following a downward trend. Social changes in Brazil explain the expansion of credit to households, especially car loans and loans guaranteed by automatic payroll deduction. However, that did not significantly affect the risk profile of the system's credit portfolio, even when taking into account the considerably larger group of new borrowers with little prior credit history and the impacts of the 2008–09 financial crisis on the domestic economic cycle. Indeed, payments overdue above 90 days for total credit to households were at a historical low of 4.98 percent in December 2010.

Credit growth was more intense for loans with earmarked resources, boosted by Banco Nacional de Desenvolvimento Econômico e Social (BNDES) and mortgage lending (see box 6.2). Total credit outstanding in the financial system reached R$1,706 billion in December of 2010, corresponding to 46.4 percent of GDP and resulting from YOY growth of 20.6 percent. The nonearmarked credit portfolio reached R$1,116 billion in December 2010, after an increase of 16.9 percent compared with the previous year. It represented 65.4 percent of the total credit of the financial system. The household credit portfolio increased by 19.2 percent, reaching R$560 billion. Loans for the acquisition of vehicles soared by 49.1 percent and personal credit, mostly for consumption, increased by 24.7 percent.[13]

Box 6.2 Housing Loans in Brazil

Early in 2011, some observers began warning about the risk of a "housing bubble" in Brazil. Joe Leahy and Samantha Pearson of the *Financial Times*, for example, wrote on May 11, "Across Latin America's largest economy, record prices for the country's commodities and surging foreign fund inflows—what the International Monetary Fund calls 'favorable tailwinds'—are driving a historic boom. Property prices are soaring, consumer credit is booming and bank profits swelling. But there are growing concerns over whether Brazil is becoming addicted to this windfall of easy money. Increasingly, there are fears that Brazil is heading for a bubble. 'Experience tells us that whenever there is a lot of credit available for emerging markets economies, especially in South America, and if that's coupled with very high commodity prices, the tendency of our economies is to spend too much,' said IMF western hemisphere director, Nicolás Eyzaguirre, a former Chilean finance minister…Anecdotes abound of beachfront apartments in Rio's fashionable Ipanema district selling for a third more than levels of late last year. In São Paulo, house prices have nearly doubled since 2008."

However, these observations did not disentangle the structural and cyclical factors behind the upswing in housing markets in Brazil, nor did they take into account the small basis upon which this segment of the credit market was growing. True, mortgage lending, whose primary funding sources are saving account deposits and the Workers Severance Fund (FGTS), accounted for a major portion of the credit expansion. For decades, however, millions of Brazilians had stayed away from the housing market altogether, because of a nearly complete

box continues next page

Box 6.2 Housing Loans in Brazil *(continued)*

lack of financing. The rapid growth in mortgage lending helped many Brazilians start access-ing the housing market. Mortgage lending in Brazil grew 56 percent in 2010, and approxi-mately 44 percent in 2011. Nevertheless, mortgage debt is still quite low (4.6 percent of Brazil's GDP), compared to international standards (table B6.2.1). In Brazil, residential real estate loans still account for only 7.1 percent of total bank loans. Given its incipient state, it is expected to continue driving housing-sector growth in the long term.

Table B6.2.1 Mortgage Loans: International Comparison

Selected countries	Mortgage loans/GDP (April 2011)	Residential real estate loans to total loans (December 2010)
Brazil	4.1	7.1
Euro zone	40.2	—
Germany	37.7	16.8
Spain	61.2	27.4
United States[a]	70.3	36.5
France	39.8	—
The Netherlands	66.1	23.6
Italy	22.9	18.1

Source: FED, Bureau of Economic Analysis, BCE, Eurostat and FSI.
Note: — = not available.
[a] December 2010.

Mortgage lending gained momentum in Brazil not just because of the credit expansion and increases in income but also because of various legal and regulatory changes over the years. For instance, Law 10.931/2004 reduced a lender's mortgage origination risk by making it easier and faster to repossess a property in the event of default.[a] Earlier, in the case of delin-quency, it took as long as six years for a bank to foreclose on a property.[b]

a. It was made possible by the use of a mechanism called *alienação fiduciária*. In a mortgage issued with this feature, the title of the property used as loan collateral is placed with a trustee who, on behalf of the lender, has the right to sell such property in case of a bor-rower default—without court proceedings.
b. Another important legal change that helped boost mortgage lending in Brazil was the Law 10931/04 that amended the civil code to extend maximum mortgage tenors from 20 to 30 years.

On average and in aggregate terms, the general credit conditions were favor-able because most of the credit expansion was taking place in lower-risk credit modalities. However, there were localized sources of risk coming from house-holds' leverage increase and excessive lengthening of loan maturities in certain credit modalities. That risk was especially noticeable in consumer credit extend-ed with loan maturities beyond prudent levels (for example, above 60 months for car loans) and with loan-to-value (LTVs) ratios incompatible with the actual quality of the collateral.

Dealing with the Challenges of Macro Financial Linkages in Emerging Markets
http://dx.doi.org/10.1596/978-1-4648-0002-3

Capital Flow Developments

In recent years, capital flows to Brazil have been related to a profound transformation of the Brazilian economy. For almost two decades, Brazil has been enjoying an environment of stability, thanks to having implemented a consistent macroeconomic policy framework. Combined with the adoption of other sound public policies, this framework enabled the country to resume a process of sustainable and inclusive growth after two decades of sluggish and irregular performance. Naturally, Brazil became an attractive destination for foreign capital, with attractive investment opportunities in numerous areas, resulting from the newly improved prospects combined with the backlog left by under-investment during the preceding decades.

Alongside these structural factors, the long history of emerging market booms and busts shows that the buildup of financial risks is usually associated with periods of capital bonanzas that fuel credit booms, asset bubbles, and exchange rate misalignments. Those episodes frequently end in sudden stops and reversals of capital inflows that endanger the financial system and the real economy. Short-term inflows in particular contribute to the buildup of financial mismatches with potentially severe financial and macroeconomic consequences arising from the combination of exchange-rate pass-through and mismanaged aggregate demand expansions.

The strong recovery of the Brazilian economy in the aftermath of the more acute phase of the global financial crisis reinforced these structural factors, such as recognition for the soundness of the policy framework and favorable long-term growth prospects. Together with temporary factors such as the difference between international and local interest rates, and excessive global liquidity, all this resulted in large short-term foreign inflows and domestic currency appreciation.

Table 6.2 describes recent developments regarding capital flows. During 2010, net capital inflows (defined as nonresidents' net flows into portfolio investments, depositary receipts, direct investment and external credits) amounted US$125 billion,[14] compared with nearly US$80 billion in 2009. Brazil had a historically high amount of equity issuance, totaling R$146 billion (mostly by Petrobras), of which 26 percent were taken up by foreign investors. External debt issuance raised another US$48 billion, approximately. Foreign direct investment net inflows amounted to US$38 billion.

Therefore, managing the effects of large capital inflows has been one of the main policy issues in Brazil since the global crisis. Brazil managed those massive inflows primarily in standard textbook fashion, with aggregate demand contraction through fiscal and monetary policies, allowing significant currency appreciation while smoothing movements through sterilized reserve accumulation, which reduced the volatility of the exchange rate without, however, aiming at distorting its structural trend.

When Brazil's credit market was affected by capital inflows, a set of measures was consequently adopted, as discussed in the next section. There was evidence that multiple sources of foreign funding were transmitted into credit markets, in addition to the confidence factors associated with periods of abundant liquidity. External funding at low cost, despite tight domestic prudential rules, creates incentives to increase risk-taking and usually ends by distorting asset prices, including the exchange rate. In Brazil, excessive capital inflows contributed to the brisk pace of domestic credit growth, which fueled inflationary pressures associated with domestic supply-demand mismatches and created fertile ground for the domestic transmission of pressures stemming from global commodity prices.

Brazil's Policy Responses to the Crisis

Brazilian policy makers relied on a comprehensive textbook toolkit of policy measures (see table 6.4) to deal with the emerging risks of macroeconomic and financial instability at the end of 2010 and in early 2011. Standard aggregate demand management was conducted using fiscal and monetary policies to dampen supply-demand imbalances and to control inflation expectations. Macro prudential measures were adopted to reduce systemic financial risk stemming from rapid credit growth and large capital inflows.

Monetary policy. On the monetary policy front, in the first half of 2011, the central bank took action and raised the policy rate by 175 bps in five consecutive monetary policy committee meetings. That followed the 200 bps increase of 2010 and totaled an overall rate hike of 375 bps.[15]

Fiscal policy. On the fiscal front, in February 2011, the government reaffirmed its commitment to a strong fiscal stance with a steady reduction of the public-debt-to-GDP ratio and proposed a fiscal consolidation of R$50 billion of expenditure cuts. In August, it announced an additional R$10 billion savings. At the end of the year, the public sector successfully delivered on its commitment to a primary fiscal surplus of 3.1 percent of GDP.

Macro prudential policy. On the macro prudential front, the central bank and the government were proactive in anticipating potential sources of risk to the Brazilian economy and its financial system. Employing macro prudential measures they: (1) increased bank reserve requirements to dampen the transmission of excessive global liquidity to the domestic credit market; (2) increased capital requirements for specific segments of the credit market (essentially consumer loans) to correct a deterioration in the quality of loan origination; and (3) created reserve requirements on banks' short spot foreign exchange positions and taxed specific inflows to correct imbalances in the foreign exchange market and to deal with the intense and volatile inflows of capital.

The scope and direction of these policies is summarized in table 6.5, using the same format as table 6.1. In terms of macro prudential instruments, most of the balance sheet vulnerabilities listed earlier were addressed either comprehensively or for specific segments of the credit market with higher financial risk; similarly, loan contracts and foreign currency liquidity were strengthened. Other features

Table 6.4 Macro Prudential, Monetary, and Fiscal Policy Measures

Policy measures	Unit	2009 Q1	Q2	Q3	Q4	2010 Q1	Q2	Q3	Q4	2011 Q1	Q2	Q3	Q4
On activity													
Selic base rate (average)	%	12.6	10.3	8.9	8.8	8.8	9.5	10.6	10.8	11.3	12.0	12.3	11.4
Selic base rate increase	(+bps)	−250	−200	−50	0	0	150	50	0	100	50	−25	−100
Primary fiscal surplus													
Target	% GDP	–	–	–	2.50	–	–	–	3.10	–	–	–	3.09
Achievement	% GDP	–	–	–	2.00	–	–	–	2.70	–	–	–	3.11
Public debt (net)	% GDP	39.1	41.2	42.8	42.1	41.1	40.0	39.4	39.2	38.9	38.6	36.3	36.4
On capital flows													
Tax on financial transactions (IOF)													
Nonresident fixed income	%	0	0	0	2	2	2	2	6	6	6	6	6
Derivative margin deposits	%	0.38	0.38	0.38	0.38	0.38	0.38	0.38	6	6	6	6	6
Equity	%	0	0	0	2	2	2	2	2	2	2	2	0
Reserve requirement on	%	n.a.	n.a.	n.a.	n.a.	n.a.	n.a.	n.a.	n.a.	Minimum between 60% of what exceeds US$ 3 billion or Tier 1 capital	Minimum between 60% of what exceeds US$ 1 billion or Tier 1 capital	Minimum between 60% of what exceeds US$ 1 billion or Tier 1 capital	Minimum between 60% of what exceeds US$ 1 billion or Tier 1 capital
Short fx open positions in													
Spot market													
External credit inflows	%	5.38	5.38	5.38	5.38	5.38	5.38	5.38	5.38	6	6	6	6
Taxable maturity	days	90	90	90	90	90	90	90	90	360	720	720	720
FX derivatives	%	n.a.	n.a.	n.a.	n.a.	n.a.	n.a.	n.a.	n.a.	n.a.	n.a.	1	1

Table 6.4 Macro Prudential, Monetary, and Fiscal Policy Measures (*continued*)

Policy measures	Unit	2009				2010				2011			
		Q1[1]	Q2	Q3	Q4	Q1	Q2	Q3	Q4	Q1	Q2	Q3	Q4
On Credit													
Reserve Requirements (RR)													
Outstanding RR	R$b	174.9	179.4	186.0	193.6	233.2	279.5	301.3	395.2	400.9	418.6	434.7	448.5
Outstanding RR	%credit	14.0	13.9	13.7	13.6	15.9	18.1	18.5	23.0	22.7	22.7	22.4	22.0
Average ratio on demand deposits	%	42.0	42.0	42.0	42.0	42.0	42.0	42.9	43.0	43.0	43.0	43.0	43.0
Average ratio on term deposits	%	15.0	15.0	14.5	13.5	13.5	14.9	15.0	15.8	20.0	20.0	20.0	20.0
Tax on financial transactions													
(IOF) on domestic credit	%	0.0041	0.0041	0.0041	0.0041	0.0041	0.0041	0.0041	0.0041	0.0041	0.0082	0.0082	0.0068

Source: Based on data from the Central Bank of Brazil.

Note: n.a. = not applicable.

were not tightened but were already in place in Brazil, such as mark-to-market rules and the obligation for all financial institutions to register any derivatives contract in a clearing house or a data repository facility. The crisis revealed that this obligation had a loophole: nonfinancial firms with foreign exchange operations could use foreign counterparties to engage in derivatives trading outside Brazil's jurisdiction. This loophole was subsequently corrected by extending the registration requirement of overseas derivatives to nonfinancial firms and demanding the disclosure on the quarterly financial statements of publicly traded companies of sensitivity analysis of three scenarios based on their derivatives exposure.

Table 6.5 Macro Prudential Instruments by Vulnerability and Financial System Component

Macroeconomic policies by area					
	2009	2010	2011Q1-Q2	2011Q3	2011Q4
Fiscal Policy	Loosening	Neutral	Tightening	Tightening	Tightening
Monetary Policy	Loosening	Tightening	Tightening	Loosening	Loosening

Macroprudential instruments by vulnerability and financial system component					
		Financial system component			
		Bank or deposit-taker		Non-bank investor	Securities market	Financial infrastructure
		Balance sheet[a]	Lending contract			
Vulnerability	Leverage	Capital ratio	LTV cap		Margin/hair-cut limit	
		Risk weights	Debt service/income cap			
		Provisioning	Maturity cap			
		Profit distribution restrictions	Margin/Haircut limit			
		Credit growth cap	Tax on household credit			
	Liquidity or market risk	Liquidity/reserve requirements	Valuation rules (for example, MMMFs)	Tax on FX deriv	Central bank balance sheet operations	Exchange trading
		FX lending restrictions				
		Currency mismatch limit		Tax on ext credit		
		Open FX position limit				
	Intercon-nected-ness	Concentration limits				Central counterpar-ties (CCP)
		Systemic capital surcharge				
		Subsidiarisation				

[a] Capital and other balance sheet requirements also apply to insurers and pension funds, but we restrict our attention here to the types of institutions most relevant for credit intermediation.

Used for some segments of the credit market

Used for all financial system components

Macro Prudential Measures in the Credit Market

This section looks at macro prudential measures used in the credit market and their results. Measures used in the credit market include reserve requirements, a tax on financial operations; and setting capital requirements for consumer loans.

The Measures

Reserve Requirements As mentioned earlier, during the 2008–09 crisis, Brazil used reserve requirements (RRs) as an important mechanism to support financial stability and to facilitate liquidity reallocation among financial institutions.[16] In particular, to support the operations of small- and medium-sized banks, the central bank allowed larger banks to draw on portions of their required reserves if these funds were to be used to extend liquidity to small- and medium-sized banks.[17] These measures were progressively reversed and, in December 2010, the central bank moved further with the recomposition of reserve requirements by gradually eliminating these reductions. As demonstrated in figure 6.1, at the end of 2010 and in 2011, the central bank used reserve requirements again as a countercyclical buffer to smooth rapid credit growth, raising unremunerated reserve requirements on term deposits from 15 to 20 percent[18] and the additional remunerated reserve requirements on demand and term deposit from 8 to 12 percent.[19]

Nevertheless, the central bank protected sources of longer-term bank funding and exempted the Letras Financeiras (LF)—a bank-issued debenture with a minimum maturity of two years—from reserve requirements.[20] Previously, the Letras Financeiras were charged reserve requirements at the same rate as term deposits. Although maturity mismatch is inherent to the banking business, it is also a source of risk to be carefully monitored, so protecting LFs as a long-term

Figure 6.1 Total Reserve Requirements/Total Deposits
percent

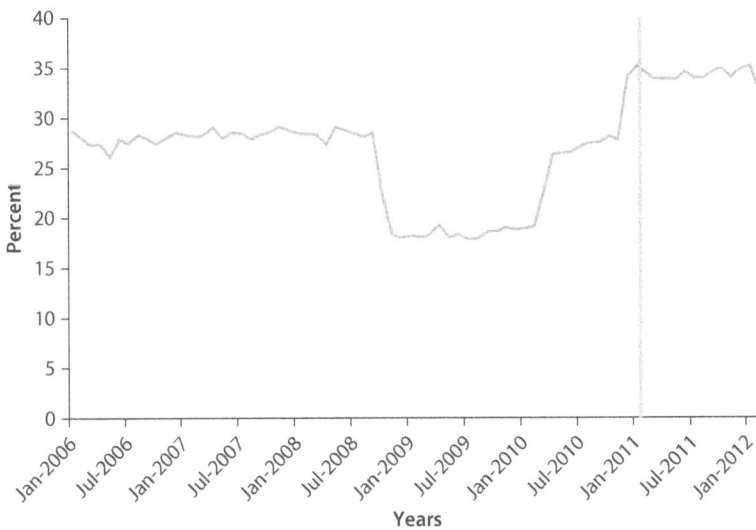

Source: Central Bank of Brazil.

Dealing with the Challenges of Macro Financial Linkages in Emerging Markets
http://dx.doi.org/10.1596/978-1-4648-0002-3

source of funding for banks, in conjunction with shortening credit maturities for consumer credit as a result of the macro prudential measures adopted, is important to mitigate this risk.

Financial Operations Tax
With the same objectives in mind, in April 2011, the government raised the tax on financial operations (imposto sobre operações financeiras; IOF) applying to credit operations for individuals[21] from 0.0041 to 0.0082 percent per day, limited to a maximum charge over 365 days. Therefore, the maximum tax rate increased from 1.5 to 3 percent.

Capital Requirements for Consumer Loans
As mentioned earlier, the diagnosis in the credit market was that the strong credit expansion to individuals, especially in car loans and payroll-guaranteed consumer loans, was increasingly done by lengthening maturities, increases in LTVs (see table 6.6), and reductions in interest rates that were incompatible with the quality of risk. These changes were translating into higher potential risk associated with higher household indebtedness and with maturity mismatches in the banking system. Since 2003, the tenors for consumption loans were extended and in some cases went beyond 72 months for car loans. As for payroll-guaranteed consumer loans, the tenors for public sector employees reached 60 months. This lengthening of loan tenors was not, however, accompanied by a similar extension in the maturity structure of banks' funding, which remained concentrated in demand deposits and term deposits with daily liquidity, thus constituting a source of financial vulnerability. The terms of some of these longer-tenor loans to households were not compatible with the quality of collateral and its associated risk. This characteristic was especially acute in vehicle financing, where the market value of pledged assets tends to decline rapidly. Given the growing size of these market segments, they represented a potential source of systemic risk if the prevailing market trends continued to go unchecked.

Macro prudential measures were thus adopted to curb the supply of excessively long-term consumer credit and car loans. In December, 2010, the central bank raised capital requirements for household loans above 24 months by

Table 6.6 Maturity Limits and LTVs Used to Calibrate Risk-Weights for Auto and Personal Consumer Loans, Brazil

Operation	Maturity and LTV	Risk Weight
Vehicles (financing and leasing)	Between 24 and 36 months and LTV > 80%	
	Between 36 and 48 months and LTV > 70%	
	Between 48 and 60 months and LTV > 60%	150%
	More than 60 months and any LTV	
Payroll-deducted loan	More than 36 months	
Personal loan	More than 24 months	
Other consumer loans		100%

Source: Central Bank of Brazil.

increasing the risk-weight factor (RWF), used for capital requirements calculation, from 75 to 150 percent on most household credit modalities.[22] In practice, the total capital required from financial institutions for those loans increased from 8 to 16.5 percent of risk-weighted assets (RWA). The rise on the RWF was not applicable to agricultural credit operations, mortgage loans, or credit for the acquisition of trucks and similar vehicles.

The Results

The reserve requirements on demand and term deposits, the IOF tax rate on consumer credit, and increases on capital requirements for consumer loans were successful in reducing the growth of household credit to a more sustainable pace. These measures affected not only the volume of new loans, as shown in figure 6.2, but also their interest rates and average maturities. The average interest rate rose to 30.4 percent p.a. in May 2011, compared with 22.8 percent p.a. in November of 2010 (see figure 6.3). In the same period, the monthly origination of new loans fell from R$11.2 billion to R$8.8 billion and the average maturities declined from 45.7 to 43 months (see figure 6.4).

Macro Prudential Measures on the Foreign Exchange Market

This section outlines the various instruments employed by Brazil to address systemic risk in the foreign exchange market, and provides an evaluation of their efficacy in the Brazilian context.

IOF Tax on Portfolio Investments by Nonresidents and on Margin Deposits on Derivatives

In October 2010, the IOF tax[23] for nonresidents' portfolio investment in fixed income instruments was raised,[24] first from 2 to 4 percent, and later in the same

Figure 6.2 New Loans: Five-Day Moving Average for Vehicle Financing and Personal Credit
R$, millions

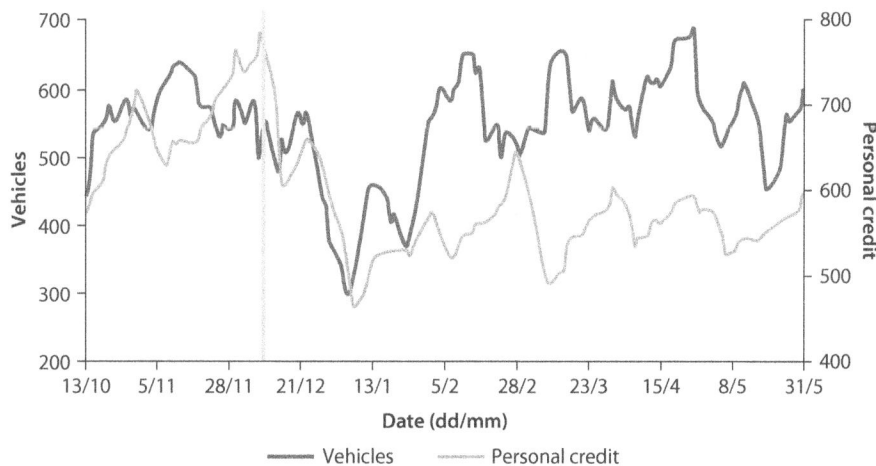

Source: Central Bank of Brazil.

Dealing with the Challenges of Macro Financial Linkages in Emerging Markets
http://dx.doi.org/10.1596/978-1-4648-0002-3

Figure 6.3 Interest Rates: Five-Day Moving Average for Vehicle Financing and Personal Credit
percent per annum

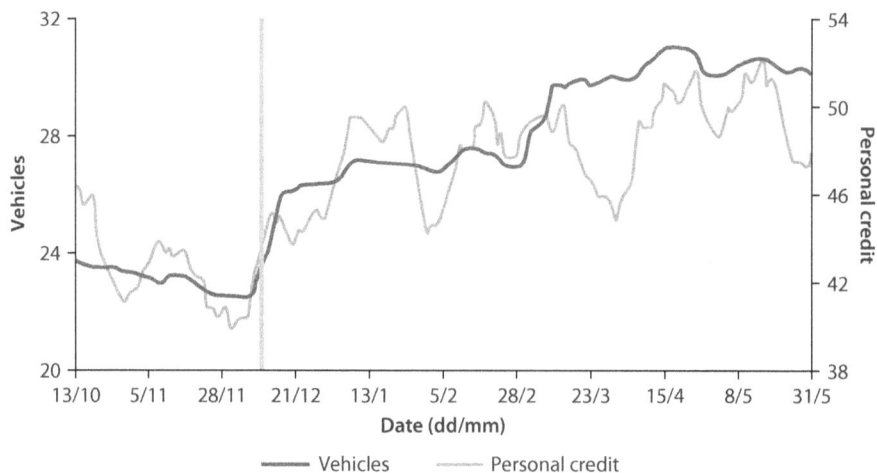

Source: Central Bank of Brazil.

Figure 6.4 Average Maturity: Five-Day Moving Average for Vehicle Financing and Personal Credit
months

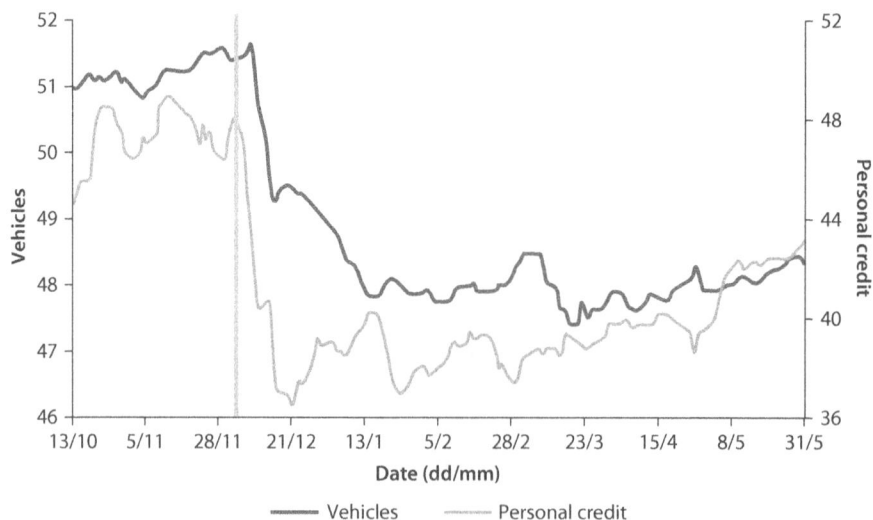

Source: Central Bank of Brazil.

month to 6 percent. The IOF was also raised to 6 percent (from 0.38 percent) on incoming remittances destined to posting collateral on derivatives positions held at central counterparties for stocks, commodities, or futures trading.[25] Inflows for equity investments remained subject to a 2 percent IOF tax rate. The IOF rate increases were meant to curb excessive short-term and speculative capital inflows and lengthen flow composition, in particular by discouraging short-term carry trades in both spot and futures markets, which were putting pressure on the domestic currency to appreciate.[26]

Dealing with the Challenges of Macro Financial Linkages in Emerging Markets
http://dx.doi.org/10.1596/978-1-4648-0002-3

Additional technical measures were subsequently adopted to close possible loopholes that would have allowed foreign investors to bypass the higher IOF tax rate on fixed-income flows. For instance, to avoid arbitrage between the different IOF rates in force, any internal transfer of nonresident funds from equities to fixed income investments was required to be accompanied by a simultaneous foreign exchange transaction subject to IOF taxation.[27] Local banks were also forbidden to lend securities to foreign investors, which would allow them to avoid the tax on derivative margin deposits. With this goal, the BM&F BOVESPA, Latin America's major securities, commodities, and futures exchange, was encouraged to exclude trust letters issued by domestic banks from the list of assets eligible as nonresident investors' collateral.

As shown in figure 6.5, the foreign net inflows to fixed income plummeted after the IOF tax rate hike in October 2010, and have not yet recovered. This happened despite the fact that, according to one estimate, when considering the domestic interest rate, the Special Clearance and Escrow System (Sistema Especial de Liquidação e Custodia; SELIC) at the time of the measure compared with the Libor rate (as a proxy for funding costs), investment in a government bond by a foreign investor subject to the IOF would break even at a about nine months.[28,29]

Conversely, carry trades on derivatives markets were not significantly affected. Because the tax on derivatives transactions applied only to margin deposits posted as collateral at the clearinghouse, and not on the actual notional exposure, it had limited effectiveness. In fact, the foreign investor could use other assets that he already possessed in the country, such as government bonds or equities,

Figure 6.5 Portfolio's Net Inflows by Asset Class, Monthly Data

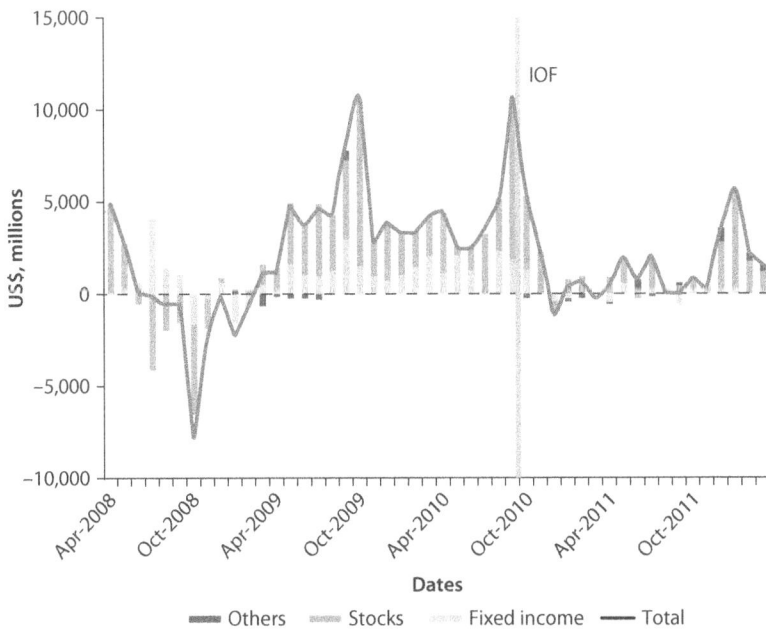

Source: Central Bank of Brazil.

to deposit as margin for his exposures and avoid the tax. Therefore, currency positions taken in the derivatives market enjoyed a favorable tax treatment compared with positions in the underlying cash market.

Bank Reserve Requirement on Open Short Positions in the FX Spot Market

In January 2011, the central bank imposed a 60 percent unremunerated reserve requirement on banks' short positions in the foreign exchange spot market exceeding either US$3 billion or Tier 1 capital, whichever is lower. In July, the limit was further tightened to US$1 billion.[30,31]

The diagnosis was that domestic banks could take advantage of the ample liquidity in global markets to significantly increase their funding abroad, and then invest those resources in Brazilian real (BRL)-denominated domestic assets, including loans, thus capturing the interest rate differential. There were concerns that such behavior could leave banks overexposed to currency mismatch and overly dependent on foreign liquidity, and hence vulnerable in the event of a large shock to the exchange rate or a rapid reversal of inflows. Technically, according to the regulations of the Brazilian foreign exchange market, banks open a short cash position when they sell foreign currency borrowed abroad resulting from drawings on external credit lines. Under those same regulations, although the operation is similar in accounting terms, when a bank contracts a direct loan or issues securities abroad (for example, commercial paper), it opens a long position. This aspect is particularly important to understanding the rationale behind subsequent IOF measures.

Indeed, throughout 2010, as shown in figure 6.6, banks increased exponentially their open foreign currency position. During that year, the financial system

Figure 6.6 Net Open Positions of Banks, 2008–12

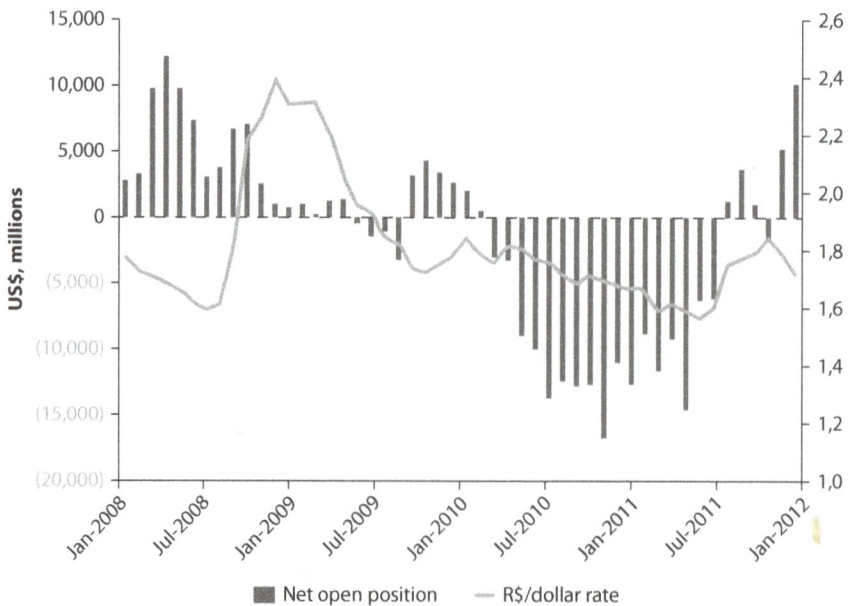

Source: Central Bank of Brazil.

came out of a long position of US$3.4 billion to a short position of US$16.8 billion by year end. Therefore, not only was the system's position as a whole excessive but also some small- and medium-sized banks built positions in very large sizes compared to their respective Tier 1 capital.

The reserve requirement on short foreign currency positions was also intended to complement the rise in the IOF tax on nonresident's portfolio investments in reducing the attractiveness of carry-trade operations through long BRL derivatives positions. That was expected to be indirectly achieved by making it more expensive for banks—usually the counterparty of nonresidents' derivatives positions—to draw on their external credit lines. It was designed to impair an important channel for carry trades while reducing vulnerabilities in the banking sector. By limiting banks' ability to operate in spot and derivatives markets, or by raising the cost of doing so, the authorities could, in theory, also make the market less liquid and potentially less attractive for foreign carry traders, even without targeting the latter directly.[32]

As shown in figure 6.7, foreign investors are on the other side of the derivative transaction, usually large international banks acting as market makers in the U.S. dollar/BRL offshore nondeliverable forward market. They take the role of bridge intermediaries between the onshore and offshore markets by relying on the domestic market to take the opposite net exposure of its offshore clients.

IOF Tax on External Credit Inflows

In March 2011, to curtail short-term speculative inflows while avoiding hampering longer-term flows, the authorities raised to 6 percent the IOF tax rate on inflows related to direct external borrowing or debt securities issued by residents[33] with maturity below 360 days. Previously, a 5.38 percent tax rate applied

Figure 6.7 FX Derivatives Exposure by Type of Investor

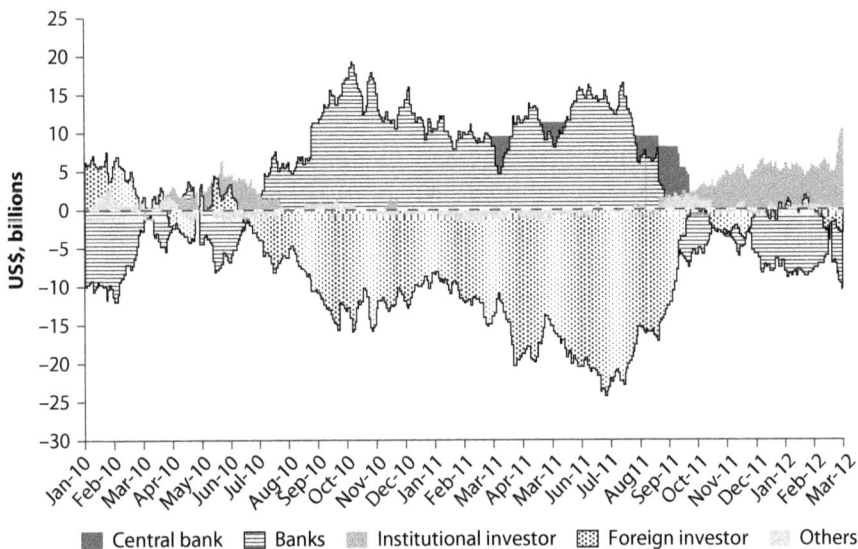

Source: Central Bank of Brazil.

Dealing with the Challenges of Macro Financial Linkages in Emerging Markets
http://dx.doi.org/10.1596/978-1-4648-0002-3

Figure 6.8 External Credit Profile Three Months Before and After IOF

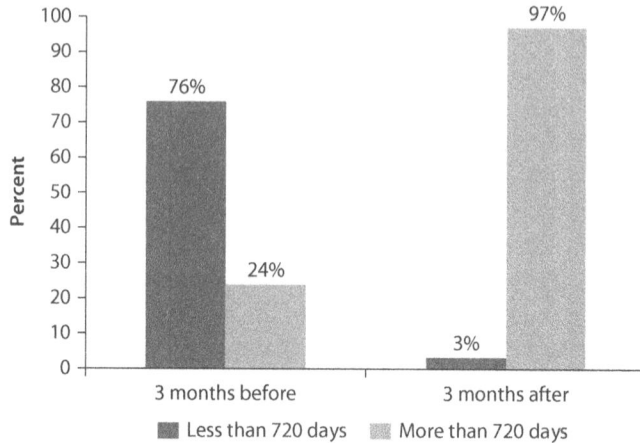

Source: Central Bank of Brazil.

only to debts with average tenors below 90 days. A week later, the minimum average tenor for IOF exemption was further increased to 720 days.[34]

Empirical evidence suggests that the IOF on external credit inflows was effective in lengthening the tenors of external credit for residents, therefore achieving its macro prudential goals (see figure 6.8). Despite the increase in the IOF tax rate, the net inflow of external credit amounted US$49.6 billion in 2011, as shown in figure 6.9,[35] a 14.6 percent increase compared with 2010, reflecting the global liquidity and strong foreign appetite for Brazilian assets.

The hike of the IOF tax rate on external credit also had a complementary function. As mentioned earlier, according to Brazilian foreign exchange regulations,[36] when a bank borrows abroad through a direct loan or a securities issue, it actually opens a long foreign exchange position. Local banks used this channel as a way to circumvent the reserve requirement on short positions while keeping their arbitrage trades.

As shown in figure 6.10, upon the adoption of the US$3 billion limit on short positions in January 2011, the authorities allowed banks to comply with the new rule and recompose their positions until April 2011. As a consequence, from January to March 2011, banks raised US$19.6 billion in net external credit. In July, the limit was tightened to US$1 billion, but this time banks were given only one week for compliance. Banks raised an additional US$8.4 billion in external net borrowing in July.[37]

IOF Tax on FX Derivatives

In July 2011, the authorities announced two new prudential measures aimed to curb excessive and concentrated short positions that could cause detrimental effects to financial stability and speculative pressures on the exchange rate.

The first was a provisional measure dated July 26, 2011,[38] which authorized the National Monetary Council (Conselho Monetário Nacional; CMN)

Figure 6.9 External Credit by Issuer, 2006–11

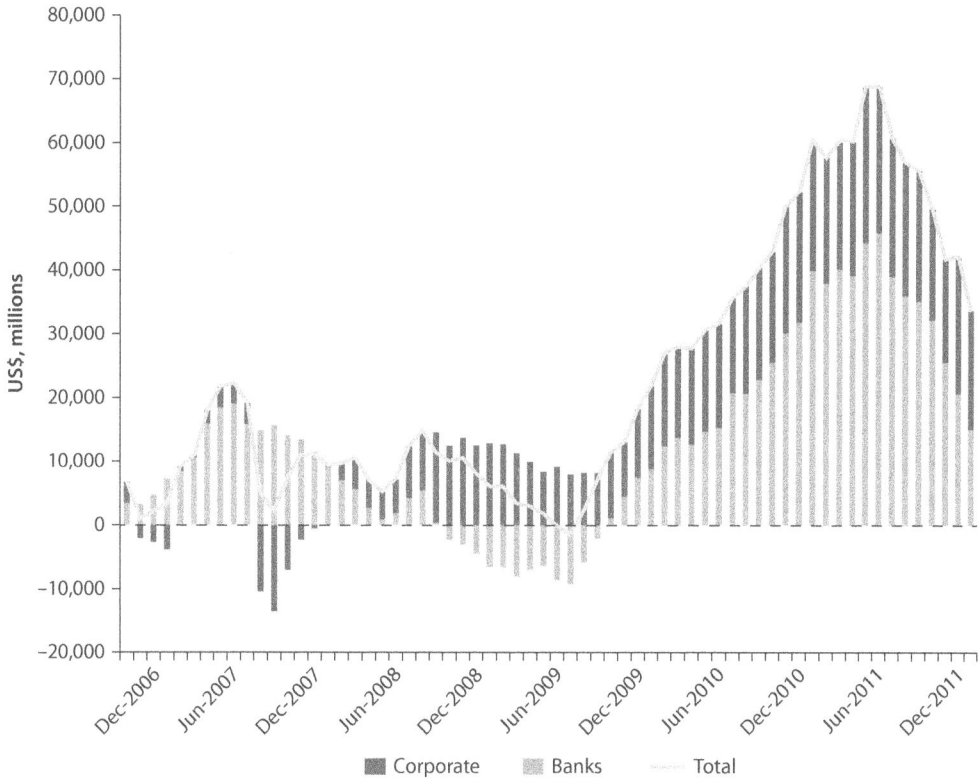

Source: Central Bank of Brazil.

Figure 6.10 Net External Credit Inflows to Banks

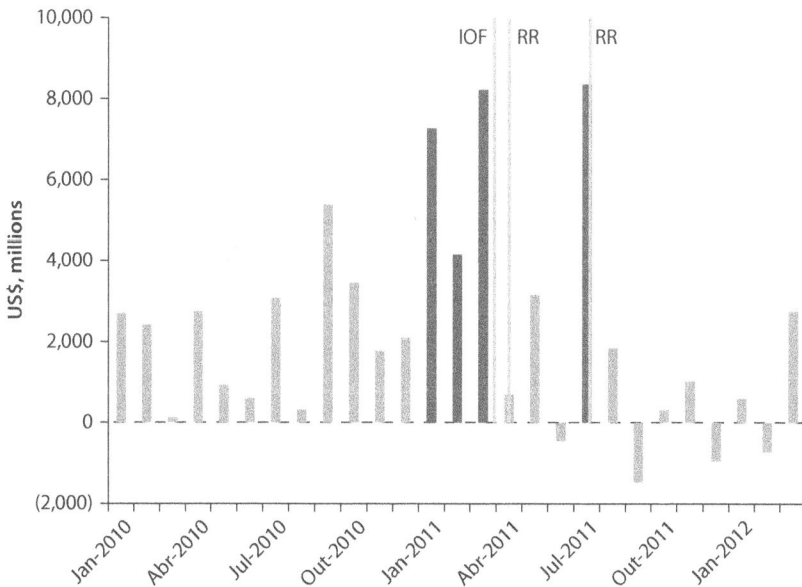

Source: Central Bank of Brazil.

Dealing with the Challenges of Macro Financial Linkages in Emerging Markets
http://dx.doi.org/10.1596/978-1-4648-0002-3

to establish specific conditions for the negotiation of derivatives contracts, for monetary and exchange policy purposes, regardless of the nature of the investor, with powers to (1) determine deposits over the notional value of the derivatives contract; and (2) set forth limits, terms, and other conditions for the negotiation of such contracts.

The measure also amended the IOF legislation, to clarify that:

- In the case of securities transactions involving derivatives contracts, the maximum IOF rate would be 25 percent. Up to this ceiling (25 percent), the executive branch can change the applicable rate at any time, considering its monetary and exchange policy goals. However, the current applicable IOF rate for derivatives transactions is 1 percent, as explained later.
- The amount of the securities transaction, for IOF purposes, is the adjusted notional value of the derivatives contract. The adjusted notional value is the reference value of the contract (notional value) multiplied by the factor resulting from the derivative's price variation with respect to the underlying asset's price variation.

It also established that to be valid, all derivatives contracts must be registered with duly authorized entities, that is, clearing houses or data repositories that have been accredited by the central bank or by the Brazilian Securities and Exchange Commission (Comissão de Valores Mobiliários; CVM) to operate with clearing, settlement, and registry.

The second measure was a decree,[39] also dated July 26, 2011, which amends the IOF regulation approved by a December 14, 2007 decree.[40] The new decree repeats many of the terms defined in the 2011 provisional measure described earlier, then states that the current applicable IOF rate to derivatives contracts is 1 percent and it is due upon the purchase, sale, or maturity of financial derivatives contracts, whenever its settlement amount is affected by the exchange rate variation and results in an increase in the net short exposure in relation to the amount calculated at the end of the previous business day. It applies both to resident and nonresident positions.

The applicable rate is reduced to zero if the purchases, sales, or maturities of derivatives contracts, at the end of the day, result in net short exposure below US$10 million. Above this figure, the 1 percent rate will apply.

The decree created a level playing field between the underlying cash market and the derivative market for nonresidents' carry trades. As mentioned earlier, initially the authorities adopted a 1 percent[41] tax rate that, although deemed insufficient to apply a burden equivalent to the 6 percent tax on fixed income instruments, apparently was enough to discourage short positions, as shown in figure 6.11.

The empirical basis for judging the effectiveness of restrictions on derivative positions is limited, given that their effects were mixed with the worsening of the global economic situation, since August 2011, and that they were imposed in conjunction with other measures. However, there is anecdotal evidence that

Figure 6.11 FX Derivatives Exposure and Exchange Rate

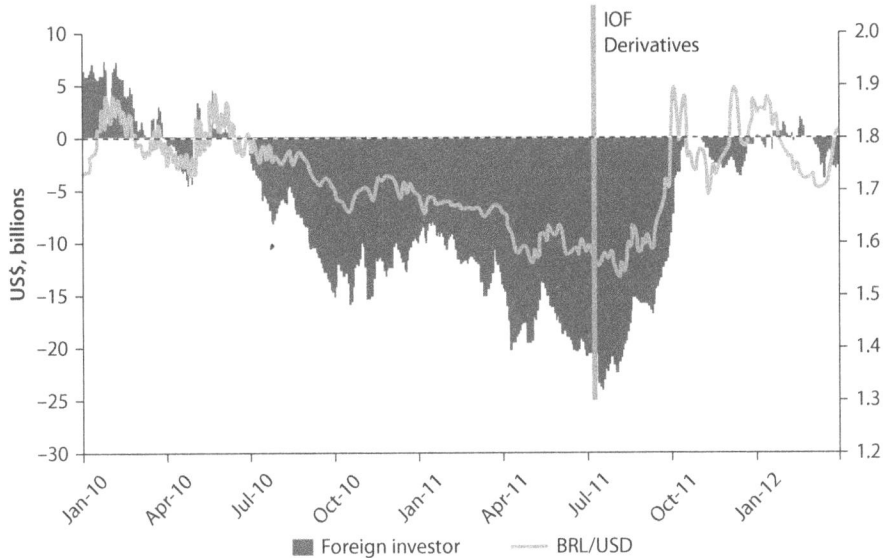

Source: Central Bank of Brazil.

the latitude given to the CMN to adopt further measures on derivatives market for monetary and exchange policy purposes, and also the establishment of the maximum IOF rate at 25 percent, had an important psychological impact on investors' mindset that resulted on dismantling excessive positions in the derivatives market.

All these measures were taken without losing sight of the fact that that there were important trade offs in taxing foreign exchange markets. First, the cost of hedging might increase for the real economy.[42] Second, the development of domestic derivatives markets, which is often a difficult-to-achieve stage of financial deepening, could be impaired or even reversed by excessive imposition of market restrictions.

Advanced Receipts of Export Agreements

In March 2012, the Central Bank of Brazil amended the rules applicable to export financing transactions involving the advancement of payment to the Brazilian exporter, commonly known as "advanced payment" (Pagamento Antecipado; PA).[43] This trade-financing modality is specifically designed to finance production by Brazilian exporters and for that reason it enjoys favorable tax treatment (0 percent rates for IOF and for income tax on interest payments).

Pursuant to the new regulation, qualifying advanced payments can be carried out only by the importer (the foreign buyer of the Brazilian goods or services) for a limited period of 360 days.[44] Before this amendment, the advanced payment could be made by any legal entity, such as the importer or a foreign financial institution, and without any time limitation.

Dealing with the Challenges of Macro Financial Linkages in Emerging Markets
http://dx.doi.org/10.1596/978-1-4648-0002-3

Figure 6.12 Foreign Inflows' Channels and Main Government Measures

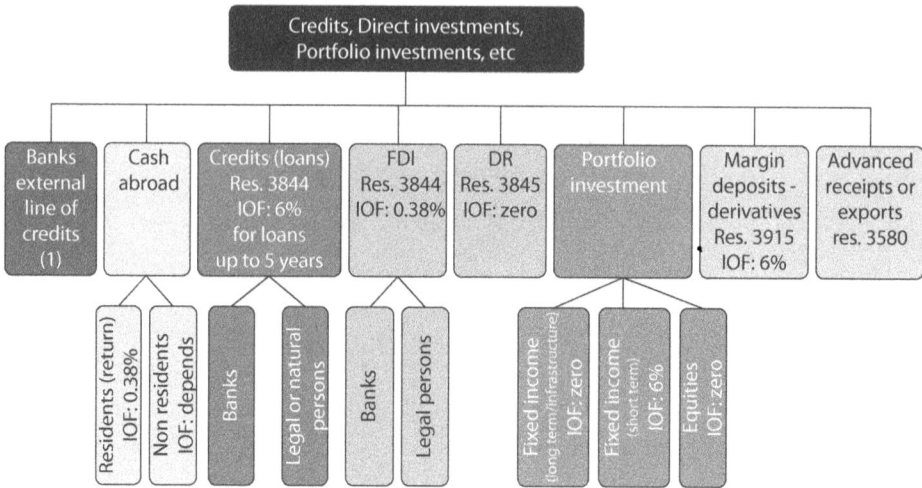

(1) There is no IOF, but short FX spot position reserves requirements may apply

Source: Based on data from the Central Bank of Brazil.

The amended central bank rules state that for values sent to Brazil as PA, one of the following situations shall occur within up to 360 days: (1) the shipment of goods or the provision of the service; (2) the conversion by the Brazilian exporter, with the prior written consent of the foreign payer, into direct investment (paying the corresponding 0.38 percent IOF tax) or external credit[45] (paying 6 percent IOF tax for operations with average maturity below 1,800 days); or (3) the return of the values sent to Brazil as PA, observing the tax regulations applicable to resources not destined to exports (paying 6 percent IOF tax on external credit and 10–25 percent income tax on interest payments).

This measure was prompted by concerns that the "advanced payment" had been diverted from its main function. It also had a complementary scope to previous measures on foreign exchange inflows inasmuch as it prevented regulatory arbitrage and closed a loophole that could otherwise be used to circumvent the 6 percent IOF tax on external credit operations. In fact, there was a strong growth of this kind of operation in January and February of 2012, when PA volume grew 46 percent as compared with the same period in 2011, while exports did not advance at a comparable pace.

Figure 6.12 summarizes the main channels for foreign inflows to Brazil and government actions to curb its excesses and improve its composition.

The Complex Conjuncture of the Second Half of 2011 and Early 2012

The results of the tightening cycle of 2010 and the first half of 2011 were positive. The policy settings were adjusted in a timely manner and were instrumental in cooling overheating pressures and gradually bringing inflation—after it reached a peak of 7.3 percent YOY in September 2011—down toward the target midpoint. Brazil was then and remains well prepared to withstand changes in the global scenario in terms of robustness of its financial sector, available liquidity buffers in local and foreign currency, and space to conduct countercyclical demand-management policies in either direction.

Macroeconomic Policies with Global Volatility and Rapid Changes in Risk Perceptions

Policy makers in Brazil were justifiably cautious as they observed the developments in the global economy in the second quarter of 2011. The global mood was one of confidence that the recovery in advanced economies (the United States in particular) was taking hold, especially after the initial boost to market sentiment brought on by the new battery of unconventional monetary easing measures, which visibly permeated through stock markets. The S&P 500 jumped from 1,286 in January 2011 to 1,320 in June 2011 and activity was indeed rebounding in the United States. Nevertheless, in Brazil, local experience with debt crises suggested that the ensuing recoveries were taking longer than usual, and could be marked by volatility. Brazilian policy makers were concerned that many structural characteristics of advanced economies had not been fully appreciated: the new levels of debt on the balance sheet of the public sector, compounded by the fiscal cost of both the rescue and the slowdown in activity, could become a serious drag on growth prospects, especially in countries with significant built-in budgetary commitments to high levels of welfare spending.

That was the case in the Euro zone, aggravated by the lack of a federal fiscal framework (especially with the discredit of the Maastricht treaty targets), lack of policy coordination, and the particular fragility of the countries at the periphery of the monetary zone. Those weaknesses were seen as having the potential to undermine the recovery and subject markets to new waves of heightened risk aversion, if not outright panic. That overall assessment was one of the reasons behind the reduction in the pace of rate hikes toward the end of the tightening cycle of early 2011 (the three last moves of that cycle, in April, June, and July, were all hikes of 25 bps each).

Toward the end of July 2011, things deteriorated rapidly. A succession of idiosyncratic policy stalemates (notably, the debt ceiling in the United States) together with a worsening in market sentiment, triggered by the Greek situation but reaching more systemic economies of the Euro zone (Spain and Italy) as well, revealed that the prevailing combination of political economy factors in the United States and in the Euro zone was pushing the balance of risks to the downside. The data coming from U.S. activity in July and August were also instrumental in affecting consumer sentiment, already negatively dented by stubborn levels of unemployment, the absence of a turnaround in the U.S. housing market, still-high levels of household debt, high gas prices reflecting buoyant commodities markets, and the downgrade of U.S. debt by one rating agency.

In that context of global deterioration, the Central Bank of Brazil was the first among its peers to reverse its stance. At the end of August 2011, it started to reduce the base policy rate. In the seven monetary policy committee meetings held since then, the SELIC (overnight) rate was cut by 400 bps (including two cuts of

75 bps each in March and April 2012). Monetary policy relaxation was accompanied by the tightening of fiscal policy in September (with the announcement of an increase of 0.1 percent of GDP in the primary surplus target), as the worsening of the debt crisis in advanced European economies discouraged any form of fiscal complacency. Despite the accumulating evidence that global economic conditions were taking a serious turn for the worse, monetary relaxation was widely criticized by market analysts who were focused on the still-high inflation headline YOY in the last quarter of 2011, despite its declining trend initiated in September.

However, by the end of 2011, domestic economic activity in Brazil was showing signs of deceleration. Eventually, growth figures surprised analysts on the downside. Vindicating the chosen policy strategy, not only did activity slow as had been expected by policy makers, but the above-mentioned worsening of global conditions affected business sentiment in Brazil by even more than anticipated, resulting in GDP growth of only 2.7 percent in 2011. Besides the obvious dent to business confidence, domestic factors may also have contributed to making the slowdown more pronounced than originally expected, including the cyclical dynamics of certain segments of the credit market (itself compounded by confidence effects) and the detrimental impact of a stronger exchange rate on industrial production. In the first half of 2012, domestic activity indicators remained as if suspended at a protracted inflexion, with flat industrial production indicators, subdued investment and business confidence, and smaller volumes of trade, while consumption continued to expand on the back of still-robust overall credit growth, resilient consumer confidence, as well as buoyant labor-market conditions, including record-low unemployment rates and rising household incomes. Activity was expected to pick up with the economy regaining momentum during the second half of 2012, led by private domestic demand, as the transmission of the monetary easing and other stimulus measures gradually gathers strength—notwithstanding some delay in transmission as rising NPLs blunted the response of lending rates to monetary policy. After growing by 2.7 percent in 2011, output did expand in the last quarter of 2012 at a faster pace but still below what was initially expected.

Inflation has been falling, but expectations—albeit decreasing marginally—remain that it will rise above the 4.5 percent target for the end of 2012, and continue to rise in 2013. After its 7.3 percent peak in September 2011, headline inflation fell to 4.99 percent YOY in May 2012. This decline reflects the activity slowdown, transitory supply factors, the progressive removal of particularly adverse inflation readings from the one-year trailing window, and the effect of the regular periodic updating of the inflation index weights. The lagged impact of moderating growth and the negative output gap on more sticky components of the index—including services—has also exerted some downward pressure on inflation. Conversely, wholesale price inflation picked up in April, reflecting pass-through—albeit moderate—from the exchange-rate depreciation observed since March.

The year 2012 saw a volatile, risk-off, risk-on environment for policy makers. After the European Central Bank's (ECB's) inauguration of long-term refinancing operations (LTROs) at the end of 2011, the new year began (as 2011 had) in a positive mood. But the implementation difficulties of the Greek program, the political economy debates about the pace of fiscal consolidation in many Euro zone countries and the missing of fiscal targets by Spain at the end of February 2012 threw markets in a downward spiral again. This negative external environment, notably the intensifying crisis in Europe, presents the most prominent downside risk in the near term. Important spillover channels include the potential for tighter external financing conditions and lower commodity prices should shockwaves from Europe lead to significantly lower global growth prospects.

Fine-Tuning Macro Prudential Instruments

With these negative macroeconomic developments, by the end of 2012, the credit market was growing at a more suitable rate and the average maturities for vehicle financing had declined. The average delinquency rate for vehicle financing in the first half of 2011 also declined 27.6 percent compared with the same period in 2010. In November 2011, the central bank decided to adjust the macro prudential measures adopted in 2010, not only to simplify the implementation and monitoring of the regulation but also to tailor it to the new economic outlook. It reduced from 150 percent back to the earlier 75 percent, the risk-weight factor (RWF) used for capital requirement calculation on all collateralized car loans with maturities below 60 months, regardless of loan-to-value ratios.[46] However, for car loans with maturities above 60 months, deemed to be riskiest, the RWF was kept at 150 percent. The impact of these changes is shown in figure 6.13.

For the payroll-guaranteed consumer loans market, the diagnosis was that the measure implemented in December 2010 to increase to 150 percent the RWF on loans above 36 months had only a modest temporary effect on the volumes of longer and riskier loans, falling well short of the desired impact. As shown in

Figure 6.13 Percent of New Vehicle Financing Loans, by Maturity Date

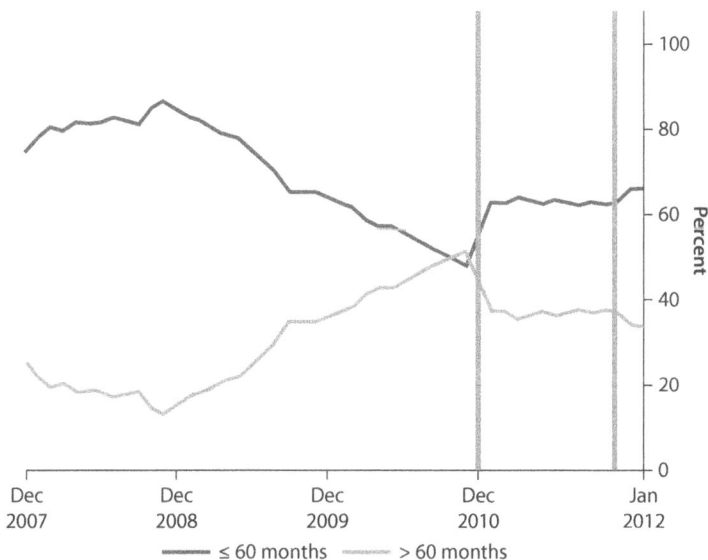

Source: Central Bank of Brazil.

Dealing with the Challenges of Macro Financial Linkages in Emerging Markets
http://dx.doi.org/10.1596/978-1-4648-0002-3

Figure 6.14 Percent of New Payroll-Guaranteed Loans, by Maturity Date

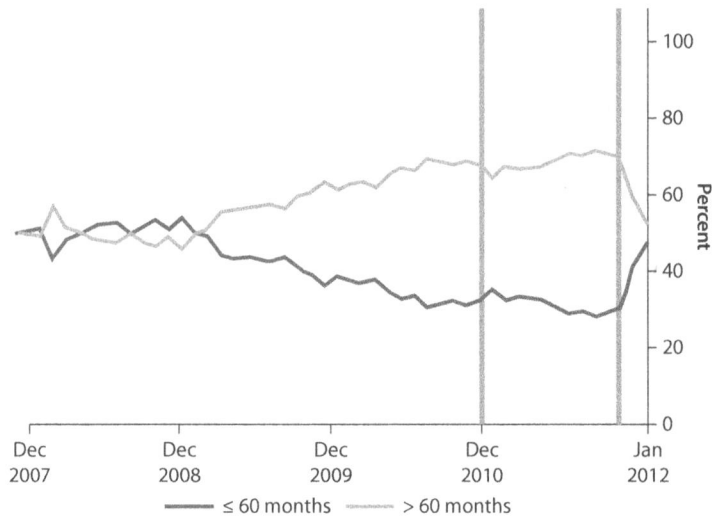

Dec 2007 — Dec 2008 — Dec 2009 — Dec 2010 — Jan 2012

―――― ≤ 60 months   ┄┄┄ > 60 months

Source: Central Bank of Brazil.

figure 6.14, the share of longer-tenor loans in the payroll-guaranteed segment declined in the months immediately following the implementation of the measure, but even that was a weak and short-lived effect, as they soon resumed the upward trend.

As a consequence, the central bank decided to increase the RWF for payroll guaranteed loans above 60 months from 150 to 300 percent,[47] and reduce it to 75 percent for the other contracts. To avoid any regulatory arbitrage or distortion in the personal consumer credit market, it also increased to 300 percent the RWF for loans above 60 months in other modalities of nonearmarked consumer credit.

In December 2011, along with other government measures to stimulate the domestic economy, the of the IOF legislation was amended[48] with respect to consumer credit transactions, reducing the rate to 0.0068 percent[49] per day (previously 0.0082 percent) for loans to individuals.

Policy Going Forward

Brazil will continue expanding its macro prudential toolbox on a precautionary basis, to increase its capacity to deal, whenever necessary, with exceptional foreign exchange volatility, destabilizing capital inflows, credit booms, and asset price bubbles. However, calibrating existing or new measures has proven to be difficult because of the economics profession's incomplete understanding of how risks to the financial system develop and how macro prudential instruments act on those risks (see Agénor, Alper, and Pereira da Silva 2009 and Agénor and Pereira da Silva 2010). Sometimes, as a result, decisions cannot be as firmly grounded in theory as one might desire; instead, Brazilian policy makers have been required to make policy judgments, drawing on analysis, market intelligence, and modeling to adopt a tentative, step-by-step approach, taking the necessary precautions and weighing the trade offs inherent to those measures to avoid excessive distortions and undesirable side effects.

Most of the macro prudential measures applied in Brazil since 2010 related to the time dimension of systemic risk, in other words to "leaning against the wind" and dealing with the cyclicality of the financial system. However, experience gained from the 2008 crisis has illustrated that, as the financial system becomes more complex and sophisticated, risks can arise not only in a single sector but also as an interlinked, systemwide issue. In fact, the Brazilian financial system is characterized by a high degree of conglomeration and concentration. It is organized around a few financial conglomerates that control over 75 percent of the system's assets. Therefore, another challenge is to develop effective indicators and to monitor cross-sectional risks related to the interconnectedness of the financial system and the real economy. The main tasks will be to assess network effects, enhance stress tests, expand the supervisory scope to include nonbank financial intermediaries, and to distill the findings from various analytical strands into a consistent macro prudential perspective on policy. Information on exposures between institutions and on exposures commonly held by institutions is crucial. Much of this information will need to be obtained not only from financial institutions, data repositories, and central depositories, but also from corporations. This aspect reinforces the understanding that the mandate that allows the Central Bank of Brazil[50] to access relevant information should be expanded to adequately fulfill its macro prudential supervisory role. Closer coordination and action between the various Brazilian supervisory agencies will, thus, be increasingly important.

In that spirit, Brazil is committed to the full and timely implementation of the Basel III framework and has reiterated its position in all G-20 fora (see figure 6.15). Most Brazilian banks can raise sufficient capital to meet Basel III requirements in the agreed timeframe mainly through retained earnings but, given new definitions and requirements, some adjustment of instruments to be eligible for Tier 1 capital will be needed. In Brazil, the traditional nonrisk-based measure of leverage, given by the ratio between total assets and equity, stands at low levels. The leverage ratios of Brazilian banks are particularly conservative considering the fact that our accounting rules are restrictive compared with international standards when it comes to netting of short and long positions. In addition, off-balance sheet exposures are not significant. Most banks should have no trouble meeting the new Basel III requirements on leverage; therefore no deleveraging process is expected in the near future.

Some refinements will need more work. On the countercyclical capital buffer requirements,[51] for example, further work may be required on its appropriate definition for a country undergoing structural changes and financial deepening because it normally relies on an automatic adjustment based on a "credit gap" indicator.[52] In line with this, the Basel Committee on Banking Supervision (BCBS) issued guidance on the operation of Basel III's countercyclical capital buffer stating that national authorities are free to use other variables as well as other qualitative information that they deem appropriate to activate the buffer.

Figure 6.15 Implementation of the Basel III Capital and Liquidity Rules

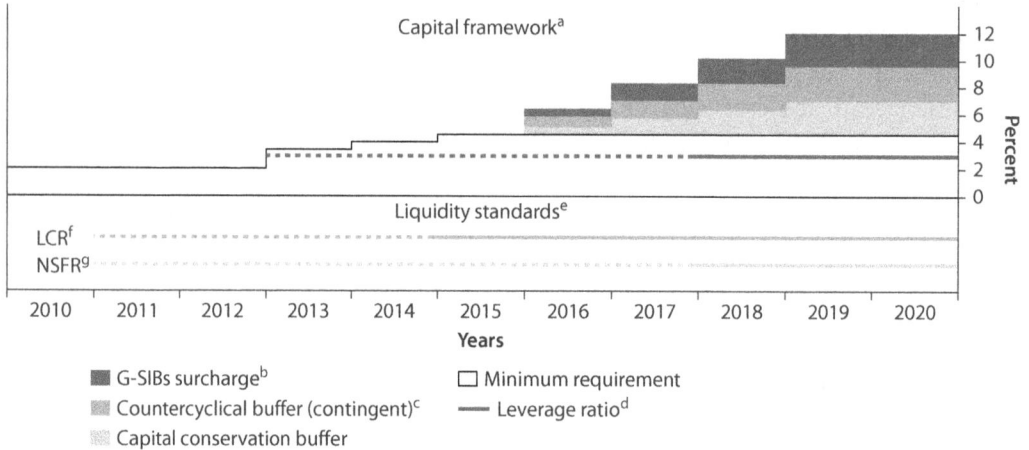

Source: Basel Committee on Banking Supervision; BIS calculations.
[a] Common equity capital requirements as a percentage of risk-weighted assets.
[b] Maximum of the countercyclical buffers to be met with common equity or other fully loss-absorbing capital, implemented according to national circumstances.
[c] Based on the results of the parallel run period, adjustments to be carried out in the first half of 2017 with a view to migrating to a Pillar 1 treatment on 1 January 2018 based on appropriate review and calibration.
[d] Capital surcharge applicable to the top bucket of systemic importance.
[e] Liquidity ratios to be monitored during the transition period.
[f] Liquidity coverage ratio.
[g] Net stable funding ratio.

Concluding Remarks: Complementing Monetary Policy with Macro Prudential Regulation

Brazil sailed well through the global financial storm. It used standard aggregate demand management instruments (combining tight fiscal and monetary policies) to deal with inflationary pressures arising from its V-shaped recovery in 2010. It maintained and reinforced its strong financial sector regulation and supervision, endorsed as a conclusion of the 2012 IMF mission conducting Brazil's Financial Sector Assessment Program (FSAP). In banking, the risk-based supervisory process is robust and with a high degree of compliance with the Basel core principles, together with insurance and capital markets supervision. Brazil also took measures to manage credit growth risks, appropriately introducing various macro prudential measures to contain financial risks in specific market segments. The Central Bank of Brazil has made clear that macro prudential measures are not a replacement for monetary policy action and are primarily geared at addressing financial stability risks.

Brazil's large macro financial linkages grew *pari passu* with improvements in the strength of the system. Brazil's FSAP stress tests show that the banking system can withstand severe shocks. After a public consultation process that ended in May 2012, the implementation of Basel III starting in 2013 will enhance the strength of the system. The interaction with the industry indicates that banks should be able to generate sufficient internal capital to manage this transition, including the replacement of deferred tax assets in their core capital base. Brazil's financial sector can also well manage shocks to liquidity and market conditions. Over 20 percent of assets in required liquid reserves are held as buffers at the central bank, and liquidity and market stress tests run by the FSAP find the system is well positioned to manage strains, including those that could arise from tail risks such as in the Lehman Brothers episode or a new bout of severe stress in the Euro zone. It is true that credit has grown quickly in the last decade (Brazil's credit-to-GDP ratio rose from 26 percent in 2004 to 49 percent in 2011) and cross-country studies have associated expansions of this duration and magnitude with risks to stability. However, as noted by the FSAP, a significant portion of the credit increase in Brazil reflects financial deepening, helped by institutional and legal reforms that have substantially strengthened creditor rights. Finally, the overall level of financial development remains low by international standards, which is associated with lower stability risks. Brazil was also innovative during and after the peak of the global financial crisis in exploring the boundaries of Tinbergen's separation principle (see table 6.7): on the one hand, we saw strong and established results that monetary policy is effective in addressing the transmission of excess demand into inflation; on the other hand, we knew that macro prudential instruments are effective in addressing the build-up of excessive financial risk. The less-explored areas were the effects of monetary policy (respectively, macro prudential policies) on financial risk (respectively, inflation and activity), and the interaction between these policies on both inflation control and financial stability. In the present stage of the global financial crisis, under the separation principle, Brazil employed two instruments (the central bank's base rate and a set of macro prudential tools) to address two objectives (the inflation target and a composite set of financial stability indicators). On the macro prudential side, a bias toward reducing excess credit growth and financial systemic risk requires a greater reliance on tighter regulation (around the Basel III framework) to reduce procyclicality.

Table 6.7 The "New" Separation Framework

	Monetary Policy (MP) One Instrument: CB Base Rate	Macro-Prudential (Map) Various Instruments: RR, LTVs, DTIs, K req (Basel rules), etc
Price Stability (Inflation)	Effective on Activity/Inflation (e.g., Flex IT, divine Coincidence, etc.)	Effects Known but issues of anchoring expectations, **timing & communication?**
Financial Stability (Risk)	Old debate about Lean Against vs Clean After	Effective on Risk (credit & asset excess growth)

Other related issues are under discussion. Financial stability remains in the mandate of many central banks but should it be conducted by a unified agency (the central bank itself) or by two separate agencies? Finally, communicating this new separation clearly to agents is important for an adequate anchoring of expectations.

Brazil had to address these issues with pragmatism, since it was painfully aware of the destabilizing effects of excessive levels of global liquidity, particularly when it transmits to domestic credit growth. Excessive capital inflows present several risks to recipient countries. They are potentially disruptive for emerging markets' price and financial stability. In the absence of any policy response, the economy may lose competitiveness and experience unsustainable trade account deficits. There is also a risk of financial instability. Banks tend to increase their foreign currency exposure and become more lenient in their credit standards when faced with higher foreign liquidity. Surges in capital inflows can lead to higher inflation and to credit and asset price bubbles. Beyond those points, the issue is whether monetary policy itself needs to be expressly concerned with financial stability objectives. And then, if the answer is affirmative, to what financial indicators monetary policy should respond? And what new set of instruments should be used as an additional component of the policy framework aimed at preventing financial crises? In short: To what extent should regulatory rules and monetary policy be combined to ensure both macroeconomic and financial stability?

That discussion is evolving alongside the emergence of analytical research, testing, and studying how these policies interact.[53] This analysis explores the roles of macro prudential regulation and monetary policy in mitigating procyclicality and promoting macroeconomic and financial stability. One avenue is to bring the qualitative insights into typical dynamic stochastic general equilibrium framework with explicitly modeled credit markets featuring some countercyclical (Basel-type) rules. There are some promising results suggesting that when both macroeconomic stability and financial stability are properly defined by quantitative benchmarks (for example, the volatility of stock or housing prices for the latter) monetary policy could go beyond its conventional mandate under inflation-targeting frameworks and address the time dimension of systemic risk—if only during a transitory period, while more is learned about the implementation and performance of the new macro prudential rules that are currently being discussed. Hence, there are promising arguments in favor of monetary policy reacting in a state-contingent manner to a credit growth gap measure, because of financial stability considerations. Nevertheless, monetary policy is not a replacement for macro prudential regulation because monetary policy cannot, in any event, address the cross-section dimension of systemic risk.

The broad direction of the new strand of literature that emerged after the crisis can be summarized in the following way: "leaning against the financial cycle" (that is, stemming excessively rapid growth in credit) can be done through a combination of monetary and macro prudential policies to avoid financial fragility and some prevention is not only recommended but achievable in an effective way. A combination of policies is effective involving monetary and macro prudential policies to act in a complementary fashion to ensure both macroeconomic and financial stability.

Brazil's recent experience with monetary and macro prudential policies to lean against the financial cycle and deal with systemic risks is an example of this new approach. We need more time to measure and assess properly whether this policy direction can be generalized and replicated with success. The present context of the global economy is challenging but it has also triggered new thinking among regulators and central bankers to be ahead of the curve for the ongoing and the next episodes of financial stress.

Annex 6A: Categorizing Brazil's Macro Prudential Instruments

Tools	Risk dimensions	
	Time dimension	Cross-sectoral dimension
Category 1. Instruments developed specifically to mitigate systemic risk		
	• Minimum capital ratio requirement above international standards (<u>Circular 3360-Sept 12, 2007</u>) • Countercyclical change in risk weights for exposure to auto and payroll loans related to longer maturities and higher LTV ratios (<u>Circular 3515-Dec 03, 2010</u>) • Prohibit payroll loan's maturity above 60 months (<u>Circular 3563 - Nov 11, 2011</u>) • Increase financial transaction tax on consumption credit operations for individuals (<u>Decree 7456 – Apr 06, 2011</u>)	• Higher capital charges for trades not cleared through CCPs (<u>Circular 3360 - Sept 12, 2007</u>) • Increase capital risk weights to exposures to mutual fund's quota (<u>Circular 3563 - Nov 11, 2011</u>)*
Category 2. Recalibrated instruments		
	• Loan loss provisioning incorporates expect losses but also incurred losses' data (<u>Resolution 2682 - Dec 21, 1999</u>) • Increase financial transaction tax on foreign inflows for fixed income investments (<u>Decree 7330 - Out 18, 2010</u>) • Increase reserve requirements on demand and time deposits and exempt "Letras Financeiras" (<u>Circular 3513 and 3514 – Dec 03, 2010</u>). • Increase financial transaction tax on inflows related to foreign credit with maturities below 720 days (<u>Decree 7457-Apr 6, 2011</u>) • Unremunerated reserve requirement on currency short open positions above certain limits (<u>Circular 3520 - Jan 6, 2011 and Circular 3,548 - Jul 8, 2011</u>) • Stressed VaR to build additional capital buffer against market risk during a boom for internal and standardized models (<u>Circular 3478 – Dec 24, 2009 and Circular 3568 – Dec 21, 2011</u>)	• Financial transaction tax on derivatives' positions that increase fx short net exposure (<u>Decree 7536 - Jul 26, 2011</u>) • Remunerated reserve requirements on time deposits conditioned upon acquisition of medium and small banks' credit portfolio (<u>Circular 3569 – Dec 22, 2011</u>)

Annex 6B: IOF Tax Measures on Foreign Exchange Transactions

IOF

TAX ON CREDIT AND EXCHANGE TRANSACTIONS, INSURANCE AND SECURITIES

MAIN MEASURES INVOLVING NON RESIDENT OPERATIONS

Date format: dd. mm yy

FINANTIAL AND CAPITAL MARKETS	Dec. 6,306	Dec. 6,391	Dec. 6,613	Dec. 6,983	Dec. 7,011	Dec. 7,323	Dec. 7,330	Dec. 7,412	Dec. 7,456	Dec. 7,632	Dec. 7,683
	14.12.2007	17.03.2008	22.10.2008	19.10.2009	18.11.2009	04.10.2010	18.10.2010	30.12.2010	28.03.2011	01.12.2011	01.03.2012
Fixed income	zero	1.5%	zero	2%	–	4%	6%	6%	6%	6%	–
Fixed income - Law 12,431 art. 1 and 3	–	–	–	–	–	–	–	–	–	zero	–
Variable income (stocks)	zero	zero	zero	2%	–	2%	–	2%	2%	zero	–
IPO	zero	zero	zero	2%	–	2%	–	2%	2%	zero	–
Emerging Companies Investment Funds (FIEE)	zero	1.5%	zero	2%	–	4%	6%	2%	2%	zero	–
Private Equity Funds (FIP)	zero	1.5%	zero	2%	–	4%	6%	2%	2%	zero	–
FDI to variable income/ stocks (migration)	zero	zero	zero	zero	–	zero	–	2%	2%	zero	–
Margin deposits	zero	0.38%	0.38%	0.38%	–	0.38%	6%	6%	6%	6%	–
Cancellation of DR into local shares	zero	zero	zero	zero	–	zero	–	2%	2%	zero	–
BDR/secondary market	–	–	–	–	–	–	–	–	–	6%	–
Deliver of Brazilian shares to issue DR[a]	–	–	–	–	1.5%	–	–	–	–	–	zero

[a] This is not IOF on foreign exchange operation, but IOF on securities.

Annex 6B: IOF Tax Measures on Foreign Exchange Transactions *(continued)*

EXTERNAL LOANS	Dec. 6,306 14.12.2007	Dec. 6,339 03.01.2008	Dec. 7,456 28.03.2011	Dec. 7,457 06.04.2011	Dec. 7,683 01.03.2012	Dec. 7,698 09.03.2012	Dec. 7,751 13.06.2012	Dec. 7,853 04.12.2012
Tax rate	5%	5.38%	6%	6%	6%	6%	6%	6%
Taxable maturity	90 days	90 days	360 days	720 days	1,080 days	1,800 days	720 days	360 days

CREDIT CARD	Dec. 7,412 30.12.2010	Dec. 7,454 25.03.2011
Credit card company obligation for client's purchase abroad	2.38%	6.38%

DERIVATIVE CONTRACTS [a]	Law 12,543 [b] 08.12.2011	Dec. 7.536 26.07.2011	Dec. 7.563 15.09.2011	Dec. 7.699 15.03.2012
Exposure:	Max IOF	1% [c]	1% [d]	1% [e]
long exposure reductions/ short exposure increases	25%			

[a] This is not IOF on foreign exchange operation, but IOF on FX derivatives.

[b] Law converted from Provisional Measure 539, de 26.07.2011.

[c] Tax applies on adjusted notional value, which results from notional value x price variation of derivatives with respect to the price variation of underlying assets. Applied to increases on short exposure.

[d] It details the calculation of the adjusted notional value and makes some aditional adjustments to this value in order to disregard foreign exchange variations (which are not related with opening or liquidation of positions).

[e] Tax = 0 on positions that increase the net short exposures acquired by exporters for purpose of hedging, up on specific conditions established in the decree.

FOREIGN DIRECT INVESTMENT [a]	Dec. 6,306 14.12.2007	Dec. 6,339 03.01.2008	Dec. 7,412 30.12.2010
FDI	zero	0.38%	0.38%

[a] General rule: tax on foreign exchange operation is 0.38%, unless specified differently.

Notes

1. Mostly from the Bank for International Settlements and not surprisingly from the Bank of Japan but also Blanchard (2000); Borio and Lowe (2002b); Cecchetti et al. (2000) and Goodhart (2000).

2. Mostly from the Anglo-Saxon academic community, for example, Bean (2003); Bernanke and Gertler (1999; 2001), Greenspan (2002); Kohn (2005), and Miskhin (2008).

3. The warning was made by Alan Greenspan during the dot-com bubble on December 5, 1996: "Clearly, sustained low inflation implies less uncertainty about the future, and lower risk premiums imply higher prices of stocks and other earning assets. We can see that in the inverse relationship exhibited by price/earnings ratios and the rate of inflation in the past. But how do we know when irrational exuberance has unduly escalated asset values, which then become subject to unexpected and prolonged contractions as they have in Japan over the past decade?" (Greenspan 1996). But questions were raised by others (see Bernanke 2001, 2002; Borio and Lowe 2002a).

4. See Miskhin (2008).

5. CIEPR (2011).

6. See Stark (2010), Svensson (2010, 2011) and Trichet (2010).

7. The Turner Review (see Financial Services Authority 2009), Brunnermeier et al. (2009), and BCBS (2010).

8. See the financial regulatory agenda of the G-20 and Financial Stability Board (FSB), Committee on the Global Financial System (2010), Galati and Moessner (2011) and IMF (2011b, 2011c). The debate on post-crisis macro financial policies was broader and can be found for example in Blanchard et al. (2010, 2012); Blinder (2010), and Borio (2011).

9. See Lim et al. (2011).

10. Mesquita and Torós (2010).

11. See BIS (2009), IMF (2011a), and Terrier and others (2011).

12. See Central Bank of Brazil (2011a) for complete description of the macroeconomic scenario.

13. See Central Bank of Brazil (2011b).

14. For the purpose of this chapter, the amounts of capital flows comes from data on foreign exchange contracts, the same criteria used for IOF (Brazil's tax on financial operations) charges. Because of these methodological criteria, the figures may differ from balance-of-payments' data.

15. The reversal of the monetary policy tightening stance in August 2011 is discussed later in more detail.

16. See Montoro and Moreno (2011), and Moreno (2011).

17. Central Bank of Brazil, Circular 3427/2008.

18. Central Bank of Brazil, Circular 3513/2010.

19. Central Bank of Brazil, Circular 3514/2010.

20. Central Bank of Brazil, Circular 3513/2010.

21. Government of Brazil, Decree 7458. http://www.planalto.gov.br/ccivil_03/_Ato2011-2014/2011/Decreto/D7458.htm.

22. Central Bank of Brazil, Circular 3515, December 3, 2010.

23. The IOF is a tax of economic nature and is applicable to several operations, such as: credit, foreign exchange, securities, and insurance transactions. Each tax origin is based on a different trigger; in the case of a foreign exchange transaction, it is the settlement of the respective foreign exchange contract.

24. The IOF on nonresident inflows for portfolio investments was used to limit excessive inflows before the crisis, from March to October 2008, with a 1.5 percent tax rate, both for fixed income and equities. In October 2009, it was introduced again with a 2 percent tax rate.

25. In Brazil, about 90 percent of the derivatives are standardized exchange-traded and cleared through a central counterparty. The BM&F BOVESPA is currently the only exchange in Brazil acting as central counterparty for every trade registered on its systems.

26. A synthetic carry trade can be performed in the derivatives market by acquiring long positions on a high-yield currency (that is, the Brazilian real) and short position on a funding currency (that is, dollars, yens, and so on).

27. Otherwise, nonresidents would be able to enter the market with a first investment in equity, taxed at the 2 percent IOF, and, later on, transfer funds to a fixed income investment, avoiding the payment of a higher 6 percent IOF rate.

28. Although the flat one-time IOF hurdle is relatively less penalizing of returns on investments held for longer terms, the tax rate hike affected the liquidity of the primary market at the long end of the yield curve, where foreign investors are usually more active.

29. Calculated as: $t = \log(1\text{-IOF})/\log[(1+e)/(1+i)]$, where $e=$ external interest rate and $i =$ domestic interest rate

30. A five-day moving average methodology was also adopted for the calculation of the short position.

31. In December 2012, BCB released Circular 3619 withdrawing this limit back to US$3 billion as the likehood of excessive short-term capital inflows was not high anymore and in order to inject further liquidity into the spot market.

32. This happens because local banks usually perform an arbitrage transaction in which they take a long foreign exchange position in the derivatives markets and hedge their exposures in the underlying cash market by drawing on an external credit line and selling the proceeds to the central bank, to another bank, or in the primary market (that is, to an importer) and invest it in BRL-denominated assets. They earn a currency risk-free arbitrage profit resulting from the difference between the onshore foreign currency interest rate—called *cupom cambial*—and the offshore external borrowing cost (Libor rate plus a spread). This transaction, in theory, does not influence the exchange rate trending path.

33. Law 4131/62 requires that the total amount borrowed abroad by a resident to be fully internalized in the country.

34. To provide more effectiveness to the measure, it was imposed on the performance of simultaneous foreign exchange operations for renewal, renegotiation, and assumption of obligation of external loan (including securities) under registration requirement with the central bank.

35. The authorities further extended the taxable average tenor from 720 days to 1,080 days on March 1, 2012 and to 1,800 days in March 9, 2012. On July 13, 2012, it returned to 720 days and on December 4, 2012 it withdrew back to 360 days.

Dealing with the Challenges of Macro Financial Linkages in Emerging Markets
http://dx.doi.org/10.1596/978-1-4648-0002-3

36. External credit flow rules are established by Resolution 3,844/2010.

37. Foreign exchange transactions related to direct investment in Brazilian companies remains subject to a rate of 0.38 percent on the inflow.

38. Provisional Measure 539/2011, later approved by the Brazilian Congress and converted in the Law 12543 of December 8, 2011.

39. Decree 7536.

40. Decree 6306.

41. The Law 12543/2011 allows the IOF tax rate on derivatives up to 25 percent.

42. On March 15, 2012, the government exempted certain exporters from the 1 percent financial operations tax levied on FX derivatives as long as they can provide evidence that the volume of their FX derivatives trades are below 1.2 times the export contracts they had in the previous year.

43. Central Bank of Brazil Circular 3580.

44. By means of Circular 3604, of December 4, 2012, this period was extended from 1 to 5 years.

45. Registered with the Central Bank of Brazil pursuant to Law 4131, of September 3, 1962, as amended by Law 4390, of August 29, 1964, and relevant regulation.

46. Circular 3563/2011.

47. In March 4, 2013, this RWF was reduced back to 150 percent.

48. Decree 7632/2011.

49. In May 21, 2012, Decree 7726 further diminished it to 0.0041 percent.

50. The Central Bank of Brazil's mission is defined as "to ensure the stability of the purchasing power of the currency and the soundness and efficiency of the financial system."

51. The size of the countercyclical capital buffer varies over time and can amount from 0 to 2.5 percent of the bank's risk-weighted assets.

52. The countercyclical capital buffer relies on a formula that considers the relation between the total lending to the country's GDP and the size of its deviation from a long-term trend.

53. For a summary of the literature see Agénor and Pereira da Silva (2012a). For an analytical solution see Agénor, Alper and Pereira da Silva (2011, 2012). The stabilizing effect of a central bank reaction function with a credit rule is stronger than that of alternative rules following a classical Taylor-rule specification even when augmented by a set of macro prudential regulations. These results hold for an open economy with a flexible exchange rate, incorporating the interaction between capital inflows (sudden floods), credit creation, and the macroeconomy.

References

Agénor, Pierre-Richard, Koray Alper, and Luiz A. Pereira da Silva. 2009. "Capital Requirements and Business Cycles with Credit Market Imperfections." Policy Research Working Paper 5151, World Bank, Washington, DC. Forthcoming in the *Journal of Macroeconomics*.

———. 2011. "Capital Regulation, Monetary Policy and Financial Stability." Working Paper 154, Centre for Growth and Business Cycles Research. Forthcoming in the *International Journal of Central Banking*.

———. 2012. "Sudden Floods, Macroprudential Regulation and Stability in an Open Economy." Working Paper 267, Central Bank of Brazil, Brasília.

Agénor, Pierre-Richard, and Luiz A. Pereira da Silva. 2010. "Reforming International Standards for Bank Capital Requirements: A Perspective from the Developing World." In *International Banking in the New Era: Post-Crisis Challenges and Opportunities (International Finance Review)*, edited by S. Kim and M. D. McKenzie, Vol. 11. Bingley: Emerald Group Publishing Limited.

Agénor, P. R., and L. Pereira da Silva. 2012. "Macroeconomic Stability, Financial Stability, and Monetary Policy Rules." *International Finance* 15-2: 205–24

BCBS (Basel Committee on Banking Supervision). 2010. "Group of Governors and Heads of Supervision Announces Higher Global Minimum Capital Standards." September 12. http://www.bis.org/press/p100912.pdf.

BIS (Bank for International Settlements). 2009. "Capital Flows and Emerging Market Economies." Working Paper 33, January, Committee on the Global Financial System, BIS.

———. 2010. "Macroprudential Instruments and Frameworks: A Stocktaking of Issues and Experiences." Working Paper 38, Committee on the Global Financial System, BIS, May.

Bean, C. 2003. "Asset Prices, Financial Imbalances and Monetary Policy: Are Inflation Targets Enough?" Working Paper 140, Bank for International Settlements, Basel, Switzerland.

Bernanke, B. 2002. "Asset-Price 'Bubbles' and Monetary Policy." In *Proceedings of New York Chapter of the National Association for Business Economics*. http://www.federalreserve.gov/boarddocs/speeches/2002/20021015/default.htm.

Bernanke, B., and M. Gertler. 1999. "Monetary Policy and Asset Volatility." *Federal Reserve Bank of Kansas City Economic Review* 84: 17–52.

———. 2001. "Should Central Banks Respond to Movements in Asset Prices?" *American Economic Review* 91: 253–57.

Blanchard, O. 2000. "What Do We Know About Macroeconomics that Fisher and Wicksell Did Not?" Working Paper Series 7550, February, National Bureau of Economic Research, Cambridge, MA.

Blanchard, O., G. Dell'Ariccia, and P. Mauro. 2010. "Rethinking Macroeconomic Policy." Staff Position Note 10/03, International Monetary Fund, Washington, DC, February.

Blanchard, O., D. Romer, M. Spence, and J. Stiglitz. 2012. *In the Wake of the Crisis*. Cambridge: Massachusetts Institute of Technology Press.

Blinder, A. S.. 2010. "How Central Should the Central Bank Be?" *Journal of Economic Literature* March: 23–133.

Borio, C.. 2011. "Central Banking Post-Crisis: What Compass for Uncharted Waters?" Working Paper 353, Bank for International Settlements, Basel, Switzerland, September.

Borio, C., and P. Disyatat. 2011. "Global Imbalances and The Financial Crisis: Link or No Link?" Working Paper 346, Bank for International Settlements, Basel, Switzerland, May.

Borio, C., and P. Lowe. 2002a. "Asset Prices, Financial and Monetary Stability: Exploring the Nexus." Working Paper 114, Bank for International Settlements, Basel, Switzerland. http://www.bis.org/publ/work114.htm

Borio, C., and P. Lowe. 2002b. "Assessing the Risk of Banking Crises." *BIS Quarterly Review*, December.

Brunnermeier, M., A. Crocket, C. Goodhart, A. D. Persaud, and H. Shin. 2009. "The Fundamental Principles of Financial Regulation." Geneva Reports on the World Economy series, International Center for Monetary and Banking Studies. http://www. princeton.edu/~markus/research/papers/Geneva11.pdf.

Caballero, R., E. Farhi, and P. -O. Gourinchas. 2008. "Financial Crash, Commodity Prices and Global Imbalances." Discussion Paper 7064, Center for Economic Policy Research, London.

Cecchetti, S., H. Genberg, J. Lipsky, and S. Wadhwani. 2000. "Asset Prices and Central Bank Policy." Geneva Reports on the World Economy series, International Center for Monetary and Banking Studies, Geneva, and Center for Economic Policy Research, London.

Central Bank of Brazil. 2011a. "Relatório de Estabilidade Financeira." April.

———. 2011b. "Relatório de Inflação." June.

CIEPR (Committee on International Economic Policy and Reform). 2011. "Rethinking Central Banking." The Brookings Institution, September. http://www.brookings.edu/research/reports/2011/09/ciepr-central-banking.

Cooper, R. N.. 2007. "Living with Global Imbalances." *Brookings Papers on Economic Activity* 2: 91–107.

Dooley, M. P., D. Folkerts-Landau, and P. M. Garber. 2009. "Bretton Woods II Still Defines the International Monetary System." Working Paper 14731, February, National Bureau of Economic Research, Cambridge, MA.

Financial Services Authority. 2009. "The Turner Review: A Regulatory Response to the Global Banking Crisis." Financial Services Authority, London, March.

Financial Stability Board. 2010. "Overview of Progress in the Implementation of the G20 Recommendations for Strengthening Financial Stability: Report of the Financial Stability Board to G20 Leaders." Financial Stability Board, June 18. http://www. financialstabilityboard.org/publications/r_100627c.pdf.

Galati, G., and R. Moessner. 2011. "Macroprudential Policy—A Literature Review." Working Paper 337, Bank for International Settlements, Basel, Switzerland, February.

Goodhart, C. A. E. 2000. *Which Lender of Last Resort for Europe?* London: Central Banking Publications.

Greenspan, A. 1996. "The Challenge of Central Banking in a Democratic Society." Remarks by Chairman Alan Greenspan at the Annual Dinner and Francis Boyer Lecture of The American Enterprise Institute for Public Policy Research, December 5. http://www.federalreserve.gov/boarddocs/speeches/1996/19961205.htm.

Greenspan, A. 2002. "Economic Volatility." Proceedings of Federal Reserve Bank of Kansas City Symposium, Jackson Hole, August 30. http://www.federalreserve.gov/boarddocs/speeches/2002/20020830/default.htm.

IMF (International Monetary Fund). 2011a. "Recent Experiences in Managing Capital Inflows—Cross-Cutting Themes and Possible Policy Framework." IMF, Washington, DC, February 14.

———. 2011b. "Macroprudential Policy: An Organizing Framework." Working Paper, Monetary and Capital Markets Department, IMF, Washington, DC, March.

———. 2011c. "Toward Operationalizing Macroprudential Policies: When to Act?" In *Global Financial Stability Report*, chapter 3, IMF, Washington, DC, September.

Kohn, D. 2005. "Financial Markets, Financial Fragility, and Central Banking." Remarks at a symposium sponsored by the Federal Reserve Bank of Kansas City, Jackson Hole, August 27.

Lim, C., F. Columba, A. Costa, P. Kongsamut, A. Otani, M. Saiyid, T. Wezel, and X. Wu. 2011. "Macroprudential Policy: What Instruments and How to Use Them? Lessons from Country Experiences." Working Paper 11/238, October, International Monetary Fund, Washington, DC. http://www.imf.org/external/pubs/ft/wp/2011/wp11238.pdf.

Mesquita, M., and M. Torós. 2010. "Considerações sobre a Atuação do Banco Central na Crise de 2008." Working Papers Series 202, Central Bank of Brazil, Brasillia, March.

Mishkin, F. 2008. "How Should We Respond to Asset Price Bubbles?" Speech at the Wharton Financial Institutions Center and Oliver Wyman Institute's Annual Financial Risk Roundtable, Philadelphia, May 15. http://www.federalreserve.gov/newsevents/speech/mishkin20080515a.htm.

Montoro, C., and R. Moreno. 2011. "The Use of Reserve Requirements as a Policy Instrument in Latin America." *BIS Quarterly Review* March: 53–65.

Moreno, R. 2011. "Policymaking from a "Macroprudential" Perspective in Emerging Market Economies." Working Paper 336, January, Bank for International Settlements, Basel, Switzerland.

Obstfeld, M., and K. Rogoff. 2009. "Global Imbalances and the Financial Crisis: Products of Common Causes." November, Discussion Paper 7606, Centre for Economic Policy Research London. http://www.cepr.org/pubs/dps/DP7606.asp.

Roubini, N., and B. Setser. 2005. "Will the Bretton Woods 2 Regime Unravel Soon? The Risk of a Hard Landing in 2005–2006." *RGE Monitor*, February 1. http://www.roubini.com/analysis/38641.php.

Stark, J. 2010. "In Search of a Robust Monetary Policy Framework." Speech at the 6th European Central Bank Conference, "Monetary Policy Revisited: Lessons from the Crisis," Frankfurt, Germany, November 18–19.

Svensson, L. E. O.. 2010a. "Inflation Targeting." Working Paper 16654, National Bureau of Economic Research, Cambridge, MA.

Svensson, L. E.. 2011b. "Inflation Targeting and Financial Stability." Keynote lecture at the CEPR/ESI, 14th Annual Conference, hosted by the Central Bank of Turkey, October.

Terrier, G., R. Valdés, C. E. Tovar, J. Chan-Lau, C. Fernández-Valdovinos, M. García-Escribano, C. Medeiros, M. -K. Tang, M. Vera Martin, and C. Walker. 2011. "Policy Instruments to Lean against the Wind in Latin America." Working Paper 11/159, International Monetary Fund, Washington, DC, July.

Trichet, J. -C.. 2010. "Reflections on the Nature of Monetary Policy Non-Standard Measures and Finance Theory." Speech at the 6th European Central Bank Conference, "Monetary Policy Revisited: Lessons from the Crisis," Frankfurt, Germany, November 18–19.

CHAPTER 7

The Operation of Macro Prudential Policy Measures

The Case of Korea in the 2000s

Jong Kyu Lee*

Introduction

The 2008 global financial crisis highlighted the need to adopt a macro prudential approach to financial stability, beyond micro prudential regulation and supervision. Macro prudential policy (MaPP) refers to a policy framework for addressing the stability of the financial system as a whole rather than its individual components, such as financial institutions or financial markets. At the international level, consensus has formed in favor of applying MaPP frameworks (FSB (Financial Stability Board), IMF (International Monetary Fund), and and BIS (Bank for International Settlements) 2011).

In reality, however, it is not easy for a country to adopt a full-scale MaPP framework. The reasons vary: that the ultimate target of MaPP cannot be clearly defined, for example, enabling it to be pursued without confusion, or that the instruments and tools necessary for MaPP have yet to be fully developed. Reflecting these difficulties, a few scholars and practitioners have begun to devote attention to MaPP instruments. To date, a variety of MaPP instruments have been suggested, but verification of their effectiveness is needed if they are to be applied in the real world (Caruana 2010; Galeti and Moessner 2011).

Many papers evaluating the usefulness of MaPP measures have appeared. For example, BOE (2011) illustrates various kinds of instruments and discusses their pros and cons. Goodhart and others (2012) analyze the effects of MaPP instruments in a general equilibrium model. Hanson, Kashyap, and Stein (2011) evaluate MaPP tools on a conceptual basis. Lim and others (2011) generalize from 49 countries' experiences on how to improve MaPP tool effectiveness. However,

* **Jong Kyu Lee** is a Senior Research Fellow at the Economic Research Institute, the Bank of Korea.

none of these papers provides detailed know-how concerning the design and operation of MaPP instruments.

This chapter reports the experiences during the 2000s of the Republic of Korea, which operated several MaPP instruments prior to the stressful events of 2008. The instruments were not based on the concepts currently discussed, but did take similar forms. The Korean MaPP scheme seemed to have been systematic; from as early as 1997 Korea applied several types of liquidity ratio regulations, designed for curing the potential weaknesses in domestic banking and foreign currency (FX) transactions, that is, covering the whole financial sector. Later, with a housing boom becoming apparent, Korean authorities introduced a loan-to-value (LTV) ratio and, even later, a debt-to-income (DTI) ratio, in order to stabilize housing prices.[1]

Notwithstanding these measures, another round of crisis-like events hit Korea in 2008. In fact, Korea had accumulated a new type of financial imbalance in domestic banking as well as in FX transactions associated in part with the housing market boom. Banks had raised funds through noncore liabilities and expanded their lending to households in line with strong housing prices. To meet the growing demand for FX derivatives transactions, meanwhile, banks had begun to rely on short-term foreign borrowings.

The Korean case in the 2000s will provide a basis for evaluating several MaPP measures from various viewpoints. For a well-defined MaPP framework, the objective, scope, and other elements for the policy need to be specified (FSB, IMF, and BIS 2011). The choices of operational options—such as single versus multiple measures, broad-based versus targeted risks, or fixed versus time-varying application—can also impact MaPP effectiveness (Lim and others 2011). The Korean case can serve as an example to question what went wrong with the operations of MaPP measures with respect to these factors.

This chapter's approach differs from other analyses of the Korean case. For example, Igan and Kang (2011) analyze the effects of the LTV and DTI regulations, but focus only on the MaPP measures for one sector. Hahm and others (2012) discuss the effects of the MaPP measures introduced in recent years since the 2008 event from a retrospective viewpoint and evaluate their effects on the key factors considered to have triggered that event. This chapter, dealing with the whole set of MaPP measures adopted before the 2008 crisis, is able to analyze the effectiveness of the measures in combination with other measures and from a preemptive perspective. In addition, it discusses various aspects of MaPP operation.

First, this chapter briefly describes the financial history of Korea since the early 1990s and the experiences of MaPP in the 1990s. Then it describes the MaPP measures applied in Korea in the 2000s. The chapter then focuses on the process of accumulation of the financial imbalances that became channels for spillover of the 2008 global liquidity contraction. Combining a consideration of these financial imbalances and of the MaPP measures operation, it then discusses what went wrong with the operations of the measures, and the limitations of these tools. Finally, it concludes with a summary and derives some implications for MaPP in the future.

Dealing with the Challenges of Macro Financial Linkages in Emerging Markets
http://dx.doi.org/10.1596/978-1-4648-0002-3

Financial Development since 1990: A Brief History

The Korean financial sector has expanded rapidly since the 1980s. As shown in figure 7.1, the financial interrelations ratio (FIR),[2] which was less than 3 in 1980, had risen to 9 in 2011. An FIR of 9 is very high, considering that per capita gross domestic product (GDP) in Korea as of 2011 was US$22,489. The ratio for the United States was only 6 in 1990, when the country's per capita GDP was similar.

Many factors have been in play in the rapid development of the Korean financial sector. Such rapid development was possible thanks to continuous efforts to maintain international competitiveness through structural adjustment, even after successful industrialization, which set the country on a path of persistently high economic growth. Economic growth increased the country's per capita GDP, and thereby created a basis for demand for financial assets.

A variety of development strategies have been pursued in the financial sector in accordance with the stages of economic development. In the early development era, the 1960s, a policy of financial repression was inevitably adopted to ensure the allocation of scarce financial resources toward the industrial sector. In the 1980s, however, the repressed financial sector began to be liberalized. This financial liberalization gave rise to the introduction of financial instruments designed to allow the market to decide interest rates; the establishment of nonbanking financial institutions, resulting in provision of a wide variety of financial instruments; and significant capital market development. The financial markets have been open to the outside world since the 1990s. In the 2000s, the government came up with measures to prevent recurrence of a financial crisis like the 1997 currency crisis, including the introduction of

Figure 7.1 Financial Interrelations Ratio—Comparison of Korea and the United States

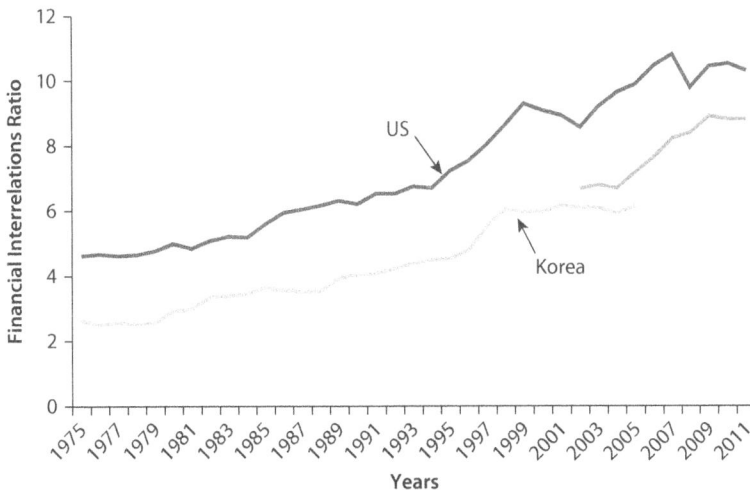

Source: The Bank of Korea Economic Statistics System, FRB, and BEA.

Dealing with the Challenges of Macro Financial Linkages in Emerging Markets
http://dx.doi.org/10.1596/978-1-4648-0002-3

global standards for financial market infrastructures and improvement of the financial supervisory system.

The process of Korean financial development, however, has been a bumpy road, and the financial sector has fallen into crises several times. The FX transaction sector has been particularly vulnerable, and has undergone two rounds of currency crisis. An Exchange Market Pressure Index (EMPI) was calculated to analyze the situation of the Korean foreign exchange market in light of this history, in accordance with the methods of Kaminsky and Reinhart (1999). When the index exceeds more than twice its standard deviation, the case is considered as a currency crisis.[3] The exchange rate and foreign reserves are based on monthly average data. As demonstrated in figure 7.2, the EMPI for Korea surpassed the upper bound in November and December of 1997 and in October of 2008, indicating the occurrences of currency crises.

The 1997 currency crisis can be considered a "typical" financial crisis, in that many financial institutions were seriously damaged by toxic assets and came to be restructured under crisis management programs.[4] The 2008 crisis, however, can be viewed as only financial market instability, in that it was not accompanied by financial institution restructuring. Nonetheless, a systemic event seems to have happened at that time, considering the observance of phenomena similar to those during a financial crisis, such as a serious weakening of function of the financial sector and consequent rapid shrinkage in the real economy.

Figure 7.2 Exchange Market Pressure Index, Korea

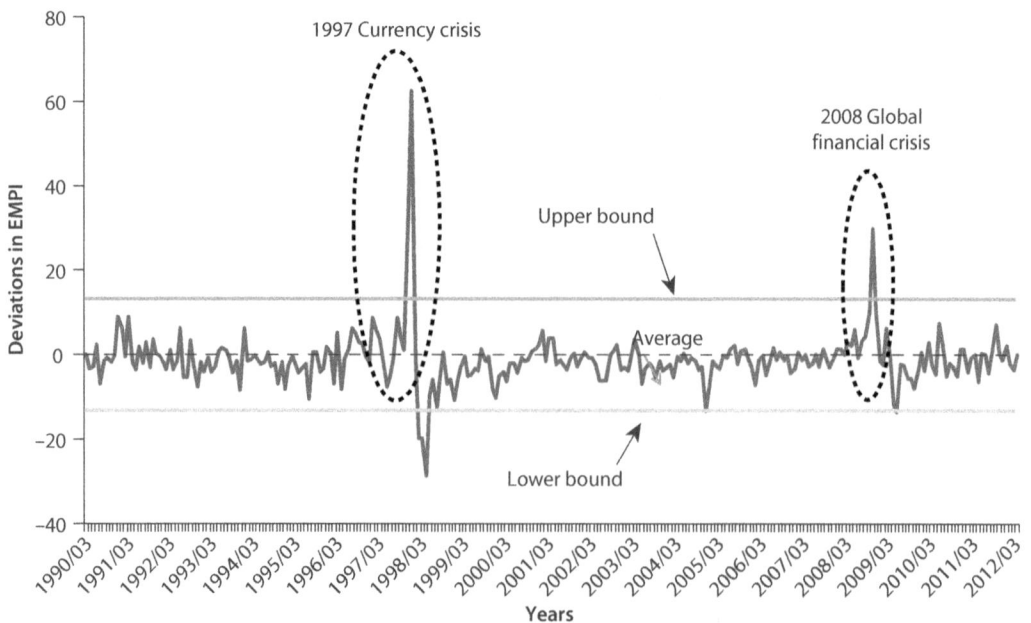

Source: The Bank of Korea Economic Statistics System

Foreign Currency Liquidity Ratio Regulation
Foreign currency liquidity ratio regulation was intended to strengthen banks' abilities to pay off their short-term foreign debts. It was based on the notion that a certain amount of liquid assets maintained by a bank can be immediately used for covering short-term debts, and, with liquid assets above a certain level, the bank may ensure its liquidity. According to the formula initially employed, banks' FX assets with outstanding maturities less than three months should be maintained at above 70 percent of their foreign debts with outstanding maturities less than three months:

$$FX\ Liquidity\ Ratio = \frac{Liquid\ assets\ with\ maturity\ of\ 3\ months\ or\ less}{Liquid\ liabilities\ with\ maturity\ of\ 3\ months\ or\ less} \cdot 100 \geq 70\%$$

This formula was similar to the foreign currency liquidity coverage ratio (LCR) under Basel III (BCBS 2010b, 2010c), but without risk-factor adjustment.[11] In addition, it differed from the BCBS's LCR in that the standard maturity was set at three months, while the BCBS's LCR has a one-month maturity.

This ratio was used as the basic regulation to ensure Korean banks' FX liquidity. Introduced in July 1997, just before outbreak of the 1997 currency crisis, it was applied initially only to general banks, but extended in July 1998, right after the currency crisis broke out, to cover special banks. In June 2000, the guideline for the ratio was adjusted upward from 70 to 80 percent in response to signs of a resurgence of banks' short-term borrowings as their FX transaction activities returned to normal with the improved creditworthiness of the Korean banking sector in the international financial markets. The guideline was raised to 85 percent in 2004, when banks' short-term foreign borrowing began to accelerate.

Maturity Mismatch Ratio
To effectively tackle a variety of risks accompanying FX transactions, the maturities were broken down into seven ranges[12] and different liquidity ratios applied. The regulation tried to limit the gap between the amount of FX assets and debts at each maturity range above a certain ratio. For example, the ratio for the maturity range of less than seven days was required to be more than 0 percent (meaning that the amount of assets with maturities less than seven days should match or exceed that of debts with the same maturity), while that for maturities of less than one month had to be larger than –10 percent (meaning that the amount of assets with maturities less than one month should exceed 90 percent of the liabilities with the same maturity).

This requirement was introduced in January 1999 in line with the recommendation of the IMF. Since then, the regulation has been partly amended, for instance, to include forward FX transactions in the coverage, and the amendments have tended to strengthen it.

Ratio of Long-Term Foreign Borrowings
This measure was introduced in 1991 to restrain the practice of setting the maturities for FX lending as long as possible in the early period of capital liberalization.

In the early 1990s, just after the capital account had begun to be liberalized, companies favored long-term FX debt as a stable source of funding. As the banks began to extend the maturities of their FX loans, their maturity mismatches were consequently aggravated. To deal with this problem, the authorities introduced this measure. According to the initial regulation, more than 70 percent of FX loans with maturities above three years had to be funded with foreign debts with maturities greater than three years.

This ratio was eased in April 1993 (from 70 to 50 percent) because it was difficult to comply with and was considered somewhat superfluous. It was difficult to comply with because, in practice, it was impossible for Korean banks to borrow long-term loans in the international financial markets because of their low credibility. It was also considered as a regulation subject to financial liberalization, and its elimination recommended by the Ministry of Finance and Economy's task force for financial deregulation at that time.

The problem with regulation compliance persisted into the 2000s. Korean banks with low external credibility had to pay additional premiums for longer-term borrowings. Thus, they tried to evade the regulation by adding clauses to their loan contracts specifying early redemption.[13] In consideration of these problems, the criterion for the ratio was lowered from maturities of more than three years to those of more than one year in September 2001, in view of the reality that most of Korean banks' foreign debts had one-year maturities.

This regulation is similar to the net stable funding ratio (NSFR) under Basel III (BCBS 2010b). The differences are as follows: it was applied to FX transactions while the NSFR is for domestic banking, and it was based on maturity only while the NFSR is based on numerical risk factors in addition to maturity.

Foreign Exchange Position Regulation

Broadly speaking, FX position regulations can be regarded as prudential regulations. They may ensure the soundness of financial institutions by reducing losses owing to changes in exchange rates. Position management can narrow the level of currency mismatches, thus reducing the possibility of currency crises.[14]

However, this regulation could be used as a means to control exchange rates. Limiting the foreign exchange positions of financial institutions, among the major market participants, to within a certain range may help stabilize foreign exchange rates. From another perspective, therefore, this measure can be criticized as regulation hindering free-market determination of foreign exchange rates.[15]

As early as 1964, Korea introduced FX position regulations. The position limit was initially set based on the absolute amount of foreign currency holding,[16] but with the foreign exchange liberalization in 1993 it was revised to be a certain ratio to capital. During the 1997 currency crisis, the overbought position limit was expanded to induce banks' holding of FX liquidity, while the oversold position limit was reduced. In July 1998, operation of the regulation was again changed to comprehensive position management, which is still applied. The position limit has also been continuously expanded, from 15 percent of total capital at the end of the previous month to 50 percent, in consideration of the view that regulating banks' FX positions was an obstacle to their autonomous management of assets (Ministry of Strategy and Finance 2007).

Recently the government has expressed an intention to abolish the FX position regulation (Ministry of Strategy and Finance 2007), based on the judgment that not much benefit has come from it since financial institutions have managed risks by themselves even after the position limit was expanded. In 2007, the ratio of position use by foreign exchange banks was 10.3 percent on average, far lower than the 50 percent maximum allowed. In addition, it was thought that prudential measures could absorb the position regulation. In fact, at the time the government expressed this intention, prudential regulation was being strengthened with the introduction of Basel II in January 2008.

These MaPP measures for FX transactions are summarized in table 7.4.

Measures for Domestic Banking

As with new regulations for FX transactions, a liquidity ratio-type regulation was applied to domestic banking. It was the major regulation for domestic banking activities, and thus much simpler than the regulation on FX transactions.

Domestic Currency Liquidity Ratio Regulation

Starting in January 1999, right after the currency crisis, the authorities began to specify a domestic currency (DC) liquidity ratio as one of the major guidelines for banks' risk management. Similar to the FX liquidity ratio, this ratio is denoted by dividing liquid assets by liquid debts of maturities set at three months or less:

$$DC\ Liquidity\ Ratio = \frac{Liquid\ assets\ with\ maturity\ of\ 3\ months\ or\ less}{Liquid\ liabilities\ with\ maturity\ of\ 3\ months\ or\ less} \cdot 100$$

Before the 1997 currency crisis, this formula was operated as the ratio of DC liquid assets to total DC deposits, and the guideline figure was set at more than 30 percent. But the formula was revised to its current form to manage liquidity risks from both the asset and the liability side and to make it consistent with international standard.

Assets and liabilities for computation of the liquidity ratio include all types of credits and debts, except for those in trust accounts. These liquid assets and liabilities should reflect the actual maturity, and the reality that assets and debts are actually payable or receivable at the due date. In this sense marketable securities are recognized as liquid assets, with no consideration given to their outstanding maturities. In contrast, noninvestment grade securities and pledged securities are excluded from liquid assets.

In March 2002, the DC liquidity ratio guideline was strengthened. Because the liquidity ratios of financial institutions had fallen below 100 percent on average from 2001, the rule was revised to send warning signals to banks whose liquidity ratios were below the precautionary level of 105 percent, and to order them to submit plans for improving their financial status.

Dealing with the Challenges of Macro Financial Linkages in Emerging Markets
http://dx.doi.org/10.1596/978-1-4648-0002-3

Table 7.4 MaPP Measures for FX Transactions

Measure	FX Liquidity Ratio	Maturity Mismatch Ratio	Long-term Borrowing Ratio	FX Position Management
Introduction	July 1997	January 1999	January 1991	1964
Objective	Strengthen banks' ability for FX debt payment	Ensure FX liquidity	Curb long-term FX loans	Reduce FX risk
Formula	$\dfrac{Assets\,(3m\,maturity)}{Liabilities\,(3m\,maturity)}\times100$	$\dfrac{FX\,Assets - FX\,Liabilities}{Total\,FX\,Assets}\times100$	$\dfrac{FX\,borrowing\,of\,3\,years\,+}{FX\,loans\,of\,3\,years\,+}\times100$	O/B position/capital; O/S position/capital
Standard	$\geq70\%$	7-day GAP: $\geq0\%$; 1-month GAP: $\geq-10\%$	$\geq70\%$	$\leq15\%$
Scope	General Banks	Domestic Banks	Domestic Banks	Domestic Banks
History				
April 1993			Lower ratio: 70% → 50%	
July 1998	Extended to Special Banks; Reporting: every 3 months → every month			Turn to comprehensive position management
April 1999				Ratio raised: 15% → 20%
June 2000	Ratio raised: 70% → 80%			
Dec. 2000			FX loan provisions excluded from FX assets	
March 2001	Forward FX included	Forward FX included		
Sept. 2001			Maturity shortened: 3-year or more → 1-year or more	
Jan. 2002	Narrower core FX liabilities	Narrower core FX liabilities	Core FX deposits recognized as stable liabilities	
April 2004	Ratio raised: 80% → 85%		Ratio raised: 50% → 80%	
July 2005				Extended to forward FX
Aug. 2006				O/B position: 20% → 50%
Dec. 2007				O/S position: 20% → 50%

However, in August 2006 the scheme was eased significantly: The precautionary ratio level was abolished and authorities allowed the banks to include reserve requirements at the central bank and CDs owned by banks in the class of liquid assets. Further, credit card receivables and other type of receivables were included in the liquid assets. This revision of the scheme meant a lower guideline in practice (down from 105 percent to 100 percent) for the liquidity ratio allowed, and much more capacity to lend domestic currency funds.

The reasons behind this easing of the liquidity ratio are unclear. The authorities said they did it to keep pace with developed countries, as the ratios of Korean banks had improved significantly (FSC and FSS 2006a). According to media reports at the time, however, financial institutions strongly requested easing of the regulation, arguing that it led to short-term lending to business firms (The Edaily 2006). At the time, long-term mortgage loans were on the increase, and the banks had been managing their corporate lending on a short-term basis to meet the liquidity ratio requirement. The bottom line, however, was that banks had to expand their loans to maximize profits, and the liquidity ratio seemed an obstacle to profit maximization.

In any case, the 2006 revision toward deregulation, or easing, was clearly a factor behind the rapid expansion in bank lending. In this regard, it should be considered a mistake in MaPP measure operation, since banks' overlending caused liquidity problems in the wake of the 2008 financial turmoil. This issue will be discussed in detail later.

Loan-to-Deposit Ratio Regulation

In the 1990s, the loan-to-deposit (LTD) ratio was a major management guideline. At that time the ratio of core disposable funds (disposable deposits + domestic currency financial debentures + capital) to loans had to be less than 100 percent, to preclude any shortage of liquidity. This requirement was abolished in January 1999, however, after introduction of the DC liquidity ratio regulation, as part of the regulatory easing efforts (FSC and FSS 1998).

Measures for the Real Estate Market

In September 2002, the authority introduced a LTV regulation to stabilize real estate prices after housing prices had soared suddenly from around 2001. The LTV ratio was first set at 60 percent, and has since then been strengthened to as low as 40 percent in some regions:

$$LTV = \frac{Mortgage\ loans + Senior\ lending\ on\ houses + Rent\ security\ received}{House\ price}$$

In August 2005, a DTI regulation was implemented because real estate prices continued to rise despite the variety of measures taken including the LTV ratio requirement. The DTI ratio has been strengthened since its introduction, and the target group for its application expanded:

$$DTI = \frac{Annual\ mortgage\ and\ other\ loan\ payments}{Annual\ income}$$

Dealing with the Challenges of Macro Financial Linkages in Emerging Markets
http://dx.doi.org/10.1596/978-1-4648-0002-3

The LTV and DTI regulations were implemented in combination with a variety of other policies. In calculating the BIS capital adequacy ratio, the risk-weighting for mortgage loans was increased. From a short-term perspective, the authorities adopted various measures to deter real estate demand; the rates of taxation for real estate ownership and transactions were raised; the administrative procedures were strengthened; and a new tax was levied on real estate development profits. Longer-term policies to expand housing supply, such as new town development plans, have also been pursued.[17]

The LTV and DTI regulations are characterized by the fact that they can target very specific areas or groups. In the early 2000s, real estate prices had begun to rise, mainly in certain parts of Seoul, and the regulations were applied first to these areas. Even after the housing price boom had spread to other regions, the regulations were applied only to some regions designated as "speculative zones,[18]" rather than on a nationwide basis. The regulations could also be differentiated in accordance with the types of financial institution they concerned, and be customized to the characteristics of individual financial institutions and users. Their flexibility was another advantage of these regulations. Whereas real estate market conditions have changed continuously, authorities have been able to change the targets of regulation flexibly, as demonstrated in table 7.5. Comparing the DTI with the LTV, the advantage of the DTI has been that it could be used to curb speculative demand among those in certain income brackets, and has been effective in curbing real estate speculation or demand for owning homes by asset holders whose incomes were unclear.[19]

Table 7.5 History of LTV and DTI Regulation

LTV Ceilings

Date	Ceiling (%)	Target Loan Type	Target Region	Target FIs
Sept. 2002	60	all	ESZ	B & I
Oct. 2002	60	all	all	B & I
May 2003	60 → 50	loans with 3-year maturity or less	SZ & ESZ	B & I
Oct. 2003	50 → 40	loans for apartment purchase with 10-year maturity or less	SZ	B & I
March 2004	60 → 50	loans for housing purchase with 3-year maturity or less	SZ & ESZ	B & I
	60 → 70	loans with 10-year maturity or more	all	all
June 2005	60 → 40	loans for apartment purchase of 600+ mW, with 10-year maturity or more	SZ	B & I
Nov. 2006	60 → 50	loans for housing purchase of 600+ mW, with 10-year maturity or less	SZ	all
Nov. 2008	(exempt)		Except 3 Dist. in Seoul	all FIs
July 2009	(reapply) 60 → 50	loans for purchase of housing of 600+ mW	Seoul Metropolitan	Banks
Oct. 2009	(extend)			all

table continues next page

Table 7.5 History of LTV and DTI Regulation (continued)

DTI Ceilings

Date	Change	Ceiling (%)	Application to	Region	FIs
Aug. 2005	Introduction	40	single under 30, married with debt	SZ	all FIs
March 2006	Extension	40	loans for housing purchase of 600+ mW	SZ	all FIs
Nov. 2006	Extension	40	all housing loans	ESZ	B & I
Feb. 2007	Extension	40-60	loans for housing purchase of 600+ mW		Banks
Aug. 2007	Extension	40-70			NBFIs
Nov. 2008	Removal		Except for 3 districts in Seoul		all FIs
Sept. 2009	Reapplication	40	3 districts in Seoul	SZ	Banks
		50	other metropolitan	Metropolitan	Banks
Aug. 2010	Exemption		debtors with less than 2 houses	non-SZ Metropolitan	all FIs

Source: Various press releases by the FSS and other authorities.
Note: SZ: Speculative Zone
   ESZ: Excessively Speculative Zone
   B: Banks
   I: Insurance Companies

The LTV and DTI regulations have drawbacks. The LTV and DTI implemented in Korea were ex-post-facto measures, rather than ex-ante ones. In other
words, they were applied after real estate prices had already gone up, and were
not effective in stabilizing prices due to these ex-post-facto characteristics.

Financial Imbalances in the 2000s, and Effects of the U.S. Financial Crisis

Notwithstanding the MaPP measures described in the previous section, a new
type of financial imbalance accumulated as the economy and financial markets
evolved. This section focuses on these financial imbalances which have amplified
the impacts of the 2008 U.S. financial crisis on the Korean economy.

The Macroeconomic Situation

In the 2000s, the Korean economy showed signs of escaping the 1997 currency
crisis and moving onto a stable path of growth (see table 7.6). Although the
economic growth rate was slower than before, it maintained a sound momentum
of 5 percent. Inflation, measured by the consumer price index, fell to about 2
percent, far more stable than the annual average of 6 percent seen in the 1990s.
In addition, the current account ran continued surpluses with the help of the
strong competitiveness of the manufacturing sector. To summarize the overall
economic situation in the 2000s, the economy maintained sound and stable economic growth momentum following the successful structural adjustment efforts
following the currency crisis.

Table 7.6 Macroeconomic Indicators in the 2000s

	2000	2001	2002	2003	2004	2005	2006	2007	2008
Economic growth rate (%)	0.0	4.0	7.2	2.0	4.6	4.0	5.2	5.1	2.3
Inflation rate (%)	2.3	4.1	2.8	3.5	3.6	2.8	2.2	2.5	4.7
Current account (Bil.$)	14.0	8.4	7.5	15.6	32.3	18.6	14.1	21.8	3.2
(% in GDP)	2.8	1.7	1.3	2.4	4.5	2.2	1.5	2.1	0.3
M2 (%. y-o-y)	2.2	6.9	11.5	7.9	4.6	6.9	8.3	11.2	14.3
Bank lending (%. y-o-y)	24.2	15.0	32.0	14.1	5.1	8.5	13.9	14.9	14.1
NBFI lending (%)	−12.8	−1.4	−8.2	2.7	4.4	9.6	14.6	19.2	17.6
Interest rate[a] (%)	9.4	7.1	6.6	5.4	4.7	4.7	5.2	5.7	7.0
Stock price (%. y-o-y)	−50.9	37.5	−9.5	29.2	10.5	54.0	4.0	32.3	−40.7
Fiscal balance (% in GDP)	1.1	1.1	3.1	1.0	0.7	0.6	0.7	3.8	1.5
Foreign reserves (Bil.$)	96.2	102.8	121.4	155.4	199.1	210.4	239.0	262.2	201.2
(% of imports)	59.9	72.9	79.8	86.9	88.7	80.5	77.2	73.5	46.2

Source: The Bank of Korea Economic Statistics System.
Note: [a] Yields on corporate bonds of AA- grade with 3-year maturities.

Financial Imbalances

Although the Korean economy enjoyed stable growth in the 2000s, big structural changes were occurring in the financial sector. Structural changes took place in domestic banking as well as in capital transactions. In parallel with these changes, prices in the asset markets surged. Financial imbalances accumulated and Korea was unable to resolve them before the outbreak of the U.S. financial crisis; thus it was hit hard by its impacts.

The process of financial imbalance accumulation in the 2000s will be reviewed for three sectors: domestic banking, the real estate market, and external capital transactions.

Domestic Banking

One of the most remarkable aspects appearing in the domestic financial sector in the 2000s was the gap in growth between the deposits and loans of commercial banks. Previously, deposits and loans had moved in parallel.[20] Beginning around 2002, however, this pattern broke down; the rate of increase in loans greatly exceeded that of deposits, and the trend continued until right before outbreak of the U.S. financial crisis (see figure 7.4a).

As a result of this phenomenon, LTD ratios increased rapidly. The ratio, which was about 80 percent during the 1997 currency crisis, soared to 142 percent in August 2008 just before the Lehman Brothers bankruptcy filing.

The rapid rise in the LTD ratio was made possible through the increase in issuance of noncore liabilities, such as debentures and CDs (see figure 7.5). From 2002, when the gap between deposit and loan growth began, the issuance of bank debentures expanded and the LTD ratio began to rise (see figure 7.4b).

Figure 7.4a Banking Sector Activities

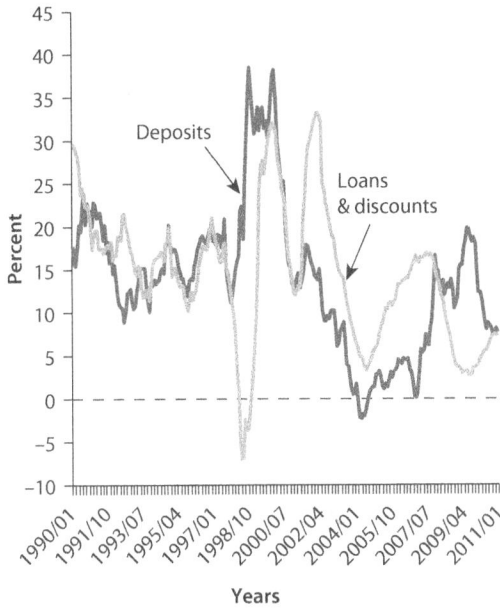

Figure 7.4b LTD Ratio

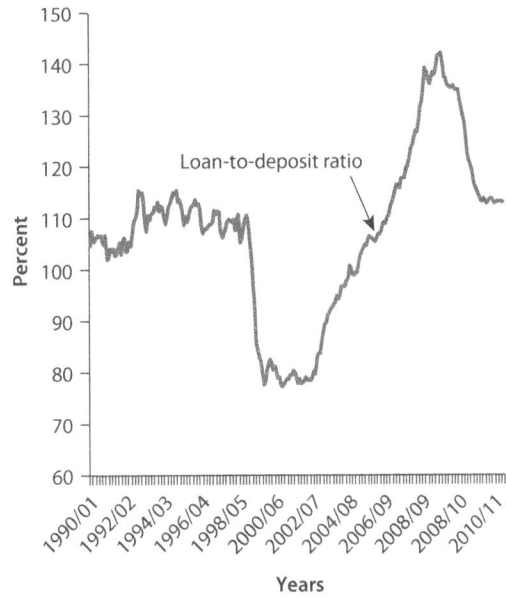

Source: The Bank of Korea Economic Statistics System.

Figure 7.5 Sources of Loanable Funds in Deposit-Taking Institutions

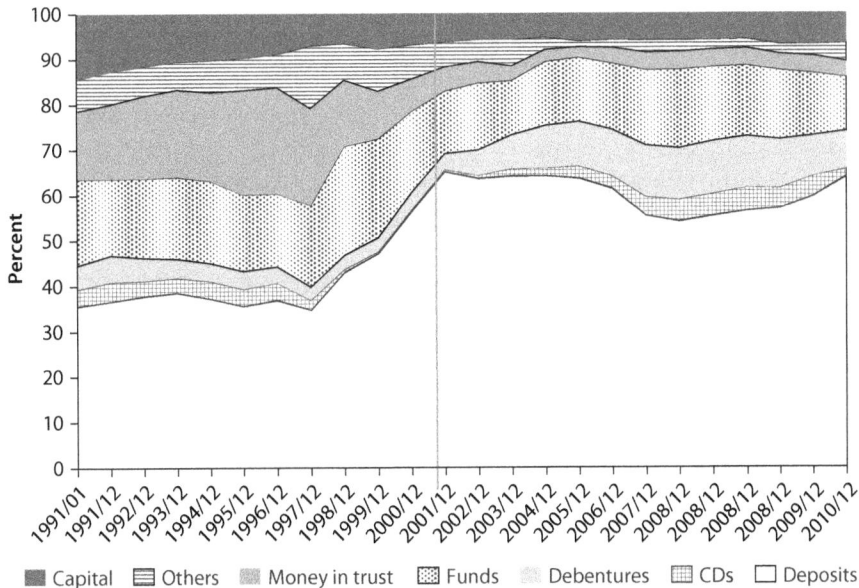

Source: The Bank of Korea Economic Statistics System.
Note: Funds include CMAs. MMFs. Beneficiary Certificates and others.

Dealing with the Challenges of Macro Financial Linkages in Emerging Markets
http://dx.doi.org/10.1596/978-1-4648-0002-3

Of course, the structural changes observed in domestic banking (as displayed in figure 7.5) might have been due to the changes in individuals' asset management practices (Khatri 2008). Individual depositors at that time preferred investment in marketable financial instruments over deposits, because of the lower interest rates paid on deposits. This meant limitations for banks in expanding their funding through deposits to meet the growing loan demand. As a result, banks could not help but rely on noncore liability issuance to raise funds to lend.

The Korean banks that had issued debentures were faced with numerous difficulties as market liquidity conditions worsened; the effects of the 2008 financial crisis become more evident as these debentures approached their maturity dates. The heavy reliance of Korean banks on noncore liabilities was pointed to as an issue by Shin (2010), from the perspective that their funding possibilities suddenly shrank with the global liquidity contraction. Banks' activities at that time may also be criticized from another point of view, that a bank's fundraising needs to be matched with its lending in respect of maturity (Berger and Bouwman 2009). Korean banks raised funds through liquid liabilities and then lent them out in the form of illiquid loans such as mortgage loans, which consequently increased the extent of their maturity mismatches. From the Berger and Bouwman perspective, we can interpret Korean banks to have been actively involved in excessive liquidity creation.

Real Estate Market

Following the 1997 currency crisis, the major users of bank loans changed from corporations to households. Business firms, which had experienced great difficulties during the currency crisis because of their high reliance on outside borrowings, began to optimize their borrowings to improve their financial soundness after the crisis. Household debt in contrast began to increase significantly right after the crisis. The rate of increase in household borrowings substantially surpassed that in corporate loans, and this trend continued until right before the outbreak of the global financial crisis (figure 7.6a). As a result, the share in total bank loans of loans to households soared from a mere 28 percent in 1998 to 50 percent when the global crisis hit, as shown in figure 7.6b.

The expansion in the 2000s in bank loans, especially mortgage loans to households, was directly related to the asset market boom accompanying the increase in real estate prices. Several other factors might have been related to the expansion in bank lending to households: the liberalization of the housing loan markets,[21] the profit maximization behaviors of banks, the severe competition among banks, the preferred treatment of household loans in BIS capital adequacy ratio calculation,[22] and others. But it should be stressed that the continuous and substantial increases in housing prices had to be the fundamental factor leading to the expansion in banks' household loans.

As shown in figure 7.7a, real estate prices began to soar about 2002, coincident with the beginning of banks' expansions in their mortgage loans. Housing prices had been stable since the early 1990s, and had in fact fallen during the currency crisis. They gained momentum after the crisis, and during 2002 posted

Figure 7.6a Loans by Borrower Type

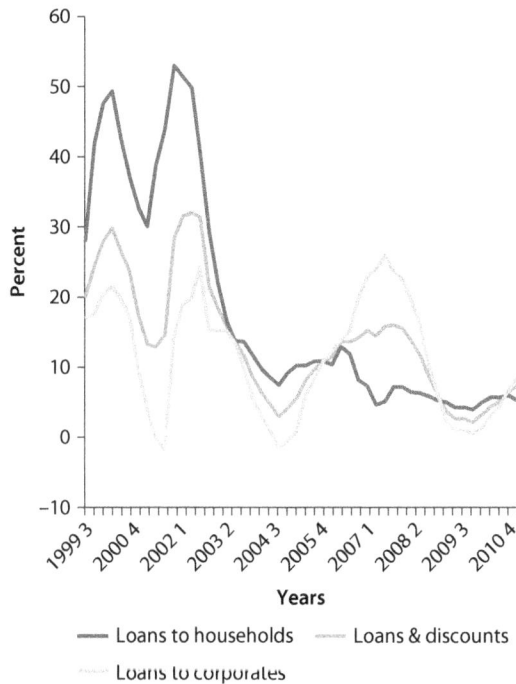

Figure 7.6b Composition of Bank Loans

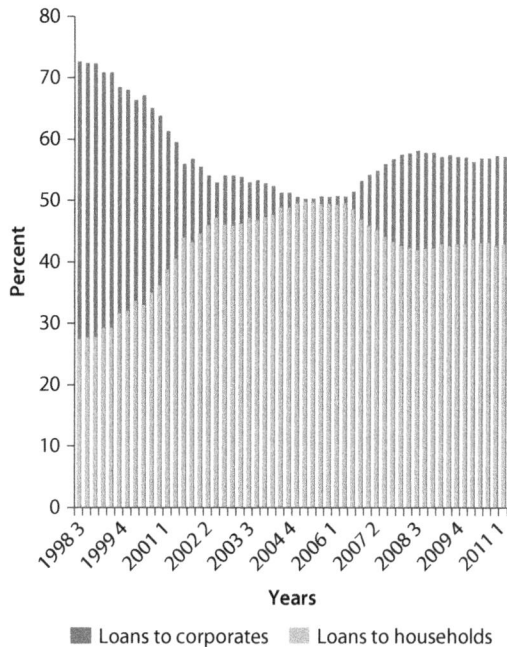

Source: The Bank of Korea Economic Statistics System.
Note: Loans to corporates include those to public entites

a greater than 17 percent increase. From that time housing prices remained continuously on the rise, despite some fluctuations, until right before outbreak of the global financial crisis. The real estate market was driven by housing prices in certain regions, specifically the three "Gangnam" districts in the southeastern part of Seoul, whose residential infrastructures were relatively well developed because of smooth traffic, high-quality schools, and numerous cultural facilities, as well as their geographic proximity to newly developed downtown areas. The rise in housing prices in these regions led to subsequent real estate price increases in neighboring areas, as demonstrated in figure 7.7b.

Foreign Exchange and Capital Transactions

The 1997 currency crisis was a critical opportunity giving Koreans an awareness of the importance of proper foreign debt management. Following the lessons of the crisis, Korea began paying careful attention to this matter. In particular, focused efforts were devoted to reducing short-term debt while maintaining the country's net creditor position. In fact, external assets began to exceed external debts in 2000, as Korea moved to a net creditor position, and the net external credit amount grew every year thereafter until 2004 (figure 7.8a). Foreign assets were held mainly in short-term assets, with the aim of ensuring FX liquidity. At least in the early years of the 2000s, Korea managed its external debt without a hitch.

Figure 7.7a Housing Price Trends

Figure 7.7b Housing Prices, by Region

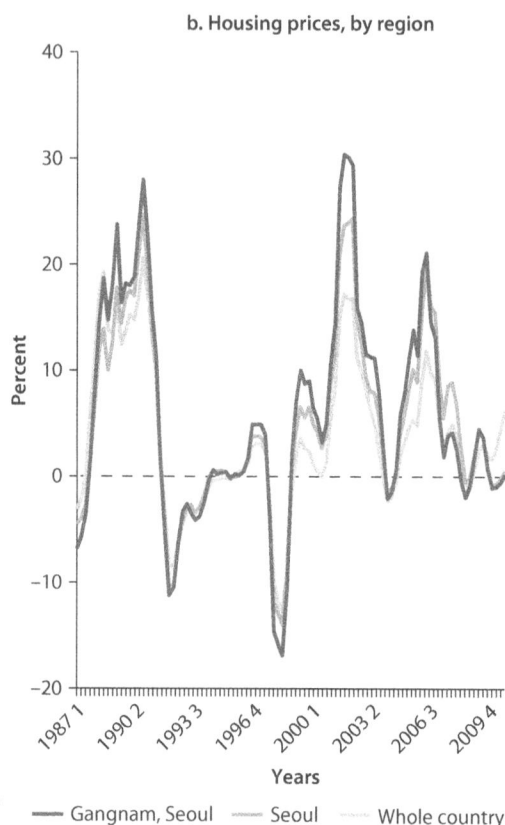

a. Housing price trends

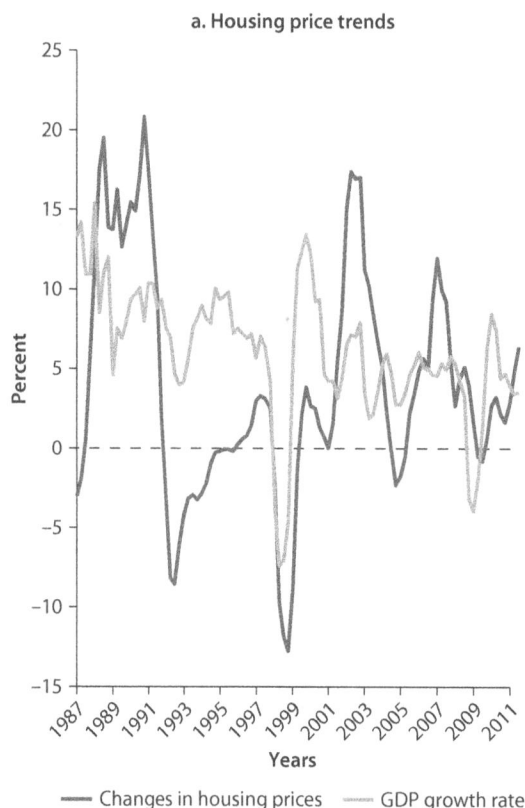

b. Housing prices, by region

— Changes in housing prices   ····· GDP growth rate

— Gangnam, Seoul   — Seoul   ····· Whole country

Source: Kookmin Bank.

In the mid–2000s, however, changes appeared in the net external credit composition. Beginning in 2005, short-term net foreign assets (NFAs) of the private sector turned negative, and the scale of their negative balance grew until right before the global financial crisis, as shown in figure 7.8b. Although the central bank's foreign reserve holdings rose continuously, the short-term NFAs of the private sector declined rapidly enough to offset this.

The decline in the private sector's short-term NFAs was a result of the lending and borrowing activities of financial institutions. Net lending (lending minus borrowing) began a rapid decline in 2005 (see figure 7.9a). This decline was caused mainly by an increase in short-term borrowing by financial institutions.

Both domestic banks and the branches of foreign banks (FBBs) played roles in the decline of short-term NFAs. Comparing the amounts of their negative short-term NFAs, however, those of FBBs overwhelmingly exceeded those of domestic banks, as shown in figure 7.9b. Short-term net debts of the former expanded from $20 billion at the end of 2004 to $114 billion in Q3 2008, just before the global financial crisis. Those of domestic banks were, in contrast, a mere $20 billion at that time. It should be noted, however, that the short-term net position of

Figure 7.8a Foreign Assets and Liabilities   **Figure 7.8b Net Foreign Assets, Short-Term**

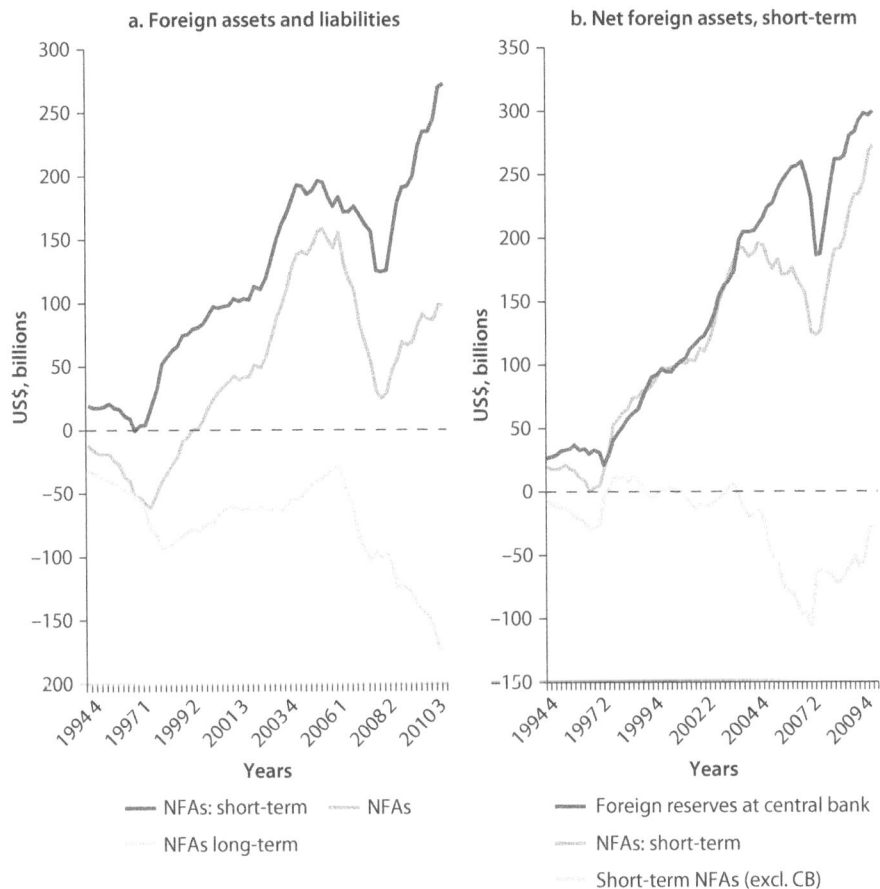

a. Foreign assets and liabilities

Legend:
— NFAs: short-term   ⋯⋯ NFAs
⋯⋯ NFAs long-term

b. Net foreign assets, short-term

Legend:
— Foreign reserves at central bank
⋯⋯ NFAs: short-term
⋯⋯ Short-term NFAs (excl. CB)

Source: The Bank of Korea Economic Statistics System.

domestic banks had turned negative in 2005, and the negative position size had gradually expanded from that time.

The jump in foreign borrowings by financial institutions was related to a sudden expansion in forward FX contracts (IMF 2008). Major exporters, including shipbuilders,[23] were selling their expected future incomes in foreign currencies in the form of forward contracts with domestic banks and FBBs. The financial institutions buying these forward contracts then needed to borrow dollars abroad to balance their FX positions.

Spillovers from U.S. Crisis: Process and Response

As mentioned earlier, Korea came close to suffering another currency crisis in 2008. This seems unavoidable, since the wide openness of the Korean economy made its exposure to global economic instability, like the U.S. global financial crisis, inevitable. However, the impacts of the U.S. financial crisis were more severe on the Korean economy than on other Asian countries. During the 2008

Dealing with the Challenges of Macro Financial Linkages in Emerging Markets
http://dx.doi.org/10.1596/978-1-4648-0002-3

Figure 7.9a Short-Term Loans and Borrowings

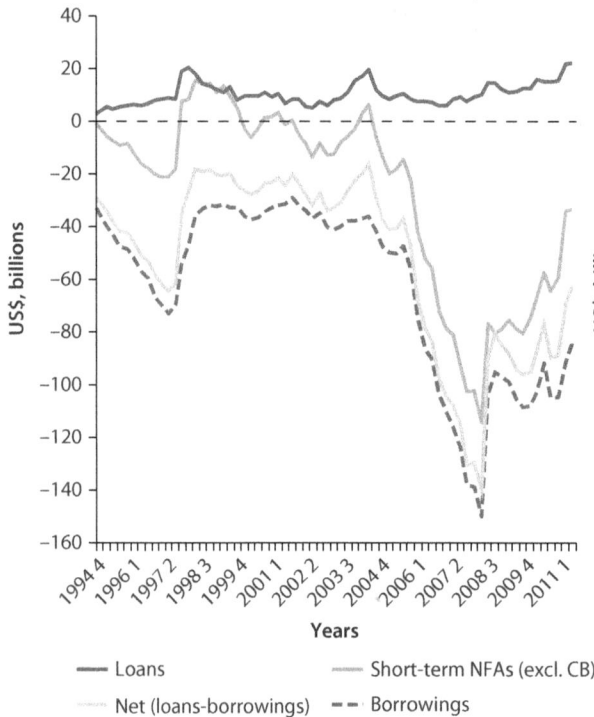

Figure 7.9b Short-Term NFAs by Type of Bank

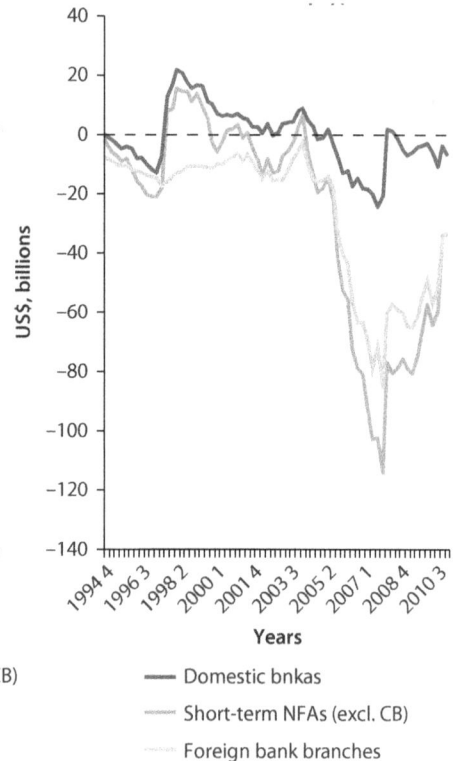

Source: The Bank of Korea Economic Statistics System.

global financial crisis, Korea was hit much harder in terms of exchange rate volatility, the jump in its credit default swap (CDS) premium, and so on. For example, the CDS premium on Korean government bonds, which had been at a level similar to those in China, Malaysia, and Thailand, rose to become much higher (figure 7.10). Korea's CDS premiums rose to a level similar to those of Indonesia and the Philippines.

This rise was due largely to domestic factors, that is, the accumulated financial imbalances in the 2000s. In the wake of the 2008 global financial turmoil, the domestic financial markets encountered liquidity freezes in several financial instruments such as bank debentures. The aggravated domestic market situation exacerbated the spillover effects on the Korean foreign exchange market from abroad.

The initial cause of the exchange rate surge in 2008 was the direct exposures of financial institutions to FX liquidity risks caused by the increases in their short-term foreign debts. In particular, FBBs had to repay their short-term borrowings from their headquarters offices, in line with the liquidity shortages faced by their parent banks in advanced countries during the global financial crisis. Domestic banks, meanwhile, having also expanded their short-term borrowings,

Figure 7.10 Comparison of Credit Default Swap Premiums

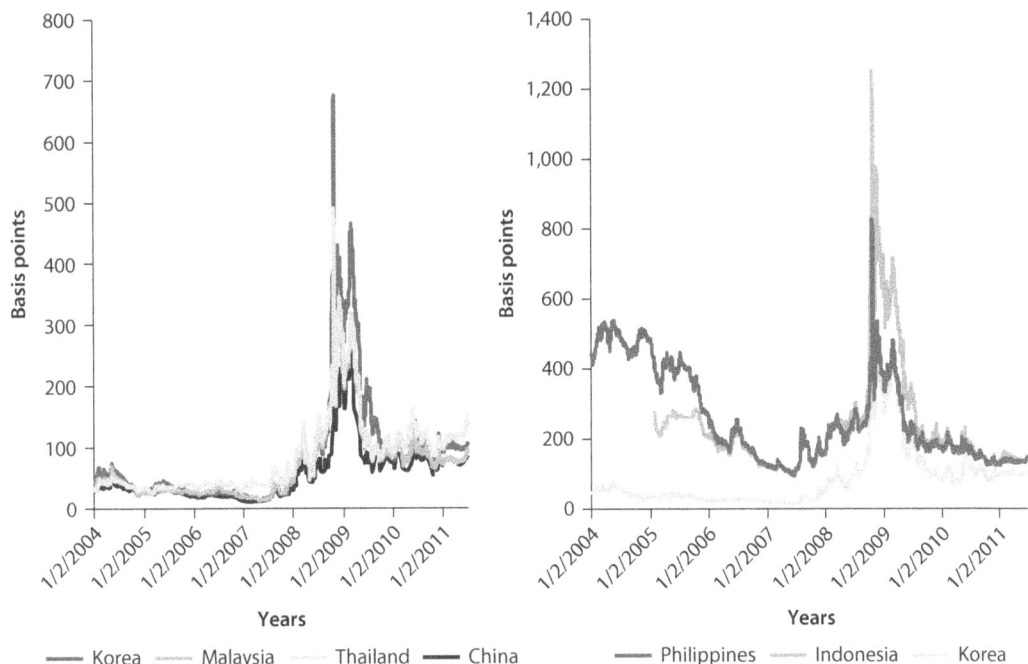

Source: Bloomberg

Table 7.7 Rollover Ratio

	2008					2009				
H1	Q3	Oct.	Nov.	Dec.		Jan.	Feb.	Mar.	April	May
97.6	99.8	39.9	52.9	60.7		92.6	89.1	100.6	111.3	97.3

Source: FSS, *Financial Supervision Information*, 2009–26 (No. 529) (2009.6.26.~7.2), and various press releases.
Note: Of general banks' foreign borrowings with maturities of 1 year or less.

faced similar difficulties repaying them. The ratio of short-term foreign debt rollover fell rapidly during the global financial crisis (table 7.7), and the cost of attracting foreign capital, measured by the spread on Korean government bonds (Foreign Exchange Stabilization Bonds), rose sharply (figure 7.11).

The FX liquidity crunch faced by domestic banks was aggravated further by the potential weaknesses of domestic banking. First, the domestic financial market situation was almost analogous to that in the United States—mortgage loans had been extended to households and housing prices had surged. Many people thus raised suspicions of a housing price bubble, and the risk of declines in housing prices leading to nonperforming loans at banks. In addition, Korean financial institutions had raised their funds for lending through wholesale financial instruments, such as CDs and debentures, a situation similar to the U.S. case.

In the process of the spillover of the U.S. financial crisis into the Korean financial markets, acute debate on the level of Korean banks' LTD ratios occurred.

Figure 7.11 Risk Premium

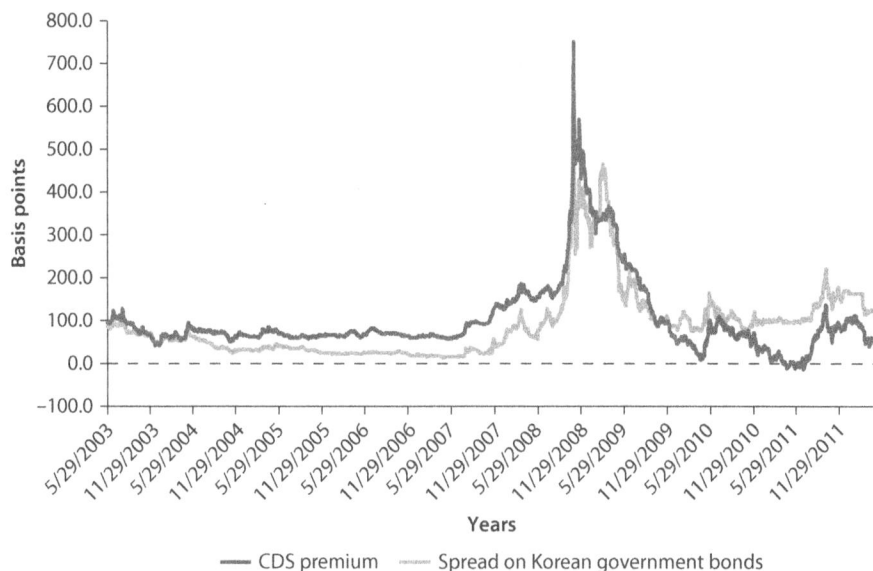

Source: Bloomberg
Note: 2–year maturity Korean Government Bond spread over US Treasury Bills.

Foreign investors (for example, Merrill Lynch 2008) and foreign media (for example, *The Economist* 2009; Wang 2008, and others) raised questions about the high LTD ratio of Korean banks. Korean banks and the authorities tried to counter by stressing the differences between Korean debentures and CDs and those in foreign countries—in Korea they were issued to individual rather than institutional investors—and by asserting that Korean banks' LTD ratio was not so high if these debentures and CDs were included in deposits. At any rate, the debate on the LTD ratio level served as momentum sounding alarms that Korean banks might have difficulties securing liquidity.[24]

Symptoms of a liquidity crunch with respect to securities appeared. The spreads of debenture and CD interest rates over government bond yields jumped to unprecedented levels (figure 7.12). Previously, bank debenture and CD yields had moved in patterns similar to those of one-year treasury bonds, but after the Lehman Brothers incident they rose to levels 2 percentage points higher than Treasury bond yields. The share of debentures in banks' funding sources declined greatly after October 2008, due to the banks' difficulties in issuing them (table 7.8).

In addition, given the economy's growing sluggishness, possibilities arose of a worsening of mortgage loan and small- and medium-sized enterprise (SME) loan performance. If the liquidity crunch in the domestic financial markets had tightened further, and financial institutions refrained from lending, then the domestic financial sector would have experienced a financial contraction through deleveraging, which might have led eventually to the outbreak of a financial crisis.

Figure 7.12 Spreads of Debentures

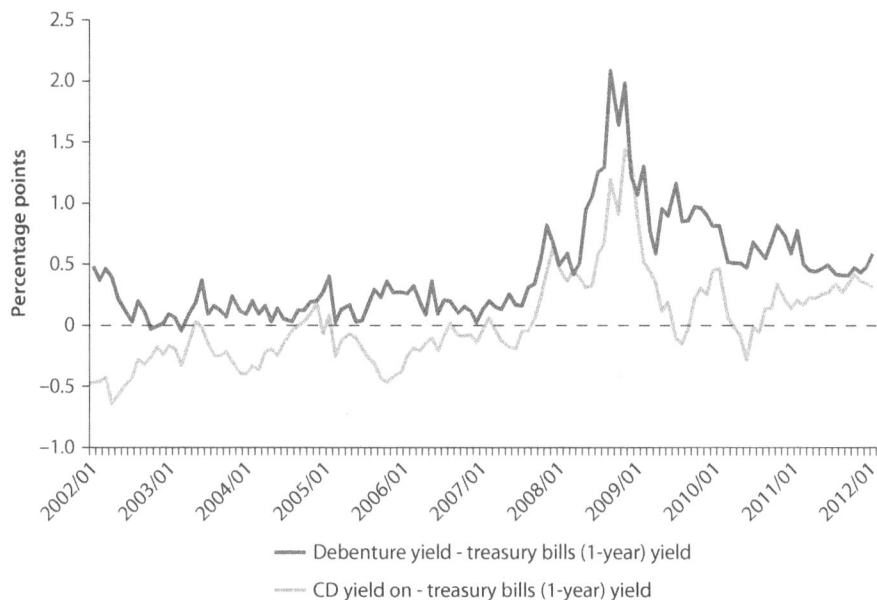

Source: The Bank of Korea Economic Statistics System.

Table 7.8 Composition of Financial Institution Debt and Capital

	December 2005	December 2007	August 2008	December 2008	December 2009	December 2010
Deposits	63.6	55.3	54.1	57.0	59.6	64.0
CDs	2.6	4.2	4.8	4.5	4.5	1.7
Debentures	9.9	11.4	11.3	10.7	8.9	8.4
Funds	14.2	16.6	17.3	15.2	13.8	11.9
Money in Trust	2.2	3.9	4.0	3.6	3.8	3.5
Others	1.4	2.8	2.6	2.2	2.6	4.1
Capital	6.1	5.9	5.9	6.8	6.8	6.6
Total	100	100	100	100	100	100

Source: The Bank of Korea Economic Statistics System.

Figure 7.13 diagrams the process of spillover of the U.S. financial crisis to the Korean economy. It shows how the U.S. financial crisis spread to the domestic Korean financial markets, and how a variety of domestic issues combined to aggravate the impacts from abroad, worsening the domestic liquidity situation and thereby giving rise to another currency crisis. The diagram stresses the fact that liquidity contractions occurred in both the domestic financial and FX markets. In addition, it shows the mutual interaction between foreign exchange market instability and the liquidity strains in the domestic financial market.

Against this backdrop, Korean authorities adopted a series of emergency measures, for example, supplying FX liquidity directly to financial institutions and providing guarantees on banks' foreign liabilities to foreign debtors, but none

Dealing with the Challenges of Macro Financial Linkages in Emerging Markets
http://dx.doi.org/10.1596/978-1-4648-0002-3

Figure 7.13 Currency Turbulence in Korea, 2008

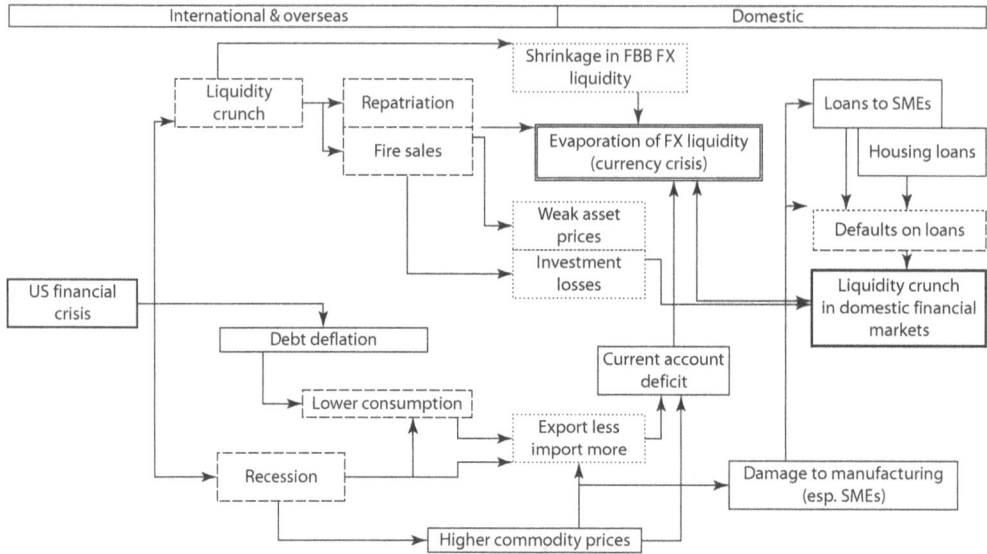

were very effective (Baba and Shim 2011). Korea managed to conclude a bilateral currency swap agreement with the Federal Reserve, however, which helped soothe market sentiment.

Emergency liquidity was also provided to the domestic financial markets. The authorities sought ways of providing liquidity to SMEs, who were suffering difficulties caused by the sharply increased exchange rate, the economic recession, and huge losses on FX derivatives transactions, as outlined in table 7.9. The Bank of Korea (BOK) opened a rediscount window to securities companies as the interbank markets froze. It also expanded the range of collateral eligible for use in its open market operations to include bonds and debentures issued by public enterprises and banks. Apart from these liquidity provision measures, the BOK cut its policy rate rapidly, from 5.25 to 3 percent in just two months between October and December 2008. The authorities meanwhile created a ₩10 trillion bond market stabilization fund and proposed a bank recapitalization fund with the aim of improving financial institutions' credibility. The supervisory authority revised the domestic currency liquidity ratio formula by reducing the maturity for calculation of the ratio from three months or less to one month or less.

Effects of MaPP Measures

In evaluating the effectiveness of the MaPP measures, this chapter will look at whether the measures achieved their ultimate purpose, that is, financial stability. Existing studies, for example BCBS (2010a) and Lim et al. (2011), considered the extents to which these measures contributed to reducing the possibility of financial crisis or systemic risk, and tended to evaluate their effectiveness positively if

Table 7.9 Crisis Management in Korea after Lehman Brothers Bankruptcy

Date	Actions and Measures	Note
Oct. 9	BOK cut of Policy Rate	5.25%→5%
Oct. 13	Government and BOK release of plan for provision of FX liquidity for international trade by SMEs	$16 Bil
Oct. 19	Government provision of guarantees of banks' foreign currency-denominated debts	up to $100 Bil
Oct. 27	BOK cut of Policy Rate	5% → 4.25%
Oct. 27	BOK inclusion of bank debentures and public entity bonds as OMO collateral	
Oct. 27	BOK introduction of auction scheme to provide FX liquidity to banks	
Oct. 30	BOK signing of currency swap agreement with FRB	$30 Bil
Oct. 31	FSC change of DC Liquidity Ratio rule	3-month → 1-month
Nov. 7	BOK cut of Policy Rate	4.25%→4.0%
Nov. 24	BOK provision of liquidity to banks participating in Bond Market Stabilization Fund	W5 Tril
Dec. 3	BOK payment of interest on banks' reserves at BOK	2.3% p.a.
Dec. 11	BOK cut of Policy Rate	4.0%→3.0%
Dec. 11	BOK inclusion of securities companies among counterparties for BOK RP transactions	
Dec. 12	BOK signing of currency swap agreement with PBOC[a]	$30 Bil
	BOK expansion of currency swap agreement with BOJ[a]	$3Bil →20Bil
Dec. 16	Bond Market Stabilization Fund launched	w 10 Tril
Dec. 18	FSC release of plan for establishment of Bank Recapitalization Fund	W20 Tril

Source: Various press releases by the authorities.
[a] The agreement was made in addition to CMI (Chiangmai Initiatives).

they made even small contributions to this end. In contrast, this chapter will evaluate the MaPP measures' effectiveness on the basis of whether they were effective in preventing the occurrence of "systemic events." This perspective seems more reasonable in the sense that the ultimate purpose of MaPP is to preemptively prevent financial imbalances in the financial sector that might lead to systemic events.

As mentioned earlier, Korea adopted several MaPP measures in the 2000s. However, a financial crisis actually did occur afterward. We can therefore assess the MaPP measures in Korea as not having been fully effective, given that they were unable to achieve the ultimate goal of "preventing system events."

We cannot deny that these policy measures had some effects, compared to doing nothing. The effects of individual policies can be examined from various perspectives and dimensions. As noted earlier, the MaPP measures in Korea were not implemented under the integrated conceptual framework of more recent years, in pursuit of the objectives that have been the basis of the current discussions.

Taking these points into account, this chapter will look into the limitations and problems of the MaPP measures used in Korea in the 2000s, as well as mistakes made in their operation to derive lessons from Korea's experience in hopes of establishing a more efficient MaPP framework. The focus will be on the major instruments, specifically the liquidity ratio regulations and the LTV/DTI regulations.

Limitations and Problems of FX Liquidity Ratio

The biggest problem of the FX liquidity ratio regulation was that the FBBs were not made subject to it. There was a perception that the parent banks in advanced countries could inject FX liquidity into their branches at any time (Khatri 2008). However, when major banks in advanced countries were hit by the global finan-cial crisis, it became impossible for them to inject liquidity into their Korean branches. FBBs, which had increased their short-term borrowings to buy forward exchange, then had to redeem their borrowings at maturity, leading domestic foreign exchange conditions to deteriorate.

Since introduction of the FX liquidity ratio regulation, meanwhile, the domes-tic banks had been in compliance with it (see figure 7.14, indicating the FX liquidity "guideline"). This compliance indicates that, even if the FX liquidity ratio is met, there are limitations in its ability to prevent the occurrence of sys-temic events. It is important to examine why an FX liquidity shortage occurred even though the ratio had been met.

Given that the indicative guideline for the ratio was 85 percent, doubts about that level might be raised. In fact, banks actually maintained their FX liquidity ratios above 100 percent, much higher than the guideline. From this perspective,

Figure 7.14a FX Liquidity Ratio, by Banking Group   **Figure 7.14b FX Liquidity Ratio, Commercial Banks**

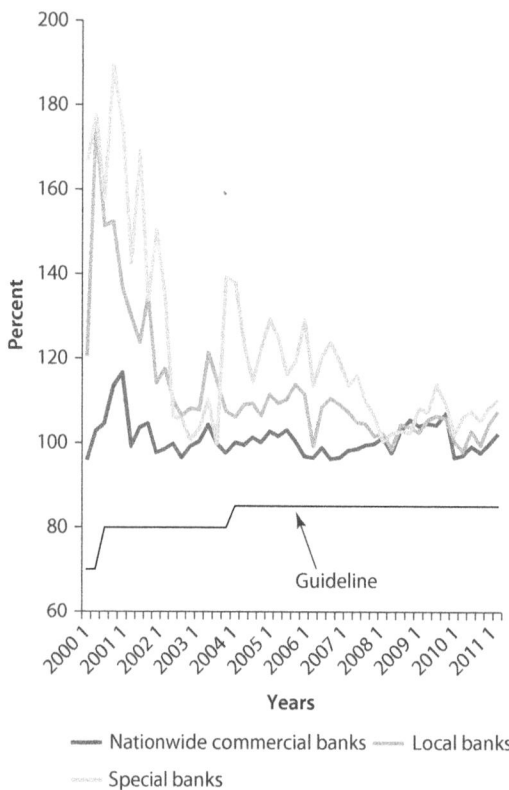

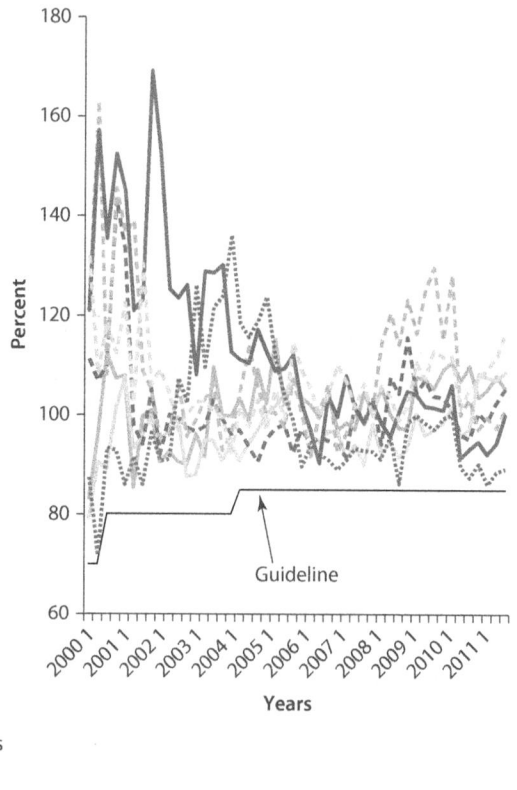

Legend:
— Nationwide commercial banks — Local banks
⋯ Special banks

Source: FSS FISIS.

the appropriate level for the FX liquidity ratio guideline can be a major topic of study going forward. However, I would like to emphasize the limitations of the liquidity regulations, as shown in the ratios of assets and debts.

The fact that a liquidity shortage occurred even though the FX liquidity ratio had been met implies that the liquidity secured through foreign currency assets was unable to meet the obligations incurred through foreign currency debts. Since it is not easy to accurately measure the liquidities of assets and liabilities, I examined their volatilities. Figure 7.15 shows the quarter-on-quarter changes in assets and debts with outstanding maturities of less than three months. The volatility of FX debts measured by their standard deviation was much higher than that of FX assets before the crisis.[25] In other words, the foreign debts fluctuated with relatively wider margins even during the normal period, suggesting differences in liquidity between foreign assets and liabilities.

There may be a shortcoming in examination of differences in liquidity on the basis of the outstanding assets and liabilities. Outstanding assets and liabilities represent stocks at a certain point in time, after adjustment of excesses or shortages in total liquidity. To measure excesses or shortages in total liquidity, it is necessary to examine the volatility in terms of flows.

Figure 7.15 Volatility: FX Assets versus Debts, Three-Month Maturity Assets and Liabilities

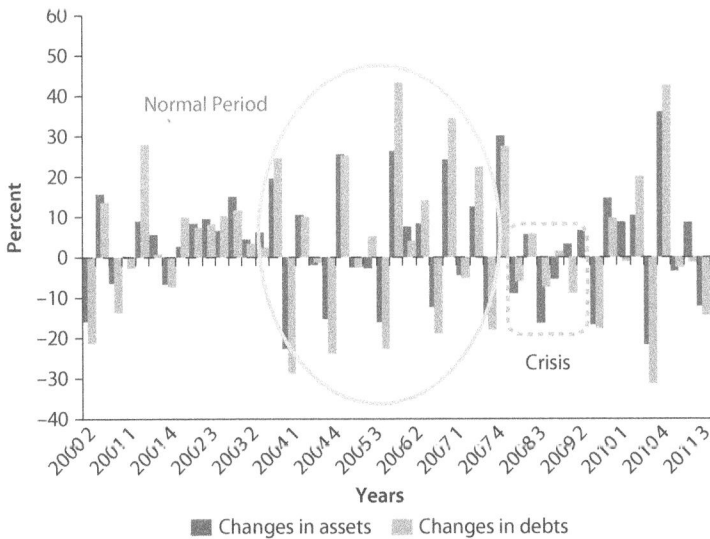

Changes in assets   Changes in debts

Volatilities in Numerical Terms: FX Assets vs. Debts (%)

	Whole Period 2003IV-2011IV		Before-Crisis 2003IV-2008III		During Crisis 2008IV-2010 I		After-Crisis 2010II-2011IV	
	mean	std	mean	std	mean	std	mean	std
Assets	2.5	15.7	3.4	16.0	−2.3	12.6	3.8	20.2
Liabilities	2.4	19.6	4.5	20.7	−3.8	9.5	1.7	25.9

Source: FSS and FISIS.

Dealing with the Challenges of Macro Financial Linkages in Emerging Markets
http://dx.doi.org/10.1596/978-1-4648-0002-3

To examine the fact that assets and debts, two components of the FX liquidity ratio, have different volatilities in terms of their flows, I investigated the relevant statistics from the capital account of the balance of payments. I used the 12-month moving sum of capital flows, based on the methodology of Rothenberg and Warnock (2006), who defined a crisis as when statistical indicators increase beyond a certain range (for example, exceeding more than twice their standard deviations):

$$C_t = \sum_{i=0}^{11} P_{t-i}$$

$$\Delta C_t = C_t - C_{t-12}$$

where,
C: 12-month moving sum of capital flows
P: monthly capital flows
ΔC: annual change.

Calculation of financial institution lending and borrowing flows, displayed in figure 7.16a, shows that borrowing went up by more than two standard deviations in 2008, with the accumulated outflows over 12 months so great as to exceed US$80 billion. Lending meanwhile did not show wide fluctuations, but

Figure 7.16 Volatility

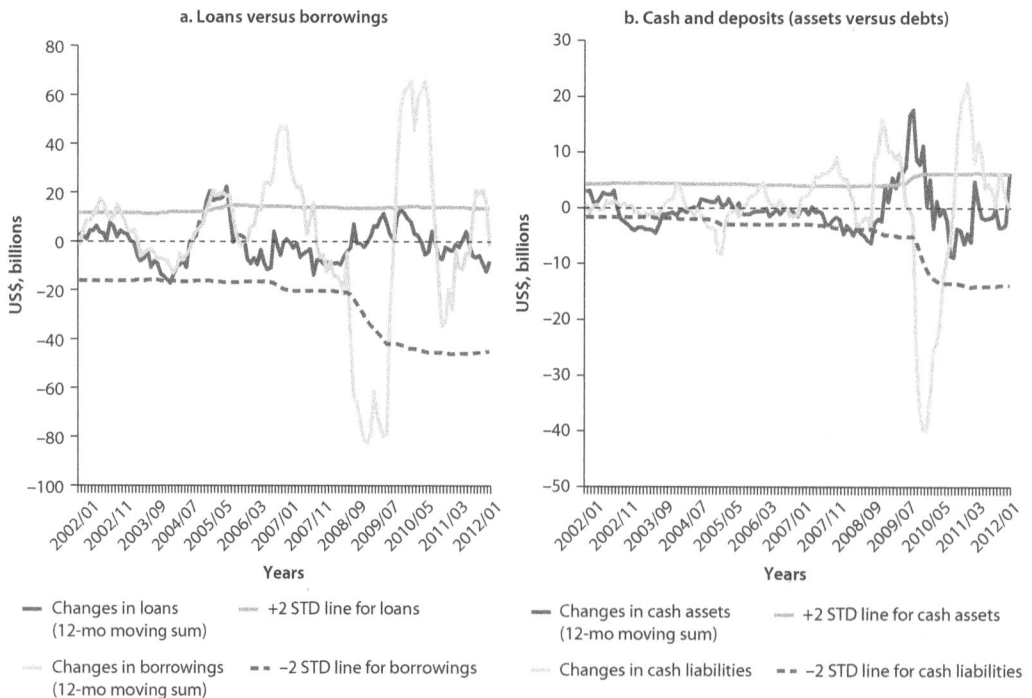

Source: The Bank of Korea Economic Statistics System.

rather remained almost stable within a certain range. In terms of cashable assets and debts including cash and deposits, both assets and liabilities showed wide fluctuations, as displayed in figure 7.16b. In terms of the ranges of their fluctuations, however, cash and deposit liabilities exhibited sharper outflows than the inflows of assets, with the accumulated outflows over 12 months amounting to US$40 billion. The inflows of cash and deposit assets also grew sharply during the crisis, but by only about US$15 billion, much less than the increase in debt outflows.[26] In sum, examination of the flows of foreign assets and liabilities confirms that the volatilities of foreign debts are larger than those of foreign assets.[27]

In conclusion, the disparity in liquidity between assets and liabilities is the limitation of the FX liquidity ratio regulation. The possibility of short-term liquid asset liquidation, in other words, market liquidity, could decline drastically during a crisis, and funding liquidity could also drop sharply. In emergencies, therefore, a situation could arise in which banks are forced to redeem their total liquid liabilities without being able to liquidate their liquid assets.[28]

Another problem of the liquidity ratio regulation is that the gap between liquid assets and liabilities could widen. With the liquidity ratio regulation in place, the actual ratio is not likely to change dramatically, but rather hover at around the regulatory level. Even with an unchanging liquidity ratio, however, the gap between liquid assets and liabilities in terms of their absolute values could widen (as shown in figure 7.17a). This possible widening is because the scale of liquid assets and liabilities with maturities less than three months could increase. In addition, the gap between liquid assets and liabilities could increase compared with nominal GDP, and as shown in figure 7.17b, this trend has been verified in Korea. The widening gap between liquid assets and liabilities may have great impact on the financial market, given the mismatch between market and funding liquidities. The ratio regulation, which expresses the relationship between liquid assets and liabilities in terms of ratios, could therefore lose its effectiveness as time passes, given an expansion in financial transactions.

Limitations and Problems of DC Liquidity Ratio

The DC liquidity ratio regulation is similar to the FX liquidity ratio in terms of its limitations and problems, in that it, too, is based on ratios expressing the relationship between assets and liabilities. Similarly, although no commercial banks' ratios went below the guideline[29] (see figure 7.18), a liquidity crunch in the domestic financial market did occur in 2008. Therefore, as in the case of the FX liquidity ratio, it is interesting to inquire as to why liquidity conditions in the domestic financial markets deteriorated in 2008, even despite all commercial banks having met the DC liquidity ratio guideline.

It is doubtful that the DC liquidity ratio represents the liquidity situation of financial institutions in the domestic financial market very well. In other words, the liquidity ratio is not closely related to actual liquidity demand in a crisis situation. As liquidity conditions in the domestic financial market deteriorated in 2008, the Bank of Korea provided liquidity. However, the relationship between the scale of this liquidity provision and the liquidity ratio is not clear. Estimation of the

Figure 7.17a Liquidity Gap   **Figure 7.17b Ratios of Gap**

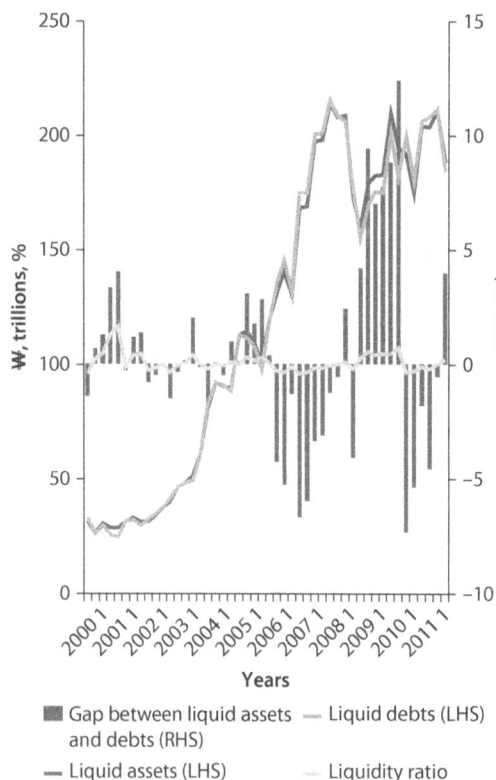

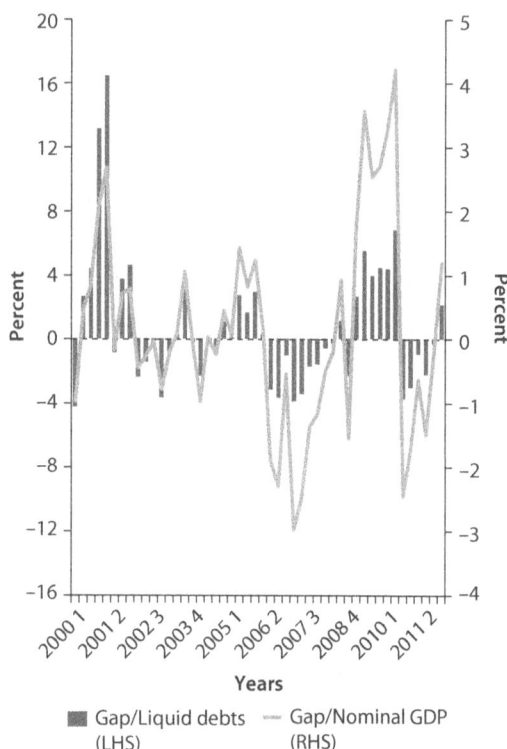

Gap between liquid assets — Liquid debts (LHS)
and debts (RHS)

— Liquid assets (LHS)   — Liquidity ratio

Gap/Liquid debts — Gap/Nominal GDP
(LHS)   (RHS)

Source: The Bank of Korea Economic Statistics System and FSS FISIS.

correlation from Q4 2008 to Q3 2009 between the ratio and borrowings from the BOK yields a correlation coefficient of near zero (see figure 7.19a). Conversely, the correlation between changes in borrowing from the BOK and in noncore liabilities was relatively distinct, showing a coefficient of –0.32 (see figure 7.19b).

This correlation implies that, amid the unstable financial market conditions at home and abroad from Q4 2008 to Q3 2009, banks that were able to reduce their noncore liabilities borrowed little from the BOK, while those unable to repay them borrowed substantially from the BOK. This analysis implies further that the sizes of liquid liabilities determine financial institutions' liquidity risks. In other words, the volatility of funding liquidity demonstrates financial-institution liquidity risks well.

It should be pointed out that the DC liquidity ratio regulation was eased in 2006, when the financial authorities de facto decided to lower the guideline (figure 7.20). This decision supported the autonomous decision making of banks, whose DC liquidity ratios had risen greatly in their efforts to consolidate their loans after the credit card distress of 2003 (FSC and FSS 2006a). The decision gave priority to bank profitability without taking macroeconomic conditions into account. At the time the decision was made, real estate prices were surging, and

Figure 7.18 Domestic Currency Liquidity Ratio

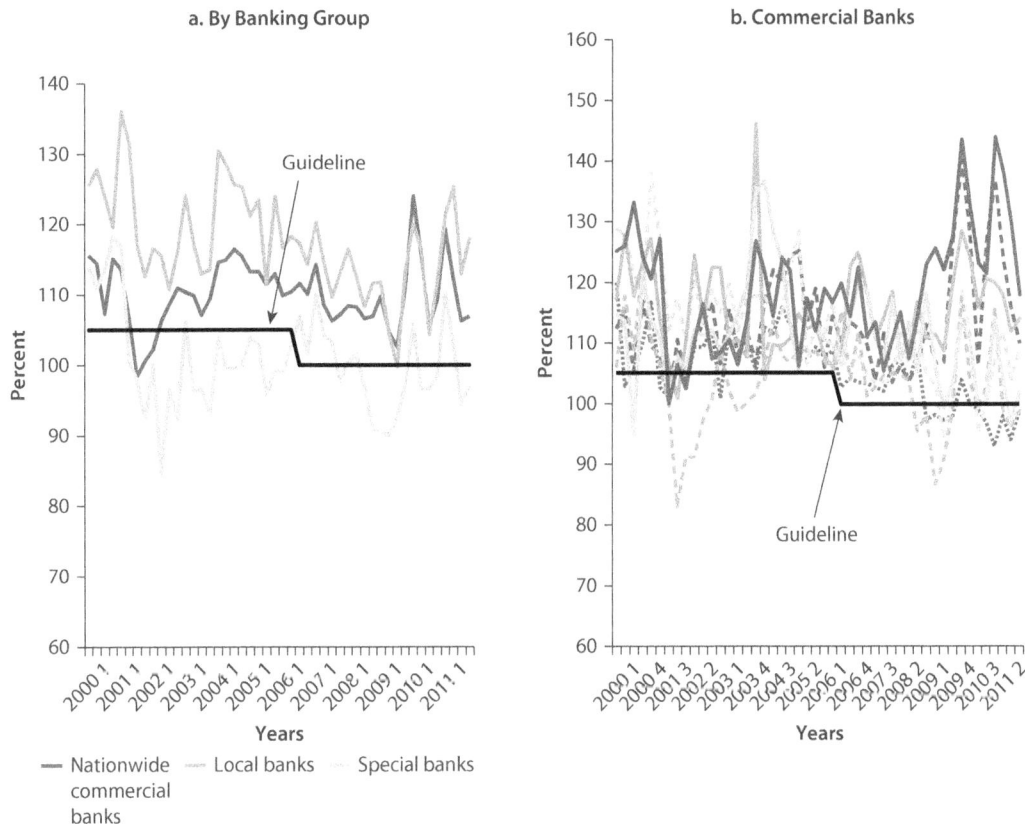

a. By Banking Group

b. Commercial Banks

Years

Years

— Nationwide   -- Local banks   ⋯ Special banks
commercial
banks

Source: FSS and FISIS

bank lending was expanding. After that, and up until just before the global financial crisis, the DC liquidity ratio continued to gradually decline, and lending by
banks with lending capacities continued to increase.[30]

Analysis shows that the liquidity ratio regulation affects the total lending
amount. To grasp the effect of the liquidity ratio on lending, I estimated the following regression:

$$\log\left(\frac{L_t}{P_t}\right) = \alpha_0 + \alpha_1 \log(y_t) + \alpha_2(R_t - \pi_t) + \alpha_3 LR_t + \alpha_4 \log\left(\frac{HP_t}{P_t}\right) + \varepsilon_t$$

where,

L_t: bank lending

P_t: consumer price index

R_t: lending rate (on newly extended loans)

π_t: inflation (changes in CPI)

LR_t: DC liquidity ratio (three-month maturity basis)

HP_t: housing price index (compiled by Kookmin Bank)
ε_t: errors.

Note: Cointegration regression analysis techniques (FMOLS, CCR) applied[31] since all level variables have unit roots; first differenced variables represented in stable time series; results of cointegration testing show existence of one cointeration relationship.

Figure 7.19 Correlation with CB Borrowing and Liquidity Ratio and Noncore Liabilities Ratio

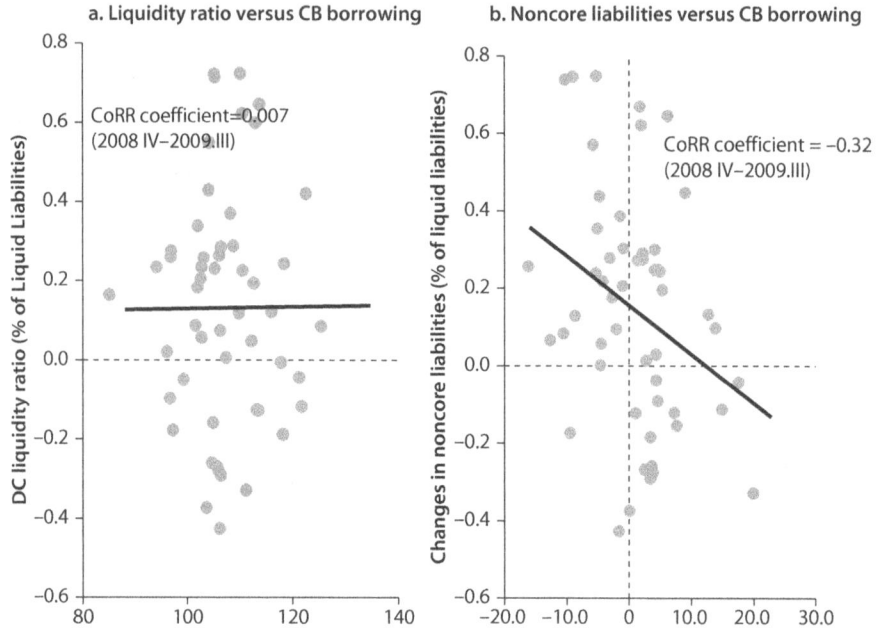

a. Liquidity ratio versus CB borrowing

b. Noncore liabilities versus CB borrowing

CoRR coefficient=0.007
(2008 IV–2009.III)

CoRR coefficient = –0.32
(2008 IV–2009.III)

Source: The Bank of Korea Economic Statistics System, FSS and FISIS.

Figure 7.20 Domestic Currency Liquidity Ratio and Bank Lending

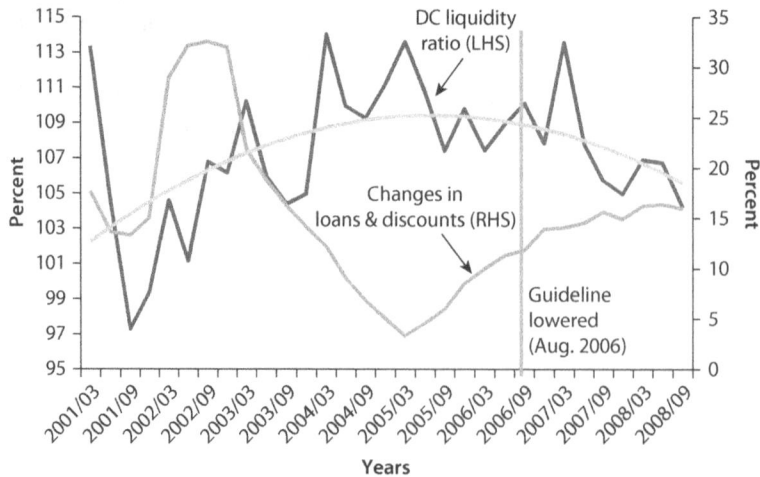

DC liquidity ratio (LHS)

Changes in loans & discounts (RHS)

Guideline lowered (Aug. 2006)

Years

Source: The Bank of Korea Economic Statistics System and FSS FISIS.
Note: The line along the liquidity ratio presents the trend.

The estimation finds that the liquidity ratio is a significant factor determining the amount of bank lending, and based upon these estimation results (table 7.10) we can infer that the easing of liquidity ratio regulations in 2006 served as a factor causing the expansion in bank lending in the second half of the 2000s. This regulatory easing appears to have been part of the background behind financial institutions' expansion in bank debenture issuance at that time.

Interpreting from a retrospective viewpoint based on this analysis, we can infer that the DC liquidity ratio regulations have been conducted to help ensure the soundness of individual financial institutions, that is, for micro prudential objectives. Macroeconomic financial conditions, including total lending, seem not to have been kept in mind. We can derive the lesson that, in order to use the liquidity ratio as a MaPP measure, it would be more appropriate to set a target variable representing macroeconomic conditions for the liquidity ratio, rather than operating the ratio simply to secure individual financial institution soundness.

Limitations and Problems of LTV and DTI

Many studies exist on the effects of the LTV and DTI regulations on housing finance. Those discussing the issue from a conceptual perspective tend to view the regulations positively. Discussions related to Korea include Chang (2010), Shin (2010), FSB, IMF, and BIS (2011) and Crowe et al. (2011). Although there are not many empirical studies on the Korean case, Igan and Kang (2011) presented results of empirical analysis in a study concluding that the LTV and DTI regulations in Korea have not had great influence on housing prices, but have affected the housing transaction volume.

Table 7.10 Liquidity Ratio and Bank Lending

Independent variable	$\log(L_t/P_t)$	
Estimation method	FMOLS	CCR
Explanatory variables		
Constant	−4.454***	−4.342***
	(0.908)	(1.002)
$\log(y_t)$	1.119***	1.114***
	(0.070)	(0.076)
$R_t - \pi_t$	−0.007	−0.007
	(0.006)	(0.002)
LR_t	−0.003**	−0.004**
	(0.001)	(0.002)
$\log(HP_t/P_t)$	0.845***	0.865***
	(0.152)	(0.158)
Adjusted R-square	0.987	0.987
Estimation Period	2000.III ~ 2009.III	

Source: The Bank of Korea Economic Statistics System.
Notes: Figures in ( ) refer to standard deviations, and ***, ** and * to significance levels of 1%, 5% and 10%, respectively.

Assessment of the LTV and DTI regulation effects can differ depending on the perspective and the standard of assessment adopted. I would like to assess the effects from three perspectives: a micro perspective to assess the effects on financial institution soundness; a perspective related to the authority's intention, that is, to stabilize housing prices; and a perspective regarding the household debt volume or level.

In the Korean case, we can assess the LTV and DTV regulations as having at least helped financial institutions maintain their soundness. Housing prices fell from the second half of 2009, after the global financial crisis, but the delinquency ratio on household loans remained extremely low (figure 7.21). This situation implies that strict implementation of the LTV ratio prevented delinquencies on household loans even after housing prices fell,[32] thus reducing financial institution credit risks despite the dramatic increase in household loans prior to the global financial crisis.[33] From this standpoint, the LTV and DTI regulations were helpful in securing financial institution soundness.

Meanwhile, the effects of the two measures in stabilizing housing prices were limited. When the LTV regulation was introduced, and during the several times it was strengthened through revisions, housing prices declined at first but then rose again one or two quarters later, as shown in figure 7.22a. In fact, the limited effects of the LTV and the difficulties in strengthening it further led to the introduction of a DTI regulation in 2005. After the DTI regulation was adopted, however, results similar to those with the LTV regulation were observed. Strengthening of the DTI regulation worked at first, but housing prices began to rise again one or two quarters later.

Figure 7.21 Delinquency Ratios of Loans to Households and Corporates

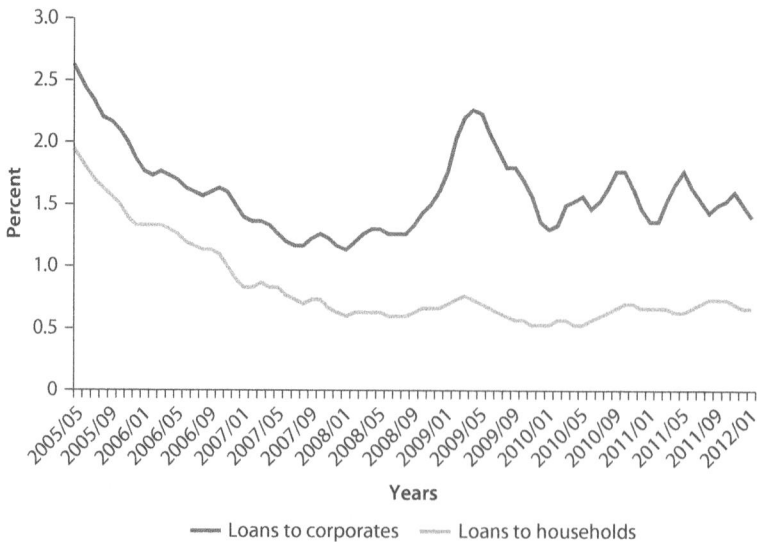

Source: The Bank of Korea Economic Statistics System.

Figure 7.22 The Impact of LTV on Housing Prices and Lending

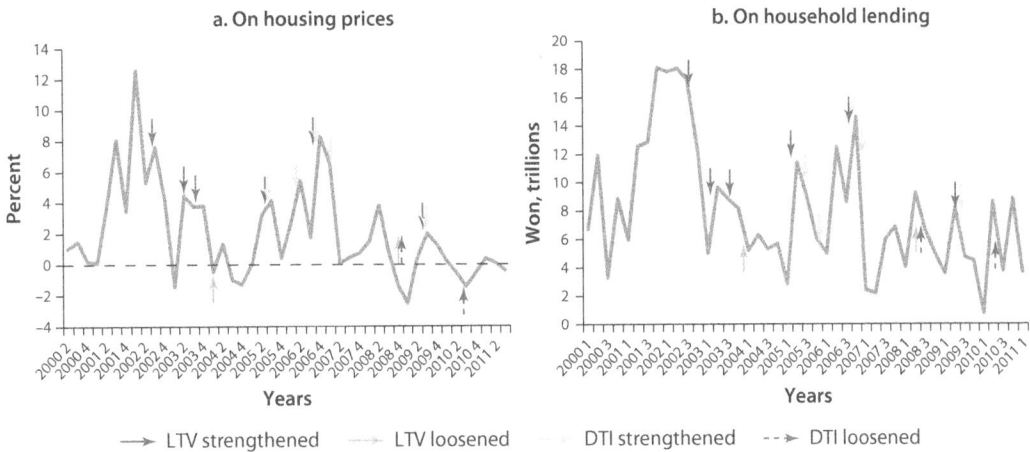

a. On housing prices   b. On household lending

The impacts of the LTV and DTI regulations in limiting household lending, shown in figure 7.22b, seem similar to their impacts on housing prices. When stronger LTV and DTI regulations were implemented, financial institutions at first temporarily extended fewer loans to households. One or two quarters later, however, they increased their household lending again, and this pattern continued until the outbreak of the global financial crisis.

To verify this argument, I estimated a simple regression for the determinants of housing prices and household lending as follows:

$$\log\left(\frac{HP_t}{P_t}\right) = \beta_0 + \beta_1 \log(y_t) + \beta_2(R_t - \pi_t) + \beta_3 \log\left(\frac{L_t}{P_t}\right) + \beta_4 LTV_t + \beta_5 DTI_t + \mu_t$$

$$\log\left(\frac{HD_t}{P_t}\right) = \gamma_0 + \gamma_1 \log(y_t) + \gamma_2(R_t - \pi_t) + \gamma_3 \log\left(\frac{HP_t}{P_t}\right) + \gamma_4 LTV_t + \gamma_5 DTI_t + v_t$$

where,

HP_t: housing price (Kookmin Bank)
P_t: consumer price index
Y_t: real GDP
R_t: lending rate (new contract basis)
π_t: inflation (changes in CPI)
L_t: bank lending to households
LTV_t: LTV ratio (minimum)
DTI_t: DTI ratio (minimum)
HD_t: household debt
μ_t, v_t: the respective error terms.

The estimation results represented in table 7.11 show the LTV and DTI ratios to have not affected either housing prices or household debt, as I could not obtain any robust estimation for the coefficient when regressing either on LTV and DTI or on their lag. The regression for the determinants of housing prices revealed a coefficient on LTV_t with a 5 percent level of significance. This estimation result seems unreliable, however, as it shows a negative sign, which is different from expectation; it is naturally expected that if the LTV is lowered (the regulation strengthened), housing prices should be squeezed.[34] Regression on the equation of the household debt determinants showed a coefficient on LTV_t and LTV_{t-1} with only a 10 percent significance level, and no significant coefficients on DTI or its lag.[35]

The reasons for the limited impacts of the measures in stabilizing house prices and limiting household lending can be found in several factors, including the nature of the housing market at that time and the competition among financial institutions. The decrease in housing supply since the time of the 1997 currency crisis had resulted in a structural housing supply shortage, leading to widespread expectations of housing price increases. Changes on the demand side were observed as well; in addition to housing quality, buyers considered the residential environment very important. These structural changes in the housing market seemed to make the LTV and DTI regulations ineffective in curbing the demand for houses, especially high-end houses. In sum, when house prices increase because of fundamental factors such as a supply-demand imbalance, or changes in housing demand patterns, the regulatory effects will be limited, as in the Korean case in the 2000s.

The expansion in mortgage lending in the 2000s was also linked to the changes in lending strategies of financial institutions. In the wake of the 1997 currency crisis, seriously insolvent banks underwent restructuring, for example through mergers and liquidations. After this restructuring process had run its course, banks began to normalize their businesses from 2004. As financial institutions regained autonomy and started to manage their businesses with a focus on making profits, they began to expand their household loans, which are stable with low risk and high interest rates. Based on the lessons from the currency crisis, companies were attempting to avoid taking out loans, making it difficult for financial institutions to expand their corporate lending. To maximize their profits, it was inevitable that financial institutions would extend more loans to households. Financial institutions were able to reap attractive profits from household loans, most of which were secured by real estate collateral such as houses and whose risk-weights in calculating the BIS ratio were low; plus interest rates on household loans were higher than those on corporate loans. Financial institutions competed vigorously with each other in a lending spree in pursuit of market share expansions or higher asset volume growth. Given these lending strategies, household loans emerged as a main focus for banks.

Table 7.11 LTV and DTI Regulations, and Housing Prices and Household Debt

LTV and DTI Regulation and Housing Prices			
Dependent Variable	$\log(HP_t/P_t)$		
Estimation method	FMOLS		
Explanatory Variables			
Constant	2.624	−4.921	0.540	−3.243*
	(3.685)	(4.536)	(3.521)	(3.895)
$\log(y_t)$	−0.520	0.152	−0.304	−0.008
	(0.387)	(0.461)	(0.370)	(0.414)
$R_t − \pi_t$	0.008	0.007	0.004	0.003
	(0.008)	(0.011)	(0.008)	(0.011)
$\log(L_t/P_t)$	0.421***	0.318**	0.355***	0.353**
	(0.127)	(0.153)	(0.121)	(0.151)
LTV	−0.002**			
	(0.001)			
DTI		0.002		
		(0.001)		
LTV(−1)			−0.001	
			(0.001)	
DTI(−1)				0.002
				(0.001)
Adjusted R2	0.859	0.809	0.842	0.823
Sample Periods	2000.III ~ 2009.IV			

Note: Figures in ( ) are standard errors. ***, **, and * imply significant level of 1%, 5%, and 10% respectively.

LTV and DTI Regulation and Household Debt			
Dependent Variable	$\log(HD_t/P_t)$		
Estimation method	FMOLS		
Explanatory Variables			
Constant	−14.562***	−14.243***	−14.074***	−13.016***
	(2.241)	(3.846)	(2.352)	(3.174)
$\log(y_t)$	1.910***	1.888***	1.871***	1.791***
	(0.180)	(0.306)	(0.189)	(0.253)
$R_t − \pi_t$	−0.026***	−0.020***	−0.024***	−0.020***
	(0.007)	(0.010)	(0.009)	(0.009)
$\log(HP_t/P_t)$	0.970***	0.864***	0.997***	0.906***
	(0.214)	(0.247)	(0.216)	(0.234)
LTV	0.002*			
	(0.001)			
DTI		0.000		
		(0.001)		
LTV(−1)			0.001*	
			(0.001)	
DTI(−1)				−0.000
				(0.000)
Adjusted R2	0.981	0.978	0.978	0.976
Sample Periods	2000.III ~ 2009.IV			

Source: The Bank of Korea Economic Statistics System, Kookmin Bank.
Note: Figures in ( ) are standard errors. ***, **, and * imply significant level of 1%, 5%, and 10% respectively.

Dealing with the Challenges of Macro Financial Linkages in Emerging Markets
http://dx.doi.org/10.1596/978-1-4648-0002-3

Figure 7.23 Household Debt

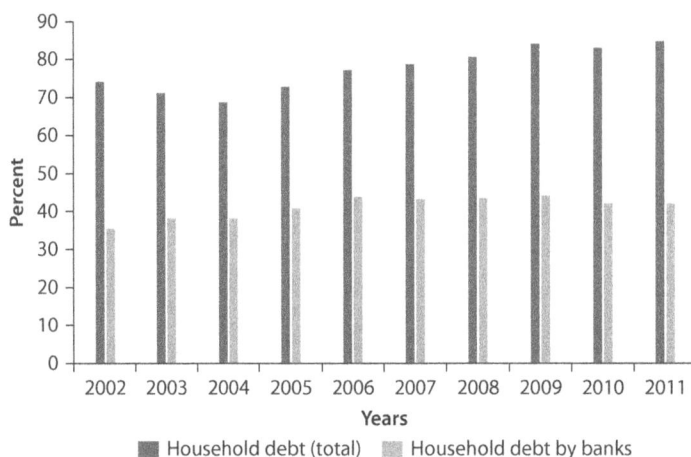

Source: The Bank of Korea Economic Statistics System.

The LTV and DTI regulations could hardly contain this bank lending strategy. Few people considered banks' expansion of household lending to be a problem at the time. There was, instead, a view that it was normal for household lending to increase in the 2000s, since funds had previously been allocated to the corporate sector, with household loan extension limited until the 1990s.

Given the limited effects of the LTV and DTI regulations, the ratio of total household credit to national disposable income has risen, from 69 percent in 2004 to 81 percent in 2008 and 85 percent in 2011, as shown in figure 7.23. Household debt is currently a critically important variable in Korea, for consideration in promoting financial stability and operating macroeconomic policies.

Lack of Linkages among Sectors

While MaPP measures have been explored for individual sectors such as the housing market, domestic banking, and foreign exchange, we should also point out the lack of a comprehensive perspective or tools taking all sectors into account. During the 2008 crisis, foreign financial institutions were reluctant to roll over the short-term foreign debts held by Korean banks, because of doubts about Korean bank creditworthiness. It was the LTD ratio that made foreign financial institutions suspicious; as mentioned earlier, acute debate on the LTD ratio level arose at that time. Although it is not easy to determine how foreign financial institutions reflected the LTD ratios in evaluating Korean banks' financial conditions at that time, the occurrence of this debate did demonstrate the possibility that domestic financial conditions affected the foreign exchange sector.

To find the correlation between the LTD ratio and financial institutions' short-term FX liquidity, a simple calculation was conducted. The coefficient of correlation between the previous quarter's LTD ratio and the quarter-on-quarter changes in short-term FX liquid liabilities was calculated.[36] The calculation was conducted for six major commercial banks during the period Q4 2008–Q3 2009,

Figure 7.24 Correlation: LTD Ratio versus FX Funding Liquidity

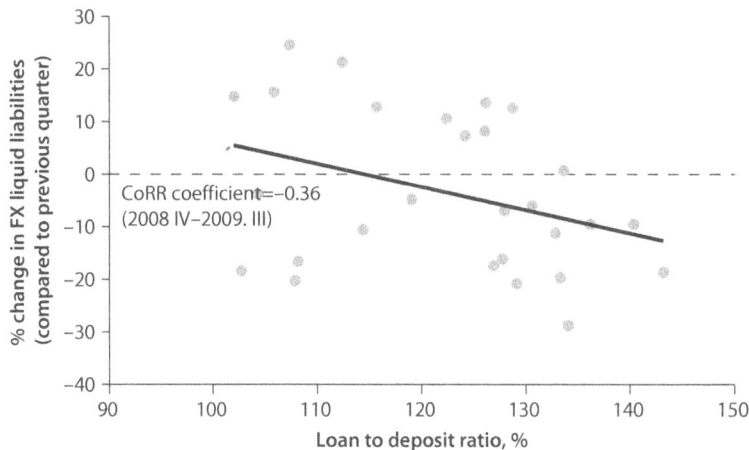

Source: The Bank of Korea Economic Statistics System, FSS and FISIS.

and the coefficient of correlation was found to be –0.36, as demonstrated in figure 7.24. Based on this result, we can conclude that the LTD ratio did affect the FX funding liquidity of financial institutions.

This finding indicates that the domestic banking and foreign exchange sectors can affect each other. Likewise, what happens in the housing market is closely linked to the financial sector. It was problematic that Korea sought MaPP measures only for application to individual sectors, rather than tools that could reflect the relationships among sectors. In this regard, it may be necessary to seek ways of reflecting domestic financial conditions in the FX liquidity ratio, and FX funding liquidity conditions in the DC liquidity ratio, as well as simultaneously considering both financial institution activities and real estate market trends when designing MaPP measures.

Summary and Implications

This section summarizes the discussions by describing the characteristic aspects of MaPP operations in Korea in the 2000s. These characteristics will then be used as a basis for deriving implications for more effective operation of MaPP measures in the future.

Characteristics of MaPP Measures in Korea in the 2000s

The limited effects of the MaPP measures in Korea in the 2000s can be attributed to several characteristics of the measures. To pave the way for deriving implications for effective future operation of MaPP measures, this chapter discusses several characteristic aspects of those measures, summarized in table 7.12.

First, the objectives of the measures were micro prudential rather than macro prudential. The liquidity ratio regulation in particular was targeted precisely at strengthening individual banks' abilities to pay their liabilities or secure their

Table 7.12 Characteristic Aspects of the MaPP Measures in Korea in the 2000s

	FX Liquidity Ratio	DC Liquidity Ratio	LTV, DTI
Primary Objective	• secure banks' capacities to repay short-term FX liabilities	• secure banks' capacities to repay debts	• stabilize real estate prices
Other objectives			• strengthen banks' soundness by reducing their credit risks
Regulator	• supervisory authority	• supervisory authority	• adopted by policy maker (government) • monitored by supervisory authority
The regulated	• domestic banks • FBBs exempted	• banks and non-bank FIs	• banks and NBFIs • adjusted flexibly

Scope	• FX-denominated assets and liabilities
	  • derivatives added
		• DC-denominated assets and liabilities
		  • Moneys in trust excluded
			• real state market FI lending activities

Character/Attributes	• quasi-regulation	• quasi-regulation recommended guideline	• order
	• prospective	• prospective	• retrospective
	• customized rule	• customized rule	• customized rule
	• general and universal	• general and universal	• possibility of modification for specific purposes
Point of Time	• quarter-end	• quarter-end	• applied to every loan contract
Time Horizon	• consistently applied and strengthened	• consistently applied, but deregulated	• changed frequently
Auxiliary Measures	• maturity mismatch ratio (GAP ratio) • FX position • minimum bound of longer-term liabilities	(none)	• DTI introduced to supplement LTV • applied with various policy measures such as taxation
Degree of Bindingness	• non-binding	• non-binding	• strongly binding
Loopholes			• bridge loans, group lending by construction companies
Side Effects		• shorter loan maturity	• expansion of NBFI and/or other lending methods
Effectiveness	• limited	• limited	• limited

Reasons for Ineffectiveness	• Exemption of FBBs
	• Limitations of ratio regulation
	  • volatility of liabilities
	• Inflexibility to new types of imbalances
		• Limitations of ratio regulation
		  • volatility of liabilities
		• Inflexibility to new types of imbalances
		• Time-inconsistency of operations
			• Limited effects in coping with fundamental changes in real estate and financial markets

	• Separately operated, while markets are interconnected (lack of comprehensive view)		

Note: FBBS = Foreign Bank Branches; FIs = Financial Institutions.

soundness. The micro prudential viewpoint of the Korean MaPP measures in the 2000s was of course, inevitable because the concept of MaPP did not exist at the time. Another reason may have been the governance of the measures; the authorities handling these measures were the supervisory authorities, whose responsibility is micro prudential regulation. In short, it should be pointed out as a characteristic feature of the Korean MaPP measures of the 2000s that they did not target macro-level variables or events critical to financial stability.

The Korean MaPP measures of the 2000s had several features that demonstrate the limitations or shortcomings of regulation. Almost without exemption, no regulation can avoid inherent problems such as boundary problems, loopholes, and negative side-effects. Because the MaPP measures took the form of regulations, these problems eroded their effectiveness. An example of a boundary problem of MaPP regulations was the exemption of FBBs from the FX liquidity ratio regulation. Cases of MaPP regulation loopholes were meanwhile relatively apparent with the LTV and DTI regulations. For example, the regulations were ineffective in curbing the demand for houses.[37] At the same time, the authorities expanded the scope of LTV regulations to NBFIs including savings banks, mutual savings banks and credit companies, in an attempt to block opportunities for bridge loans by these NBFIs. Negative side effects were not small. Banks endeavored to expand to housing loans, which have longer-term maturities. To meet the liquidity ratio obligation, however, they had to reduce the maturities of their loans to business firms. This reduction was neither ideal nor desirable from the perspective of banks' basic function of maturity transformation, particularly in the Korean situation where viability of the economy depends on smooth business firm activities in exporting and transactions.

The flexibility of MaPP measures is an important factor that can impact their effectiveness or determine the validity of the MaPP scheme. In the history of MaPP measures in Korea, the tools were revised frequently and promptly in accordance with changes in market conditions. However, these frequent revisions did not lead to success in achieving the measures' primary objectives. This failure implies that it might be necessary to adopt a new series of regulations to deal with newly emerging potential risks, rather than adjusting existing regulations. In this regard, Korea was not flexible in adopting new types of MaPP measures in line with the appearance of new potential risks accompanying structural changes in its financial markets.

Another characteristic aspect of the Korean MaPP measures may be examined from the viewpoint of their time dimension, that is, whether they were applied ex ante or ex post. It is clear that the LTV and DTI rules were applied ex post. The introductions and amendments of these rules accompanied changes in housing prices, and their time dimension operational characteristics were thus reactive. This aspect is the opposite of the MaPP perspective, which preempts potential risk factors.

The scope of the MaPP measures is another important characteristic. The Korean MaPP measures were confined to certain areas. Although simultaneous, they were operated separately, without coordination or harmonized adjustments.

In this regard, the operational characteristic aspect of the Korean MaPP measures can be described as an ad hoc approach, which contrasts with the comprehensive viewpoint recommended by the current conceptual framework for MaPP.

A final point about the characteristics of the Korean MaPP measures is that the focus of the regulations was on ratios. The liquidity ratio, for example, a comparison of asset volume with total debt size, has an inherent inability to catch signals of financial imbalances in advance and prevent their accumulation. In addition, the assets and debts of financial institutions have different properties with regard to financial stability: banks' liabilities may become volatile in an emergency situation, moving beyond a range that cannot be covered by the liquidity of the assets that a financial institution holds. In sum, a liquidity ratio is unable to fully and flexibly reflect all aspects of structural changes in the related financial markets, and cannot prevent accumulation of financial imbalances. Reliance on a few ratios, therefore, even though applied from the MaPP perspective, is not sufficient for securing financial stability.

Implications for MaPP Operation

This chapter closes with some implications for the effective operations of MaPP, based on evaluation of Korean experiences of MaPP measure operations in the 2000s.

Objective Setting in a Macro Prudential Dimension

For the successful implementation of MaPP measures, it is important that their objectives be set from a macro prudential dimension. It would be ideal to set as objectives indicators reflecting procyclicality, systemic risks, or interconnectedness. In reality, however, it is necessary to find alternatives for these macro prudential indicators, because their formulation for use in the real world is not easy. Better candidates would be lending or borrowing aggregates of certain sectors, for example, whose developments can be monitored, since most financial imbalances usually accumulate in the forms of excessive lending or borrowing. The Korean case provides evidence, at least, supporting the argument that micro prudential objectives should be avoided in the design of MaPP measures.

Supplementing for Problems of Ratio-Style MaPP Measures

The Korean case illustrates the inherent limitations of liquidity ratio regulation because of the differences between asset liquidity and liability liquidity. Even though the risk factor weighting of liquidity ratios, as considered under Basel III, may lessen this problem to some degree, it cannot resolve it completely. In extreme cases, like during the 2008 global financial crisis, a higher liquidity ratio will not make any difference in preventing a liquidity crunch. In this regard, liquidity ratio regulation may need to be supplemented with, for example, a cap on total borrowing.[38]

The Korean case also raises the issue of the liquidity ratio level. During the 2000s, the liquidity ratios for DC- as well as FX-denominated transactions did not constrain banks' risky activities; almost every bank maintained its liquidity ratio above the guideline level. This may indicate that the level for the liquidity ratio guideline has been lax. The appropriate level for the guideline can thus be an important issue related to regulation effectiveness, and could perhaps be raised to far above 100 percent.[39]

Minimizing Boundary Problems

In Korea, similarly to the U.S. case, the financial imbalances began in areas not subject to regulations. It is clear from the Korean experience that MaPP measures should be devised in a way that reduces the possibility of regulatory arbitrage or minimizes boundary problems of regulations.[40]

Maintaining Time Consistency of MaPP

It is natural to expect a situation in which the MaPP measures need amendment or revision as economic and financial circumstances change. Especially when amending or revising MaPP measures in the direction of deregulation, it will be important to maintain their intended purposes. Authorities should evaluate the impacts of MaPP measure amendment from various perspectives because, as in the Korean case of its 2006 DC liquidity ratio deregulation, a change can be rational from one side but suddenly lead to an imbalance in an unexpected way, which might be very difficult to correct ex post.

Harmonizing MaPP Measures and Combining Subsector MaPP Measures

The financial system consists of many subsectors, for example the domestic banking and FX sectors in Korea. As in Korea, MaPP measures may be designed to target individual subsectors. However, in reality these subsectors are interconnected. Separate MaPP measures targeting specific subsectors will not be able to cope with events occurring across several subsectors. Thus, MaPP measures designed for specific subsectors should also consider activities in related sectors.[41] For example, the Korean case suggests that the FX liquidity ratio scheme needs to also incorporate an indicator for domestic banking activities, such as the LTD ratio.

The operation of MaPP measures would work best if harmonized with those of the whole scheme of measures. This issue may be similar to that of coordination between MaPP and monetary policy. The point is that, when several MaPP measures are applied simultaneously, consideration should be given to coordination and the interrelationships among them.

Overcoming the Limitations of Readymade Rules

MaPP measures, like any regulations, have inherent limitations, such as their tendency to lag behind changes in the financial markets and to have loopholes. For the sake of MaPP-measure effectiveness, they should be supplemented with non-regulatory measures, such as the activities of the authorities concerned with financial market and economic monitoring, analysis of potential risks, recommendation of risk avoidance means, and so on. These measures might be articulated as belonging to the realm of "macro prudential policy," rather than "macro prudential regulation." From this point of view, it would be reasonable to operate the MaPP on two tracks: the MaPP regulatory measures supported by the MaPP policy activities.

Notes

1. These measures can be matched with the MaPP type of Funding Liquidity Standards and Collateral Arrangements considered by Galeti and Moessner (2011), who classify the MaPP measures into 10 categories (see Galeti and Moessner (2011),10).

2. $\dfrac{\text{Total Financial Assets}}{\text{Nominal GDP}}$, which indicates the size of financial sector relative to the real sector (Goldsmith 1959).

3. The monthly data during the period of April 1990 through March 2012 were used for the calculation, because the government allowed the exchange rate to be freely determined in the market from March 1990 (Rhee and Lee 2004).

4. For more details on the 1997 financial crisis, refer to Chopra and others (2001).

5. The government pursued liberalization of interest rates in 1965, but as a result witnessed only adverse side effects such as expansion of curb markets, and it therefore returned to a policy of suppressive interest rate regulation. Refer to Kim and Lee (2010) for more detail.

6. One extraordinary phenomenon was the expansion in lending by NBFIs, which later became a cause of the 1997 currency crisis but was not recognized as a financial imbalance at that time.

7. Refer to Giordano (2009) for more details on the objectives of financial supervision.

8. At that time, strengthening of regulation was considered unacceptable given the social mood and sentiment valuing pursuit of political and social freedom.

9. Initially 7.25 percent was applied, which was later raised to 8 percent in 1995.

10. Korea has employed several other tools that can be regarded as MaPP measures, such as the BIS capital adequacy ratio, reserve requirements on deposits (in both foreign and domestic currencies), and restrictions on lending (especially FX lending) to certain borrowers. This chapter excludes such measures from discussion.

11. In 2009, Korea revised the formula to incorporate the risk factors for various assets (FSC and FSS 2009).

12. From zero to seven days, from eight days to one month, from one month to three months, from three to six months, from six months to one year, from one to three years, and exceeding three years.

13. The loan contracts set the maturity at more than three years, but contained put option clauses giving the borrowers the right to ask for early redemption, so that the actual maturity would be shortened to one to two years.

14. Goldstein and Turner (2004) expressed the view that currency mismatch is a problem typical to any currency crisis.

15. There has been debate on global introduction of FX position regulations, but objections have been raised from this perspective (see for example Hartman (1994)).

16. Limited to within a certain ratio of past performance.

17. Real estate policy and monetary policy were implemented separately during this time (BOK 2003).

18. An area was designated as a speculative zone in the case where: (1) its monthly nominal house price index (HPI) had risen more than 1.3 times the nationwide inflation rate based on the consumer prices index during the previous month, and (2) either (a) its average HPI appreciation rate in the previous two months had been higher than 1.3 times the average national HPI appreciation rate during that time, or (b) its average month-on-month HPI appreciation rate over the previous year had been higher than the average month-on-month national HPI appreciation rate for the previous three years (Igan and Kang 2011). In the most extreme cases, "excessively speculative zones" were designated, in which certain specified types of transactions were prohibited.

19. The problem, however, was that it was discriminative against members of the younger generations with relatively low incomes, since it could possibly prevent them from owning houses.

20. Except during the period of the currency crisis when deposits at NBFIs were relocated to the banking sector and lending declined significantly due to economic recession.

21. In 1996, Korea Housing Bank was converted to a commercial bank, and from that time other commercial banks were allowed to deal in mortgage loans. Commercial banks had previously focused mainly on corporate finance, and Korea Housing Bank, a specialized bank, had been in exclusive charge of housing finance.

22. Household loans had higher interest rates than corporate loans, and unlike in credit-guarantee funds, securing of deposits was not mandatory. Risk-weights were just 50 percent in estimation of the BIS capital ratio with respect to household loans because the houses were the collateralized. The risk-weight application for corporate loans, in contrast, was 100 percent.

23. In addition, overseas portfolio investment by domestic investors increased rapidly from 2006. Investors sold forward contracts to hedge their investments to avoid foreign exchange risk.

24. The suspicions about Korean banks might also have been aggravated by memories of the 1997 currency crisis.

25. However, the standard deviation of their quarter-on-quarter changes was relatively smaller during the crisis period, presumably because the range of fluctuation in debt narrowed because of unfavorable debt financing conditions.

26. Meanwhile, the time it took for the cash and deposit assets of domestic financial institutions to exceed two standard deviations was significantly less than what it took for debt outflows. We need to devise a plan to use this as a crisis forecasting index.

27. In the case of Korea in 2008, the rapid reduction in foreign borrowings was attributable mainly to foreigners. In this sense, the event could be categorized as a "sudden stop" rather than sudden flight (refer to Rothenberg and Warnock [2006] for detailed discussion of this issue).

28. Recently, a way of numerically reflecting the possibility of liquidation has been considered. However, it is possible that liquidity might not be ensured as much as expected in this case either, if many financial institutions try to liquidate assets at the same time.

29. The ratios of the government-owned specialized banks were lower than the guideline, but they did not cause the liquidity shortage in 2008.

30. In response to this expansion in bank lending, the Bank of Korea raised the reserve requirement ratio in November 2006 to curb the pace of bank lending expansion. This did not pay off, however, because of the inclusion of reserve requirements in liquid assets in DC liquidity ratio calculation.

31. FMOLS: fully modified ordinary least squares method; CCR: canonical cointegrating regression.

32. The lower household loan delinquency ratio in Korea may be due to legal factors. In general, Korean law allows the right of recourse to the creditor, which weakens household incentives for foreclosure. Fitch Ratings (2010) compactly describes the legal aspects of Korean housing loans.

33. The conclusion of Wong and others (2011), who reported relatively positive empirical analytical results for Hong Kong regarding the LTV effects, is based on this logic.

34. This estimation result may reflect the ex post property of the LTV regulation, which was lowered after the jump in housing prices had been observed.

35. To obtain concrete statistical evidence of the effects of the LTV and DTI regulations on housing prices and household debt, it may be necessary to apply more detailed econometric estimation techniques that can determine the interrelations among the variables used in the estimation.

36. Since the liquidity ratio could not reflect the liquidity conditions for banks, as analyzed here, the changes in FX liabilities are selected as the needed proxy for FX liquidity conditions.

37. Up to that time, an LTV ratio of 40 percent had been applied to loans for houses priced above 600 million Won with maturities of 10 years or more. On loans for houses of the same value, but with amortized repayment over 10 years with one-year grace periods, the LTV ratio was meanwhile 60 percent, as the authorities believed these loans were not motivated by speculative purposes. In fact, however, the latter form of loan came to comprise the majority in those days, with most taken out for the purpose of avoiding the regulation (FSC and FSS 2006b).

38. Regarding this issue, Perotti and Suarez (2011) expressed views similar to those in this chapter.

39. The Korean authorities have recently announced a plan urging mandatory minimum holdings of safe FX assets, sufficient to cover FX liquidity needs in times of low roll-over ratios as seen during the recent crisis.

40. Caprio (2010) argues that the ineffectiveness of Spanish dynamic provisioning has been due to the boundary problem. See Goodhart (2008) for a general discussion of the boundary problem.

41. The notion here may be similar to the idea of the "look-through" approach suggested by Caruana (2010).

References

Baba, Naohiko, and Ilhyock Shim. 2011. "Dislocations in the Won-Dollar Swap Markets during the Crisis of 2007–09." Working Paper 344, Bank for International Settlements, Basel, Switzerland, April.

BCBS (Basel Committee on Banking Supervision). 2010a. "An Assessment of the Long-term Economic Impact of Stronger Capital and Liquidity Requirements." BIS, Basel, Switzerland, August.

————. 2010b. "Basel III: International Framework for Liquidity Risk Measurement, Standards and Monitoring." Bank for International Settlements, Basel Switzerland, December.

———. 2010c. "Basel III: A Global Regulatory Framework for More Resilient Banks and Banking Systems." Bank for International Settlements, Basel, Switzerland, December (revised June 2011).

BEA (Bureau of Economic Analysis). http://www.bea.gov.

Berger, Allen N., and Christa H.S. Bouwman. 2009. "Financial Crises and Bank Liquidity Creation." Paper presented at "Conference on the Financial Crisis." Centre de Recerca en Economia Internacional, Universitat Pompeu Fabra, Barcelona, May 7–8.

BOE (Bank of England). 2011. "Instruments of Macroprudential Policy." Discussion Paper, December.

BOK (the Bank of Korea). 2003. "Monetary Policy Report: January 2002–February 2003." May.

———. ECOS (Economic Statistics System), http://ecos.bok.or.kr.

Caprio, Gerard, Jr. 2010. "Safe and Sound Banking: A Role for Countercyclical Regulatory Requirements?" Policy Research Working Paper 5198, World Bank, Washington, DC, February.

Caruana, Jaime. 2010. "Macroprudential Policy: Working towards a New Consensus." Remarks at the high-level meeting, "The Emerging Framework for Financial Regulation and Monetary Policy," Bank for International Settlemetns Financial Stability Institute and International Monetary Fund Institute, Washington, DC, 23 April.

Chang, Soon-taek. 2010. "Mortgage Lending in Korea: An Example of a Countercyclical Macroprudential Approach." Policy Research Working Paper 5505, World Bank, Washington, DC, December.

Chopra, Ajai, Kenneth Kang, Meral Karasulu, Hong Kiang, Henry Ma, and Anthony Richards. 2001. "From Crisis to Recovery in Korea: Strategy, Achievements, and Lessons." Working Paper 01/154, October, International Monetary Fund, Washington, DC.

Crowe, Christopher, Giovanni Dell'Ariccia, Deniz Igan, and Pau Rabanal. 2011. "Policies for Macrofinancial Stability: Options to Deal with Real Estate Booms." Staff Discussion Note 11/02, International Monetary Fund, Washington, DC, February 25.

The Economist. 2009. "Domino Theory: Where Could Emerging-market Contagion Spread Next?" Economics Focus, February 26.

The Edaily. 2006. "Liquidity Ratio Regulation, to be Changed or Not to Be?" June 20, Seoul, Republic of Korea (in Korean).

Fitch Ratings. 2010. "Asset Bubbles in Asia." Asia, Excluding Japan, Special Report, January 29.

FRB (Board of Governors of the Federal Reserve System), http://federalreserve.gov.

FSB (Financial Stability Board), IMF (International Monetary Fund), and BIS (Bank for International Settlements). 2011. "Macroprudential Policy Tools and Frameworks." Update to G-20 Finance Ministers and Central Bank Governors, February 14.

FSC (Financial Services Commission) and FSS (Financial Supervisory Service). 1998 "Revision of Bank Supervision Regulations and Procedures for Bank Supervision Regulations." Press release, November 27 (in Korean).

———. 2006a. "Improvements of Domestic Currency Liquidity Ratio Regulation." Press release, July 27 (in Korean).

————. 2006b. "Strengthening Risk Management for Housing Loans." Press release, November 15 (in Korean).

————. 2009. "Supervision for Financial Institutions' FX Soundness Strengthened," Press Release, November 19.

FSS (Financial Supervisory Service). FISIS (Financial Statistics Information System), http://fisis.fss.or.kr

Galati, G., and R. Moessner. 2011. "Macroprudential Policy—A Literature Review." Working Paper 337, Bank for International Settlements, Basel, Switzerland, February.

Giordano, Claire. 2009. "Prudential Regulation and Supervision Instruments and Aims: A General Framework." In *Financial Market Regulation in the Wake of Financial Crises: The Historical Experience*, edited by A. Gigliobianco and G. Toniolo. Rome: Italy: Bank of Italy.

Goldsmith, Raymond W. 1959. "Financial Structure and Economic Growth in Advanced Countries: An Experiment in Comparative Financial Morphology." In *The Comparative Study of Economic Growth and Structure, edited by* edited by R. W. Goldsmith, 114–23. Cambridge, MA: National Bureau of Economic Research (NBER).www.nber.org/books/unkn59-1.

Goldstein, Morris, and Philip Turner. 2004. *Controlling Currency Mismatches in Emerging Markets.* Washington, DC: The Peterson Institute for International Economics. April 2004.

Goodhart, Charles A. E. 2008. "The Boundary Problem in Financial Regulation." *National Institute Economic Review* 206 (1): 48–55.

Goodhart, Charles A. E., Anil K. Kashyap, Dimitrios P. Tsomocos, and Alexandros P. Vardoulakis. 2012. "Financial Regulation in General Equilibrium." Working Paper 17909, March, National Bureau of Economic Research, Cambridge, MA.

Hahm, Joon-Ho., Frederic S. Mishkin, Hyun Song Shin, and Kwanho Shin. 2012. "Macroprudential Policies in Open Emerging Economies." Working Paper 17780, January, National Bureau of Economic Research, Cambridge, MA.

Hanson, Samuel, Anil K. Kashyap, and Jeremy C. Stein. 2011. "A Macroprudential Approach to Financial Regulation." *Journal of Economic Perspectives* 25 (1): 3–28.

Hartman, Philipp. 1994. "Foreign Exchange Risk Regulation: Issues for Industrial and Developing Countries." Working Paper 94/141, International Monetary Fund, Washington, DC, December.

Igan, Deniz, and H. Kang. 2011. "Loan-to-Value and Debt-to-Income Limits as Macroprudential Tools: Evidence from Korea." Paper presented at The Bank of Korea-International Monetary Fund workshop, "Managing Real Estate Booms and Busts," Seoul, April 11–12.

IMF (International Monetary Fund). 2008. "Republic of Korea: 2008 Article IV Consultation—Staff Report; Staff Supplement; Public Information Notice on the Executive Board Discussion; and Statement by the Executive Director for the Republic of Korea." Country Report. 08/297, IMF, Washington, DC, September.

Kaminsky, Graciela L., and Carmen M. Reinhart. 1999. "The Twin Crises: The Causes of Banking and Balance-of-Payments Problems." *The American Economic Review* 89 (3): 473–500.

Khatri, Yougesh. 2008. "Korea's Banking Sector—Liquidity Risk Management in the Face of Structural Trends and Deregulation." Republic of Korea: Selected Issues, Country Report 08/296, International Monetary Fund, Washington, DC, September.

Kim, Joon-Kyung, and Chung H. Lee. 2010. "Finance and Economic Development in Korea." Working Paper 10-A05, Institute for Research in Finance and Economics, Seoul National University, Seoul, Republic of Korea.

Kookmin Bank, *Monthly Housing Prices*, various issues. http://nland.kbstar.com.

Lim, C., F. Columba, A. Costa, P. Kongsamut, A. Otani, M. Saiyid, T. Wezel, and X. Wu. 2011. "Macroprudential Policy: What Instruments and How to Use Them? Lessons from Country Experiences." Working Paper 11/238, International Monetary Fund, Washington, DC, October.

Merrill Lynch. 2008. "Asia: Risks Rising." *The Asian Macro Navigator*, October 3.

Ministry of Strategy and Finance. 2007. "A Plan for Improvements of Foreign Transaction Regulations in Pursuit of a Market-friendly Foreign Transaction System," Press Release, November 8, (in Korean).

Perotti, Enrico C., and Javier Suarez. 2011. "A Pigovian Approach to Liquidity Regulation." Paper presented at 12th Jacques Polak Annual Research Conference, November 10–11, International Monetary Fund, Washington, DC,

Rhee, Gwang-Ju, and Eun Mo Lee. 2004. "Foreign Exchange Intervention and Foreign Exchange Market Development in Korea." Working Paper 24, Bank for International Settlements, Basel, Switzerland, December 3.

Rothenberg, Alexander D., and Francis E. Warnock. 2006. "Sudden Flight and True Sudden Stops." Working Paper 12726, National Bureau of Economic Research, Cambridge, MA, December.

Shin, Hyun Song. 2010. "Macroprudential Policies Beyond Basel III." Policy Memo, Princeton University, Princeton, NJ, November 22.

Wang, Tina. 2008. "South Korea Is Looking Like East Asia's Weakest Link." Market Scan, *Forbes*, October 6.

Wong, Eric, Tom Fong, Ka.-fai Li, and Henry Choi. 2011. "Loan-to-Value Ratio as a Macro-prudential Tool – Hong Kong's Experience and Cross-country Evidence." Working Paper 01/2011, Hong Kong Monetary Authority, February 17.

Environmental Benefits Statement

The World Bank is committed to reducing its environmental footprint. In support of this commitment, the Office of the Publisher leverages electronic publishing options and print-on-demand technology, which is located in regional hubs worldwide. Together, these initiatives enable print runs to be lowered and shipping distances decreased, resulting in reduced paper consumption, chemical use, greenhouse gas emissions, and waste.

The Office of the Publisher follows the recommended standards for paper use set by the Green Press Initiative. Whenever possible, books are printed on 50% to 100% postconsumer recycled paper, and at least 50% of the fiber in our book paper is either unbleached or bleached using Totally Chlorine free (TCF), Processed Chlorine Free (PCF), or Enhanced Elemental Chlorine Free (EECF) processes.

More information about the Bank's environmental philosophy can be found at http://crinfo.worldbank.org/crinfo/environmental_responsibility/index.html.

green press
INITIATIVE